Literacy and the Practice of Writing
in the 19th Century:
A Strange Blossoming of Spirit

For Nancy and Ben

Literacy and the Practice of Writing in the 19th Century: A Strange Blossoming of Spirit

Ursula Howard

Published by **niace**
promoting adult learning

© 2012 National Institute of Adult Continuing Education
(England and Wales)

21 De Montfort Street
Leicester
LE1 7GE

Company registration no. 2603322
Charity registration no. 1002775

NIACE has a broad remit to promote lifelong learning opportunities for
adults. NIACE works to develop increased participation in education and
training, particularly for those who do not have easy access because of class,
gender, age, race, language and culture, learning difficulties or disabilities,
or insufficient financial resources.

You can find NIACE online at www.niace.org.uk

Front cover image: The Ballad Monger by Richard Dadd, 1853.
© The Trustees of the British Museum. All rights reserved.

Cataloguing in Publications Data
A CIP record for this title is available from the British Library

ISBN 978-1-86201-564-7 (print)
ISBN 978-1-86201-565-4 (PDF)
ISBN 978-1-86201-566-1 (ePub)
ISBN 978-1-86201-567-8 (online)
ISBN 978-1-86201-568-5 (Kindle)

Cover design by Book Production Services.
Designed and typeset by Kerrypress Limited, Luton, UK.
Printed and bound in the UK.

They continue their dreams,
And shall wake soon and long for letters,
And none will hear the postman's knock
Without a quickening of the heart,
For who can bear to feel himself forgotten?

WH Auden, Night Mail

And so, my little cracked treasure, worn and polished by time and usage, remains a cherished symbol of those fragmentary, yet imperishable moments, crystallised by the passing years ... a strange blossoming of spirit in an odd corner of strife and poverty.

Alice Foley, A Bolton Childhood

Working-class literature is bound to be different.

Leah Hood, Manchester, 1986

I don't know where the ideas come from, but they must have been there, just not in words before.

Voices on the Page, 2007

Images from the past crowd in my head and half the time I cannot tell whether they are memories or inventions. Not that there is much difference between the two, if indeed there is any difference at all ... When I look back all is flux, without beginning and flowing towards no end, or none that I shall experience except as a final full-stop.

John Banville, Ancient Light

I used to scribble with chalk and things like that on the pavements. And remember things. I always had a big old handbag tucked under my arm and my mother would say 'let me have a look what you've got in that'. Snippets of paper I'd collected fell out. Anything that was written down, I'd keep it.

Margaret Bearfield, Brighton 1987

School was a series of bad events. It was my ambition to leave and then to learn to read and write – one of those ambitions you never get round to, like trekking across the desert. I was forced to start, on day-release and it was completely different: 'write something down and enjoy doing it'. Writing about school, I exaggerated situations, making characters absurd, which to me they were. It was either go back and smash somebody's head, or write badly about someone. The art side of writing progressed from there.

John Glynn, Manchester, 1989

Anxiety attends riches: handwriting taken from the Johnson Collection at the Bodleian Library
Courtesy of the John Johnson Collection at the Bodleian Library

Contents

Acknowledgements

Thanks are due to the Institute of Education, University of London, for periods of study leave during which I began to develop my University of Sussex DPhil into this book. Several colleagues at the National Research and Development Centre (NRDC) for Adult Literacy and Numeracy at the Institute kept me going, despite the intensity of our research on present-day literacy policy and practice. First I thank David Mallows, without whose constant encouragement, critical reading and editorial gifts I would have lost heart. For long periods, the project hung by a thread. David and John Vorhaus commented constructively on chapters, while never holding back on criticism. At NIACE Virman Man, followed by David Shaw and Sarah Turner, have offered exemplary support, skill and patience. I have been deeply impressed by Nicola Proudfoot's meticulous editorial skills. I have had invaluable practical help from Jenny Rhys-Warner in preparing final drafts. The large cast of colleagues in literacy theory, history and practice who have kept me going with opportunities to share my work, feedback and supportive nudges to get on with it include: Jane Mace, Mary Hamilton, Alan Tuckett, Peter Lavender, Sue Grief, John Field, Alan Cole, Deborah Brandt, Norah Hughes, Irene Schwab and David Barton. I am grateful to Sally Alexander, Cora Kaplan and Alistair Thomson for incisive comments on my research for the thesis. Anna Davin was characteristically generous with source material. Annabel Hemstedt pointed me towards Elisabeth Gaskell and other writers, and my mother Nora Howard combed the Dickens novels she knew deeply for anything related to literacy: thick envelopes dropped through the letter-box. I was lucky to have an inspirational teacher in Geoffrey Hemstedt, a superb doctoral supervisor who opened my eyes to different ways of seeing, questioning and excavating the meanings of writing for 19th century working-class people. Timothy Ashplant and Stephen Yeo may not realise how important our animated discussions about working-class autobiography over the last few years have been. Despite all the 'really useful knowledge' I have been given, mistakes in the book are mine alone.

Many present-day literacy learners and new writers contributed their experiences and insights to this book and influenced my thinking profoundly. Brief quotes, selected from many interviews I conducted between 1984–1990 appear at the front. I thank Margaret Bearfield, John Glynn, Leah Hood, Peter Goode and all those who wrote pieces for NRDC's 'Voices on the Page'.

I am grateful to the librarians at the John Johnson Collection, Bodleian Library, University of Oxford, the Stockport Local Heritage Library and Christine Bradley at Colne Library for their help locating documents and permission to publish. Thanks also to the Museum of London, the Mary Evans Picture Library, the British Library, the Victorian Web and the Bridgeman Art Library for permission to use images.

Stephen Yeo is the person I thank from the bottom of my heart for enabling me to keep faith with this book, offering precious insights, deep historical knowledge, creative thinking, and ideas about social class, associational culture and writing. Above all I am grateful for his careful, patient ways of listening to and interpreting what people have to say and what they actually practice: that is what this book tries to do.

Introduction

I

This is a book about literacy in nineteenth-century England. More specifically, it is a book about writing. It explores, through autobiographies and other personal accounts, why and how working-class people learned and practised writing and what their writing meant to them. It is partly a cultural, educational and social history; partly a contribution to literacy studies past and present, especially adult literacy; and partly an engagement with cultural theory about the role of writing in society. Why writing? Of the two literacy practices, writing has historically been the most problematic, contested and difficult for people to access. Much past and present-day literacy research has put reading first or worked on the basis that the two do not need to be distinguished. The vast majority of books about literacy and histories of education have done the same. Discussion of writing has often been almost totally absent in research and policy. Since the nineteenth century, literacy policies have consistently focused more on reading, and mostly measured literacy in terms of reading ages, fixed standards or levels. Adult literacy teaching over two hundred years has, for various reasons which will be explored, found it harder to prioritise writing than reading. The book will argue that writing matters in its own right, and ask why it was that unbidden writing practices thrived at a time when there was no expectation or pressure for working-class people to write.

The writers

At the heart of the book are people's experiences and views about learning to use writing. My aim is to turn up the volume of the voices of

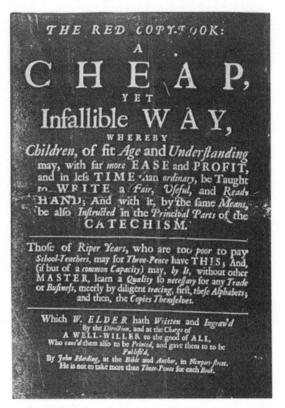

A copybook for children and adults, designed for Sunday School use
Courtesy of Stockport Local Heritage Library

ordinary people who did extraordinary things in producing poems, letters, autobiographies or diaries (or fragments of them), whether their work was published or not. The process of unearthing how people used their writing skills and what writing meant to them in their lives led me to an interest in the deeper meanings of literacy and the effect of writing on the development of an inner self and a subjectivity as someone with the capacity to write about their life. My explorations of this are located in the self-referential nature of the project: how people wrote about the processes of learning to write and use writing, and, in some cases, developing an identity as a writer.

Nineteenth-century people who taught themselves literacy skills wrote in different settings for different reasons: to make a living, to communicate with distant family and friends, to participate in social and religious organisations, to explore their own lives at different levels, to write for writing's sake and to seek an audience. Why did writing matter so much to them? One reason is that through writing they could become historical actors, and their complex writing certainly defies the generalisations about lives of uniformity or passive victimhood. For nineteenth-century working-class people writing was itself a hard-won act of human agency. Unsurprisingly, the profound and diverse meanings which attached to writing, for people who managed to learn and practise it, are often rooted among the difficulties they experienced in the process: without schooling, in poverty, with little time and often in the face of trenchant opposition. In the autobiographies and diaries explored here, this story is told in many different ways. There is a common preoccupation with how a person came to write. In general this is less about the writerly difficulties of putting words on paper – the frustration of writer's block or the pleasure in turning a phrase – and more about how they managed to learn to write at all, their learning methods and the changes to social being which writing brought or promised to bring. There is pleasure in the achievement and confidence of having reached a point where they could write for others, as well as, for those whose work was published, ambivalence about 'being a writer' in society. Satisfaction in their writing, given its provenance, is often more apparent than the pain of creativity. Another reason why writing was so compelling is that it was increasingly visible in the world around them and seemed to them to be invested with power. Books proliferated and, if they were mostly beyond reach, access to Bibles and other sacred scripts and to cheap tracts, ballads, poems and broadsheets was possible. Postal services grew and fell in price. Writing was in the air, and getting nearer to every community.

The context

As far as possible, this book works through the voices of people who wrote, or those who worked closely with them. But the learning and practice of writing did not develop in a vacuum and the context for people's writing practices is critical. The nineteenth century began in the middle of the Napoleonic Wars, with bread shortages and terror of the spread of the French revolutionary spirit. The movement of people from the countryside to the cities to work in the mills and factories of the Industrial Revolution was changing lives and landscapes swiftly and dramatically. The learning, teaching and practice of reading were broadly met with approval and grew fast. But there was a growing consciousness of public hunger to read and write radical publications – tens of thousands of copies of Thomas Paine's *Rights of Man* (1791) were circulating within a few weeks of publication. The book was quickly banned, but continued to circulate, read in secret. The creation of undesirable reading material was one reason writing was strongly opposed, along with fears that it would enable forgery and encourage people's ambitions to rise above their ordained station in life. Access to literacy was at the core of fears of unrest. This led to the harsh suppression of 'seditious' literature, and other reading material seen as dangerous. Meetings in public and private were banned for fear of subversive, radical organisations including trade unions. Autonomous literacy practices went into hiding. There was widespread opposition to mass education and Education Bills failed.

By the 1820s the pendulum had swung back in favour of education and debates intensified, Britain was already a culture in the process of becoming literate. The question was not whether literacy, but which literacies, and how to teach and contain them. The next decades saw intense activity in state formation, educational development and cultural production. The use of the written word grew at an unprecedented rate to unprecedented levels: in public institutions and bureaucracies, parliamentary activity, surveys and information gathering, postal and communications systems, surveillance activities, and education, science and the arts. Among the middle class and officialdom there was intense interest in education and in which literacies were appropriate for working people to learn and practise – to the point of obsession. Religious, educational, voluntary and commercial organisations, as well as radical organisations, aligned with working-class people, struggled over the means and methods of developing literacy for the poor and culturally powerless. While the case for universal reading skills was made early on in the century, the teaching of writing was initially opposed, then evolved in tense and constantly changing relationships between those who promoted (and practised) writing, and the establishments of church and state as they sought to define and shape those literacies which should be practised. At the beginning of the nineteenth century people learned to read and write through a range of informal, self-selected, more (or less) haphazard methods. People learned at home, at work, in Sunday schools, and in a wide variety of private day schools in the local community for which 'dame school' became the shorthand. But by the end of the century, following a series of education acts from 1870 onwards, universal, compulsory elementary education for all children was established, and a uniformity of experience was imposed through the Board schools and national Standards. By then, illiteracy had become strongly stigmatised and literacy was believed to be universal.

How the book is organised

The first part of the book is about the social and political context of literacy learning and how the teaching and learning of writing developed. The first chapter explores the adoption of writing by churches and the state, parliamentary debates and public attitudes about writing and schooling. From an official viewpoint, distrust of writing, and the secular, subversive or potentially criminal misuses of it was replaced by uneven, then concerted efforts to define and develop methods for teaching writing appropriately. I also look into the ideas about teaching writing developed by social organisations and individuals who supported working-class interests before the state's grip on education tightened. The second contextual chapter explores the ways in which the literary culture of the period gave voice to attitudes towards working-class literacy and joined in with debates about education and working-class life. The imagined – and for some, directly observed – nature and symbolism of working-class literacy practices, including in social movements, were a preoccupation for several prominent novelists. Fictional characters who were illiterate or struggled to learn and practise writing stalk the pages of numerous books, especially those with a critical social edge and moral vision. The writers in this chapter had large readerships and cultural influence. This chapter also looks at some other ways in which working people themselves invested literacy with mythical, powerful meanings inherited from oral cultures.

Official literacies and the powerful stories of working-class life by established writers are more than a context: they are also a counter-story. Supported by cultural theory and critical historical perspectives, the book mainly sees the world, including their own worlds, from the point of view of working-class writers themselves. For them the spread of literacy was unstoppable. Even in the harshest times, when writing was banned or discouraged, hairline cracks in the repressive structures around them enabled many people to slip through if they wanted to pursue their own literacies strongly enough. Writing was a singular kind of cultural produc-tion which proved impossible to stamp out or completely contain, whether in published or unpublished forms. It was already becoming too widely available at a relatively low cost. The technological means were there. And writing was too strongly desired and too central to human creativity and the need to communicate to be sealed off for long inside the patrolled borders of class or gender.

The second part of the book explores community-based social forms of writing practices. Chapter 3 explores how literacy was learned and practised in families and communities and challenges myths about the individualistic nature of autodidactism and 'self-improvement'. Learners invented new ways of blending individual, family and social learning and practices through informal groups and mutual improvement societies. Their ambitions and their ambivalence towards the educational prescriptions of churches, charities and the state invoke a sense of loss as well as gain about the arrival of universal schooling and the dismissal and dismantling of their methods of learning. They did this in ways that often challenged a hierarchical approach to acquiring knowledge and skills. This chapter also introduces a theme which recurs later: the typology and roles of significant other people, known and unknown – who have usefully been termed 'sponsors' by one historian – in enabling, or hindering, people in their efforts to write.[1] In the context of debates and developments about postal services and their impact on working-class life, chapter 4 explores the uses and meaning of letter-writing as the key means of communication between people in and away from families and communities, separated by circumstance, compulsion or choice. Although this chapter puts letter-writing and its meanings at the centre, writing, receiving and sending letters feature as a seminal literacy practice throughout the book, as a means of connection, but also a means of enacting change which could be both powerful and precarious.

The third part of the book focuses on autobiographies, exploring the characteristics of nineteenth-century experiences and events as unfolded in life stories, including the stories of writing itself. Chapter 5 looks at the reasons why autobiography as a genre suited the purposes of working-class writers best: what it proclaimed, what it revealed and concealed, and how it related to its intended audience. Chapter 6 explores the nature of creativity in relation to working-class writing, the origins of writers' creativity and the connections they made between their writing and other cultural and aesthetic practices. Writers' uses of memory and dreaming reveal a deeper, darker and more complex relationship to earlier life experiences and feelings in texts which, at first reading, can feel like watching a water-boatman skidding fast across the waters of a pond. Chapters 7 and 8 explore the subjective meanings of writing for women and men who attributed the transition to a different selfhood to learning and practising writing. For many, especially women, writing led to conflict, challenge and change. It carried a significance that transcended its historical, social meanings and could only be represented or interpreted through mythic narrative structures and the investing of a metaphoric energy in the minutiae of learning and the fairy-tale appearances of real and mythic others in the enactment of change. Writers recalled, celebrated and sought to justify the changes in identity that were facilitated by literacy.

Historical sources and concepts

The sources for this book range from official government documents and parliamentary papers to scraps of scribbled writing. But autobiographies are its main source. As the basis of historical record, they are a rich, problematic but indispensable source for understanding the ways of life, beliefs, thoughts, feelings and aspirations of people in the nineteenth century, particularly from subordinated communities. They are reconstructions of complex selves, drawn from memory and with an imagined audience, even if that audience is only the writer creating a sense of themselves for posterity. Some historians have insisted they are not reliable, formal historical records, useful rather for correlating harder forms of evidence. Novels are a further stretch from authenticity as capital H History, though I have used them too. But parliamentary papers and minute books are also reconstructions of events, written from a subjective point of view. Each of these sources had its live, critical, correcting audience response which we only partially know. For the purposes of digging for meaning and interpreting it, autobiographies are the most fertile terrain for yielding some understanding of working-class experience, mentalities and mores through the voices of people who lived them. In this book, that also means what writing itself signified to writers.

Even though the language autobiographies use may often seem straightforward, even plain, the texts here offer more than simple narratives which reflect simple lives. An autobiography exposes many aspects and layers of a person's lived experience. This book also explores the meaning of writing itself in remembering and reconstructing a life, adding another dimension to the sense of complexity of the stories being told. I hope it is self-evident that the book does not claim to be a linear, comprehensive history of literacy practices, more a qualitative exploration of literacy as a cultural practice in one country in the nineteenth century. Richard Altick's *The English Common Reader* opened up historical studies of reading practices. Years later, in the 1970s and 1980s, John Burnett, David Vincent and David Mayall began to discover, collect and work on autobiographies and made it possible to study writing through the eyes of over a thousand nineteenth-century writers previously hidden from history. This work changed the landscape of research on working-class life. Because so many autobiographies were found, communality and differences of experience can be extracted from individual stories, giving weight to the exploration of what their individual writings can say about life and literacy more generally. Vincent's further work on literacy and popular culture analysed the experiences of dozens of people, especially men's. His work has, literally, made this book possible. Jonathan Rose has since drawn on many autobiographies to investigate thoroughly the scale of informal working-class adult learning and the breadth and character of their reading practices.[2]

There is also much scholarship on how state education for working-class people developed and swept away learning organised 'from below'. Economic and social historians of the nineteenth-century literacy have used both statistical and qualitative methods to investigate the relationship between literacy and economic and social development.[3] Then there are the numbers. Statistics reveal that the greatest quantitative leap forward in literacy took place before the introduction of universal state education. By 1700, nearly half the male and a quarter of the female population of England were able to read and write. As literacy levels rose, labourers and women were least likely to learn to write, but the expansion of the reading public was the essential foundation for the growth of writing. By the 1760s, 40 per cent of women and 60 per cent of men wrote their name on marriage registers; by 1840, between 50 per cent of women and 75 per cent of men; and by 1870, 77 per cent of all brides and grooms.[4] A signature is a very crude measure of literacy. However, most of those who signed the register, rather than marking it with an 'x', would also have had some reading skills, which were taught first. Many would have been able to write a little more than their name. There is ample statistical evidence that compulsory full-time schooling did little more than top up the earlier efforts of children and adults to create their own literacy education. And although the literacy demands of the present age are far more complex, it remains the case that we still have an adult literacy problem, which means 15 per cent still struggle with functional literacy in their lives despite years of schooling. Why? Finally, there have been more American than British studies of nineteenth- and early twentieth-century literacy learning that have cast light on writing practices.[5]

Working-class writing and literary conventions

Many writers in this book filled no more than an exercise book in their lifetimes – a diary or fragments of a life story. Others became well-known as authors and poets, reaching audiences way beyond a contemporary working-class readership, and their work has endured. John Clare stands out as a highly-rated poet, even though it took him nearly two hundred years to escape the label of 'peasant poet'. This book does not attempt literary criticism or judgements about quality. Nevertheless, I have tried to include pieces of writing which strike me as beautiful, as well as pieces which are there mainly because they explain things. There is scholarship on the pre-existing literary models which writers drew from, and for poets, on their uses of poetic conventions and diction. The extent to which they succeeded in literary terms is for others to pursue. What is clear from autobiography is that some writers were so confident of their story, they just wrote it, while others show more diffidence and intellectual deference. For many, there is a sense of grappling with what writing is supposed to be like. For yet others, the literary sources include oral story-telling, fairy tales, the Bible and their reading of the religious and secular literature which clearly inspired them.

Literacy and social practice: why literacies?

As well as historical scholarship, multi-disciplinary literacy studies offer support for a historical and cultural analysis of literacy through life stories. Over the last quarter century, the 'New Literacy Studies', particularly the ground-breaking work of James Gee, Brian Street, David Barton and Mary Hamilton, have worked on the concept of literacy as a social practice, part of social being. Literacy is for a purpose and always about communication. It happens through processes, termed 'literacy events' in people's lives. In this conceptual framework, literacy, in the singular, is only one aspect of a literate culture. Twenty-first-century society has an array of official literacies. But in this society as well as in societies

9

becoming literate like nineteenth century society, literacy is also a set of practices which people use in their own lives for their own purposes. Historically, literacies are multiple and contested and the social practices approach is in tune with my own. So I use the terminology of 'literacies' wherever possible to denote differences and contests between official literacies and the unofficial literacies people elect to practise. I take this further. Who is practising literacy makes a difference to what literacy is, as do the provenance and power of a particular form of literacy. Some literacies are officially-sanctioned, coercive and 'domesticating': they try to police other literacies. In a distinction which goes back to Paolo Freire's work on literacy, elective, socially-relevant literacies are self-generated, independently produced, culturally dynamic and individually or mutually liberating.

There is another relevant strand of literacy studies which focuses on the relationship of literacy to consciousness and the transition from 'primitive' to 'advanced' societies. This book engages at the level of subjective meaning about ways in which writing changes consciousness. At a societal level, debates were triggered by Jack Goody's famous and deeply influential argument that literacy, the technologising of communication, is a key factor which enables societies to develop economically and culturally. Debate over the decades since has inevitably led to discussion of the condescension of literate societies towards societies perceived to be more 'primitive' because they are oral. This book is about a society in flux and asks what difference becoming proficient at writing made to groups of people in a not-yet-fully literate society, people who might easily have remained illiterate. If they had, it would have been less socially and culturally remarkable than the achievements and practices of literacy they actually managed to realise. As literacy gained pace, they would have become more stigmatised and marginalised. However, people lived in the nineteenth century, as many live now, without literacy adequate to their purposes and many prospered. I do not want to seem to make judgements about their lives. Because the focus of this book is literacy and the changes it can bring, a persistent question hangs in the air unaddressed: what about those people who did not learn to write, what can we know of their subjectivity and their abilities and means of changing their lives? They are hidden from history and their absence serves to make literacy as an agent of change and a measure of competence feel more important than it may be. That much seems likely from the complexity of the lives and skills of people who struggle with literacy in our own times.

Cultural theory

This book is also informed by cultural studies, including cultural Marxism. Raymond Williams explored concepts which help to illuminate literacies historically. Several facets of his work inform this study. These include historical explorations of education and culture in *The Long Revolution* and elsewhere. The first is the notion of culture understood as a way of life, as 'ordinary' (everyone's), rather than belonging to an artistic or literary domain inhabited by the few. This idea enables different ways of seeing the culture of excluded people. This is related to Williams's concept of 'cultural division', which he argues persists in contemporary British society, and affects who has access to the most powerful literacies. I have also found that Bordieu's concept of 'cultural production' helps to capture the processes from which writing emerges. Walter Benjamin offers the metaphor of digging to excavate meaning from memory. 'Digging' into texts for the workings of memory reveals the richness of the experience and creativity of writers which are present in seemingly straightforward, relatively unproblematised accounts of life. Finally, in exploring how autobiographical writing needs to engage with the complexity of memory, dreams and the surfacing of material from the unconscious, I have, without any claim to expertise, used Freud's writing to draw attention to the psychological dimensions of autobiographies.

Class

I have used the terminology of social class throughout the book: working-class writer, working-class writing, middle class and so on. I do not apologise for this in 2012. Other terms do not address the issue of cultural production by relatively powerless social groups, or the cultural processes which the people in this book struggled with for themselves and on behalf of those in their situation. Twentieth- and twenty-first-century social terms such as 'disempowered', 'disadvantaged' or 'socially-excluded' are often policy-generated and are ephemeral and more passive terms in comparison to class. They will not do for the nineteenth century. Lower classes, inferior classes, lower orders or simply 'the poor' were terms often used in nineteenth-century public documents and used by social 'superiors'. I have stuck with 'working class', conscious of it as a generalisation which does not fully represent how all the writers in the book described themselves (particularly women), or the diversity of their cultural backgrounds and their consciousness of 'difference' as writers.

The subjects of the book also differ widely in terms of their work. There are manual workers; artisans – the skilled craftspeople so often associated with learning; factory workers; domestic servants and others. Many had a variety of work during their lives. The activists among them, such as Chartists, Trade Unionists and political party members, came from manual as well as skilled craft occupations. Those who have struggled most with literacy are not necessarily those in the most skilled jobs. Domestic servants are an interesting group. In the 1851 census, there were 751,641 females in service and 848,251 males, including young children. This is out of a total female population of England, Scotland and Wales of 10.7 million. The numbers of servants continued to rise rapidly over the next 20 years. Domestic servants started young and tended to have the least education, and many were agricultural labourers' children, or orphans and paupers from workhouses – and if they had any schooling it was likely to have been at the workhouse rather than the well-to-do home they were sent to. However, people from the occupational groups I have described as working class shared a subordinated status, a sense of belonging with other workers and a struggle for literacy and education. Servants were the most isolated from any support, or sponsorship of their learning, and least able to organise with others, for education or better conditions. And their masters and mistresses did not see it as their duty to educate them, even if a few did.[6] My analysis is based on the argument that there are class-based identities and actions within which there are also individual identities and actions. In this I acknowledge E.P. Thompson's account of the growth of working-class consciousness in the early nineteenth century, which, as he argued, was developed in part through the literacy practices in social, cultural and political activisms. The idea is not to use class as a reified single concept, but as happenings, struggles for change.[7]

II   Why I wrote this book

It is often said that history is written about the present for the future. The motivation to write this book, which started as a DPhil at Sussex University, came from years working as an adult literacy teacher and organiser from the 1970s onwards, when the first post-war campaign for adult literacy was launched. Through history, I wanted to get to the bottom of why literacy problems persist, in order to inform policy and practice. Elementary schools for all had resulted in the assumption that universal literacy had arrived. Opportunities for adult literacy learning quickly vanished. Long-standing providers of adult literacy, such as the Adult School Movement, gradually ceased teaching writing and by the 1930s had virtually abolished their 'First Half Hour', Sunday morning session.[8] A few 'Elementary' classes continued for a time, for example in the WEA (Workers' Educational Association), Local Authority technical schools and the armed forces, tucked away from mainstream adult education provision. Illiteracy was a stigma and assumed to be restricted to people with learning difficulties. 'Remedial' courses survived in pockets.

Growing up in the 1950s and 1960s, my first encounter with literacy as a concept was Hoggart's *The Uses of Literacy* published in 1957, which strongly influenced discussions about working-class culture – or the perceived lack of it. In the post-war decades, literacy practices themselves were invisible, taken for granted. Hoggart's book marked the beginning of a resurgence of interest in working-class life and poverty as well as new literature and drama, some written by working-class writers like Alan Sillitoe and Bill Naughton. Hoggart drew on his working-class childhood for an analysis of reading practices, mostly in relation to leisure pursuits. The contrasts made possible by the book between popular and 'high' culture were sharp. In Hoggart's evocation of daily life, active uses of literacy were minimal, hangovers from nineteenth-century life. Writing needs were provided for by scribes and local autodidacts; in families, mothers mainly took responsibility for whatever minimal writing was needed to keep alive relationships with absent members.

> *Socially … each day and each week is almost unplanned. There is no diary, no book of engagements, and few letters are sent or received. If a member of the family is away, a weekly letter is somewhat painfully put together on Sunday. Relatives or very close friends who have gone to live away are likely to be communicated with only by Christmas card.[9]*

Hoggart suggested that the uses of literacy had become superficial and derivative, and that a hand-to-mouth economic existence carries over into cultural and social life. For Hoggart an 'unplanned' existence means an absence of certain kinds of literacy, for example diaries and timetables. It does not mean 'spontaneity', rather a lack of written systems for the control and organisation of life, compared with social groups whose elaborate writing practices are taken as the norm. He didn't seem to see all

13

the literacy practices which nearly everyone is unavoidably faced with in everyday life in a society powerfully shaped by controlling institutional literacies, as well as those needed or chosen by less powerful groups. Hoggart's comment that letter-writing is a painful exercise carries a faint echo of the deeply-held association, expressed in nineteenth-century literature and political debate, that working-class people were not physically evolved to be literate and had difficulty adapting to holding a pen properly. In this regard they were sometimes seen as living closer to animals than to middle-class persons.

The settled twentieth-century view of literacy levels and practices was turned on its head in the 1970s. The campaign for adult literacy, 'A right to read', which started in the university settlement movement in 1973 questioned the consoling myth of universal literacy, together with the commonsense view that literacy was not much needed, used or wanted in working-class communities. It was a shock for Britain to discover there was still an adult literacy problem. Media coverage, including prime-time television programmes run by the BBC, replanted illiteracy in public consciousness. A new era of modestly-funded adult literacy courses in voluntary organisations and local authorities was launched, supported by central and local government funding. The thousands of adults who flocked to courses were overwhelmingly working class, including black and Asian people.[10]

In some views of adult literacy, the individuals bore the brunt of responsibility for their problems. Complacency, back-of-the-class bad behaviour and truancy were frequently suggested reasons. Some emphasised psychological problems rather than social factors in a failure to learn. For others, low literacy meant low intelligence and ignorance as it had done in the nineteenth century. Some learners blamed themselves, internalising negative views. It took a life event, a prospective transition or a crisis point in their sense of self to bring some people back into learning. Yet others had a positive identity as resourceful survivors, as well as people who could more than get by. Many, too, had a good understanding of the social and economic forces and educational values which had failed them and left them to fend for themselves in adult life without the skills to practise literacy to their satisfaction.

I was among those practitioners who wanted the 1970s literacy campaign to be a social movement, a response to social inequality: poverty, poor schooling, homelessness and cultural 'disadvantage'. For practitioners, under-education was not about failure by individuals but about individuals being systematically failed by schooling. In their analysis, this meant understanding how class, gender and ethnicity affected educational under-achievement, social subordination and poor prospects. Teachers argued that adult literacy problems were one measure of failure in British education and the education provided in the former colonies, particularly the Caribbean islands, the Asian sub-continent and East Africa. Under-funding and the low priority given to children and adults struggling with their education had perpetuated educational and social inequality across generations. Discrimination was also cultural. At a time when different cultures were opening up, more people were seeking a voice, women's hidden writing was emerging and community-based writing was beginning to flourish, it was natural that writing took centre-stage in adult literacy. As well as seeking empowering ways of engaging adults, and learning from them, there were practical reasons. No adult reading materials existed. So learners wrote for other learners, especially life-story writing. In this way, a body of writing by working-class people was published which other learners felt was relevant and stimulated them to write. Booklets, anthologies, student newsletters, magazines, pamphlets and course materials expressed shared experience.[11]

From the mid-1980s, teaching through writing declined and has struggled to recover. Literacy policy was dominated by initiatives to address unemployment, offering measurable, skills-based training, which concentrated on individualised work-related skills. Getting any job was a more important outcome than sustainable gains in literacy, or developing the habit of writing for its own sake. The policy discourse shifted away from the humanist paradigm of self-realisation of the 1970s and early 1980s, which placed expressive writing at the heart of literacy, and replaced it with an instrumental, utilitarian paradigm divorced from learners' experience. The priority ever since has been 'basic skills' improvement measured by formally-assessed levels, reskilling for employment.

By the mid-1990s, adult literacy as policy had faded to near invisibility. In practice, it had remained an integral part of adult learning, surviving through droughts and gluts in funding, keeping learners' needs at the forefront. And public consciousness never sunk back to pre-1970s levels. From the mid-1990s, everything changed. Research by the Basic Skills Agency, set up by government in the 1970s, suggested that the number of adults in 1993 whose literacy was inadequate to their needs or to those of employers was an estimated 15 per cent and higher for numeracy. An influential survey by the OECD (Organisation for Economic Co-operation and Development), published in 1997, and subsequent UK government research bore this out.[12] The exposure yet again of the extent of the literacy problems caused almost a moral panic and humiliation at the UK's position near the bottom of the league table of developed countries' skills. A committee of enquiry was established, and, following its report, a comprehensive multi-billion pound ten-year strategy or 'crusade' to improve literacy, numeracy and English language, 'Skills for Life', was launched by the Labour Government in 2001.[13] The strategy has been ambitious, characterised by its top-down mechanisms to define and fund desired literacies, with the emphasis firmly on skills rather than on the infinite variety of social practices. Practitioners have not been in the driving seat: more the uncomfortable beneficiaries of unprecedented funding, higher professional status and prescribed pedagogical systems resources. Learners have benefited from better funding and new curricula. However, the strongest emphasis has been placed on reading, and writing has often been relatively neglected in favour of preparation for skills-based tests. Government-sponsored assessments for adults examined only reading skills, through multiple-choice papers.

The continued prioritising of reading in policy and educational discourses sits more and more awkwardly with fast-changing practices in real life and work. It feels anachronistic in an age when a powerful shift is underway. Writing is overtaking and reshaping reading practices in many spheres, fuelled by technologies which support interactive writing practices, whether transactional, social or creative. The nature of working life in particular is changing fast, facilitated and driven by writing. Research has shown that practitioners have persisted in teaching writing, encouraged to do so or not. Practices varied from creative writing to the composition of texts related to daily life, to the widespread practice of limiting writing to spelling individual words. Learners and teachers continued to value writing and despite pressures to conform to assessment regimes and achievement targets, efforts were made to support teachers and rekindle a culture of writing through writing competitions and the publication of anthologies.[14] Skills for the economy still outweighed social practices in policy and official discourses of literacy, even though social justice was another explicit aim of Skills for Life. There were community literacy programmes in support of social inclusion, and family literacy projects which enabled adults to help their children's (and

16

grandchildren's) prospects of success in the National Curriculum, while improving their own literacy and numeracy. Research evidence showed the value to both generations of adult learning, a key finding as so much evidence made clear that literacy and numeracy problems ran from generation to generation.[15] Yet, work-related skills to support the economy have had the highest priority in Skills for Life, underpinned by the ideology of individual improvement, employability and the promotion of 'social cohesion'.

English for Speakers of other Languages (ESOL) for immigrant, migrant and refugee communities was somewhat reluctantly included for some years in the funding of Skills for Life, alongside policies for promoting British culture and citizenship skills.[16] ESOL funding was eventually cut back, a victim of high levels of participation and a policy panic in part related to immigration debates. ESOL is unavoidably linked to any account of literacy, since so many language learners also have literacy needs. Like their nineteenth-century predecessors, the adults who join present-day literacy or ESOL-literacy courses, or belong to community writing groups, defy simple characterisations of their many skills, capabilities, cultures, values and creative potential. Policy makers might have benefited from listening to learners more carefully. As it is, their official surveys show very limited success despite good intentions and massive funding.[17] And still, beyond the world of literacy and language practitioners, there is no subtle understanding of learners' problems, hopes and needs; the low confidence they report, the prejudices they encounter, and their search for a more positive sense of identity.

There was once an independent culture of literacy practices in working-class life. Undoubtedly it was silenced and lost confidence over decades, all but drowned out by an aggressively divisive and unequal culture, by the popular press and mass media. Nevertheless, the number of people who write, and the quantity and quality of writing produced by people and groups who are neither perceived to be nor expected to become writers, has been underestimated. Many people still write for their own purposes. Time and again, exercise books or dog-eared notepads filled with autobiographical writing or poems are unearthed in the course of conversations in adult literacy groups and community activity. In such literacy 'events', writing may turn out to be a continuing practice. Sometimes long-completed pieces of writing lie at the back of a sitting-room cupboard and other people's interest is met with astonishment. Life-stories and poems – handwritten and word-processed – are regularly submitted to local writing groups for critical feedback or in the hope of publication. Independent community publishing ventures have survived continuously since the 1970s. Groups have worked together across the country, most powerfully in the Federation of Worker Writers and Community Publishers (FWWCP); and some high profile commercially-published memories of a childhood in poverty also helped to motivate others to write.[18] Working-class culture and autonomous literacy practices thrive in different ways in different pockets, not least through writing and social networking on the internet, private and political. It has never been easier to access ways of writing for individual and social purposes. Community-based interest groups and cultural action for change have not died either. Research has pointed to the continuation of writing cultures as part of 'local literacies', which have never ceased to be practised.[19] In recent years, a body of quantitative and qualitative research has confirmed learners' accounts of their experiences and life-chances, much of it from the National Research and Development Centre for Adult Literacy and Numeracy.[20] It confirms social class, poverty, housing and other social deprivation indices as key determinants in educational success or failure which passes from one generation to another. Research and practice also show that nearly all adults who have literacy problems now manage to read and write a little, if not to their satisfaction, or get others to help them write notes and letters. Scribes are still part of modern life.[21]

Literacy learners face challenges every day: relating to bureaucracies, and the workplace, or functioning as parents of children in a competitive school environment, as well as being able to 'read' and 'write' the bigger picture of a constantly changing environment in the places they live and work.[22] None of the condescending assumptions, residual and active, about the people perceived by others to lack or barely use literacy could survive unscathed through a single week of working with the complexity of learners' lives. The reality of persistent and growing inequality today, different as it is from the nineteenth century, still provides the lens through which to look closely at the literacies of working-class people in the past. As it was in the nineteenth century, learning to write, to be able to say something about yourself in writing, beyond instrumental communication for jobs or the practical business of daily life, is still a desired and motivating aim. And life stories, letters and poetry are still favoured forms for writing, on paper or online.

III   Note about historical periods and use of tenses

Some indication of my method, language and the presentation of this book is needed. The chronological sequencing of this book may seem eccentric. The 'long' nineteenth century up to the First World War is the broad framework, but I do not work chronologically with the 'period' in a linear account of historical developments in literacy. The situating of experience which is recorded in autobiography at a particular time cannot in any case be fitted into a neat chronology. To do so would ignore the workings of memory and the psychology of the construction of events. Writers refer to different events or experiences at different times. The feelings they unearth may be attached to a particular event in adulthood, or to the faint traces of an earlier buried event. People also wrote life stories at different points in their lives. For example, a woman of 80, writing in the early nineteenth century of a recent experience, might be writing about the same world as an 80-year-old woman writing towards the end of the century, recollecting and reconstructing her early childhood during that same period. Their births and deaths are almost a century apart. Their writing skills could have been learned in the same decade, or separated by decades and their stories written in different epochs. But I have included both. I have also strayed a little further into the twentieth century when the themes in which I am interested demand it. The decision to include or exclude a writer has been more about their social and cultural position and how this affected their access to the literacy and education they desired.

My use of tenses and names, particularly in chapters 7 and 8, needs explanation. It is difficult to disentangle tenses in describing the content of writing as a literary text, when texts are also part of a historically attributable account. I have used the present tense in offering readings and interpretations, except where references are so clearly and publicly historical that the use of a past tense seemed more appropriate. This is not always possible to distinguish, and ambivalence about the relationships between fact, memory, reconstruction and fiction, and the fluidity of time in memory are part and parcel of the different meanings of autobiography. I have referred to writers, men and women, by their family names, but where they are referring to earlier selves, the central characters in reconstructed narratives of the past, it sometimes seems more appropriate to use first names. There are quotations which use writers' own spelling and syntax. Where there is any ambiguity about whether there is a typographical error, I have tried to draw attention to it.

I have quoted from many autobiographies. To avoid long lists of individual page numbers in separate notes, I have 'bunched' references which come from a single source into one note which covers a particular story, episode, preoccupation or idea and listed the relevant pages together.

Notes

1 See Brandt, 2001, pp.17–24, 105–45.
2 See Burnett, *et al.*, Vols 1–2, 1984–7; Vincent, 1982, 1989; Rose, 2002.
3 See Graff, 1979; Cushman, Kintgen, Kroll & Rose, 2001, pp. 211–33; Sanderson, 1991.
4 See, e.g., Schofield, 1973, p. 437; Vincent, 1989; Stephens, 1987.
5 See, e.g., Brandt, 2001; also Howard, 2008, which refers to American historical studies of writing.
6 See Burnett, 1974, pp. 136–7, 167–8; Steedman, 2007, pp. 64, 110–27, which describes how employers of domestic servants might be prominent in their communities in setting up schools for the teaching of the poor, yet were not concerned that their own servants could not write.
7 E.P. Thompson, 1968, chapter 16.
8 Freeman, 2010, p. 481.
9 Hoggart, 1958, p. 135.
10 See Hamilton & Hillier, 2006: offers a history of the period between the 1970s and the present, particularly concentrating on fluctuations in policy interest and developments in practice.
11 For the testimony and creative writing of learner-writers, see Write First Time, a broadsheet of student writing with editorial comment, written and produced by students and tutors, Bedford, 1974–85. Archive held at Ruskin College, Oxford.
12 OECD, International Adult Literacy Survey, 1997.
13 DfEE, 'A Fresh Start: improving literacy and numeracy. Report of the working group, chaired by Sir Claus Moser', 1999; DfEE, 'Skills for Life: the National Strategy for Improving Adult Literacy and Numeracy Skills', 2001; Department for Business Innovation and Skills (BIS), 2011, BIS Research Paper 57: 2011 Skills for Life Survey, Headline findings.
14 See Grief, Meyer & Burgess, 2007, pp. 8–9; also NRDC (National Research and Development Centre for Adult Literacy and Numeracy) & NIACE, Voices on the Page, 2007–8, accessible at http://www.nrdc.org.uk; for the changing balance of writing and reading, see Brandt (2009), pp. 117–40; pp. 141–76.
15 De Coulon, Meschi & Vignoles, 2008; Bynner & Parsons, 2006 and 2007.
16 For an historical account of ESOL, see Rosenberg, 2008.
17 DfES (Department for Education and Skills), The Skills for Life Survey: a national needs and impact survey of literacy, numeracy and ICT skills, 2003. A follow-up representative survey in England confirmed the figures as largely unchanged, despite the ten-year funded 'Skills for Life' intervention (Department for Business Innovation & Skills (BIS), 2011, BIS Research Paper 57: 2011 Skills for Life Survey).
18 See, e.g., reports of FWWCP groups, such as QueenSpark Books in Brighton (http://www.queensparkbooks.org.uk); see also Morley & Worpole, 1982; Gregory, 1991, pp. 109–20; Woodin, 2005a, 2005b.
19 Barton & Hamilton, 1998.
20 NRDC, based at the Institute for Education, University of London, is an independent research centre funded by government as part of 'Skills for Life', 2002–8.
21 See, e.g., Mace, 2002; Kalman, 1999.
22 Edmondson, 2003, pp. 49–71.

PART ONE

POWERFUL LITERACIES: STATE, CULTURE AND SOCIETY

CHAPTER 1

Teaching and learning writing

I Landscapes of writing development

This chapter explores the teaching and learning of writing in the nineteenth century, from formal institutions to informal ways and means. The emphasis is on the institutional and political formation of school-based literacies in an age which saw rapid development in systems and curricula, resulting in universal elementary education in the 1890s. But educational development was diverse and contested. Besides the political and institutional histories, a sense of the attitudes and practices of learners, social organisations and commercial publishers is needed to create a more rounded picture, so these perspectives are included. I aim to offer insights by delving into policy and practice to paint a landscape from which this under-researched area of educational history can be explored further.

From the start of the century, people were learning to write in a multitude of ways: off and on as time and circumstances permitted. Children learned through local organisations, informal networks and private, community-run schools. These included dame schools, day schools, Sunday schools and, more rarely, dedicated writing schools. After the 1833 Factory Act, reading and writing were also taught in factories to children and adults. Writing was part of educational developments throughout the century. In the competing educational initiatives by churches, government and philanthropic educators detailed attention was paid to writing: who should have access to it, at what stage, and which methods and materials should be used to teach it. Until the 1830s, there was strong resistance to teaching any writing skills to the lower classes: the

A school for mill operatives at Mr Stirling's mill, lower Mosley Street in Manchester. Date:1862
Courtesy of Mary Evans Picture Library

struggle for writing will be explored in chapter 2. From the 1830s onwards, as state grant-aid increased, government influence over how writing should be taught grew. The Revised Code of 1862, and subsequent amendments to it, and the Education Acts of 1870–90, which established elementary education for all, saw the curriculum organised and stratified into Standards 1–V1 and created a structure for standardising the teaching of writing to children.

The milestones in adult literacy learning in the nineteenth century were not marked by Acts of Parliament, but by individual, voluntary, social or political initiatives: adults attended community-run night schools; Sunday schools; studied alone using what materials and manuals they could find; formed independent mutual improvement societies; or got together with others in local informal learning associations, sometimes attached to a social or political organisation. The periodicals of reforming social movements show how they prized education, and writing in particular. Movements such as the Owenism and Chartism put literacy at the heart of their activities. The *Northern Star*, the *Poor Man's Guardian* and other radical newspapers, such as the *Chartist Circular* and the Owenite *New Moral World*, regularly published advertisements for self-help writing lessons and 'Reading Made Easy' courses. There were advertisements for Writing Masters and for community-based and affiliated schools, as well as numerous announcements of the opening of Mechanics' Halls, literary institutes and the like. Such notices appeared in practically every issue, and alongside news and political features, stories and poems by readers and activists were published.[1] Sunday schools, starting with Robert Raikes's Gloucester School founded in the 1780s, mushroomed into large-scale provision, their popularity dependent on whether they offered writing classes. And the Quaker-led Adult Schools, which started in 1811, expanded enormously after 1845 and remained a major provider of writing tuition until 1914. Working men's colleges were founded in the mid-century. Ruskin College was started by radical-thinking US benefactors in 1899 as a correspondence and residential college. And the Workers' Educational Association (WEA) was founded in 1903 by Albert Mansbridge, its first branch opening in Reading in 1904 and its first tutorial classes in Rochdale and Longton, Staffordshire in 1907. Essay-writing was key to all the colleges' and WEA tutorial courses.

Mechanics' Institutes, literary institutes, libraries and lyceums were founded by working people or their middle-class benefactors, sometimes jointly. Writing was taught in most of them, for those with time and money to take advantage. Many people also learned within their families, and among friends or workmates. The most striking characteristic of the ways in which children were taught literacy before the establishment of universal elementary education after 1890 was, as David Vincent comments, 'their sheer variety'.[2]

The most common feature of working-class education, however, even after 1890 and the introduction of the half-time system, was that a child's schooling ended prematurely.[3] After that, most people, however keen, could do no more than squeeze a little education for themselves into the short waking hours outside work – paid or domestic – in whatever local organisations existed.

The proliferation of writing materials on the market before and after the ground-shifting Education Act of 1870 reflects the scale of personal interest as well as a growing labour market for skilled writers, including clerks and local scribes. Stationery and other writing equipment were widely sold by pedlars and street-sellers as well as booksellers and stall-holders. The social investigator Henry Mayhew wrote in the mid-nineteenth century of London's flying stationers, standing patterers and itinerant pedlars, describing them as among the most 'literary' of the multitudes of street-sellers. They produced elaborate written placards, recited poems, told lurid stories and could 'hold forth to a gaping multitude for ... some few minutes continuously'. 'Paper-workers' sold both writing equipment and reading materials, pocket-books, paper, pencils, pens, sealing wax and 'many bladed pen-knives', throughout London and at any 'mail', 'stage' or railway station – 'as if a man could not possibly quit the metropolis without requiring a stock of such commodities'. Mayhew illustrates the contradictions of literacy practices among unschooled workers: the extent of the costermongers' and other street-sellers' reading habits. In his estimation only one in twenty women sellers could read, and 'not one in forty could write'.[4] Yet the motivation to learn to write was widespread and intense. The materials which children and adults used in informal learning and daily life, on which to write, prick out or scratch notes varied from scraps of re-used paper and stone steps to walls, fabric and sand. Pieces of stone, chalk, slate, and pins served as 'pens'. The better-off and clerks used quills and the knives to sharpen them. Steel pens and ink were unknown or a sophisticated luxury for most people in the first half of the century, but they were rapidly introduced into schools and became the key tools of a late-nineteenth-century clerk.

'Learning to write' has never been a simple concept or practice. The phrase 'learning to write' carries complex meanings, because writing is simultaneously a technical and motor skill, a conceptual process and, above all, a means of communication. A thinking process is needed to memorise shapes and strokes, letters and words and apply them, particularly as all this effort must come together simultaneously to generate and compose meaning (a letter, word or sentence). It is more straightforward to write down text which has been dictated or memorised. Yet writing skills which are often seen as relatively mechanical, for example if they are defined as 'handwriting' or 'spelling' or 'copying', in reality also involve complex mechanisms of physical, technical and visual coordination together with cognitive, affective and even creative processes. Decisions are needed at each minute step. All these processes, successfully achieved, result in meaningful marks that are decipherable by self and others and convey messages clearly. The multiplicity of meanings and possibilities is also influenced by other factors for any one person. These include inner, psychological pressures, such as the motivation to learn to write, the ability to persist or the level of confidence; and external pressures, such as the compulsion to attend school, the constraining forces of curriculum

26

structure and content, the literacy requirements of a workplace, or opposition to learning.[5] For nineteenth-century would-be learner-writers, material constraints such as time, poverty, exhaustion, lack of space and privacy added to the weight of all the forces which affected the possibilities and meanings of learning to write.

Writing skills are not the automatic corollary of reading skills. Writing does not follow seamlessly from being able to read. Nevertheless, the two key elements of literacy are interactive and reading is one of the most important activities from which writing skills can be developed. The traditional separation of reading and writing instruction was reinforced in the first two-thirds of the nineteenth century, because most private day and evening schools taught the two subjects separately. Many community-based schools charged additional fees for writing, which prevented large numbers from learning to write at all. The development of specialist writing schools further separated the two. Philip Gardner argued that in private working-class schools writing was 'scarcely ever tackled concurrently with reading'.[6] The result was that by the time a young person had a grasp of reading, they left schooling behind to start work. Writing was a highly prized but secondary skill and as autobiographers make clear, this skill often had to be learned later in life. It was a male province, and far fewer women taught it. Her Majesty's Inspectors, established in 1839, noted though that 'specimens of fine writing' were used to advertise schools, and a schoolmaster who was a proficient penman could attract large numbers to his school.[7] Writing was the more profitable subject, attracting higher fees. Boys and men saw writing as a way into clerical work. Gardner argues that men thus 'endeavoured to monopolise the more lucrative end of the market in basic skills'. Additionally, the rarity of writing schools, their cost and the lack of other ready opportunities to learn writing by comparison with reading go someway to explaining the far greater significance attached in later life to learning to write.

New writers of English faced any number of difficulties quite apart from lack of time or money to learn. There was the complexity of written English with its several clusters of phonemes and complex spelling resulting from the multiple languages from which it developed. Before the 1890s people did not learn to read and write by methods which emphasised a consistent relationship between speech sounds and certain clusters of words, nor was the emphasis on whole words or on meaning.

Learners had to grapple with the inadequacy of the 'consonant-vowel-consonant' method of spelling, which was taught as part of reading, and therefore mainly spoken out loud, rather than attached to the writing lesson. Pupils learned lists of syllables from primers – 'ba be bi bo bu' – which had hardly changed since at least the beginning of the eighteenth century. Moves towards phonic and synthetic methods of teaching gathered pace during the 1840s, but until the elementary system was firmly established, literacy learning was marked by its traditional approaches and methods rather than by any of the new systems which were being rapidly developed and marketed as pedagogically effective as well as scientifically and socially respectable.[8]

Regional speech differences were highly significant to the learning of writing. Given the short periods of time spent concentrating on print in school, and with other printed matter unaffordable, writing was bound to be influenced by the spoken language of teachers and learners. Yet the proliferation and extensive sales of grammar and spelling books for working people are evidence of high levels of awareness of the increasing importance of competence in 'standard' rather than regional varieties of English. Awareness of the looming presence of a dimly perceived set of absolute rules which such publications generated must have inhibited many learner-writers who spoke regional varieties of English. Their vocabulary was only partially available in dictionaries, should such a luxury be accessible. The poet John Clare's Northamptonshire dialect illustrates the point. Learners could scarcely have avoided a consciousness that their English was not acceptable as written communication, other than for purely personal notes. On the other hand, manuals and grammars provided at least some guidance, grounded in written conventions at a time when little education was available. The journey into literacy was even more complicated because so many texts used for learning, such as catechisms and other religious readers, the King James Bible, *Pilgrim's Progress* or *Paradise Lost*, and now obscure books such as James Hervey's *Meditations among the Tombs* and Richard Baxter's *Saints' Everlasting Rest*, were all written in an archaic English very different from varieties in contemporary usage, and must have been a strenuous read for adults new to literacy. But these books had meaning: they were often held dear as tenets of belief or because they were the only books a family possessed.[9] And as E.P. Thompson noted, the fact that they represented truth and spiritual guidance as well as being symbols of aspirational literacy – they were, literally, teachings – had a profound influence on the ways people wrote.[10]

Working-class autobiographers often include an account of their first experiences of learning to write, and progress to discussions of grammar and writing as a compositional, creative form of communication. Although reading and spelling generally preceded writing and ciphering in small private schools, it was not until the Revised Code of 1862 took an iron grip on the curriculum that an absolute hierarchy of writing skills was mapped out. There was no compositional writing of any kind. Any remotely creative writing, such as a short letter or composition, became a practically unattainable target for most children, since even after the relaxation of the Revised Code in 1871 it was available only in Standard VI – the highest level. This consisted of 'a short theme or letter or an easy paraphrase'. So it was 30 years after the introduction of the Penny Post in 1840 before composition became an element of the curriculum, and even then it was only offered to pupils at the top Standard within a tightly restricted framework. Many children left school before they reached this stage. The careful control of the curriculum demonstrates the increasing effectiveness of attempts to shape what and how people learned. Writing skills for working-class people were in general to be limited to the most basic skills required for the functions which in the eyes of the state it was useful for them to perform. Approved activities included writing simple letters to be sent by the Penny Post and the acquisition of skills to ensure a supply of labour for the market in clerical work. Favoured methods and materials for teaching writing and reading promoted moral improvement, to counter the malign influence of popular literature. The ascendancy of the mechanical (e.g. copying) over the conceptual (e.g. dictation, composition) in writing was reified by the Revised Code. However, the intentions of governments, powerful establishments and professional educators should not be confused with people's actual practices and purposes in and out of school. Not everyone learned to write by working through a hierarchy of skills from basic letter formation to complex composition. The motivation to learn often came from the desire to write a particular text – to communicate or express thoughts and feelings arising from acute hardship or happiness. Nevertheless the enshrining of conventional stages and levels in formal education provided the context for the variety of ways in which literacy was actually learned and practised. And official, hierarchical patterns of literacy learning increasingly took hold.

Writing lessons for all ages generally began with copying simple strokes, letters and words. The most popular and the cheapest method of learning to write was to copy a found text, using the most basic materials. For learners with a rudimentary reading ability who were picking up writing skills on their own, or helped by family or friends, copying was the most obvious method. Letters, words and texts, wherever found – on stray papers, letters, scraps, in books, on tombstones or placards – were used to shape and compose letters, words and sentences. The meaning of these materials to learners will be explored in later chapters.

Copying as a method was less inventive but more systematised in schools and adult institutions. Formal opportunities to learn to write began to sprout up in the early years of the century, not only because of the growth of Sunday and day schools, night schools and other adult institutions. The Adult School Movement became one of the main providers of writing teaching for adults throughout the nineteenth century, with classes sometimes exceeding 100 pupils, rarely fewer than 20. Classes were held in many towns and cities. In 1901 there were over 45,000 learners and 400 Adult Schools. The movement was buoyant until 1914, but declined sharply between the wars. Developing from Sunday schools, the first opened in Nottingham in 1798, then in Bala, Wales in 1811, followed by Bristol in 1812. After that, schools proliferated. The movement was led by Quakers, though Baptists were early initiators. The core Adult School model was a one-hour or one-and-a-half-hour session, of which the 'First Half Hour' was mainly devoted to writing: copying or dictation.[11] When Thomas Pole described the schools' method of teaching writing in 1816 he praised copying as an aid to memory and a contemplative activity as much as the practice of a mechanical skill.

> *When the learners have advanced to joining hand, instructive Scripture texts are placed before them, which being written over and over again, six or eight times on the slate, it becomes much more indelibly impressed on their memories than by hearing them once read; … in writing, there is the exercise of a mental, as well as a mechanical, operation, each tending to fix those religious truths in the mind, which may become subjects of future instructive contemplation.[12]*

In the Scarborough School, where the learners included a bricklayer, a labourer and two painters and decorators, 'The teachers would set out three or four copy books, write a line of a text at the head of a page, search in another desk for half a dozen Bibles and then begin to read – and wait' for the scholars to arrive. As well as writing, Sunday morning studies included arithmetic, Bible study, using the library and managing money. Savings and funeral funds were part of Adult Schools' purposes – and social events like tea parties and outings – 'Pleasant Sunday Afternoons' – were regular features. There was resistance to overt proselytising: 'I did not come here to learn religion, but writing' said one learner to which the teacher replied: 'do we not teach writing?' Organisers knew writing was the lure: a leader William White remarked that 'they will come if you advertise the school for reading and writing. Being crafty, we catch them with guile.' Finding writing teachers – no qualifications asked for – was not always easy. A typical advert ran: 'We are in want of a writing teacher. Will someone kindly help us?'[13]

There is evidence from autobiographers that copying stimulated thinking, reflection and creativity. Adam Rushton was born in 1821 in High Hurdsfield, near Manchester, the son of tenant farmers. His formal education was limited to a Sunday school, to which he was attached from the age of four to thirty. In his Sunday school, as was common practice, writing lessons were offered once competence at reading was achieved. In *My Life*, Rushton describes his progress:

> *In all the Bible classes at that time writing was taught. I worked hard and strove eagerly to get into one of these classes, and very soon did so. And then came the glorious times of straight strokes, pothooks, and ladles. How fascinating these elementary characters seemed! How, in admiration, I fixed my gaze upon them, and how easily, to my surprise, I made them! Then, more exhilarating still, came forth words, and sentences, and even my own name, written in large, strong strokes of my quill pen. No engineer, inventor, discoverer, or commander could have felt more exquisite pleasure in their moments of conquest and triumph, than was experienced by me in mastering the art of writing.*

Rushton remembers the intense pleasure of anticipation, a sense of power and the rewards of achievement. There was no dreariness for him in repeatedly copying the strokes and curves before he progressed to copying letters and words. The language of adventure and discovery is bound up with the practical mechanics of learning. As for many learners, learning to write his name was a significant act. Modern pedagogy might allow that for Rushton the end, the pleasure of achievement, justified the means:

31

repetition, mindless copying and rote learning. But he insists that pleasure lay not only in the achievement of literacy but in the process itself, in the contemplative and imaginative release which copying facilitated and the pleasure of creating accurate shapes on the page. He developed this theme, asserting that copying was no 'barren conquest'. For Rushton and others who learned to write by copying, it was a way of actively reading and thinking through writing. Copying made space for ideas to spark and provided imaginative inspiration for composition. Rushton wrote of the Sunday school hymns used for writing practice that 'by writing them down in my copy-book, they became a rich and lasting treasure'. 'Pondering over' was a creative process. They'd 'fill my mind with sentiment and song'. He thought physical writing exercises had also helped his intellectual and political development.

> *By these writing exercises my mind was led out into ever-broadening streams of thought and investigation. In some book … I found a poem entitled* The Covenanter's Crave. *I wrote it down and became deeply interested in it, and eagerly sought for further information concerning the Covenanters' sufferings and noble deeds … Another poem, entitled* The Pilgrim Fathers, *which I copied, greatly excited me. No rest could I have until I had learned more of these heroic people.*[14]

Rushton's response to repetition in writing was not unique. In 1852, Harriet Martineau wrote *Household Words* about a learner in a Unitarian women's Adult School in Birmingham. The woman wanted to write a love letter:

> *The patience with which these women sat at their pothooks makes us marvel. One woman made 'o's' in her copybook for weeks and the delight of being able to add a stroke to this so that she could form 'd' and write the first letter of her name, was extreme.*[15]

But learners were not to be patronised, even if that is exactly what often happened: 'One woman complained that she was being treated like a child in having to learn o + x = ox, and on being asked what it meant, she said "as if everybody did not know a' ox is a cow" '. Motivation ran high: 'the learners stick to their writing, as if nothing could discourage them'. To encourage absent learners who might have lost momentum through illness, bereavement or 'idleness' writing skills were used to 'send a message of comfort'. Making writing useful and relevant to real life was a much-discussed aspect of the curriculum.[16]

II Towards a national model: the Lancaster and Bell systems of teaching writing

From the early nineteenth century, learning to write became a possibility for more urban working-class children. Many charity and community-run private schools, including dame schools, Sunday schools and some writing schools, provided, with financial contributions from families, the means to some learning. The state and churches jostled for influence and position, and a growing interest in education for the 'lower classes' hardened into a determination to develop provision and mould it to their vision. Philip Gardner has convincingly argued that the powerful educational movements which emerged at the beginning of the century gradually evolved, with the intervention of the state, into a coherent and zealous assault on private schools run by the working class, which ensured their eventual eradication. The founding of the two great rival educational societies, the non-conformist British and Foreign School Society and the Anglican National Society marked the beginning of the intensification of attempts to counter, through mass education, what were seen as the morally and politically unwholesome influences of working-class mores. Their goal was a properly orchestrated education system. Dame schools and other independent working-class institutions were seen at best as worthy but ineffectual, at worst as educationally and morally harmful. More practically, they could only take small numbers of children. Through their pioneering new systems, the Societies could multiply exponentially the number of children who received a basic education.

The educational system sponsored by the two Societies was known as the monitorial system. Older, often just-literate pupils taught and supervised younger pupils in huge halls divided into rows with just one teacher presiding over all. The British and Foreign School Society was founded by Joseph Lancaster, a Quaker. His first school opened in Borough Road, Southwark, London, in 1798. The National Society was founded by Dr Andrew Bell in 1811. Bell's earlier experience in education, in particular the monitorial experiment in Madras, India, became the model for this mode of instruction. Lancaster's claim that by using monitors up to a thousand pupils could be taught by one teacher was attractive, reflecting in education the efficiencies of the new factory system. By 1833, when both societies were well established, approximately two pupils in five received an education outside informal local educational networks, although these practices remained resilient for some decades. Participation in the new forms of education varied in length from a matter of days to a few weeks, but rarely extended beyond a year.

If moral education rather than literacy skill was the primary driving force of the monitorial movement, reading and writing were solid planks of the daily school routine. The education was normally free, apart from the fee of 3d for writing-books. The cost of writing was a problem for all providers of education, but Lancaster and Bell came up with two of the most popular solutions. Bell favoured the sand tray as the cheapest medium for first steps in writing rather than paper, and Lancaster 'found that slates from a demolished house made a good writing surface, and thus gave to nineteenth century education one of its most characteristic symbols'.[17] Lancaster's invention was a constantly recurring symbol of schooling and the learning of writing in autobiography and continues to be so well into the twentieth century in memories of Board School education. Albert Goodwin, a pupil, writes of:

> 'that great asset, the Slate'. The piece of very thin slate was enclosed in a wooden frame and according to size and extras on it cost 1½d (very small) to 4½d (very large). If it had lines on one side they cost an extra ½d and if the first size letters of the alphabet were grooved in the top line a penny more etc. If you got one of the best the overall cost was sixpence but few of us had these. On purchasing a slate someone, usually your father, bored holes with a heated poker in the top and bottom bar of the frame and from these a piece of string, a leather lace or even a piece of staylace if your mother had broken hers and saved the pieces, was passed through the holes and knotted in such a way that a big loop was formed through which you put one arm and your head and so carried the slate on your back.[18]

Mabel Cutts's life story mentions the importance attached to starting each day 'with a clean slate', and the cleaning of the slates at the end of the day, under the direction of the pupil chosen for 'slate duty'.[19] So powerful was the image of the slate for the conscientious objector and Labour MP George Tomlinson, it stayed with him throughout life: his biographer quotes him saying 'I do not remember using an exercise book except at an examination – slates were used instead. I well remember the number of my slate – 41085.'[20] Others remembered the slates as unhygienic, wiped clean each day with grubby rags which pupils wore round their necks.[21] The servicing of writing was delegated to monitors who were also responsible for ruling copy-books and preparing pens.

The method of teaching children their letters inherited by the early-nineteenth-century church societies had survived from medieval times. This was a system of learning by disconnected syllables 'followed by columns of monosyllabic words which might then be grouped into sentences of a relentlessly spiritual or moral quality'. One innovation of the new 'Madras' system was its concurrent teaching of reading and writing, introduced only because 'the processes of acquiring each skill were thought to be mutually reinforcing' and 'mere "learning" remained a secondary concern'.[22] Regardless of the motivation in introducing this approach, it seems to have offered more than just increased efficiency in teaching technical skills. It was also a way of developing conceptual skills. The inspector John Allen, reporting in 1841/2 on Derbyshire schools, noted that far more emphasis should be placed on writing, for reasons of strengthening both memory and understanding:

> *It would be a much greater step in leading them to use their understanding if the reading lessons were tested by written answers to written questions, or by requiring an abstract of the lessons to be written from memory.*

Allen also noted the merits of Bell's system of contemporaneous teaching of reading and writing because 'It affords a change of employment, and the forms of the letters are better fixed on the child's memory by the attempt to copy them'.[23]

James Bonwick was a pupil at the Lancasterian School in Newington Causeway, Southwark, early in the century. He provides a lengthy account of sand, slate and copy-book writing and spelling, each presented as a separate item. He gives writing far greater prominence than reading – his schooling began with the 'Oriental' style of making letters in the sand, carried out at a specially designated 'sand desk'. A letter was drawn by the monitor ('my little teacher'), who shouted its name and the children repeated this out loud. The sand was then smoothed by the children with a stick in preparation for their formation of the letter. The name of the letter was repeated in chorus. The process was repeated for the next letter. Bonwick observed that Bell's Madras system was still in operation when he visited schools in Bombay later in life. In a century which saw methods and materials change rapidly, Bonwick saw learning to write as a shared point of reference across time and cultural differences: 'My education ... began at the very point where little ones had begun the noble art of reading and writing in far off eastern lands, doubtless thousands of years ago.'[24]

Writing was the only relatively quiet activity in the hubbub of a school day. Reading was learned aloud and spelling was drilled by chanting syllables and by 'zealously practised' dictation so that 'from the beginning to the end of the school day the classroom was filled with the sound of the human voice'.[25] It was 'always sufficiently loud to stun the visitor'. Writing was learned, after sand-writing, on slates and afterwards in copy-books. 'The slates were ruled for three hands.' Slower ones were taught separately, 'in the quietude of others at writing'.[26] Quill pens for copy-book writing had to be repaired by the monitors with the help of pupils. All the materials belonged to the Society, and when the writing lesson was finished, the copy-books were preserved for the next day. Every last detail of their careful storage and redistribution was thought of by the Society.[27] One of Bonwick's vivid memories is the 'Christmas Pieces', 'gaudy' pictures of Bible stories, with a space in the middle, into which the pupils copied verses. Like many others, Bonwick keeps a significant memento of learning to write next to him as he writes his autobiography: 'done when I was eleven years old, the daub of colour depicting Jehu driving furiously'.[28]

Lancaster and Bell's monitorial methods sought, as Bell put it, to be 'the steam engine of the moral world',[29] an educational version of the factory system. A serious criticism was that pupils 'who were little more than infants, without training, without special instruction, with no qualifying test, were set to waste their own time and that of their still younger companions under nominal supervision of the teacher'.[30] The system of monitors was replaced by pupil teachers following the establishment of the government's Committee of Council on Education (CCE) in 1839. Two points complicated the paradigm of Lancasterian schools as the socially-controlling engine of instruction and demonstrated how close opposing political and social ideologies could be. First, there was Lancaster's idea that allowing pupils to make a noise meant they would never consider schooling a drudgery to be taught. This is reminiscent of the utopian socialist and communitarian Charles Fourier, who proposed that hordes of little boys would willingly be cleaners and drudges in his

36

'phalansteries' because they loved getting dirty. Secondly, Lancaster's humour and scatty humanitarianism undermined the authoritarian framework of his own schools.

The method of teaching writing in the schools run by the British and Foreign School Society may have seemed as mechanical as factory production. The Society's pedagogy was ruled by the principle of skills acquisition in a moralising context rather than to expand knowledge or nurture creativity. However, writing was a core element of the whole curriculum, not as elsewhere an additional option to attract a higher fee. And the method of teaching reading and writing concurrently potentially offered a stimulus to cognitive development, forging connections between reading and writing and the linguistic content of each, which could facilitate an interactive learning process in which a child could absorb material and recreate it in writing.

In the *Handbook to the Borough Road Schools*, which explains the teaching process, cost-effectiveness sits alongside educational concerns. Pupils were divided into sections of 50, with the lowest sections '*on slate*' while the more advanced worked with paper. This division was to enable pupils to learn body and hand positions and letter-formation 'before the expense of writing on paper is incurred'. However the Handbook urges speedy progression to copy-books on the grounds of raising achievement: 'The additional trouble entailed by the use of pen, ink and copy-book, is more than repaid by the better means of training and improvement which they afford'. The writing lesson proceeded as follows:

> *The teacher now prints on the blackboard one of the letters learned, and questions on the direction and comparative length of the lines composing it; bringing out the ideas straight, curved, vertical, horizontal, oblique, or parallel. He then pursues the same course with the rest of the letters which form the subject of the lesson, the children imitating them on their slates, first from the teacher's copy, and afterwards from dictation. The alphabet is thus quickly and easily learnt, while at the same time the minds of the children are developed and much useful information imparted respecting words and things.* [31]

This lesson is concerned with more than mechanical skills. It aims to promote understanding of abstract concepts, the 'bringing out' of mathematical and spatial terms such as 'curved, vertical, horizontal, oblique', with an emphasis on mental development. Writing was understood as a set of graphic skills to be taught overtly, but with the secondary aims of encouraging thought processes, increasing vocabulary and widening knowledge. Even if the purpose behind these aims was also to subordinate, control and morally indoctrinate learners they could nonetheless be empowering because they were transferable to other purposes and practices.

Lancaster's intention, like Bell's, was to provide a moral education and literacy skills for thousands of children, not to create aspirations beyond possessing the rudiments of reading, writing and arithmetic. But he appears to have been happily aware that knowledge gleaned through his system could escape its intended confines. He remarked that one clever boy at the Borough Road school wrote constantly, composing paragraphs for newspapers, stories, a reply to Thomas Paine's *Rights of Man* and more:

> *In all these attempts he wasted many quires of paper, rose in the morning early, neglected his meals, and was often wholly swallowed up in the subject with which his mind was engaged. What was the result of all these laughable attempts? He insensibly acquired the art of thinking intensely and clearly on any subject on which his mind was engaged; and, in the end, attained a concise, familiar style of writing, which, it is probable, he never would have acquired by any other means.*[32]

Lancaster was a disastrous manager of money, even though he shared with all his contemporaries in education the belief that education for poor children should cost next to nothing. Despite the cost he thoroughly approved of the capabilities which writing skills could bring. He made the connection here between writing, thinking and the role of the unconscious in learning, and noticed that concentration, clarity of thought and creativity can be developed by trying to express ideas as well as facts in writing. As Frank Smith argued, compositional writing can only happen if there is a reason for saying something, the desire to say it, and a 'transformational grammar' is developed enough in the brain to convert 'deep structures of meaning' into conventional prose.[33] A narrow skills-based instruction was enough for this motivated learner to answer Paine in writing. Writing does need mechanical skills, to enable words surfacing from the unconscious, processed and crystallised in the conscious mind, to take shape on paper. That Lancaster, the inventor of an educational conveyor-belt, should have been aware of such issues is as surprising as that he should find a child 'wasting' paper amusing. And although the Society's schools did provide paper free to some pupils, there was normally a charge – with waivers. The accounts of 1802 show that two reams of paper for 160 books were 'gifts for those unable to pay for them'.[34]

III   Writing and the State: The Committee of Council on Education (CCE) and Her Majesty's Inspectorate (HMI) 1839–50

Historians of working-class education and literacy have rightly emphasised that the motives for 'one of the strongest of the early Victorian obsessions'[35] sprang from a condemnation of working-class mores and the need to compensate for the negative influences of the family through state-sponsored schools acting *in loco parentis*. Education, at least from the 1840s, was, in HMI Henry Moseley's words, the last 'great hope of staying … this flood of evil' which was seen to engulf the working-class child with rising crime rates and pauperism. Education would counter the 'great tide of human calamity'.[36] In this view, the malign influence of working-class parents was caused by poverty and ignorance, compounded by susceptibility to crime, superstition, political subversion and demagoguery. A forceful counter-influence was widely deemed essential. The strategies initiated by the Privy Council worked from the start to replace the majority of community-run schools by grant-aiding the two Societies to reform and improve their teaching and facilities. They sought to professionalise teaching. In this respect, the monitorial system and the 'bawling' lessons in these 'engines of instruction' had gone out of favour because of their lack of discipline and effectiveness. From the late 1830s, the careful training and monitoring of pupil teachers and teachers began, to ensure that they developed from skills instructors and childminders to effective educators and custodians of moral welfare. During training, their writing skills were rigorously tested.

The HMI began its work at a time when the argument that writing should be part of working-class education had largely been won. The old prejudices and fears about the consequences of writing had been outstripped by institutional and commercial forces in favour. Parliamentary Enquiries paved the way for the introduction of the Penny Post in 1840, led by Rowland Hill. There were educational clauses to the 1833 Factory Act, requiring the youngest children allowed to work in factories – aged nine to 13 – to receive two hours of education per day, and their working hours not to exceed nine hours (for 13–18-year-olds, 12 hours). Factory inspectors were appointed. Subsequent Factory Acts provided more improvements in conditions and educational provision for children, the result of sustained campaigns to alleviate harsh conditions and long hours. These Acts also reflected some recognition that employers were beginning to voice interest in a more literate workforce, minimal as their conception of literacy for operatives was. And since people were taking it on themselves to learn in growing numbers without help, official support for literacy followed the gathering pace of practices on the ground. Evidence of changing ideas is provided by the state's first major initiative. The Committee of the Privy Council on Education and HMI were created in 1839 to report on schools of every kind across England and Wales, each inspector reporting on a geographical region or 'district' and sometimes also a particular aspect of education. They moved swiftly to professionalise the writing curriculum by giving 'full support to the introduction of a "rational basis" for instruction in writing: "Formerly ... the method of teaching to write, from the absence of any acknowledged system, was necessarily abandoned to the inventive powers of the master" '.[37] For centuries writing was taught in Latin – for example to middle-class boys in grammar schools. Some of the Writing Masters' methods were rejected and some, like note-taking, were now desired.[38] Writing was becoming a serious subject and its perceived amateurism was to be replaced by a system that could be properly evaluated. Inspectors provided detailed accounts of the teaching of writing as well as statistics on levels of reading and writing. Their reports built on factory inspectors' reports of literacy levels and attendance patterns among factory children in the reading, writing and arithmetic classes provided in factories after the 1833 Factory Act. The CCE issued careful instructions and recommendations to HMI about the new writing practices to be promoted in their work with schools.

HMI has been widely perceived as working within the ideology of the educational reforms of the state and churches, the embodiment of middle-class patronage. Yet their reports reveal that as a group of establishment and literary figures, they held diverse, independent-minded and critical views. They were not simply aligned with the forces of social control. Their attitudes to popular education were sometimes crushingly certain, sometimes exploratory, sometimes questing, and often critical of mechanical learning. More often than not, they sought to promote a deeper level of educational development and breadth of knowledge. Their undoubtedly patronising social views were tempered by enthusiasm for intellectual development and their belief in education as morally and socially uplifting. Henry Moseley in particular realised that it was important to look beyond the moral universe of the middle-classes and understand a profoundly different way of life:

> *The inner life of the classes below us in society is never penetrated by us. We are profoundly ignorant of the springs of public opinion, the elements of thought and the principles of action among them.*[39]

HMI's work revealed the complexities and tensions in the development of national education systems. Their stances are well illustrated by their reports on writing instruction which offered detailed accounts of the state of writing in schools across the country. They covered a wide range of social, economic, pedagogical and health-related concerns from teaching methods to posture, hygiene, furniture and the arrangement of classrooms. If the desks for writing were placed facing the wall (the traditional arrangement for monitorial systems), they commented, then newer 'synthetic' whole-class methods of teaching using a blackboard were impossible. By the 1840s the use of the monitorial system was actively discouraged. The 'synthetic' method was applied to reading and writing and involved breaking words (or letters in the case of writing) down into component parts, which learners then synthesised, in effect a mixture of traditional and new approaches.[40] The writing skills of monitors and pupil teachers were subject to inspection, which assessed whether monitors and pupil teachers were able to write with ease and skill; decently; imperfectly; or not at all. Inspectors report on the numbers of pupils learning writing 'With Chalk on the Wall or on a Board', 'On Slates', and 'On Paper' in all levels of classes. Grammar and Linear Drawing were also among the subjects to be inspected.

The inspectorate noted every detail of the physical environment, and proposed reforms. The shape and furnishing of classrooms were crucial to their concept of teaching and their dual purpose of minimising costs whilst accommodating as many children as health and hygiene would allow. One of the Council's early recommendations was that desks should be built facing the front, at an inclined plane, adjustable with hinges and moveable brackets, not least so that extra scholars could be fitted in on Sundays. 'The classes which are writing or ciphering being

41

thus arranged along the sides of the room, the middle will be left open for the classes to stand out whilst reading.' The Committee was concerned that the walls should be 'lined with a broad belt of black board, or prepared with mastic, painted black, for lessons in chalk-drawing and writing'. In 1839 they proposed the depth, width and height of desks and forms, with boards nailed to desks on which dictation and class marks should be posted.[41]

In those schools inspected from the 1840s, writing lessons suffered from lack of materials, especially expensive items such as copy-books. So pupils started on sand or slates and progressed to copy-books if and when they could be afforded. But slates got lost or broken, and blackboards were increasingly recommended. Inspectors remarked on whether the walls were lined with blackboard 'for lessons in chalk drawing and writing'. Blackboards also facilitated the teaching of large classes by one teacher, and for this reason also inspectors noted their absence and urged their use. Paper, which was costly and rarely used for early stages, gradually became more attainable. Moseley reported in 1845 that paper was now machine-made and almost duty-free. Bellair criticised the prevalence of 'bad writing' in the Western Districts, blaming the stubby pieces of pencil, hard for children's little fingers to manipulate. 'The left hand was used to support the slate which fell to the left hand side, causing the fingers of the right hand to be "cramped and doubled up" '.[42]

Before 1891 fees were charged in nearly all schools at varying levels. Private and local church schools relied entirely on fees, and were often more expensive than grant-aided voluntary schools, and writing usually cost extra. Yet the success of these schools reflected demand for a more organic provision, in which there was not the social gulf between community and school that was fast developing. At one Derbyshire Congregational school at Mill St, Bakewell, which was inspected in 1842–3, reading and writing were core subjects, taught in a 'package' with others at 3d–6d per week depending on further subjects taken. But the materials needed pushed the fees for writing higher. At one boys' school in Penzance, 1d a week extra was charged for writing paper.[43] At Bakewell, a home exercise book was an additional 2d; copy-books 4d; a framed slate 4d; slate pencils ½d; drawing pencils 1½d; drawing paper 1d. In this school, nevertheless, the take-up of writing was high. More children had begun writing than were thought able to read. Some gender differences existed. More boys (approximately 60 per cent) wrote on paper than girls, who wrote longer on slates, with only 35 per cent writing on paper.[44] One inspector commented that 'a graduated scale of payments, according as the child may be taught writing and accounts as well as reading, acts, as far as my experience teaches me, very ill. The master ordinarily neglects the less advanced pupils to give an undue share of his time to such as bring the largest school fee.'[45] Those who could afford to learn to write thus received extra attention. However, the system also militated against many children learning even the most basic writing skills, since, as autobiographers have testified, many families could not afford the extra fee. Graduated fees also worked against an integrated curriculum. Where reading and writing were taught at the same levels, it was more difficult to separate out the fees and charge for individual components of the curriculum.[46]

One of the first aspects of the writing curriculum the inspectorate addressed was the allocation of time to writing. Precise timings were recommended for each component of the school day, one of many drives to control 'the use of time by the labouring poor'.[47] The consensus about how much time should be spent on a writing lesson was a maximum of half an hour on grounds of health:

> *The lesson in writing in a copy-book should not occupy more than twenty minutes or half an hour; after a short period the delicate frames of children become incapable of that precision and freedom of movement indispensable to good writing.*[48]

In some schools inspectors noted that writing was taught each day for 15 minutes; in others half an hour, including bookkeeping and the correcting of false grammar. The recommended period excluded the preparation and repair of pens, which inspectors proposed should be outside school hours. The danger otherwise was that teachers would be busy mending pens 'or copying out returns for the overseers of the poor'.[49]

Detailed reports criticised teaching and learning practices, the levels of literacy in the communities visited and the methods used in schools. Content and methodology were among concerns about the place of writing in the curriculum. Lack of meaning and 'mechanical processes' in lessons were targets for improvement. In his reports on many aspects of schooling in the mining district of South Wales, HMI Samuel Tremenheere charged schools with a lack of meaningful content in the writing curriculum. 'A pile of detached covers and leaves too black for further use … betoken[ed] the result of long struggles with unmeaning rows of spelling'. He noted that in only 18 of the 47 day schools visited were 'the principles of English grammar taught' and that the teaching of reading and writing was confined to 'the mechanical processes'. This was in a community where a sample survey of 24 families had shown that no-one was able to write. The lack of the kind of 'intellectual proficiency' that would allow individuals to gain 'situations of responsibility' was noted.[50]

Inspectors set more store on quality than quantity and for this reason they commended the graduated scheme of writing offered by the new Mulhauser method of teaching writing. They argued that systems for the evaluation of learners' work should be introduced. Writing about boy pupils, one inspector remarked that they 'should be encouraged to judge of their own work, and perhaps that of each others'.[51] Dictation and the writing of abstracts of lessons that had been read were further aspects of writing lessons favoured by inspectors. A number of inspectors' reports lend as much importance to understanding and imagination in writing lessons as they do to the skills components. Their recommendations were not couched only in the language and philosophy of utilitarianism, promoting mechanical inculcation of facts or rote learning of bodies of knowledge. Indeed one inspector reported that 'we cannot expect them to be interested in that of which they do not in some measure apprehend every part'. Allen advocated the development of language and vocabulary through reading and writing. He criticised the practice of learning words and spelling by rote from set books, advocating instead the association of 'new words with ideas previously acquired'. At one level this reflected a concern with accuracy. He suggested the creation of sentences in which pupils could test whether a word could be replaced by a 'supposed synonym' without changing the sense. At another level, however, the discourse centred on the building up of ideas and expression through language, where 'every fresh term rightly conceived by the mind becomes the centre of a new cluster of ideas, adding substance and compactness to what has previously come under observation and making the acquisition of treasures more easy'.[52]

The CCE put forward the Rotterdam Poor School as a model for the inspectorate, chosen for its 'order, propriety, decorum and subordina-tion', and because of its solid attention to skill 'though without any brilliancy'. Writing was prominent in the curriculum of this model, and by the second class (of three levels) emphasis was laid on the fact that skills acquisition should not be 'merely in the mechanical part of those

44

branches', for example the development of 'writing, as a means of stating their thoughts'.[53]

One inspector recommended following the Bell system, bringing together the reading and writing lesson.

> *It would be a much greater step in leading them to use their understanding if the reading lessons were tested by requiring written answers to written questions, or by requiring an abstract of the lessons to be written from memory.*

> *It seems very desirable that Dr. Bell's rule of beginning to teach writing contemporaneously with reading should, if possible, be always adhered to; it affords a change of employment, and the forms of the letters are better fixed on the child's memory by the attempt to copy them.*[54]

The 1844 Minutes of the CCE on the teaching of writing recommended that writing be taught from the outset of a child's education, and even that writing might precede reading instruction. Their approach recognised a child's ability to imitate, and made writing central to every subsequent form of instruction or subject: writing was the means of instilling and facilitating learning. They emphasised the pleasure and ease of learning and the advantages of a system which a child saw as a pastime rather than work.

School inspectors were agreed that there was room for rethinking the teaching of writing, though their analyses of what caused or consti-tuted good or bad practice varied. The educational establishment often looked to models from Switzerland or Germany: patented educational packages of proven success, wrapped in the respectability of scientific language and academic recommendations. The inspectorate were encouraged to adopt the Mulhauser writing system, imported from Switzerland and used at the Battersea Training College with pupil teachers. Another common approach was to promote the writing lesson as an aspect of moral education, reflected in the British and Foreign School Society's eagerness to provide pupils with 'good copies'. In 1844, HMI Watkins was concerned that schools in the northern counties of England were becoming too liberal in their approach to writing. He deplored an approach by schools which considered 'common copies' as 'beneath their notice'. Schools favoured extracts from 'real' literature rather than the copy-book texts which offered admonishing or thought-provoking homilies: 'Anxiety attends riches', 'Patiently bear trials', 'Oppression is hateful'. The Chartist William Lovett good-humouredly remembered his experience of learning to write from copies at his boys' school:

> *This master was … a bit of a wit; for he being too busy on one occasion to set me a copy requested me to write one for myself. From some curious notions I had formed of royalty, I wrote for my copy – 'All kings have long heads', which, when my master saw, he wrote on the opposite page, 'All horses have longer heads'.* [55]

The use of 'real' texts would have saved the cost of buying commercial copy-books with pre-printed texts, and may also have been introduced as an improvement. The inspectors' reports show that some copy-books were of poor quality with 'thin and spongy' paper, home-made by teachers, parents and children. To save paper, one copy was written over another. The inspector complained that 'one can hardly find the beginning, and can never hope to reach the end'. The system of writing a chosen text into home-made copy-books gave pupils access to popular books and other copy drawn from real life, conveying the message that reading literature was valuable as well as writing neatly and accurately. Another inspector disapproved on several counts:

> *Passages from all kinds of books are preferred, and copied carelessly and incorrectly. Amongst these I have found a 'Letter-Writer' with letters beginning 'My dear charmer', 'My lovely Emma', and the like. In a boys' school there were others addressed to 'William Honest', 'Job Troublesome', Etc. complaining of 'badness of times', Etc. In several I observed 'notes of invitation to dinner', 'to a party at the theatre', messages 'of inquiry', of 'condolence', Etc. There were also passages of poetry of a questionable tendency, hymns in extravagant or presumptuous language, Etc.*

HMI Moseley joined the debate, criticising the daily copying of model phrases. He opposed the subjugation of the individual to 'the huge animal having a single volition', which prevented learners from any opportunity 'to write on paper from dictation, or to express their own thoughts under any form whatever in writing upon paper'. In his view, the success of education for the labouring classes depended on

> *teaching them to reason about and understand things which are connected with their ordinary pursuits. With the labouring man these are things so engrossing that, whatever other process of instruction we may begin in his mind when a little boy at school, the consideration of these will infallibly take the place of them when he comes to be a man.*

Writing about dictation, Moseley wrote:

> *In the hope of making them fine writers – for the accomplishment of which a long practice of large-text writing is assumed to be necessary – they are deprived of the practice of the art of writing under that form in which alone it will ever be of any use to them; and the process of their education is left without that exercise of the intelligence which is implied in the exposition of the thoughts in writing – an element which no other can replace.*

Moseley notes that 'in our own education' mentally demanding writing exercises were of 'great importance', adding that this system would influence working-class attitudes to education for the good, because parents would see the usefulness of their children's learning.[56]

IV   Teaching writing: radicals' responses

Diverse approaches to teaching skills, knowledge and moral responsibility collided. Many church educators in the early nineteenth century, including the Adult School founders, were convinced that learning to write by copying was neither an intellectually nor a morally empty exercise. J.J. Mayer of the Stockport Sunday School expressed similar sentiments to the Adult School promoters when he wrote that:

> *You may say, without being able to read we could not obtain a knowledge of the scriptures. And I reply, without writing they would never have been handed down to us. Is there any more harm in writing a chapter from the Bible, than in reading it? Nay, is not the former better than the latter? Because that will impress it upon our memory much more than this ... I have found that those who have been taught writing, have been more serious, and more circumspect in their conduct ... and for this, among*

other reasons, they have hereby acquired greater ability to make themselves better acquainted with their duty.[57]

Social movements were actively engaged in education and no less concerned to provide a moral and political education, along with literacy skills. Education was seen as integral to activity for social change and many people joined not least to learn and practise literacy. Middle-class fervour for education was matched by working-class hunger for literacy as well as debate and action, evidenced by articles and correspondence in the columns of the radical press, a variety of educational tools and pedagogical publications. Empowerment through 'Really Useful Knowledge' lay at the heart of the educational aims of social movements and writing instruction was a prominent feature in many organisations' educational efforts. The Chartists William Lovett and J. Collins developed an educational plan in which writing was a vital element. In *Chartism, A New Organisation of the People*, 1840, which they wrote in prison, Lovett and Collins set out their educational proposals, emphasising the mental and moral processes of learning as strongly as the inspectors. In their proposed system, the starting point for learning to read was word-creation through 'writing'. A linguistic concept (e.g. 'it is a pea') was agreed and the lesson moved from concept to the physical creation of written words which were then used for reading. A learner picked letters from a 'letter case' to make the phrase 'it is a pea'. The writing lessons were similarly thought through:

> *We come now to the writing department, and here we must suppose that the children have been taught the forms and proportions of letters in the writing-alphabet in the infant school; if not, they should be taught in classes by the means of diagram-boards placed before them, on which the letters should be drawn, and which the children should copy on their slates. The teacher should direct their attention to the peculiar forms and proportions of the letters, and the easiest method of copying them. As soon as they have acquired some skill in making the letters, they should be taught to write down the names of objects on their slates, and a number of objects which are easily spelt should be given to each class for that purpose. After they have had some practice with one set of objects, another should be given them; and eventually they should begin to describe at length their qualities, uses, etc.*[58]

48

These methods of teaching writing have been described as purely physical skills.[59] But while they may be limited with regard to developing thinking skills or creativity, Lovett aimed at far more than imparting technical skills. His references to the progressive Swiss educator Pestalozzi (who drew on Rousseau's ideas, and promoted learning through activities and working with relevant objects or things) show the importance to radical and working-class movements of new pedagogies, marked by attempts to develop creative aspects of writing. Once the basic skills of writing had been grasped, Lovett proposed the development of observational skills, the power of seeing as the catalyst for the development of compositional, expressive writing. Walks and outings added additional visual stimuli for writing tasks. His proposal prefigures the less ambitious 'composition' and 'object lesson' of the reformed Revised Code later in the century. It is a bold departure from the drier methods of synopsis, comprehension and dictation through which the inspectors sought to promote understanding and the capacity to absorb knowledge. Below is a flavour of the Chartist approach:

> *When they can write tolerably well on their slates, they should be provided with writing-books, into which they should copy their compositions on objects, as well as descriptions of such places, scenes, or occurrences as they may have witnessed in their walks with the teacher. It should also be his duty to point out to them particular objects for this purpose, and to question them at the time as regards their several features or peculiarities, in order to call forth the descriptive powers of their children: they should write the matter down first on their slates, and, when approved of, into their copy-books.*

Examples of pupils' writing were given:

> *Last Saturday afternoon our teacher took us to Mr. Carefull's [sic] farm, and showed us the tools and implements used in farming. We saw spades, picks, hoes, rakes, pitchforks.*

For Lovett descriptive writing was an intellectual end in itself. A radical imprisoned for his political activity, he was as keen as the most conservative educationalist to develop moral values, sobriety and cheerful diligence. But as well as fostering creative talent and 'moral qualities', he advocated learning a sense of justice: during writing lessons, children were to be taught 'to describe any act of cruelty or injustice, or of kindness or affection, they may have witnessed in their rambles'. Lovett expected learners' initial efforts to be 'very crude', but an educational system that would develop their 'knowing and reasoning powers' would ensure they succeeded eventually. They would be spurred on by the knowledge that 'they will have to describe certain objects they see in their walks, they will observe them with greater care and attention than they otherwise would'. Teachers' attitudes were critical to success: learning should be 'rendered pleasant by the clear-headed and light-hearted disposition of the teacher'.[60]

Lovett was not alone among radicals and reformers in creating educational materials. This chapter will also look at grammar and writing, and the teaching methods of William Cobbett and the cooperator George Jacob Holyoake.

V   Heads, hands and the introduction of the Mulhauser method

Tensions grew between the concern to teach working-class people 'to reason about and understand things which are connected with their ordinary pursuits' and the dedication to copying, which reflected the overriding importance of precise, graphical presentation, not least for work purposes, but also because it was associated with neatness and uniformity, elevated to moral virtues. Handwriting became pivotal to the writing curriculum as state-sponsored schooling developed. To some extent, dictation bridged the two concerns and became increasingly popular as a valuable mental exercise as well as testing accuracy and handwriting. One advantage of the system of teaching reading and writing simultaneously, some argued, was that it supported an improved supply of good writers, i.e. good 'hands'. Emphasis on the production of good 'hands' gradually came to eclipse the idealistic aims of teaching compositional writing to everyone. Yet the teaching systems which reflected this growingly mechanistic approach claim that the concentration on handwriting was also in the interests of mental and moral, if not creative, development.

In the 1840s, a Swiss writing system developed by M. Mulhauser was adopted widely in England and Wales. The new system was enthusiastically received because it claimed to meet several dearly-held pedagogic objectives. Mulhauser was Inspector of Writing for the Primary Schools of Geneva. His system was designed to tackle the uneven levels of achievement at writing in schools. The haphazard distribution of copies for imitation favoured brighter children and the majority laboured with unsatisfactory results. Precision in copying for all children by specially designed templates was attractive. Mulhauser revived the old system of forming strokes and loops prior to assembling letters and words to a 'necessary science'. The four elements, the straight line down and up, the curve down and up; the loop down and up and the crotchet, were matched by the four principles which governed the design of the system. Mulhauser's writing method claimed to be scientific in arrangement, uniform in shape, artistic in design, legible and beautiful in form. This high-minded approach was accompanied by practical exercises and controls. Each letter, made up of the appropriate elements, was to be fitted into specially designed 'rhomboids', providing uniformity of shape, size and slope.

The Mulhauser method was based on reducing the units of meaning to the smallest possible element, a kind of visual morpheme, based on small script characters. The CCE and the HMI were persuaded that the Mulhauser system had the capacity to develop powers of thought: 'in vain will their memories be loaded with a variety of knowledge if, in the midst of this abundance, their thinking powers remain uncultivated … we must return to more rational methods and escape from the routine which converts instruction into mechanism and the child into an automaton'. Mulhauser became an officially-recommended system which was designed to teach children reading through writing. The method of breaking down letters into component parts presented learners with signs which were gradually built up into letters which, if all the parts were correctly assembled, resulted in a recognisable letter of the alphabet. If the letter was not recognised in the combination of signs, it could be spotted and corrected: 'The synthesis, or re-composition of these elements into letters and words, is the process by which the child learns to write. He combines the forms which he has learned to imitate'. Meanings were created through these formations. They emerged from a mysterious process rather as photographic prints from chemicals mixed in the right proportions or pictures from jigsaw puzzle pieces.

Although the system relied on dictation of sounds which represented each element, disconnected from any meaning, the system was not judged to be mechanical. As the Director of the Normal School at Versailles enthusiastically proclaimed, Mulhauser provided 'enigmas', which 'both amuse and force the children to reflect'. It was claimed that the system thus challenged the intelligence through play. English inspectors were more cautious, but declared their satisfaction that the success rate seemed to outstrip any previous system, economising on time and improving the standard of handwriting.[61]

The value placed on handwriting, already evident in educational texts early in the century, grew much stronger over time. In Lovett's words, the dual aims of 'elegance and expedition' reflected the needs of the labour market as well as individual aspirations to achieve good presentation of work.[62] Pens and ink were tricky to control. So properly-crafted writing materials, correctly designed desks and benches, correct and incorrect ways of holding a pen and a writer's posture all became the focus of educational enquiry. The challenges to perceived bad practice can be summed up in the British and Foreign School Society's questions to its own schools:

> *Are the books kept clean, free from blots, and without the corners being turned down? Do you furnish the boys with good copies, avoiding those which have improper contractions? Have you a black board on which you write in chalk for the lower boys unable to write?*[63]

It is uncertain exactly how widely the Mulhauser system was used. Government and educationalists recommended it. High costs would have made it prohibitive in many private working-class schools, and there is no evidence of its use in informal or self-education. But J.H. Cowham's *Mulhauser Manual* was still in print at the end of the century.

VI   Pedagogy and the market for writing materials

The market in popular writing manuals and copy-books had already been growing in the early 1800s. Copy-books and handwriting manuals offering a plethora of approaches had appeared in a steady trickle for centuries before education for the 'lower orders' became such a national concern. Supply increased throughout the century to meet the needs of Sunday and day schools, as well as self-help groups, individuals and families. J. Boardman, addressing the Society of Schoolmasters in 1810, denounced the growth of 'quackery' and the 'talismanic kind of tuition' in manuals and schools which promised quick results, and put forward his own method, a combination of 'design' (art) plus 'execution' (science).

The basic element was the 'fundamental stroke'. He cited soldiers and seamen as proof that there was 'no station in life' in which writing 'with clearness and dispatch', if not 'finely', was not important. A steadily swelling stream of text books and copy-books appeared from the 1810s, offering systems both for schools and for 'self-instruction'. A 'campaign' to improve handwriting began in 1854 after a complaint from Lord Palmerston that the 'great bulk of the lower and middle orders write hands too small and indistinct, and do not form their letters'.[64]

The official sanctioning of Mulhauser widened the market for guides on handwriting methods and techniques. A range of manuals continued to flow onto the market with titles such as *Writing without a Master* (1858) targeted at young people as well as 'persons of a more mature age'. Manuals took on the language of empirical science, referring for example to 'dissected' writing copies. Price and value for money were selling points. Typically conscious of affordability, Butterworth's 'durable' copy-book advertised itself as time-saving and low cost, recommending special ink and ink remover so that its pages could be reused more than a dozen times. Gradually, the speed at which the system could be learned and writing as a means to upward mobility and economic betterment became the key selling points. The claims to scientific principles and the discarding of more ornamental scripts enabled writing to be marketed to 'all persons, even the most ignorant', who could acquire a 'bold, fluent and business-like style of writing in a short space of time' and in 'a manner to him incredible'.[65]

From 1870 the number and variety of publications and pedagogic approaches proliferated. There were plenty of reasons for this: the Education Act; the interest of the CCE; a number of Parliamentary Inquiries into the uses of literacy; the rapidly developing labour market for clerical work; the growing pressure to become literate; and the increasing market for many types of writing materials and resources – copy-books, spelling books and grammars. Many publications claimed scientific status, and guaranteed success, citing testimonials by academics and prominent public figures, including Palmerston. Mulhauser combined the older idea of writing as an art with newer claims for writing as science or, alternatively, as Sir James Kay Shuttleworth put it, as one of the 'almost mechanical arts'. Writing was now a virtue and defined more freely to serve the educational aspirations of the age. The early defenders of the teaching of writing to the working class had emphasised its enriching value as an art, and its moral qualities. By the middle of the century, writing was an applied science and its teaching reflected the precision techniques of modern manufacturing production. As the status of 'penmanship' in education grew so too did the handwriting industry.

From the 1870s, as the use of the steel pen became more widespread, there was a significant increase in commercially-produced manuals and systems. All emphasise four great virtues: the speed with which the system can be learnt; the virtues of the system in promoting health and hygiene and, by implication, moral rectitude; neatness; and lastly accessibility, a system by which anyone can learn. In 1873 William Stokes published a popular do-it-yourself handbook on writing and his verse introduction (severely shortened below) to *The Art of Rapidly Teaching Writing* covers all these concerns as well as testifying to the 'shame' which was beginning to attach to illiteracy:

> *In this Book upon Writing you quickly will find*
> *Suggestions for guiding the hand and the mind …*
>
> *I have given such hints as most surely must guide …*
> *The 'thick headed' – 'the sleepy' – 'the slow,' and 'the dull;'*
> *For, I have an idea, – and I think I am right, –*
> *That in all such as these, there exists out of sight*
> *Of the vulgar who sneer, and who give these mean names,*
> *The spark and the fuel, which might produce flames*
> *Of lively intelligence …*
>
> *The nominal 'teacher' may be a retarder,*
> *Making easy things hard, and hard things much harder.*
> *Such teachers as these have the world been affrighting,*
> *Quite scaring away from the effort of writing.*
> *And thus with our boasted intelligence – shame,*
> *There are thousands of men cannot write their own name*
>
> *But heed well these hints, it shall be in your power*
> *To teach this in less than the fourth of an hour!*[66]

Stokes's claims for training memory through writing and vice versa reflect the need to flatter the intelligence of potential customers of all ages and abilities. His system aimed simultaneously to develop memory, powers of thinking and the artistry of scripts with ornamental flourishes. It was one of many sales pitches to convey the multiple benefits that learning to write offered. However, over the following decades the ethos of the Revised Code of 1862 and mass elementary education sharpened the focus on the technical features of writing at the expense of broader creative purposes.

In 1885 Daniel Walter Kettle's *Pens, Ink and Paper* looked to a golden future for writing as a universal practice, saying goodbye to the bad old times with a reference to Dickens's archetypal illiterate character, Bill Stumps in *The Pickwick Papers*, whose 'mark X ... was his Long-hand and Shorthand combined'. Noting the 'lamentable' fact that still so many people could not read and write, he welcomed the coming of the 'millennium' in compulsory education, whereby 'Bill Stumps will be effaced in time, by the benevolence of the Tax-payer and the labours of the School Board Officer in "running in" the Arab, *nolens volens*, to study the three Rs'. Kettle pleaded for a return to high standards of Penmanship, and to the 'good old moral maxims of the Round and Small Hand *copy-slips* of our Fathers'. In 1888, J.C. Sharp's *Writing and How to Teach It* presented a system that met the requirements of the Education Code, and provided a system of drill based on lined copies, free of theoretical claims or embellishments, and with no connection whatsoever to a wider framework of literacy and language learning, memory training or cognitive development. This system offers a handwriting style, pure and simple, neat and swift, and recommends the correct furniture and posture to achieve success. In this increasingly common model, handwriting was no longer part of education, but simply the training and drilling of a skill.[67]

Nevertheless, teaching the mechanics of handwriting continued to include a moral dimension of sorts. The debate between protagonists of different systems of teaching handwriting in the 1890s demonstrated how far the teaching of writing had travelled from the high-minded reports of the inspectors and the joyous copy-exercises of learners like Adam Rushton. Morality had returned, linked to a utilitarian ethos, with less Godliness and more emphasis on secular concerns such as punctuality, speed, efficiency and conformity, with a nod to the aesthetic in the promotion of elegant styles with flourishes. This reflected middle-class anxieties about health and hygiene among the poor. Well may they have worried. John Sykes, who left school at 13 to go to the mill as a 'half-timer', described his daily reality, the lot of many:

The half-timers ... often came to school with bleeding fingers. When the fingers had become injured they were swollen and like strips of raw beef attached to the palms of their hands ... Bleeding heads and bleeding hands were oft their portion, and with this type of fingers they were expected to write. No wonder they sometimes fell asleep in the effort.[68]

Writing and How to Teach It provides a system for teaching large text and round-hand styles. Drill, precision, (bodily) position are key words in a system in which 'the orders are given': 'Position' ... 'Pens' ... 'Write' ... 'Stop writing' ... 'Pens down' ... 'Blot copy'... 'Close books' ... 'Collect'. There is no mention of other subjects to which the writing exercises might be connected, no hint of 'moral' copy texts and lines and no discussion of intelligence. Yet there was still debate in the 1890s about the relative virtues and evils of different kinds of handwriting. *Jackson's System of Upright Penmanship and Hygienic Writing* produced a version of Civil Service Handwriting, widely used in the commercial and public sectors, and claimed to have been adopted by many school boards and praised in Blue Books.[69] It is a comprehensive system, including a manual and copy-books. Jackson advocates upright handwriting as a replacement for the various degrees of slope which had been the fashion. Upright writing was claimed to be superior on grounds of scientific and moral superiority, hygiene, legibility, speed, ease of teaching and learning and economy. Jackson attacked sloping writing, its very name for him indicative, like Trollope's Mr Slope, of its untrustworthy character.

What significance – and what a demoralizing significance – there is in the words oblique, slope, sloping, etc., whereas in the terms upright, upright-ness, erect, etc., there is nothing but what is elevating. Vertical writing is exact, definite, and reliable, whilst sloping writing is ambiguous, delusive and untrustworthy. Vertical writing is vigorous and stimulating as opposed to the enervating and vacillating character of all slanting penmanship.[70]

A compromise between these two opposing systems was proposed in the 1890s by G.C. Jarvis in *Semi-Upright Writing* (1897). He argued that a system was needed which would avoid the tendency of upright writing to slope backwards, which would be an even greater evil than a forwards inclination; and also avoid the tendency of 'Italian' sloping handwriting to 'degenerat[e] into an illegible scrawl'. The good qualities of each would be combined into Semi-Upright Writing, the title of his book, subtitled *The Golden Mean in Penmanship*.[71]

Ambidexterity was another of Jackson's ideas, the ultimate in work-force effectiveness. He believed that employers would benefit from the left hand of a copyist taking over when the right hand was exhausted. A change of hand was also more healthy, he argued:

> *If all our sailors and soldiers, our surgeons and sportsmen, our artists and artizans, our clerks and cricketers, and all other manual operators, were as adept with the left hand as with the right, what a revolution would be effected ... !*[72]

However, ambidexterity was not encouraged in schools, and left-handed writing was often forbidden. George Baldry's autobiography illustrates typical attitudes towards left-handed children. He made no progress with his right hand and as his copies were constantly being crossed through, he slipped the pencil into his left hand, 'keeping one eye on the teacher'. He was caned on his left hand to stop him using it, which 'cured me for life of writing with it, though there's many a job to this day I'd sooner use my left hand for'.[73]

Schools' tightening grip on the writing curriculum and the quest for perfect neatness and accuracy meant that 'bad' writing, whether hand-writing, grammar or punctuation, was punished, and writing itself came to be used as a punishment. Mary Smith, a radical schoolteacher, recalls ordering a girl 'to write a verse' in detention for a misdemeanour although her own childhood memories of verse-writing are associated with pleasure.[74] At Randall Place School in London, one parent 'removed her daughter from the school because' she was made to 'do 100 lines as a punishment for scribbling on the doors'. The mother was angry that the teacher would punish 'such a little thing'. The teacher then caned a girl for the same offence the next day. The school's logbook reports that 'several girls have been punished this week for writing on the newly-painted school walls'. Writing lines of copy as punishment became entrenched in schools, but the officious exercise of power engendered its own resist-ance.[75] Untidy writing became synonymous with poor performance and bad behaviour: 'blotting your copy-book'. But it worked both ways, writing also became a transgressive art form: graffiti, satirical versions of hymns and commands, notes handed round the class. Families could use writing to enforce authority too: Will Thorne tells how he forced his child to sit down and write a statement promising never to run away from home again.[76]

Traditional gendered approaches to teaching handwriting gradually waned. The 'hand' long deemed more suitable for girls and women, 'Ladies' Angular Hand', was gradually replaced by newer, simpler and more practical styles suitable for clerical work, as more and more young girls and women took it up. Stokes claimed that women were 'as quick with the Pen in Business Houses' as men, and had more stamina for continuous writing. Angular hand had been thought 'neat and pretty', but also often 'unintelligible', due to 'the small letters being based upon the horizontal zigzag, which causes great similarity in ... i, u, n, m'. Angular hand became obsolete and a London School Board inspector noted in 1876 that girls were now 'taught a good round legible hand'.[77] Angular hand persisted longer in girls' private schools, and became associated with leisured correspondence. Board School 'roundhand' reflected the practical needs of employers or of teachers of large classes marking batches of homework. Handwriting experts nearly all promoted variants of roundhand and reassured readers that the new systems were suitable for girls. Jackson answered criticisms that upright roundhand would not be 'natural or proper for girls to write', arguing that 'Vertical writing is just the very style for Girls, the only hygienic, and the only proper system'. It was the 'simply superb' handwriting of 'popular celebrities', pointing to Elizabeth I, George Sand and Caroline Norton as the best exponents of the art. Caroline Norton is a telling choice of 'model' writer. She was a wit and society beauty, but became a campaigner for divorce-law reform and women's custody rights. She wrote poems on social justice in 'A Voice from the Factories' (1836) Copy-books published specifically for girls, such as Pitman's *Domestic Copy Book for Girls* (1879) featured domestic hints and 'homely maxims' ('Have a place for everything and everything in its place'), taught feminine etiquette of social and family correspondence but also supported practical ambition with suggested wording for letters of application for clerical jobs.[78]

VII Grammar and composition

Grammar featured prominently in literacy learning, whether for individuals, informal groups, schools or Mechanics' Institutes. 'Dr Syntaxes', as the cooperator and grammarian George Jacob Holyoake joked with political edge, were needed to contest the 'daily triumph' of 'the wealthy and educated ... over the ignorant and poor'.[79] The problem he saw was not a lack of grammar books but the number of them available, offering as many different methods. Holyoake noted that one author offered nine parts of speech, and another only one, with as many in between. William Cobbett and Holyoake both promoted grammar to working people as a tool for empowerment, while commercially-oriented texts drove home grammar as an essential component of state and church school systems. Grammar books were a profitable venture for numerous publishers. Both kinds were widely in use, as their numerous editions and reprintings show.

Little is known about how learners actually responded to Lindley Murray, Lennie, Cobbett or other popular grammars, or whether their teachings were applied much at work or at home. But they were household names and sales of spelling, grammar and letter-writing guides were high. From the early nineteenth century, many working-class people were conscious that a grasp of standardised grammar was a requirement for entry to clerical work and journalism, radical or otherwise. Grammar classes flourished in night schools and crop up frequently in autobiographies. For Cobbett, 'ignorance, mystery, and authority reinforced each other to oppress the majority of the population'. As late as 1900, Robert Blatchford wrote of 'good books and bad books' and the horrors of mixed metaphors, platitudes and clichés, driving home to a working-class readership the message that good grammar was essential to all forms of writing.[80]

Although employment as a copyist did not require a sophisticated command of grammar, the ability to write Standard English was essential for higher-level administrative or clerical work involving composition of texts. In addition, some people were motivated to express themselves to a public readership, and they did not want eccentricities in their writing to be exposed. And some writers were conscious of the widening gap between spoken and written language. Grammar books exploited their awareness of correct and incorrect usages. The belief that working-class and regional varieties of English were inappropriate for written language became almost universal. Dialect societies gradually promoted regional differences more as an art form than a defensible literacy practice. They celebrated the value of local cultures through public readings and booklets, and kept them alive by writing down what once had been spoken language. But their intention was to complement, not to replace, a standard, grammatically-uniform English. The lengthening social reach of education diminished the status of regional varieties of English. Thomas Hardy, writing in 1908, lamented that:

> *Education in the west of England, as elsewhere, has gone on … reducing*
> *the speech of this country to uniformity, and obliterating every year many*
> *a fine old local word. The process is always the same: the word is ridiculed*
> *by the newly taught; it gets into disgrace; it is heard in holes and corners*
> *only; it dies; and, worst of all, it leaves no synonym.*[81]

Samuel Partington, a defender of dialect writing, also pointed the finger at 'Railways and the Schoolmaster', but in particular at the education system, for the ironing-out of language differences which followed the 1870 Act: 'Educationists have … shown scant respect and consideration for folk speech which retains the ancient words … The attempt to grapple with folk speech to final extinction has been overdone.' He proposed a movement for the inclusion instead of exclusion of words.[82] The farm worker Adam Rushton wrote about his day school that 'the uncouth sounds of letters and words I learned here, I had … to unlearn in later days'. The 'great hubbub' in his school days, with pupils shouting out words together, prevented the identification of 'bad' pronunciation.[83] His view was echoed by many adult writers re-learning written language.

The radical educator William Cobbett was one of the most popular teachers of grammar. His *Grammar of the English Language* reached its fifth edition by 1823. The first edition was dedicated to William Benbow, a shoemaker of Manchester, political activist, and member of the Hampden Club who was imprisoned for illegally manufacturing and supplying pikes. Benbow's pamphleteering was 'typical as the very first product of an autodidact whose capacities are in absolute contrast with the opportunities of education and development offered him in his youth. It is clumsily written as regards grammar and spelling, but the style is forceful and imaginative.' Cobbett wanted to match the ability of young people with real educational opportunity. His claims for grammar were ambitious and use the ubiquitous nineteenth-century metaphor for education: 'In the immense field of this kind of knowledge, innumerable are the paths, and GRAMMAR is that gate of entrance to them all.'[84]

For Cobbett, grammar was essential to communicate learning and spread knowledge. Never self-serving, grammar 'teaches us to make use of words'. Knowledge was not the property of the literate: people were not ignorant because they could not write. Cobbett believed in the 'natural genius' of the people who, liberated by grammar, could be effective communicators of truth and challenge the 'false pretenders to erudition', the 'insolent and ignorant great and powerful' because 'tyranny has no enemy so formidable as the pen'. Cobbett's advocacy of grammar was motivated by the part he believed literacy could play in the assertion of rights and liberties, although in his dedication to Queen Caroline in the fifth edition, he also enthused about its capacity to turn 'genius into a perennial source of wealth, strength and safety to the Kingdom'.[85]

Cobbett's *Grammar* and his *Advice to Young Men* were popular, not least because of their accessibility. He chose to present them as 'Letters', 'in order that I might be continually reminded, that I was addressing myself to persons, who needed to be spoken to with great clearness'. There were no short cuts to learning grammar, but Cobbett advocated 'First to read the grammar from the first word to the last very attentively, several times over; then, to copy the whole of it very correctly and neatly; and then to study the chapters one by one'. Far from conceding this to be an arduous process, Cobbett challenged his readers: 'And what does this reading and writing require as to time? … Not more than the tea-slops and their gossips for *three months*.' Learning was to be as easy for every ploughboy as he and his children had found it. Cobbett, writer and farmer, swept aside the idea that people were '*ignorant* merely because they cannot make upon paper certain marks with a pen'.[86]

The popularity of Cobbett's *Grammar* also lay in its politics. W.E. Adams, who 'picked up' English grammar from Cobbett, found it 'an intensely interesting work, if only because of the characteristic way in which the author makes political friends and political foes supply examples and illustrations of good and bad English'.[87] For Cobbett, literacy itself did not shape thought, but it did enable its effective expression through grammar by teaching people 'how to make use of words'. Citing the seventeenth-century dissident William Prynne, he offers readers an example of someone whose use of grammar enabled him to achieve acts 'by which his name has been thus preserved, and which have caused his memory to be held in honour'. Cobbett also shared the view that literacy provided a means to immortality through written records, a challenge to the anonymity and obscurity of the lives and deaths of individual working people.

George Jacob Holyoake was an Owenite, a cooperator, Mechanics' Institute lecturer and a secularist who was imprisoned for blasphemy. He also wrote a grammar explicitly directed at working-class learners. His *Practical Grammar and Handbook*, subtitled 'for the use of those who have little time for study', ran into its fifth edition in the year after it was first published in 1846 at a cost of 2s 6d. By 1857 it had reached many more editions and was still reprinting in the 1870s. For Holyoake language was 'the doctrine of signs, or the art of expressing thoughts by words'. Holyoake understood language to be primarily the expression of subjective sets of meanings, 'for describing our impressions of the nature of things'. History could be seen as 'an ocean of events' viewed from a 'promontory of Time', which enabled a general system or grammar of the world to appear. There was a grammar of nature, of the world, of life and society. Thus, 'the knowledge of the agreement and arrangement of the words to which [*sic*] express what we thus see, hear and understand – is grammar'.[88]

Holyoake made ambitious claims for grammar as art and science. While other popular contemporary grammarians, such as Murray, defined grammar as 'the art of using language with propriety', for Holyoake it was hard knowledge. The cost of ignorance of grammar was 'perpetual reproach'. Nothing could atone for its deficiency, which was impossible to conceal: 'there can be no greater imputation on the intelligence of any man, than that he should talk from the cradle to the tomb, and never talk well'.[89]

Holyoake and Cobbett both conveyed the message that political tyranny is a symptom which grows on 'ignorance and incapacity'. To learn grammar was to attack the cause rather than fight the symptom, part of the toolkit of the agitator. Holyoake's language echoed Cobbett's when he wrote that 'the ignorant man is at the mercy of educated opinion': to be without grammar is to be defenceless. 'Grammar ... gives a man more useful arms than those which Magna Charta permits him to carry.' The belief in the power of literacy, and a new equation of illiteracy with ignorance is developed in a continuing metaphor of war and tactics: 'The battle of liberty is now fought with the tongue and the pen ... without practical grammatical knowledge, those who move in the ranks of gentlemen betray that they are strangers there.' Holyoake's call was for collective self-help, using the language of class: 'we' and 'others', 'Intellectual bondage is worse than physical because the physical chain is riveted by others, the mental by ourselves.'[90]

Holyoake's *Grammar* is simply written. He continued Cobbett's method of teaching fewer essential parts of speech. And his *Grammar* includes a basic writing course, 'The Writing Book', in which reading and writing are simultaneously taught, emphasising the view that writing ('making') letters is a surer way of remembering them than reading them. Although Holyoake makes no explicit mention of any connection between the skills of letter formation and the compositional skills he teaches in the grammar sections, literacy and language are presented as aspects of the same essential learning.

Beyond the intellectual allies of the uneducated, educators and publishers jostled to sell their opinions in grammar books and pamphlets. But James Tilleard, Corresponding Secretary of the United Association of Schoolmasters, still felt that insufficient attention was being paid to grammar in the 1850s. He complained that the teaching of writing was pegged at too low a level. The systemisation of writing in schools by the adoption of the Mulhauser system was let down by a paucity of new thinking about grammar. Ignoring the radical tradition in grammar, he regretted the uselessness of teaching 'scientific grammar', and the use of textbooks which blindly followed the well-established Lindley Murray grammar, such as Lowth, Priestly, Blair and a host of others – many of which appear in autobiographers' memories of learning to write. Although Tilleard advocated a grounding in grammar, he criticised mechanic teaching methods for their overemphasis on correction without explanation.

> *Plans have been proposed for teaching children ... grammar by purely mechanical means, such as the writing out of good English, the correction of bad, for instance, provincialisms, according to such a standard. This is very well in its place ... but I trust we are not yet so utilitarian as to give our pupils any kind of knowledge without, at least, the endeavour to improve their minds.*

Grammarians often cited each other, referring regularly to Lindley Murray and others. New grammars adapted earlier ones, or claimed theirs was an improvement on the most popular ones. They had their favourites: Tilleard recommended Morell's grammar. Citing HMI Moseley, he separated the two essential and complementary purposes of grammar as 'forms and usages' and 'intellectual training', arguing that both should be at the heart of schooling from the earliest age.[91]

Matthew Arnold, reporting as HMI in 1867, expressed his own ideas about the aims of teaching grammar. He denounced the 'rubbish' given to children in Standard V as popular poetry, and argued for simplicity of expression in contrast to what he saw as the tendency of the state system to ape the worst features of middle-class education. He cited two letters to make his point: one from a working-class girl, '*Father cannot spare Willie, so*

I have as much as I can do to teach him to cipher nicely; and one from a middle-class private school pupil, '*and time has sped fleetly since reluctant my departing step crossed the threshold of whose indulgences and endearments their temporary loss has taught me to value more and more*'.[92]

For people at the receiving end of teaching or engaged in self-education, experiences of grammar were mixed. The priority placed on it by Adam Rushton's night-school teacher forced him to meet with 25 other learners an extra night a week, from nine until ten, to try to keep up. They chose Lennie's grammar but found the terms (orthography, etymology, syntax, prosody) 'puzzling and frightful'. One of their group, Peter Mackenzie, a coal-miner and lay preacher found it objectionable that the grammar made no reference to the Bible. Many autobiographers railed against the scorn which met their way of speaking and writing English. Will Thorne spoke out against grammar, and John Clare famously rejected both grammar and punctuation, 'that awkward squad of pointings called commas colons semicolons etc.'. Unsettled by reading that 'a person who knew nothing of grammar was not capable of writing a letter nor even a bill of parcels', he set out 'quite in the suds' to learn. He used a text book, but soon gave up. Those who eventually learnt what George Lansbury called 'decent grammar' in Board Schools, thought it was as important as logic, but, as Alice Foley wrote, 'taught on the blackboard, mainly parsing nouns and verbs ... our ... young minds were rarely ever stirred or fertilized'.[93]

The value which radical and cultural activists placed on Standard English continued into the twentieth century. Robert Blatchford in his 1925 handbook *English Prose and How to Write it* reflects on how he had 'been asked again and again by young men to tell them how they might learn to write good English prose' and even by one 'woman worker' asking for his help with writing.[94] His handbook is an eclectic set of points on grammar, tips on style, favourite quotes, a mini thesaurus, recommended writing tools and advice on 'English Composition', a term by then well-established. In adult education, attention to the development of writing and grammar was a key element of the WEA University Tutorial classes from 1907. Articles in the WEA magazine *The Highway* and how-to-write manuals with titles such as *First Aid to Essay Writing* accompanied this new movement in which a pledge to write a minimum number of essays was the centrepiece of the course. Adult School attendees were urged to follow this advice in their journal *One and All*. Albert Mansbridge and G.D.H. Cole were among teachers who saw good writing as central to the realisation of their ambitions for the 'Higher Education of Working Men' and wrote pieces of practical advice in journals.

Teaching and learning grammar overlapped with composition, which entered the official curriculum as a subject in 1871, though it had long been taught in voluntary schools and adult classes. In local mutual improvement societies, reading and discussion of a member's essay was the cornerstone of learning. And in radical traditions, too, composition featured as good practice. A correspondence between 'Educationist', 'Pencil'em' and 'Nemo', for example, in the *New Moral World* in 1841 promoted the teaching of English grammar, composition and rhetoric in Owenite 'social schools and lectures' because of the need to have followers capable of 'an unanswerable exposition of our principles':

> ... *how many members have we ... with a fluency of language, only equalled by a fertility of ideas and an almost miraculous intimacy with the principles, who, if set down to transfer their thoughts to paper, would find the task utterly impossible. The sight of the white sheet seems to congeal their ideas, which can flow forth only in sight of a human countenance.*

Good speakers were to teach good writers and vice versa. The overriding purpose was to improve the quality of written argument in favour of Owenite ideas:

> ... *many of the most original thinkers belonging to our body, whose conceptions, if properly embodied in writing, might adorn the pages of their weekly organ, are useful only in a limited sphere, for want of the practice of composition ... How much more effectual and powerfully interesting might the* New Moral World *become, if its pages contained more of the effusions of such men.*[95]

Short essays were advocated, in suitable subjects such as political economy. Such exercises would harness writing skills to the promotion of 'really useful knowledge'. Work would be read aloud. Each student would produce his corrections and the reasons for them in addition to discussion of the subject matter. This method was adopted almost universally by mutual improvement societies and in courses offered by institutions such as the People's College, Working Men's College, Birkbeck, lyceums, the education departments of cooperative societies and, later, the WEA.

In some schools, HMI Tremenheere reported children being asked to 'write their thoughts' on the subject of 'confirmation' and thought them worth publishing in his report. Moseley reported of one school in 1847–8 that 'a child in the lowest class but one … is told to write the names of its brothers and sisters, of all the things in the house where it lives, of all the birds, or trees, or plants that it knows'. A second stage in this system was to associate qualities (adjectives) with things. Moseley approved of this method which he considered should be 'adapted to each stage in a child's intellectual growth' and would promote thought and the expression of thought. Compositional writing was one area of the curriculum which inspectors clearly aimed to expand. HMI Allen advocated it as a daily exercise, albeit only for the 'more forward pupils'. Another popular form of composition was letter-writing. One teacher reported asking 'the bigger boys' to write a letter about reaping, hay-making or another activity. Their parents would help with the task with 'a good deal of pleasure … But such letters it is almost impossible to imagine.' His dismay at the disorder of their work prompted him to design systematic exercises for the improvement of accuracy and order in composition.[96] The approach of pedagogues to composition, including later promoters of essay-writing such as Mansbridge and Blatchford, was on the style, manner and order of ideas, to complement the systematic approach to language offered by grammar, and the presentation skills of handwriting. Learners' responses to composition as a formal subject varied. George Lansbury admitted learning 'some sort of skill in composition' at school but considered that this was due to 'nature' more than to education. Alice Foley liked 'dictation and composition' and yet remarked that the teaching omitted 'the wonder and splendour of our great literary inheritance', as if she wished some connection to be made between literature and her own writing efforts and was disappointed that none was made.[97]

Many learners found essay-writing hard-going. In the early years of the WEA's university tutorial class movement, this was the most common reason for 'retiring' from the class. Chesterfield students reported that 'our tutor thinks there is nothing difficult in essay-writing – but we beg to differ'. R.H. Tawney, the first tutor of the tutorial classes, suggested students get started with an autobiographical piece, or compiling a family budget. At the Rochdale branch, courses in essay-writing were set up. At Longton, the course organiser held an extra evening every week to coach students in writing skills. But most commonly, students formed self-help groups to support each other with essays. On the literature course in Reading (where 21 of the 27 students were women), 'essay-writing was of course a problem for those unaccustomed to using the pen. Determined to carry out their undertakings they frequently met outside class hours for advice and practice in writing.[98] Whilst the WEA imposed academic standards of excellence in written work, driven not least because their grant-aid depended on stipulated volumes of written work, the students themselves responded in ways that reflected other traditions – cooperation and mutual self-help.

VIII   Coda

The accounts of autobiographers and cultural activists as well as formal evidence of the way writing teaching developed raise some critical questions. Autobiographies often paint elaborate pictures of the diverse ways and means of acquiring writing skills. Historians have focused more on institutional pressures, school curricula and the superficiality and drudgery of much instruction. Paradoxically, many autobiographers described with enthusiasm the same building blocks which HMI referred to as 'mindless' and were at pains to drop in favour of more meaningful activities. Autobiographers claim to have found value, even creative stimulus, in mechanical learning. When motivation and purpose are strong, perhaps any process or method, however narrow, can trigger and enable wider learning and deeper thinking.

Perhaps it was also the scarcity of material resources for learning such as paper, copy-books and writing tools which invested them with meaning. Working-class autobiographers often celebrate the rituals and artefacts of the writing process and, by treasuring them, break down the division between the material, mechanical aspects of learning and the creativity, emotion and meaning which they have found in the process. Once compulsory universal state education was established, time and materials were more plentiful, though regimented, while the space for human agency in determining the connections between creativity and skill seemed to have diminished. Boundaries became more fixed. Political and social priorities changed and the curriculum changed accordingly. Nevertheless, the ways in which people learned, though affected by these changes, were not altogether contained by them. Church educationists, HMI and successive governments did not set out to promote an education which enabled people to challenge dominant ideas or their social position. People were not encouraged to define their own purposes and ambitions in learning. Yet the educational methodologies proposed, at least by the HMI, provided a context in which some learners could develop cognitively and creatively. It was always just possible to exploit, subvert or profit from some aspect of a plural approach until the 1860s when rigid systems, rigidly controlled, were refined, narrowing the range of possibilities and cultural practices.

The story of the development of writing as part of officially-sanctioned literacies shows how attempts to submerge or destroy cultural and educational activities owned by working people were not always totally successful. The state's educational project was itself not a unified effort. New educational approaches developed as part of the state's growing stake in education, which unintentionally served others' ends. There were competing commercial interests, dissenting views, new thinking and independent practices. Writing was at the centre of a fermenting cultural mixture. Sometimes learners' purposes chimed with emerging or dominant values. Sometimes they diverged deeply and their stories reveal their dissent. Prescribed teaching methods, and their ideological determinants, could not altogether predict how a person's learning would actually unfold. People learned what was on offer; but many searched out what they needed for themselves and wrote their own accounts.

Notes

1   See, e.g., *Northern Star*, September 1839, 14 December 1839; *Poor Man's Guardian*, 20 July 1833, p. 236, 6 September 1834, p. 258, 25 October 1834.
2   Vincent, 1989, p. 67.
3   The 1880 Education Act made it compulsory for children to attend school from age five to ten. After this, they were exempted for half-days to work part-time in factories, as long as an appropriate educational standard was reached.
4   Mayhew, 1985, pp. 104–5, 194–5, 148.
5   F. Smith, 1983, p. 84.
6   Gardner, 1984, p. 20; see also pp. 29, 30, 112–13.
7   Vincent, *op. cit.*, p. 76.
8   *Minutes of the Committee of Council on Education* (cited below as 'Mins CCE'), 1844, pp. 139–151; Vincent, *op. cit.*, pp. 76–7.
9   James, 1976, pp. 28–9.
10   E.P. Thompson, 1968. See also Cooper, 1851; Maidment, 1987.
11   *One and All*, 1891, Vol. 1, No 8, p. 138. For the decline of Adult Schools, see Freeman, 2010.
12   Pole, 1816, p. 75.
13   *One and All*, November 1892, Vol. 2, No 11; Currie Martin, 1924, pp. 78, 114–15; *One and All*, September 1891, Vol. 1, No 9.
14   Rushton, 1909, pp. 23–4.
15   Currie Martin, *op. cit.*, pp. 232–3.
16   *One and All*, January 1892, Vol. 2, No 2, p. 24.
17   Sturt, 1967, p. 21.

18 A. Goodwin (b. 1890), untitled MS, held Brunel University, pp. 34–5.
19 M. Cutts (b. 1894), untitled MS, held Brunel University, pp. 4–5.
20 Blackburn, 1954, p. 4.
21 'From a woman textile worker (b. 1893)', in *Bolton History Project*, Tape 155a 2(f).
22 Vincent, *op.cit.*, pp. 75–6.
23 Mins CCE, 1841–2, p. 165.
24 Bonwick, 1902, p. 9.
25 Vincent, *op.cit.*, p. 79.
26 Bonwick, *op. cit.*, p. 10–11.
27 British and Foreign School Society, 1854, p. 7.
28 Bonwick, *op. cit.*, p. 50.
29 Quoted in R. Williams, 1965, p. 157.
30 H. Craik, *The State in Relation to Education*, 1896, quoted in Lawson & Silver, 1973, p. 243.
31 British and Foreign School Society, 1854, p. 27.
32 Sturt, *op.cit.*, p. 26.
33 F. Smith, 1982, p. 108.
34 Quoted in Sturt, *op. cit.*, p. 26.
35 R. Johnson, 1970, p. 96.
36 Mins CCE, 1845, pp. 265–66.
37 Mins CCE, 1840–1, p. 22, quoted in Vincent, *op. cit.*, p. 78.
38 See Ferreira-Buckley & Horner, 2001, pp. 190–1, 195–7.
39 Mins CCE, 1845, pp. 226–7.
40 Mins CCE, 1844, pp. 139–47.
41 Mins CCE, 1841–2, pp. 38–50.
42 Mins CCE, 1841–2, p. 165; 1845, p. 233; 1844, p. 188.
43 Mins CCE, 1844, p. 189.
44 M. Johnson, 1970, p. 38, pp. 96–7.
45 Mins CCE, 1841–2, p. 165.
46 Higher fees for writing with strictly separated processes for reading and writing were the norm in other European countries. See, e.g., Furet & Ozouf, 1982, pp.112–13.
47 See Vincent, *op. cit.*, pp. 180–193, on the ways in which literacy facilitated the transformation of time from the traditions of natural cycles to 'a more ordered, formal and public notation'.
48 Mins CCE, 1842, p. 183.
49 Mins CCE, 1842–3, p. 50.
50 Mins CCE, 1839, pp. 177–9.
51 Mins CCE, 1842, p. 183.
52 Mins CCE, 1842, p. 50.
53 Mins CCE, 1839–40, p. 73.
54 Mins CCE, 1842, p. 183.
55 Lovett, [1876] 1967, p. 4. There are a number of copy-books, used and unused in the John Johnson Collection, Bodleian Library, Oxford, with moral sentiments and proverbs as typical lines of copy.
56 Mins CCE, 1844, p. 257; 1840, p. 40; 1845, p. 232.
57 Mayers, 1798, pp. 26–7.
58 Lovett & Collins, 1841, p. 97.
59 See Vincent, *op cit.*, p. 77, n. 117, and p. 297, where Vincent refers to the Chartists' mode of teaching writing, described elsewhere in this chapter.
60 Lovett & Collins, *op cit.*, pp. 97, 100–1, 105.
61 Mins CCE, 1840, p. 40; 1844, pp. 147, 148; 1842–3, p. 558.
62 Lovett & Collins, *op cit.*, p. 97.
63 From the *Manual of the System of Primary Instruction* pursued in the Model Schools of the British and Foreign School Society (1839), quoted in Mins CCE, 1846, p. 389.
64 Boardman, 1810; see e.g. F. Webb, *Dissected Writing Copies*, undated; Anon, *Writing without a Master*, 1858; Stokes, 1873, pp. 6–7.
65 Anon, *Writing without a Master*, 1858.
66 Stokes, *op. cit.*, pp. 6–7.

67 Kettle, 1885, p. 27; Bill Stumps in fact 'wrote' all but the final 'L' in the inscription in stone which so puzzled Mr Pickwick and his friends, and which they were convinced was a runic tablet of 'unquestionable antiquity' (see Dickens, *The Pickwick Papers*, 1986, pp. 125–7, 136–7); Sharp, 1888, p. 27, p. x.

68 I. Strickland, *The Voices of Children*, 1970, pp. 169–70, quoted in Springhall, 1986, p. 79.

69 Blue Books date from the fifteenth century as a tool of parliament to report on and record information about events, policy implementation and compilations of statistics.

70 Jackson, 1895, Introduction.

71 Jarvis, 1897, Introduction.

72 Jackson, 1905, pp. 14–15.

73 Baldry, 1939, pp. 59–60.

74 M. Smith, 1892, pp. 38, 45.

75 Randall Place School Logbook, London, 7 October 1881, Greater London Record Office.

76 Thorne, 1925, p. 145.

77 Stokes, *op. cit.*, pp. 165–6; PP, LSB Inspectors' Reports, 1876, p. lix.

78 Jackson, 1895, pp. 163–4; Pitmans, 1879.

79 Holyoake, 1847, p. 7.

80 O. Smith, 1984, p. 1; Blatchford, 1900, pp. 28–9.

81 Quoted in R. & M. Williams, 1986, p. 205.

82 Partington, 1917, p. 12; see also Partington, 1920.

83 Rushton, 1909, pp. 17, 45.

84 Cobbett, [1819] 1984, esp. pp. 8–10; Cobbett, [1830] 1856. On Cobbett's radicalism and views of literacy in relation to class, see also R. Johnson, 1979, pp. 89–91.

85 Cobbett, [1819] 1984, p. 10.

86 Cobbett, [1830] 1856, Letter One.

87 Adams, 1903, pp. 112–13.

88 Holyoake, *op. cit.*, p. 8.

89 Murray, quoted in Holyoake, *op. cit.*, pp. 5–9.

90 Holyoake, *op. cit.*, pp. 5–9.

91 Tilleard, 1855, pp. 2–8. A plethora of popular grammars appeared, such as *Progressive Exercises; or easy Steps to the Knowledge of Grammar, by the author of Flora's offering to the Young; A Grammatical Game, in Rhyme by a Lady* was recommended in *Books for Youth*, Darton & Harvey, London, undated.

92 Arnold, 1910, pp. 122–4.

93 Rushton, *op. cit.*, p. 202; Clare, 1983, p. 6; Lansbury, 1935, p. 26 ; Foley, 1973, pp. 33–4.

94 Blatchford, 1925, pp. 1, 3–9.

95 *New Moral World*, April/May 1841, p. 225.

96 Mins CCE, 1846, pp. 622–3; HMI Allen quoted in Ball, 1983, pp. 185–6.

97 Lansbury, *op. cit.*, p. 26; Foley, *op. cit.*, pp. 33–4.

98 Souch, 1954, p. 12; see also Oxford University Extension Delegacy Tutorial Classes Committee Report, 1910; Mansbridge, 1913.

CHAPTER 2

Literacy and literature, culture and class

I

Raymond Williams provided a clear distinction between writing and other 'formations in cultural production' such as painting, sculpture, drama and music. Writing, he argued, had a 'radically different status, as a technique'. This status is defined by its capacity to exclude: 'Thus while anyone in the world, with normal physical resources, can watch dance or look at sculpture or listen to music, still some forty per cent of the world's present inhabitants can make no contact whatever with a piece of writing'. Both 'producers' and 'receivers' need specialised training. For this reason, 'the most difficult problems in the social relations of cultural practice revolved around the question of literacy'.[1] This is still the case: in the 30 years since Williams wrote this, successive international literacy surveys have shown that the situation, world-wide, has even deteriorated.

Williams locates the first half of the nineteenth century as the moment of change following two thousand years of 'cultural division' when writing was known only to a minority. When a majority of people in that period of fundamental economic and social change rapidly achieved at least 'minimal access' to writing, a 'confusion of developments' resulted. Following this argument, there is still tension about access to cultural production and consumption in the twenty-first century. In the nineteenth century contradictions and conflicts erupted as widespread acknowledgement of the social and economic advantages of literacy met apprehension, even fear, of its dangerous consequences. A glowing picture of educational progress among a soberly industrious

One night I was sitting in the chimney-corner with my slate, expending great efforts on a letter to Joe.
'Joe Gargery and Pip' by Felix O. C. Darley, c. 1861
Scanned image and text by George P. Landow, courtesy of Victorian Web
(www.victorianweb.org)
Dickens, Charles. Great Expectations. Volume 19 of the Edition de Grande Luxe. Ed. Richard Garnett. London: Merrill and Baker, 1900.

working class was met by its distorted mirror image – a society disturbed and deformed by the effects of literacy. There were visions of working-class pretensions to upward mobility and of criminal misuses of literacy if control of access to print spiralled away from church and state into the hands of the writers and sellers of politically subversive literature. Condescension, moral concern and fear contributed to a confusion of attitudes. This was a new situation, with no simple certainties to draw on. And the urgent, earnest tones of contributors to both sides of the debate, as well as the scramble of each side for the moral high ground, hardly registered two significant facts. First, neither church nor state possessed the power to prevent people from learning to write. Literacy could only be made more difficult and less public. Secondly, large numbers of working-class people living in cities or remote villages were already taking steps to learn literacy skills on their own cultural territory: the relatively private and informal spheres of home, community or local organisations. David Vincent, John Burnett, Jonathan Rose and others have provided ample evidence of that.[2] Pessimistic interpretations of nineteenth-century learning as a minority pursuit persist, but literacy learners at the very least constituted a large and significant minority.

Nineteenth-century novelists such as Dickens, Gaskell, Emily Brontë, Kingsley and Hardy often focused on illiteracy or a particular character's attempts to learn to write, as a simple way of creating authenticity in depictions of working-class life. In *Our Mutual Friend*, the character of Betty Higden is typically situated through her relationship to literacy: 'for I aint, you must know … much of a hand at reading writing-hand, though I can read my Bible and most print'.[3] But when the focus on literacy becomes more central, driving the plot or acting as a key to unlock wider meanings, evidence emerges of a strong belief that the spread of writing skills, or even simply the availability of writing as a mode of communication for large numbers of people has become a powerful instrument of change. Further, literacy is perceived as a tool that works in treacherous as well as beneficial ways, to effect personal and social change. Of course, that sense of the dramatic potential of writing as a transformative force is found in many working-class writings though in these it is almost always an affirmative concept, in which authors seem to coax other working-class people into taking advantage of the tools and skills of writing to catalyse a religious conversion, to encourage learning for its own sake, to engage in social action or simply to enable silenced voices to speak.

II   Writing and power: dangerous weapons and useful tools

In Gaskell's novella, *My Lady Ludlow*,[4] the narrator Margaret Dawson looks back from the mid-nineteenth century, the railway age, to its early years. She surveys the change from the time when letters came three times a week, and remembers 'a two days' journey out of what people now go over in a couple of hours with a whizz and a flash and a screaming whistle'. She explores dynamic social change through education: especially the lower classes learning to write. The novella engages with early nineteenth-century debates about writing skills from several angles, including the social and political alliances that were forged or split by the issue. Writing is used as a metaphor to unlock the meanings of myriad changes which seem set to cast aside the values of late eighteenth-century rural society. Writing describes and prescribes an emerging new social order. As the elderly landowner Lady Ludlow sees it, the spread of writing skills represents the chaos of the new times. Writing is associated with revolution, treachery, foreignness and much else besides: moral confusion, uppitiness, not knowing one's place, modernisation in agriculture, the mutual spilling-over of city and country life, changes in women's work, and the role of the church. The old oral ways of going about your business, based on trust, are perceived as being replaced by written transactions, contracts and records. The construction of the narrative as a story told by the fireside from one woman to another symbolises the disappearing way of life.

Lady Ludlow's trenchant belief in the dangers of education is depicted as anachronistic and even ridiculous. She represents the decline of the social and cultural values of the eighteenth-century landowning class, defending traditionally fixed master/mistress and servant relationships against 'new fangled' ideas, in particular demands for education for the lower orders. Every set of relationships in the story expresses some aspect of the depth and breadth of economic, social and cultural change that is under way.

Mr. Horner, the steward of Lady Ludlow's failing estates, which are beset by old fashioned agricultural methods, 'wanted to make every man useful and active in this world, and to direct as much activity and usefulness as possible to the improvement of the Hanbury estates, and the aggrandisement of the Hanbury family, and therefore he fell into the new cry for education'. His modernising utilitarianism allies him with the new vicar, Mr Grey, whose desire for education is motivated by religious zeal. He intends to spread and improve knowledge of the scriptures. They agree the same means to different ends: establishing a Sunday school. Gaskell was well aware that 'Mr. Raikes had set up his Sunday-Schools; and some clergymen were all for teaching writing and arithmetic.'[5] The Sunday school movement had spread fast since the 1780s. Strong differences arose over the morality and wisdom of teaching writing on Sundays, particularly within Methodism, and public debate followed. Lady Ludlow's notion of 'keeping a Sunday' means she is violently opposed to a Sunday school. Horner's motivation is more worldly. He also 'hoped for a day-school ... to train up intelligent labourers for working on the estate. My lady would hear of neither one nor the other: indeed, not the boldest man whom she ever saw would have dared to name the project of a day-school within her hearing'. The cry for education and for writing was one signal of the end of the 'moral economy', of that degree of responsibility for material and moral nourishment which had been customary from employer to servant or tenant in exchange for loyalty and quietude. The development of the wage economy during the eighteenth century, the draining of the rural population to the industrialising cities and the impersonality of the relationship between employers and workers fundamentally changed the context within which cultural and educational activities were experienced.[6] The aims of non-conformist and socially improving clergy coincided with the rise in opportunities to use writing at work. They stressed a knowledge of scripture, but literacies learned for worship could not be disentangled from their potential applications in work and daily life.

Economic modernisers and reforming preachers were toppling a long-established system in which servitude and loyalty were higher callings than working for a wage in commerce or manufacture, and in which, however much they abused their powers, employers might claim to be the guardians of their servants' souls as much as the clergy. Lady Ludlow's views are a parody of the attitudes of the pre-industrial age to education, yet at the same time they reveal a consciousness of the moral censoriousness of the Victorian era when the story was written.

My lady would have none of this; it was levelling and revolutionary, she said. When a young woman came to be hired, my lady would have her in, and see if she liked her looks and her dress, and question her about her family ... Then she would bid her say the Lord's Prayer and the Creed.

75

Then she inquired if she could write. If she could, and she had liked all that had gone before, her face sank – it was a great disappointment, for it was an all but inviolable rule with her never to engage a servant who could write.

At that time, writing was seen as closely related to arithmetic, or ciphering. Both skills were linked with employment, trade and the practical competencies of self-reliance, as this passage illustrates:

I have known her ladyship break through it, although in both cases in which she did so she put the girl's principles to a further and unusual test in asking her to repeat the Ten Commandments. One pert young woman – and yet I was sorry for her too, only she afterwards married a rich draper in Shrewsbury – who had got through her trials pretty tolerably, considering she could write, spoilt it all, by saying glibly, at the end of the last Commandment, 'An't please your ladyship, I can cast accounts …'. 'Go away, wench,' said my lady in a hurry, 'you're only fit for trade; you will not suit me for a servant.'

Gaskell astutely assesses the consequences and characteristics of literacy across the changing social spectrum, if anything overstating the case. The young woman's writing leads to exactly the change in social station which Lady Ludlow dreaded, going from a life of rural servitude to affluence in the world of urban trade. In fact the view that teaching writing would cause shortages in the market for domestic labour was widely and publicly expressed.[7] Before this candidate is dismissed from the house, she is given a Bible and Lady Ludlow's warning to 'beware of French principles' which have led to regicide, reflecting the widespread fear in England that the French Revolutionary spirit could ignite in England, as well as the belief that the spread of writing skills and radical publications were inciting political and social unrest. Lady Ludlow's idealised notion of Englishness is an unschooled population living in contented stability, serving their betters, who in turn will look after them. She exhibits the characteristics, if eccentrically expressed, of the conservative educational ideology of her time.[8]

E.P. Thompson's *The Making of the English Working Class* showed the importance of the Corresponding Societies as sites for the development and dissemination of radical thinking. The ideas born of the French Revolution were reaching unprecedented numbers of readers – and listeners at public and private readings – featuring books such as Paine's *Rights of Man*.[9] In *My Lady Ludlow* the theme of writing as the means to betrayal and treachery is explored in private as well as public spheres. Mr Horner decides to teach the young son of a local tenant farmer, Job Gregson – 'a notorious poacher and evildoer' – to read and write. That Harry Gregson was the 'brightest and sharpest' of the farm boys was more important to Horner than the fact that he was the 'raggedest and dirtiest'. He intends to train him as foreman on the estate. Lady Ludlow learns of this when the boy confesses to knowing the contents of a letter to her from Mr Horner, which he was delivering. He has lost the letter, but not before reading it. At this point one of the key moral arguments of literacy's opponents is explored: 'My boy, as you have got possession of edge tools you must have some rules how to use them. Did you never hear that you were not to open letters?' The boy replies that he had thought it 'good for practice, all as one as a book'. Lady Ludlow continues to appeal for 'honour as regards letters'. Her sermonising reached back into the traditional, oral world, and she seeks his assurance that he would never eavesdrop. He replies that: 'I always hearken when I hear folk talking secrets; but I mean no harm.' Their moral and material worlds are poles apart. Her terror mounts: the tools of writing in the hands of the poor, without the aristocratic code of honour, will lead to immorality, revolution and crime. Literacy means a loss of innocence. The poor will look at the world through 'wicked and mischievous eyes', seeking to survive by any means. With material gain comes the demand for rights.[10] Lady Ludlow has been personally affected by the curiosity of a newly-literate boy messenger during the Reign of Terror in the French Revolution, which led to the betrayal and execution of her own aristocratic friends. In her view, revolutionary forces are released by the subversive consequences of literacy. Through the production and dissemination of dangerous ideas about the rights of man, democratic ideas reach the poor and previously illiterate. And the scale of rewards for the rich and privileged is revealed before the greedy curiosity of the lower orders, whose appetite for emancipation and self-improvement has been whetted by the secular possibilities of literary skills and ambitions for political change.

The association of writing with crime was often put forward during this period. Writing in 1816, Thomas Pole, founder of the Adult Schools for the teaching of reading, writing and arithmetic to the poor, tried to soothe fears that the spread of writing skills would encourage forgery.

That teaching the poor to write, would be placing in their hands a power of committing forgery, is a sentiment which it is to be hoped need not occasion any alarm to the public mind. It cannot be expected that in these humble seminaries they will be made complete penmen; or that they should arrive at that degree of perfection that is required to exercise the atrocious practice in question.[11]

The view that working–class people should not acquire writing skills or a fluency in handwriting comparable to the middle classes persisted for decades, as the minutes of the Select Committee on Education in 1834 show.[12] Of course, forgery was a real issue as well as an excuse to frustrate the cause of education and this will be explored further below.

The growth of literacy did break barriers that had restricted circulation of information. Confidentiality, as Lady Ludlow realises, could never be so secure again. The existence of a growing reading public, alongside other forces that were changing economic and social relations, broke up the intimate world of servile personal allegiance and trust, signified by unsealed letters like the one Harry Gregson has read. The need to make a point of insisting on confidentiality, and to set up systems to secure it, formed part of the growth of anonymous systems and functions based on writing, which further eroded personal business relationships and oral transactions. The medieval historian Michael Clanchy examines the growth of transactional record-keeping as a foundation of modern 'official' literacies in Norman England, including the imposition of French over the English language. But he argued that overdependence on writing by one group to the exclusion of others directly causes the growth of other literacies that can challenge that power:

Making records is initially a product of distrust rather than social progress … The harsh exactitude of Norman and Angevin officials with their writs and pipe rolls caused churchmen and ultimately even laymen to keep records of their own.[13]

The argument is relevant to the early nineteenth century. Lady Ludlow had not been told that Horner's clerk was teaching Harry Gregson the tools of managing her business. Horner himself embodies the old school of loyal retainers but he is also a moderniser, determined on education for his workers: his conflict of loyalties ends with a fatal accident. The transition from old to new systems results in 'dynamic confusion' and tragedy. Harry rises to be schoolmaster and eventually vicar of Hanbury. But there is a severe cost to his self-improving journey. He is permanently crippled by an accident while running across country to catch the post, carrying an important letter for Horner. His fall, an event significantly associated with literacy, represents a symbolic, evocable break with manual life and labour. But he is also 'broken' by the new timetabled world of postal collections, emblematic of the accelerating pace of commercial life, with its growing adherence to the clock and its dependence on the rapid exchange of documents. Up to this moment, Harry has no prospect of becoming more than rudimentarily literate, nor of reaching a higher social status. But his disability makes it safe for him to continue learning. Additionally, his life journey reconciles the split between learning for worldly purposes and learning for spiritual life. Harry shares with other 'exceptional' working-class people a status that does not threaten the social order, whilst providing a model for others' aspirations to benign self-improvement. The growth of individual aspiration reflects the growth of a guarded middle-class acceptance of a limited upward mobility.

III   Writing and gender

My Lady Ludlow stretches the writing metaphor to cover one further aspect of social change. Miss Galindo, Lady Ludlow's clerk, anticipates transformations in women's work and the tension between independence and servitude. Miss Galindo, well-read and efficient, represents possibilities and problems for single women in the early nineteenth century, especially women from the impoverished gentry. She must earn her own living in a respectable manner. Her modernity is discussed first through her administrative role, albeit in a domestic setting: only towards the end of the century were women to work in offices in large numbers. More unusually, Miss Galindo aspires to be an 'authoress'.

Gaskell uses Miss Galindo's role to parody the business-like, masculine persona Miss Galindo adopts as a clerk, although this is matched by a familiar spinsterly feminine persona: penny-pinching, subservient and garrulous. She emerges as an idiosyncratic character, good-humoured, independent and professional, ridiculed but also admired:

> *'I have had to sit up pretty late to get these sleeves made' – and she took out of her basket a pair of brown-holland over-sleeves, very much such as a*

grocer's apprentice wears — 'and I had only time to make seven or eight pens, out of some quills Farmer Thomason gave me last autumn. As for ink, I'm thankful to say, that's always ready: an ounce of steel filings, an ounce of nut-gall, and a pint of water (tea if you're extravagant, which, thank Heaven, I'm not) … and there's my ink ready for use; ready to write my lady's will with, if need be.'

Feeling resented by Mr Horner, Miss Galindo parodies the steps women take to play down the threat of their presence in a male sphere:

I try to make him forget I'm a woman, I do everything as ship-shape as a masculine man-clerk. I see he can't find a fault — writing good, spelling correct, sums all right … I have gone good lengths to set his mind at ease. I have stuck my pen behind my ear, I have made him a bow instead of a curtsey, I have whistled … I have said 'Confound it!' and 'Zounds!'

But Horner 'looks glummer than ever, just because I'm a woman'. The novelty of women clerks was still striking male commentators as late as 1863, although by then in public settings.[14] The social observer Arthur Munby's diaries describe a visit to Caldwell's public dancing rooms in London where he was shocked to hear a girl say 'I came straight from business' and that she had 'been writing all day'. He questioned her and discovered she was 'A bona fide female "city clerk" ' carrying out the same work as male clerks. He commented on her difference from 'other girls of her own class' and struggled to make sense of the complexity of suitable occupations and behaviours for women who wrote for a living. The dignified, frank and sober manner of the girl whose 'sleeves get worn with leaning on the desk and [whose] white cuffs get dreadfully inked', and who treated him with casual confidence, did not flirt with the male clerks, travelled first-class on the underground, and called herself a lady, outraged Munby's sense of 'women's decorum, if not purity'. Finally, Munby decided that the girl's pleasure-seeking nature, her 'evil and unlovely parts' were checked and disciplined by her 'masculine employment', since 'the independence and keen sense fostered by her city training have probably preserved [her] from a woman's worst catastrophe'.[15] Munby appeared to find the blurring of the dividing-line between angelic and fallen women, so central to Victorian male constructions of the feminine, disquieting and confusing.

For Gaskell and Munby, women writing for a living, whether for clerical work or as 'authoresses', whatever the moral dangers, offered the possibility of women determining their own patterns of work and even leisure. For Gaskell, even literary ambitions might be possible for many more women. From the 1870s onwards, women began to enter clerical work in increasingly large numbers at the same time as social, educational and political movements were revitalised by the pressure from both educated and working women to shift attitudes, property and marriage rights, to obtain the vote on the same terms as men, and to loosen some of the tightest restrictions on women's activity. By the turn of the century, a revolution in clerical work had taken place and employment for women in offices was a commonplace in towns and cities. Between 1851 and 1914 the number of women clerks rose from 2,000 to 166,000, 20 per cent of the clerical workforce.[16]

IV No sin to write: dangerous practice, divine art and useful science

Sunday schools, more than any other type of organisation, had introduced and spread the teaching of writing to working-class people since they were founded in the 1780s. They also contained the strongest opponents of the practice. In 1824, correspondence appeared in the *Bolton Express and Lancashire Advertiser* about the merits and demerits of teaching writing on Sundays. One correspondent accused his opponent of 'disgraceful innuendoes', bringing 'disgrace upon their author' whose letter the previous week was 'the mere cloak under which he wished to conceal his dagger'. The practice this writer most deplored was that:

> *The School-room has been turned into a bazar [sic] for the Sunday sale of copy-books, slates, and pencils, and perhaps, under his idea of sanctifying the whole, of Bibles and Testaments; and further, that nothing might be wanting to exhibit the evil in its strongest light, the Sunday-School circulating library has, in a few instances, also been opened on the Sabbath for receiving and returning books, with their hire and fines … These are lamentable facts.*

Advocates of writing, however, spoke of the 'almost divine art of writing whereby thoughts may be communicated without a voice, and understood without hearing'; by writing 'we treasure up all things that concern

81

us in a safe repository'. Most ambitiously, they observed that John Wesley himself, with a 'playful smile', had approved of the work of the Bolton Sunday School and that 'the wealth and grandeur of Great Britain is maintained by this means'.[17] In addition, it was still a common view beyond the sphere of religion that writing would teach 'the labouring classes of the poor ... to despise their lot in life instead of making them good servants ... it would make them fractious and refractory ... it would enable them to read seditious pamphlets ... it would render them insolent to their superiors ... the legislature would find it necessary to direct the strong arm of power against them'.[18]

The *Bolton Express* exchange illuminates wider views about the wisdom of the poor learning to write, and especially on Sundays. Advocates of writing on Sundays argued that writing was a 'Divine Art', which should not be denied to people who could only learn on Sunday. However worldly their motives, copying and writing sacred scripts would enhance devotion, not diminish it. The industrialising north was the heartland of Sunday schools, but the argument over writing was not confined to Bolton or Lancashire. It exercised Methodist leaders such as Jabez Bunting and others at the top of the church hierarchy. Teaching writing was a 'calumny' to be 'corrected'. In this view, it was a secular skill and teaching it on the Sabbath was wrong. Deep rifts in the Bolton Sunday Schools and elsewhere resulted from the prohibition of writing lessons. In 1834, the Methodists lost nearly 1,000 scholars to a new Sunday school which did offer writing. Sunday schools were hugely popular, and their cavernous buildings often dwarfed the chapels to which they were attached. Numbers mattered.

The debate about writing extended beyond Methodism and the Sunday school movement; but within Methodism it centred mainly on the theological question of whether teaching a purely temporal art on Sundays was an 'unjustifiable infringement of the sanctity of the Sabbath', rather than on the wisdom or desirability of teaching of writing at all.[19] One thread of the story of teaching writing is how it changed from the status of a refined Art taught by professional 'Writing Masters' to privileged social groups for the expression of ideas and beliefs, for polite communication and to oil the wheels of commercial and bureaucratic concerns, to a skill to be taught to everyone. The halting and cautious extension of writing to all social classes gradually changed its status from Art to a practical branch of science, providing vital skills to the commercial and industrial world.

Other protagonists of writing took up the argument. Adult Schools, from the first one in Nottingham in 1798, believed that the religious advantages of writing, such as its importance to intellectual development and greater harmony in family and social life, were all factors which influenced piety and sobriety and helped 'to improve and perfect the character of man'. Pious writing practices were part of Sunday school culture, including the writing of testimonials by the dying, and in memory of pupils who had died, notably in Stockport.[20] The idea of writing as a Divine Art, but for practical use by everyone, was developed in a pamphlet by Joseph Barker, a prominent radical Methodist. His autobiography suggests that writing had been significant for him since childhood, because his dissolute father's religious conversion was associated with learning to write. He connects learning literacy so closely with his father's discovery of faith that it is uncertain which is the primary transforming experience. In 1837 Barker published his pamphlet *Teaching the Children of the Poor to Write on the Sabbath Day*, in reply to the continuing virulence of anti-writing forces in the Dissenting denominations. It is a passionate treatise in favour of teaching writing, fired by his political views as well as by the potential for writing in religious conversion. Of his father he wrote: 'he could never rest until he had learnt how to write and sent my mother the story of his happy change'.[21]

For aspiring learners, the implications of the writing controversy were far-reaching. Sunday was the only free day for most workers, so to rule out writing in Sunday schools was to deny any teaching to vast numbers of people. The hope of escape from poverty and manual labour through better-paid employment forced the issue from the bottom end of society. For some working-class people, gaining clerical or administrative work did become a reality. Then there were those who wanted to write for self-improvement or communication with family members. There has been much historical debate about the extent of demand for literacy, from above and below, but some consensus that hope fed the motivation to learn even if, for most people, a change in social status through literacy remained a dream.

Barker's pamphlet was published at a time when Chartist and Owenite Sunday schools as well as church and chapel Sunday school pupils (for example at Bolton's Hope Street School) in Lancashire and Yorkshire were campaigning for the right to write. On occasion teachers and pupils took to the streets to demonstrate in support of writing on the Sabbath, with slogans such as 'No sin to write' on their banners. Strong demand for writing was also a factor, since schools that did not teach writing were losing scholars to those which did.[22] Barker's argument was that teaching writing to the poor is 'a work of mercy' and thus 'proper employment for the Lord's Day'. Without the help of writing, people would 'sink into a savage state', equivalent to slavery, with no means of upholding their liberties and rights. Barker argued flamboyantly that reading is not enough: it is writing that empowers people to shape their own lives:

> *He who reads and does not write may be likened to a man who plucks up many plants in his neighbour's garden, but never sets them in his own … But he that reads and writes may be likened to a man who collects as many plants as the other, and sets them orderly in his own ground where they all flourish and come to perfection.*

A person who can only read, he added with a fresh metaphor, 'gathers money to put into a bag with holes: he that writes gathers as much, and puts it into iron coffers'. At the same time, writing makes people 'wise and holy'. The interest of Barker's treatise lies in its synthesis of spiritual and earthly concerns as positive elements of a moral vision. Those who fought the spread of writing upheld the tradition of a sharp separation of everyday and spiritual concerns to protect the Sabbath. Thus, since it was argued by no one that writing was not a skill with practical, secular applications, the struggle for its supporters lay in showing how this-worldly and other-worldly benefits were mutually reinforcing. Barker pointed out the hypocrisy of 'those who unaccountedly pronounce the art of writing wholly secular, and represent it as a thing of little moment, [and] have come near to the summit of ministerial excellence, by the constant use of this art'.[23]

Barker was with those who spotted double standards at work. It was because its socially-conforming and its actually or potentially subversive uses were inseparable, that life-changing powers were attributed to writing in so much nineteenth-century literature. Those who had managed to achieve a higher cultural status did not necessarily want other ranks to join them. As long as only a limited proportion of the population had access to cultural production, society and culture could be more easily shaped and contained to reflect the habits and aspirations of the literate middle and upper classes. Their cultural grip was naturally felt to be in danger of slackening, especially as the pressure for popular education could upset the inexorable readjustment of political power in favour of the ascendancy of the property-owning middle class, a process in which the 1832 electoral Reform Act was a towering landmark. In the first years of the century, the ruthless suppression in a series of Acts of Parliament, of radical societies, the unstamped press, 'seditious' literature, swearing of oaths and pledges and meetings of social and political organisations like corresponding societies – in fact meetings of practically anyone – was evidence of how central the uses of literacy had become to both social change and social control.

Fears of forgery resulting from the spread of writing skills were expressed in parliamentary debates as well as church circles. Reports in the press were common, including in the radical press: the *Northern Star* reported a substantial number of paper forgery cases in the 1830s and 1840s. One report in 1838 describes how two men had been 'found in possession of false papers to the amount of 400,000f.' and that John McCormick, an unemployed Manchester bookkeeper, was accused of forging a cheque. However, the same radical newspaper sought to correlate crime with ignorance rather than literacy skills.[24] Forgery was a treasonable offence which was not reduced to a felony until the Forgery Act of 1861. It had a strong hold on the popular imagination. As we have seen from *My Lady Ludlow*, Gaskell was well aware of the association, as was Dickens: Magwitch, the escaped convict in *Great Expectations*, was transported to Australia for forgery after learning to write. Copying by hand was the machinery of nineteenth-century communication in business and bureaucracy and, in purely technical terms, it was similar to forgery. But clerical and copying skills – as Dickens's many clerks and copyists from Bob Cratchit to the opium-addicted pauper Nemo in *Bleak House* reflect – were ever more essential to manufacture and commerce, as well as to the growth of official and voluntary bureaucracies. So, beyond the immediate anxiety that more people would be capable of forgery, educationists were exponentially multiplying the number of people who could copy other people's work. Copying, a standard pedagogical tool for writing instruction could provide millions of children and adults with much-needed skills to meet employers' demands. As Alexander Galloway, a master engineer, reported in 1824, 'a man is not much use to me unless he can read and write; if a man applies for work, and says he cannot read and write, he is asked no more questions'.[25]

If copying was a double-edged sword, at least it was an approach to writing and draughtsmanship that could not be easily connected to the imagination, another site of concern about teaching writing. Creativity and imagination were not what teaching writing to the lower classes was for. But the notion of creative originality took hold once the entrenchment of literacy in society was firmly grafted on to the ideology of 'possessive individualism'. In *The Long Revolution*, discussing the emergence of romanticism, Williams argues that the gradual shift from 'imitative' to 'creative' original art was developed significantly at this time, promoting the artist as someone who is the fount of vision and creativity. The celebration of the gifted individual writer and the primacy of imagination in writing was gaining ascendancy at the same time as pressure to extend the skills of writing to all were first seriously considered.[26] Of course the concept of working-class people as creative beings was beyond the parameters of two dominant streams of thought and feeling: romanticism and utilitarianism. Dickens understood this too. The early chapters of *Hard Times* caricature the suppression of the imagination, 'fancy' and the glorification of 'fact' in Victorian education for the working class. The vast commercial potential of writing, realised during the late nineteenth-century revolution in communications, could not yet be fully grasped. So the movement in favour of writing came from many quarters: from the working class itself and radical 'organic' intellectuals such as Joseph Barker; from those who saw the benefits of writing to the systems of a bureaucratising state; from forward-thinking employers; from the liberal intelligentsia; and, for practical and humanitarian reasons, from social reformers and educationists.

The emergence and growth of a new social group of copyists, clerks and other office workers was a further complication of social groupings through upward mobility, which gradually expanded the skilled working class, the lower-middle class, many of whom aspired to educate, improve and express themselves after spending their days writing other people's words.[27] It seems no coincidence that many working-class autobiographers and poets had been clerks, postal workers or teachers, earning their living by practising writing. Often, their attempts at creative writing as young people and in later life were met with repression, disdain, condescension or possessive patronage. If there was a slight slackening of the middle-class grip on cultural power, allowing newcomers into the writing trade – and this was certainly true of Grub Street, popular fiction, serialised novel and autobiography – it was at the margins. Before ceding the need to pursue writing skills for all, the movements against writing early in the century could be seen as attempts to delay, minimise and control the extent of cultural inclusion.

V The magic of writing

Much nineteenth-century writing is self-reflexive in its exploration of the writing process, from accounts of literacy learning to the trials of the jobbing writer. Writing was becoming an industry in the mid-century, as the reading public expanded and the number of writers on 'Grub Street' proliferated.[28] In a period of rapid change, with widening access to reading and writing, the qualities specific to writing and its changing status in relation to the spoken word particularly exercised those who practised it, and took them in several different directions.

The belief in writing as more portentous than the spoken word is often evident in working-class writing. However, the ways in which successful literary figures such as Dickens and Gaskell cast access to literacy (both reading and writing) suggest that there was a continuously shifting social border between those who successfully achieved the status of a writer or author, and those for whom literacy was just within reach, but for whom the processes, practices and products of literacy were less easy to acquire, manipulate or disseminate. Perhaps recently successful cultural producers are best placed to see and understand how new categories of marginality and exclusion are created, and how hard it is to become a recognised writer. They could have responded by closing the door behind them. But many nineteenth-century novelists and social commentators looked outwards and strove to understand but also celebrate the importance of writing in working-class life. There was ambivalence, as in Dickens's testy relationship with John Overs, a working man he befriended and yet 'seem[ed] to treat … as the kind of person he might have become if he had not been successful'.[29] Dickens, Kingsley and Emily Brontë are among those who included access to literacy as part of their critique of social injustice; other writers, like Gaskell or George Eliot, who had become successful despite prejudice against women writers, accepted the need for writing skills but with caution, asking if all working people were morally ready or physically fit to practise literacy.

Most working-class writers seem also to have believed strongly that writing is more powerful than the spoken word. Writing is a legacy; it lasts and defends against a 'destiny obscure'. W.J. Ong argued that the 'vatic quality' of writing is the major difference between oral and literate cultures. The author is powerfully positioned because he or she is divorced from the text and cannot be directly challenged. A text cannot be refuted because 'even after total and devastating refutation, it says exactly the same thing as before'. In this argument, writing is 'inherently contumacious'.[30] Barthes argued the opposite: that 'speech is irreversible; a word cannot be *retracted*, except precisely by saying that one retracts it. To cross out is here to add ... paradoxically, it is ephemeral speech which is indelible, not monumental writing.'[31] Working-class writers lived this paradox. They came from a culture that was still largely oral, but they were increasingly surrounded by print, and well aware of the availability of literacy and its power to exclude them. In the profusion and confusion of cultural and educational change, they longed to own literacy and then try to make sense of its powers in their lives.

A sense of the vatic quality of writing was an important element of nineteenth-century popular belief systems. To take one example: spiritualism was a faith with many working-class followers, including the autobiographers Allen Clarke, Fred Edwards, Joseph Gutteridge and others.[32] A key part of spiritualist practice was automatic and spirit writing, in which the dead communicate with the living through the medium of writing. Logie Barrow's study of the widespread belief in spiritualism among 'English plebeians' drew attention to its systems of education, scientific belief and culture.[33] Later in the century these included the spiritualist lyceums, where alongside a Sunday school style education, and a correspondence college, an independent culture of writing and publishing flourished. Their periodical, the *Lyceum Banner*, encouraged and published letters and poems and ran regular essay competitions. There was a professed 'poetess of our movement, who like many of our most noted workers and writers ... was cradled in dissent'.

Alex Owen analysed the phenomenon of 'passive writing' as part of working-class spiritualism. The medium wrote, 'simply holding a pen over a blank sheet of paper, clearing the mind of unpleasant thoughts, and allowing the spirits to guide the hand'. The medium Florence Theobald recalled that 'hundreds of pages of deep wisdom and of marvelous [*sic*] beauty were poured through my hands ... and so rapidly was page after page written, that what was given in ten minutes by the spirit-writing, would take me an hour or more to copy'. Regardless of who literally did the writing, passive writing is a phenomenon which exemplifies the difficulties for subordinated groups in this period, including women, in expressing an imaginative or psychological life, and of the power of writing to release feelings too difficult and painful to be acknowledged. Florence Theobald spoke of messages of 'shocking or indecent import'. Writing released knowledge and feelings from the unconscious, of which women and children were supposedly incapable in pre-Freudian constructions of the feminine. Spirit-writing also demonstrated how writers could be 'influenced' by belief or ideology. Another case shows passive writers in dialogue not with the spirit voice, but with the writing technique itself as the 'other': 'Passive writing and I – dialogued together for hours at a time. I was very lonely and this intercourse so fascinated me that for several days I did little else than enjoy it'. In another instance, Christ suggested that a woman should 'cast off the trammels of authority'. External sources of authority and authorship enabled writers to write imaginatively from different perspectives in different voices than those with which their conscious social self was associated. Writing in spiritualism emphasised the power of writing itself, confirmed its irrefutable status and gave credibility to mediumship for many spiritualists: 'passive writing … convinced countless novices of the authenticity of spirit communication'.[34] This eccentric practice offers some understanding of the power invested in writing. The spiritualist espousal of the magical power of writing extended even further, to 'Direct Spirit Writing', whereby messages from beyond the grave were 'written' without human mediumship. In 1894, the *Lyceum Banner* printed a facsimile of a letter written by 'two gentlemen' who instructed a Mr Everitt to place an initialled piece of paper in a locked box with no pencil, in a locked wardrobe in the room of his daughter, who was sensitive to 'direct writing' and trembled when it took place. On investigation, the message had been written and its facsimile provided the comforting spiritual message, irrefutably confirmed in writing, to the readers of the *Banner* that 'death does not end their existence'.[35]

Another story about the belief in writing's magical and transformative properties appeared in the Owenite journal *The Crisis* in 1832. 'Difficulty in Comprehending the Art of Writing, a "Mariner's Account of the Tonga Islands" ' describes a meeting between Finow, King of the Tonga Islands, and a group of Englishmen. Finow, encountering a letter for the first time, puzzles over it, but cannot draw any meaning from it. He asks 'Mr. Mariner' to write something for him, and requests that he 'put down me'. He complies, 'spelling it after the strict English orthography', 'Feenow'. The King then orders him to turn his back and instructs another Englishman to read it out. Hearing his name, he turns the paper over and expresses amazement: 'This is neither like myself, nor anybody else! Where are my legs? how do you know it to be I?' He immediately orders a series of names: of other people, places, things, and even a dictated love letter, putting them all to the same test. He expresses curiosity and astonishment at this 'witchcraft', then reasons that perhaps it is 'possible to put down a mark or sign of something that had been seen both by the writer and the reader, and which should be mutually understood by them'. Tests are then carried out, involving reading the dictation of the names of people who've never been seen – in particular one who had been assassinated by the King himself, and 'Tarky' a garrison chief. Finow 'was yet more astonished'. He asks the writer whether Tarky was blind or not, 'putting writing to an unfair test'. When the mariner writes to dictation 'Tarky, blind in his left eye', and explains that writing can be used to send messages across the world 'and that the histories of whole nations were thus handed down to posterity', Finow begins to analyse the implications of the discovery. It would not do for Tonga. The result would be 'disturbances and conspiracies'. He could lose his life within a month. He would like to learn it for himself and for 'all the women to know it, that he might make love with less risk of discovery'.[36]

The story is more than a quirky tale of exotic cultures, though radical journals included all sorts of tall tales and sensational reporting. This is likely to have felt relevant to Owenites: the state of writing and publishing in England in the 1830s offered an analogy with writing in Finow's kingdom. Publishing 'must not freely be trusted in the hands of the people, because it may lead to "disturbances and conspiracies" '.[37] Yet working–class people, individually and mutually, were learning to read and write on a massive scale, and social movements circulated their journals as widely as they could. Growing numbers of people bought papers, poetry broadsheets and books and, if they could not afford them, read other people's copies of publications which reflected their experiences, living conditions and hopes for social change – and satisfied an appetite for stories, including weird and gruesome ones. And there were the illiterate who 'in times of political ferment ... would get their workmates to read aloud from the periodicals' and 'the illiterate worker' who 'attached a talismanic virtue to ... favoured works which he was unable, by his own efforts, to read'.[38] In the 1830s and 1840s significant numbers wished to write for themselves and for publication. Letters, poems, ballads, articles and personal advertisements signed by 'operatives', 'cotton spinners' and political prisoners were regularly printed in Owenite and Chartist papers, church magazines and cooperative journals. The *Northern Star*, also conscious that 'in the present turbulent times ... no man is safe, even in his correspondence', prominently published advertisements for 'A Secret System of Writing ... so simple that any person may read it in five minutes, whether he can write in the ordinary way or not'.[39]

Such accounts capture the way magic was attached to writing, which could symbolise immovable power and authority as well as human possibility. Comparable accounts are found in anthropological studies of societies in a state of development, such as Lévi-Strauss's study of the Nambikwara people who had no written language or Niko Besnier's study of what he calls 'incipient literacy' in Polynesia.[40] Back in nineteenth-century England, the shoemaker cited in *The Making of the English Working Class* 'who called punctually each Sunday on W.E. Adams to have "Feargus's letter" read to him, was nevertheless the proud owner of several of Cobbett's books, carefully preserved in wash leather cases'. This episode is drawn from the life story of a writer who even as a mentor and one who read out loud for others, still saw himself as subordinate and newly literate.[41]

For Ong, it is only oral cultures who attribute magic to words in the ways described by Owenites in *The Crisis*. Typographic cultures experience words as 'assimilated to things, "out there" on a flat surface. Such "things" are not so readily associated with magic, for they are not actions, but are in a radical sense dead.' Ong uses the meaning of names as an example of the difference between oral and written cultures. Names, he argues, convey power over things in oral cultures, whereas typographic cultures see names as 'labels', 'tags imaginatively affixed to an object named'.[42] But is such a split between oral and written cultures applicable to the first half of the nineteenth century in England, when the number of people becoming literate was dramatically increasing as millions spent snatches of time, often over years, persistently learning these skills? In 1834, The National Society reported over one million attenders at their schools, including Sunday schools. In the Stockport Sunday School alone in 1825 'above one thousand young persons' were reported to attend writing classes. As late as 1878, 5,000 adults were recorded as literacy learners in Birmingham's Adult Schools, attending classes between 7.30 and 9.30 on Sunday, the 'First Half Hour' of which was usually dedicated to writing.[43]

How can we best describe a society which is at the same time both oral and literate, and caught up in a dynamic process of change? The concept of 'incipient literacy' helpfully defines recent instances of increasing literacy practices by people who have previously been excluded from cultural and political power – practices in which literacy can have multiple, contradictory, subjective meanings, for both the newly literate, and the established classes who have received a more extensive education and dominance in literacy practices. So a second, more speculative question to ask of societies that assume almost universal literacy and boast a rich literary culture is whether there may still exist, both for the minority which remains culturally excluded, and for the literary establishment traces, faint or firm, of a sense of magic, and of belief in the irrational power of some forms and practices of literacy. The written word, as Vincent argued, not only recorded and communicated knowledge about traditions, superstitions and the supernatural, but was itself part of their rituals. There is evidence that this is so, and it is expressed particularly in the evocative use of names and in the vocabulary of identity and selfhood. That sense of power may be buried in the unconscious, it may exist as unexplored psychic realms of feeling, or it may be recognised and manipulated consciously as the power of writing to connect lost memories and feelings to consciousness.[44]

VI Names, signatures and identity

Writing a signature is part of a person's identity and has formal, often contractual, significance in a literate culture. In the nineteenth century, signing the marriage register was for many people the only public evidence that they could write, and so amounted to a meaningful statement in itself. The ritual of signing one's name or an 'X' in the marriage registers symbolised belonging to or exclusion from official literacies, and reinforced the significance of names and signatures. They had become part of an iconography of literacy, and 'owning' your own name was part of a significant process of creating an identity and subjectivity shaped by a consciousness of the growing importance of literacy.

At that time, signatures and writing one's name also carried deeper meanings for selfhood. And the act of writing a signature can still invoke feelings about the self or trigger memories. The novelist John Updike wrote:

> *When I sign my name … I find it increasingly difficult to get past the*
> *'d' … This unprompted hesitation, in what should be a fluent practised*

signature, I think of as my self – a flaw that reveals my true, deep self, like a rift in Antarctic ice showing a scary, skyey blue at the far bottom.[45]

Ong proposed that 'oral peoples commonly think of names … as conveying power over things' and that 'names do give human beings power over what they name'. For many newly-literate people in the nineteenth century, situated at the margins of a society increasingly obsessed with writing, the power of writing was expressed through the importance attached to signatures, the formal, official symbol of a literate self as well as part of self-identity. Even totally illiterate people who were otherwise indifferent to the literacy of those close to them, set store on as many signatures as possible appearing on their marriage certificate rather than crosses. The appearance of names in writing offered status, and perhaps a deeper ceremonial significance.[46]

Charlie Chaplin, who was born in poverty in south London in 1889, the son of a music-hall singer, described in *My Autobiography* how he and his brother witnessed their mother break down on stage and saw her committed to a lunatic asylum, after which they descended deeper into poverty and were forced into the workhouse and an industrial school. He describes his time at the Hanwell Schools for Orphans and Destitute Children as 'a most formative year, in which I started schooling and was taught to write my name "Chaplin". The word fascinated me and looked like me, I thought.' He recalls a fleeting encounter on the street, when a man he instinctively, instantly, knew was his father, asked his name; he 'feigned innocence' and replied 'Charlie Chaplin'. His father kept silent. For Chaplin this meeting connected isolated incidents in which his name was significant in attempts to create an identity for himself.[47] In *The Autobiography of Joseph Arch*, the writer repeats his name insistently, to witness milestones in his life: 'All I can say is, they did not know Joseph Arch'; 'The name of Joseph Arch will never be disgraced'; 'I only remembered I was Joseph Arch, MP'; 'Joseph and his brethren had accomplished their object'.[48] The repetition of his name emphasises his sense of self and the growth of power and agency in his life, but also betrays his astonishment at his achievements. The sense of self-esteem jostles with a plea for recognition. Writers more certain of their cultural standing would have had less need to remind others of their identity. For less confident writers, a changing sense of identity and selfhood surfaces in the spelling out of names and pride in signatures – as 'literacy events'. These signal the strength of feeling about the unexpected realisation of their human potential, to which the literacy has been critical.

An article in the Adult School journal *One and All* about a Women's School in the 1840s reported that 'the most striking feature of this first night was the great desire shown by all the women to learn to write, and great delight was expressed by some of them when they could write their names'. Another note, from the Cradley Heath Adult School, described a man attending the school in the early 1890s, who 'stated that he was 63 years of age and four months ago could not write his own name. He had learned to write it since then, and thought it looked better than a cross'. It was said there were frequent reports of similar cases circulated in the schools.[49]

In working-class childhoods, tombstone epitaphs played an important role in learning to read and write. The diarist Moses Heap of Rossendale copied out all the epitaphs on his rambles and other autobiographers recall how they offered models for the composition of verse, including satire. Writing inscriptions or mock epitaphs for graves was another pastime, as Marianne Farningham and others remember. For some, inscriptions offered inspiration and practical suggestions for writing. Epitaphs are a direct symbol of deeper meanings which a new consciousness of literacy enabled people to unearth. In becoming literate, people discovered that writing created ways of exploring memories and feelings, and reflecting on a changing sense of identity, and rites of passage.

A piece of autobiographical writing, an epitaph, a signature or a scrap of handwriting offered an alternative to the anonymity and oblivion of illiteracy. As M.K. Ashby wrote in her account of mid-century village life: 'Not a vestige of my grandmother's handwriting remains, and almost the only worldly goods she left were a row of books. Could any woman be more obscure?'[50]

In Dickens's representations of working-class life, and his biting criticisms of the workings of economic and social power, education was a central driver of changes in identity and circumstances. He elaborated the symbols and metaphors of gaining literacy that were common to working-class autobiography. Like his other novels, *Great Expectations* is socially and historically rooted but it is unique in several ways. It is narrated in the first person by a working-class orphan. It explores human relations in powerful psychological depth and uses fairy-tale and folklorish metaphors. In the opening lines Pip tries to explain his name and who he is. At first his tone is cheerful and assertive: 'My father's family name being Pirrip, and my christian name Philip, my infant tongue could make of both names nothing longer or more explicit than Pip. So, I called myself Pip, and came to be called Pip … I give Pirrip as my father's family name.' He has never known his parents. But authority for Pip's sense of who he is comes from the engravings on the family tombstone in the local graveyard, where he gains his 'most vivid and broad impression of the identity of things'. Pip's imaginative recreation of the dead parents he has never seen is 'unreasonably derived' from gazing at their names:

> *The shape of the letters on my father's, gave me an odd idea that he was a square, stout, dark man, with curly black hair. From the character and turn of the inscription, 'Also Georgiana Wife of the Above', I drew a childish conclusion that my mother was freckled and sickly.*

A sense of loss and abandonment suddenly intrude on Pip's wistful fantasy. Out of the engraved letters and names comes a grim self-discovery:

> *My first most vivid and broad impression of the identity of things, seems to me to have been gained on a memorable raw afternoon towards evening. At such a time I found out for certain, that this bleak place overgrown with nettles was the churchyard; and that Philip Pirrip, late of this parish, and also Georgiana, wife of the above, were dead and buried; and that Alexander, Bartholomew, Abraham, Tobias, and Roger, infant children of the aforesaid, were also dead and buried; … and that the small bundle of shivers growing afraid of it all and beginning to cry was Pip.*

His self-invented name gives Pip his ambiguous identity. It reflects an orphan's uprootedness and the fragile threads which tie him to a lost family known only through writing after death. The scene in the graveyard, which is interrupted by the terrifying appearance of the convict Magwitch who threatens his life, is already one of crisis: Pip's sense of desolation about being alone in the world and dependent on the willingness of relatives to look after him – Joe Gargery the blacksmith and his wife Mrs Joe, Pip's older sister and the only other survivor of the family, who is bringing him up 'by hand'. Pip runs home to fetch a file and food for Magwitch and is beaten by his sister for being out late. 'Mrs Joe', who remains significantly nameless, is neither companionable nor motherly. Joe is her sole defender, despite her violence towards him too. She's a 'tall and bony' woman, harsh and anxious, who is aggrieved at her social position and fiercely determined to encourage Pip's social progress.

Joe, a generous, forgiving and witty man is Pip's loving, collusive companion. Dickens explores literacy through their relationship, poking fun at Mrs Joe among other good-humoured exchanges: Mrs Joe is 'given to government' and 'not overpartial to having scholars on the premises', out of fear that an educated Joe might become rebellious. Dickens, as so often, satirises a public mood. He makes connections between profound life experiences catalysed by the writing process and written symbols, and the mundane tasks and repetitive processes necessary to learn to write. In a caricature, he also sneers at the local evening school, run by an old woman in the village, adding to the many middle-class voices clamouring to see such institutions replaced by proper schooling. However, it is grudgingly admitted that Pip learned to read, write and cipher there. He recalls the time he first read the names in the churchyard – he 'had just enough learning to be able to spell them out'; and how at evening school, he undertook the arduous process of writing with slate and copying of passages from a book 'to improve myself in two ways at once by a sort of stratagem'. A letter to Joe, with all Pip's spelling mistakes and misplaced capitals marks the start of Pip's educational journey: 'mI deEr JO i opE U', etc. Joe attempts to read it, but only manages his name, misspelt:

> *'I say, Pip, old chap!' cried Joe, opening his blue eyes wide, 'what a scholar you are! An't you?'*

> *'I should like to be,' said I, glancing at the slate as he held it: with a misgiving that the writing was rather hilly.*

> *'Why, here's a J,' said Joe, 'and a O equal to anythink! Here's a J and a O, Pip, and a J-O, Joe'.*

Joe's failure to learn to read is one symbol of Pip's developing sense of difference and his eventual abandonment of Joe, who realises that Pip's education will separate them. Pip remembers how on the previous Sunday he has accidentally held the prayer-book upside down, without any reaction from Joe. Now Pip asks him to read a whole letter he has written. Joe picks out more J's and O's and does not immediately admit to Pip he cannot read; indeed he goes on to say how much he enjoys reading. His admiration for Pip's learning and reticence about naming his own illiteracy are measures of the gap opening up between them. When

Pip probes gently, marking the development of the 'modest patronage' with which he begins to treat his companion-father, Joe reveals the reasons for his lack of schooling. His violent, drunken father had made it impossible; his mother's encouragement was hopeless. Joe's tolerance of Mrs Joe's violent episodes is associated with his horror at his mother's frailty, cruel treatment and early death. She (Mrs Joe) is 'a fine figure of a woman'.

So Dickens's understanding of working-class literacy practices avoids a simplistic and anodyne picture of learning in families. He chooses the more conflicted and topical issue of children outpacing their parents, and the emotional fallout that often resulted. The complexity of relationships is acknowledged again when Joe goes on to describe to Pip the poem of reconciliation he composed for his father's epitaph: 'Whatsume'er the failings on his part, Remember reader he were that good in his hart'. Only poverty has prevented Joe from having his verse carved in stone: 'poetry costs money'. Through Joe, Dickens challenges the equation of illiteracy with lack of sensibility or insight. The graphic 'reproduction' of Pip's first clumsy text and Joe's attempts to read displays the discrepancy between a ponderous learning of letters and the dancing literary style in which Dickens describes it. But there is also acknowledgement of a continuum in the use of letters, a sense of how Dickens developed his own brilliance as a writer despite childhood hardship, and in key episodes, a belief that the ability to compose and recall significant lines can be achieved, as with Joe, in total ignorance of reading or writing skills.

For Dickens, like Gaskell and Hardy, working-class literacy practices could be a treacherous business – in this and other novels. Pip falls into Orlick's murderous trap when he responds to a 'very dirty letter'. He is saved because he accidentally drops it on the floor, where it is found by his friends who rescue him. In the right hands, writing is to be welcomed. Long afterwards, Joe is successfully taught reading and writing by his second wife, Biddy. In Pip's voice, Dickens writes in humorously patronising tones of Joe's 'unbounded satisfaction' with his new-found skills at letter writing, labouring over 'up-strokes' and 'down-strokes' with a pen, and how he managed to complete and sign a letter triumphantly, despite being 'tripped up by orthographical stumbling blocks', blots and smudges.

In the final chapter, Pip returns to the graveyard with little Pip, the son of Joe and Biddy: 'I again', and has him read the tombstone engravings in a happy domestic sequel to his own forlorn childhood discovery. Again Dickens places the scene immediately before a startling encounter. In the happy, revised ending, Pip finds Estella, since childhood the 'irresistible' object of his hopeless love. They meet in Miss Havisham's desolate garden in a scene of reconciliation. The cold mists are the same as ever; but the metaphors of identity, the tombstone names and epitaphs no longer represent abandonment, estrangement or threatening violence. Warmth and domesticity, friendship and hope re-emerge as Pip sees no 'shadow' in a future bathed in 'tranquil light'.[51]

Hareton Earnshaw is a relatively minor character in Emily Brontë's *Wuthering Heights*, but the one who most sharply reflects attitudes to working-class literacy. Hareton is cast as rough, but easily hurt; illiterate but aware of the power of books. He is treated as a servant even though he is a member of the Earnshaw family which owns Wuthering Heights. The narrator Lockwood's first impression of Wuthering Heights is the carving, date and inscription above the door, which reads 'Hareton Earnshaw'. Names, inscriptions and drawings on mildewed books in the abandoned room of the long-dead Cathy Earnshaw (Linton after marriage) are part of the 'weird goings on' that Lockwood and Nellie Dean narrate: a 'ledge … covered with writing scratched on the paint … nothing but a name, repeated in all kinds of characters, large and small'. Brontë's consciousness of the significance of writing – random scraps and serious books – of working people's struggles to be literate and of autodidactism is clear from descriptions of Hareton trying to learn on his own by secretly stealing and collecting books. His relationship with Catherine Linton, daughter of Catherine Earnshaw and his cousin and neighbour, is played out through books, learning and attitudes to illiteracy. Catherine and Linton Heathcliff, the frail son of Heathcliff, form a close relationship, and together they mock Hareton. His inscribed name above the door becomes significant again later in the book, as narrated by the servant Nelly Dean. Hareton, conscious of his lack of education and 'sensitive to suspected slights', is ridiculed as almost sub-human by Catherine and Linton, who share a delight in books and write to each other. The focus of her scorn is his illiteracy:

> *I heard Cathy inquiring of her unsociable attendant, what was that inscription over the door? Hareton started up, and scratched his head like a true clown. 'It's some damnable writing,' he answered. 'I cannot read it.'*

> *'Can't read it?' cried Catherine. 'I can read it … It's English … but I want to know, why it is there.'*

Linton and Catherine discuss possible reasons for Hareton's inability to read, whether he is a 'colossal dunce', 'simple ... not right' or merely lazy. Linton decides Hareton's illiteracy is caused by his 'frightful Yorkshire pronunciation' and parodies Hareton's dismissal of 'book-larning'. Their response to his reply, 'Where the devil is the use on't?' is laughter at his expense. Nelly Dean's sympathies lie with Hareton and his uneasy consciousness of humiliation. As Linton and Catherine draw closer, their relationship develops through their clandestine exchange of books and letters – a bond between them which distinguishes them from the world signified by Hareton's ignorance.

The inscription above the door reappears at critical points in his progress, firstly when he tells Catherine he can read it: 'He spelt, and drawled over by syllables, the name – "Hareton Earnshaw".' His name is the first step towards literacy; and at the same time the emergence of Hareton as a character who grows beyond being subordinate and reactive to the emotional storms of powerful and educated others. Hareton's self-education is the theatre in which he experiences: new feelings of ambition, resilience, love and jealousy. At first, Hareton mistakes his mastery of the threshold of learning – his name – for all the knowledge and skills of literacy: 'He imagined himself to be as accomplished as Linton ... because he could spell his own name; and was marvelously [*sic*] discomfited that I didn't think the same'. Until that moment, Hareton's name has been out of reach, a symbol of his inability to take possession of his own identity and inheritance. Nelly Dean understands what it is to be dominated by the presence of literacy as a symbol of power and social class, but at a point in time and place when social and cultural structures were not developed enough for those who would become excluded to be clearly aware of the nature of their position. The boundaries between the educated and the unschooled ensured that the world of the educated is invisible and impenetrable, yet those who cannot gain entry know it is becoming the most important place to be.[52] Other novelists expressed this groping for what literacy could mean and not mean. In Hardy's *Jude the Obscure*, Jude is acutely disappointed to discover that the Latin grammar book, which he knows is a key to success, cannot be learned by cracking a simple code, as he had imagined: 'there was no law of transmutation ... but that every word in both Latin and Greek was to be individually committed to memory'. It is a moment which drives home the near impossibility of his ambition to seek an education. And in Kingsley's *Alton*

Locke, a near-illiterate farmer assumes that incanting lines from books can 'conjure' up his lost son.[53]

Hareton suffers setbacks and misunderstandings in learning literacy. It is assumed he merely steals books to hide in his room 'as a magpie gathers silver spoons'.[54] Eventually, his solitary learning is replaced by Catherine's teaching, which she approaches gingerly, leaving books for him to read despite his refusal to have anything to do with learning. Its climax is her present to him of a book inscribed with his name. Gradually, learning literacy becomes the process through which his life is transformed. Spurned by Catherine, Hareton burns her books. But the sickly Linton dies shortly after he and Catherine are forced to marry and eventually Catherine and Hareton are reconciled. Catherine persists in befriending him, persuading Hareton to trust her, breaking down his fear and suspicion, making him presents of books and promising to teach him to read. At the end, Hareton accepts he loves her. He and Catherine marry and some of the deep family and class conflicts and personal feuds find a sense of resolution. In small part, amid the novel's strangest happenings, enmities and alliances, learning and literacy are among the symbols of longing, growth and connection.

VII   Writing: contingency and chance

Literacy was a symbol of progress and human agency in the nineteenth century, besides the deeper meanings attributed to written communication and its association with permanence and power. But literacy was also recognised as an elusive and fickle instrument of change. The growth of literacy practices in daily life was experienced as placing power in a fragile and unpredictable medium. The tension between the unassailability and vulnerability of documents, and their significance as both permanent and ephemeral, is a recurrent theme in nineteenth-century fiction. There is an exploration of the part writing and letters play in maintaining, developing – and betraying – human relationships. Letters bring the shock of bad news as well as good. The essence of writing as final and flimsy, contractual and unchangeable yet vulnerable to loss, misdirection, contradictory interpretations and theft, gave rise to a consciousness of literacy as a newly significant and sometimes fateful factor in relationships, evident in contemporary literature.

Once daily life became dominated by documents, as Dickens constantly emphasises and satirises, not to write became less of a choice, and, in some circumstances, dangerous. Once writing was available, silence, or the absence of written communication, carried a different meaning from the silence of an oral culture. Letters in nineteenth-century fiction and autobiography were the sole medium for communication in situations where people were separated from each other. They were also symbols of chance, coincidence and contingency; of what might not have been and of the limits to human agency in a complex and irrational world of interdependent factors. Letters in particular were represented as powerful because of the uncontrollable aspects of their production, delivery to the right destination and how they would be received. The hard-won technical skill of writing was attractive, and people sought it, often innocent of the pitfalls. Although problems of contingency and chance mishaps were occasionally articulated in autobiography, in novels, working-class writing practices are beset by calamity and ill-fate. It is as if the middle-class literary imagination struggled to come to terms with the idea of working people as writers. As Boffin says to Silas Wegg in *Our Mutual Friend*, 'it's too late for me to begin shovelling and sifting at alphabeds [*sic*] and grammar-books'. Dickens satirised what many felt; writing by the wrong people was somehow unnatural and susceptible to failure.[55]

Fiction frequently explored the problem of living without literacy in a literate world and the meaning of becoming literate. Raymond Williams writes of Hardy as deeply and consistently aware of 'the problem of the relation between customary and educated life; between customary and educated thought' and of the state of mind captured by Jude Fawley's arrival outside 'Christminster' (Oxford) of belonging to one world and desiring entry to another. The meaning for writers who lived this tension, or, like Hardy, have either imaginatively entered it or been subject to condescension is one where the literate world, alien to those living without literacy, is credited with overwhelming and decisive power.[56] Literacy itself is seen to drive that world to the extent where 'customary feelings' become negligible without it.

By the time Hardy was writing, education had become more systematised and the stigma of illiteracy was stronger than in earlier decades, but for him, the journey from illiteracy to literacy also carried the pain of living at the threshold of change and possibility. Differently and more sympathetically than in George Eliot's earlier description of working people labouring over their letters at night school in *Adam Bede*, Hardy's illiterate or newly-literate characters are aware of their social disadvantages and the scorn they attract. Turbulence erupts, exposing not only their social frailty but also the narrowness, vanity and ruthlessness of the literate world they seek to join. 'On the Western Circuit' explores the power of literacy from two points of view: that of Edith, a lonely, unhappily married woman, and her servant, the illiterate young woman for whom Edith scribes letters to the professional man who has seduced and abandoned her. The scribe gradually falls in love with her correspondent, but even more with the romance of writing as she increasingly uses her own words. The lover responds, imagining the working-class girl he has seduced is after all refined and eloquent. A miserable ending for all three is the inevitable consequence of the deception.[57] For those who lacked literacy skills, perceptions of its reach and dominance were bound to be distorted, and they were easily cheated of their own language and emotions. Being able to write for others as well as yourself offers powers unknowable to those who can't write for themselves. Those at the border of literacy and illiteracy, trying to second-guess the best way of communicating embody the difficulty educated and uneducated people face in sustaining balanced, let alone equal relationships with each other.

In *Mary Barton*, a novel about Manchester working-class life, Gaskell's advocacy of social and political progress uses writing to plead caution and prescribe an emancipated, moral world for the working classes, wrought by persuasion rather than 'physical force'. The practice of literacy indicates depth of feeling, cultural sensibility, and promises justice and redemption, but it also facilitates violence and treachery. Mary Barton is a factory worker who lives with her Chartist father John. In the reformist political spirit of the book, literacy is dangerous in John Barton's hands because his political convictions are let down by poor judgement and an unstable character. His uses and interpretations of literacy are underhand and subversive. John Barton uses his copyist's job in a hospital to discover facts about industrial accidents. He reads, in particular, the Chartist *Northern Star*. He is chosen to join a group taking the Chartist Petition to Westminster. John's weakness and 'wildness' lead him to kill Carson, the son of the mill owner. In doing so, he uses a scrap of paper as wadding for his gun, on which a Valentine had been written to Mary by her sweetheart Jem Wilson. On this scrap she has also later copied out a poem by Samuel Bamford, a working-class writer and political activist. Gaskell contrasts Bamford with Barton as a moderate figure in the Chartist agitation for electoral reform that dominated working-class activism during the 1830s and 1840s.

Jem Wilson, Mary's lover, is Gaskell's portrayal of an honest, literate, self-improving working man, who is wrongfully arrested for the murder of the mill-owner's son. A key character in his release is Esther, Mary's aunt, a 'fallen woman', who has sought redemption by 'saving' the innocent Mary from Carson's predatory attentions. Esther later intercedes to reconcile Mary and Jem, but then discovers John Barton's scrap of paper by chance, in a ditch.

> *And what do you think she felt, when, having walked some distance from the spot, she dared to open the crushed piece, and saw written on it Mary Barton's name, and not only that but the street in which she lived! True, a letter or two was torn off, but, nevertheless, there was the name clear to be recognised. And oh! what terrible thought flashed into her mind; or was it only fancy? But it looked very like the writing which she had once known well – the writing of Jem Wilson, who, when she lived at her brother-in-law's and he was a near neighbour, had often been employed by her to write her letters to people, to whom she was ashamed of sending her own misspelt scrawl. She remembered the wonderful flourishes she had so much admired in those days, while she sat by dictating, and Jem, in all the pride of newly-acquired penmanship, used to dazzle her eyes by extraordinary graces and twirls. If it were his!*

Through this dramatic moment, Jem's status in the community is compared with Esther's. Gaskell is sensitive to differences in working-class communities. Esther is a fallen woman, Jem (until his arrest) is a pillar of the community. Literacy is one metaphor of the qualities which separate them. But it is Esther who makes the awful discovery of Jem's handwriting on the scrap of paper, bearing Mary's name in Jem's handwriting. Esther's conclusion that Jem is guilty is associated with the dangers of semi-literacy. For Mary, who is more literate, it reveals that her father is the murderer. The meanings of this literacy 'event' are dramatised as Mary gazes at the 'stiff, shining, thick writing paper'. She notices how the piece of paper fits with the torn-off remainder: 'jagged end to jagged end, letter to letter; and even the part which Esther had considered blank had its tallying mark with the larger piece, its tails of ys and gs'. The finality of the evidence in writing – handwriting style and quality of paper – feels as devastating as the gravity of the crime and the treachery which this scrap of literacy has laid bare. For Gaskell, the poetry of Samuel Bamford has been traduced. She suggests that he is too good for his class: the wilder

103

men will take his message too far, and use 'physical force' rather than 'moral force' or the power of the pen. They will take Bamford's cry for social change to the barrel of a gun. This is a betrayal of the power of literacy itself. The trust between father and daughter is instantly destroyed. Mary had copied Bamford's words as a gift for her father. Doubly treacherous, the original paper was a Valentine card from Jem Wilson, wrongfully charged with murder, and whom Mary realises she loves. Jem's innocent and honourable message of love has been sullied and betrayed. And yet Mary's father has killed the rich, callous man who would be her seducer.

Possession of written proof of her father's guilt forces Mary to confront her own timidity and vacillation which had made her prey to the mill-owner's son. Until this discovery, her literacy practices have reflected her passive character. She rejects Jem as her lover then regrets it, but is persuaded not to write to him. She receives letters and Valentines, but does not write back. Jem, in contrast to Mary and John Barton, continually educates himself, writing for his own purposes and as a scribe for others. He writes an emotional letter from prison, preparing for self-sacrifice. Now, writing gives Mary the power to become an independent actor. From the moment she discovers her father's guilt and Jem's innocence, she is empowered to act, and through her actions wins Jem by saving his life and name. After the trial, when Mary falls dangerously ill, Gaskell continues to explore the significant ways in which different life events may be characterised by the uses or absence of literacy. Jem 'was constantly anticipating that … every scrap of paper was to convey to him the news of her death'. But he did not hear because Job Legh, who was caring for Mary, had not thought to write:

> *Any necessity for his so doing had never entered his head. If Mary died, he would announce it personally; if she recovered, he meant to bring her home with him. Writing was to him little more than an auxiliary to natural history; a way of ticketing specimens, not of expressing thoughts.*[58]

Mary Barton explores the ways literacy practices engineer and reflect change, enable learning and self-expression, carry the business of everyday life and work, and pin down the truth irrefutably through documentation. At the same time, the use of torn scraps of paper and chance discoveries points to a fear of over-reliance on the ephemeral quality of writing as much as its solid permanence. Misunderstandings portend misfortune and even tragedy; and oral communication is still the safest way of telling. During the trial, only the physical presence of Will Wilson who arrives by boat, against the tides and wind, to bear true witness carries the day in court. The novel combines the elemental and the artificial in determining human relations. Under Gaskell's anthropological and moralistic gaze, her sense of ambivalence about the unchecked spread of literacy in turbulent times is revealed. Her preoccupation with literacy also draws attention to her own unlikely position as one of a new and tiny group of respected women writers, although her life experience was very different from the tough childhood and truncated education out of which Dickens became another celebrated writer for whom literacy was a prominent social issue. Perhaps some successful writers, consciously or not, explored the relationship between literacy and literature in working-class life from their own experience.

Charles Kingsley wrote his novel *Alton Locke* in the form of a working-class autobiography and as a didactic treatise against 'physical force' Chartism. He too places an innocent in the dock. Alton Locke is redeemed by a note, also a 'dirty scrap of paper', announcing 'a labouring man' as the key witness.[59] Kingsley, like Gaskell, is a promoter of education for working people. But they both express unease about the susceptibility of literacy skills to supposedly wrongful and morally-distorted uses, associating the danger with ignorance or lack of mental or moral discipline rather than education. Moral judgement is not the preserve of the educated, though. While both writers reinforce the solid borders between an educated literate life and the life of manual labour and the soil, it is honest working men who ensure justice: the witness who saves Locke is an 'English peasant'. John Bedford Leno, who was taught by Kingsley, has a telling story of how he expressed his gratitude and admiration to Kingsley for *Alton Locke*: 'His reply was … that I had misunderstood his motives in writing the work … and in a word, that he did not require my thanks. I was hurt and puzzled.'[60] The exclusive power to imagine and interpret the lives of subordinate others was a cultural given, even for reforming well-wishers. Comment from the subjects of writing was not required.

The borders between literacy and illiteracy became more permeable later in the century as literacy and time in school grew. Hardy's Tess Durbeyfield classically inhabits the interface between traditional rural patterns of life and the lifestyles of the educated, poised between them as 'a mere vessel of emotion untinctured by experience'. 'The dialect was on

105

her tongue to some extent, despite the village school.' The marginal social position of her family is defined by her father's fanciful pretensions to higher social status, and their literacy is a mix of the old, the superstitious and the modern, exemplified by books like 'The Compleat Fortune-Teller' and Tess's mother's letter to her, written in a 'wandering last century hand'. As a working girl, Tess is observed by three scholars, 'young men of a superior class' looking on with desire and the curiosity of anthropologists at a country dance. One is Angel Clare, the well-meaning vicar's son who marries her against the will of his family, deserts her and, in a narrative which makes letter-writing pivotal to the course of their doomed relationship, returns too late to halt her death on the gallows.

Tess of the D'Urbervilles explores the impact of change on families, particularly women, trapped in marginal positions as new social and cultural formations took shape. Education gave rise to aspirations that outpaced the changes that were possible in class or gender relations. Families were mostly still dependent on manual labour, whatever their literacy skills. But Tess might have become a teacher if her parents' dreams had not turned their heads. To be the wife, as opposed to the mistress, of a middle-class man was not a realistic aspiration. Through plot devices, *Tess* exposes tensions resulting from the tenuous nature of literacy practices in unequal relationships. The certainty and authority that literacy brings is matched by its unpredictability and dependence on chance. In *Tess* if, when and how written messages are received and understood cannot be foreseen, controlled or corrected.

When they promise to marry, Tess tries to write to Clare, to confess her earlier seduction by the wealthy and unscrupulous Alec D'Urberville. Innocent of moral and social rules and the 'double standard', she supposes he will forgive her. Her tentative efforts to broach the issue 'by word of mouth' are repeatedly interrupted. The idea of writing occurs to her as 'another way' – it is not her chosen way. She writes at night, loses her nerve and destroys the letter, fails again to speak, and tries writing again. She senses the decided nature of writing and the way in which it enables control over difficult communication. Using writing, the story of Tess's past could be written as 'a succinct narrative', on 'four pages of a note-sheet' put into an envelope, directed and carried to Clare. She pushes the letter under his door, but cannot know that it has slipped under the carpet, and he will never see it.

Writing permits a temporary evasion of the emotions involved in direct communication. For Tess there is a suspension of feeling during the task of writing itself, followed by extreme anxiety about the consequences of her letter. Writing provides a controllable space to act, but also loss of power to adjust and negotiate narrative and response, which 'word of mouth' might have offered, especially for the tentative new writer. Hardy plugs into the fear of documents being lost or stolen, which haunts the psychic structure of literate societies. In the world that Tess inhabits, poised between Williams's 'customary' and 'educated' cultures, neither the old nor the new routes to communication can be travelled surefootedly.

Writing continues to be a strong driver of the story after Angel and Tess marry. Angel leaves the country immediately after discovering Tess's sexual experience. Writing continues to carry some of the additional burdens of mean-spiritedness and class-related misunderstandings Tess suffers. Jealousy and doubt about Angel's affection and loyalty drive Tess to make several more attempts at writing, but eventually she decides to visit his parents to seek comfort and advice. She reflects on the oddness of her 'technical claims on such a strange family only by the flimsy fact of a member of that family, in a season of impulse, writing his name in a church-book beside hers'. When she reaches their village, she overhears dismissive comments that emphasise the unbridgeable social divide between Angel and the 'dairy maid' he has married.

When Alec D'Urberville reappears, Tess begins letters to Clare and discards them, unable to assert her moral claim on him. The emotional register of each letter measures the strength of her will to resist D'Urberville's renewed pursuit. She manages to send Clare a letter asking him to return. There is no reply and at the point where her resistance to Alec is breaking, she writes another letter, an angry denunciation of his betrayal, abandoning all 'polite' letter-writing conventions.

> *O why have you treated me so monstrously, Angel! I do not deserve it. I have thought it all over carefully, and I can never, never forgive you! You know that I did not intend to wrong you – why have you so wronged me? You are cruel, cruel indeed! I will try to forget you. It is all injustice at your hands!*[61]

There is no reward for Tess's acts of agency. Chance is against her and determines the outcome. Events are played out beyond predictable social patterns of life or communications. Letters reach Angel too late. Writing might have changed the course of events, but Hardy interprets writing as too fragile to support the exercise of human agency by the socially powerless. Once the chain of actions connecting writer and reader is broken, writing is useless. Both Tess and Angel depend on writing to urge, defend and receive each other's emotional truths. Their passions are mediated by social and cultural norms, by the double standards in gender relations; they are supported by the possibilities of love in a time of social and educational progress. But by making chance and mistiming more influential in the tragic closure than Tess's emotional hesitance, and more significant, finally, than the cultural barriers of class between them, Hardy seems to confirm the doubts that still attached to working-class literacy. He associates it more with fate, the downside of magic, than with a social or rational role in human relations. At the same time as universal elementary education was becoming a reality, the suspicion that written communication was untrustworthy was still deeply lodged.

Notes

1   R. Williams, 1981, pp. 93–4.
2   Vincent, 1982; Burnett, 1982; Rose, 2002.
3   Dickens, *Our Mutual Friend*, [1864–5] 1985b, p. 246; Baynham (2008) usefully explores constructions of literacy in Dickens's *Bleak House* and Gaskell's *Mary Barton*.
4   Gaskell, *My Lady Ludlow and other Tales*, [1858] 1890. All quotes are from this edition.
5   See Lacqueur, 1976, for the history of the growth of Sunday schools, the place of secular education and the teaching of writing.
6   See, e.g., E.P. Thompson, 1971 and 1991.
7   Pole, 1816, p. 56.
8   Gaskell, *My Lady Ludlow*, pp. 2–3, 14, 23–5, 345, 51–2, 56–7, 129.
9   E.P. Thompson, 1968, pp. 22–23.
10 Gaskell, *op. cit.*, pp. 56–7.
11 Pole, *op. cit.*, p. 56.
12 PP: Mins of Evidence to SC on Education, 1834, p. 97.
13 Clanchy, 1979, p. 7.
14 Gaskell, *op. cit.*, p. 129.
15 Quoted in D. Hudson, 1974, pp. 155–6.
16 See, e.g., Zimmek, 1986. My own great great aunt, Annie Howard, b. 1847, sister of the social reformer Ebenezer Howard – stenographer, inventor and founder of the Garden City movement – is reported to have been the first woman typist in the City of London, reflecting the active connections between social reform, modernity, the communications revolution and the emancipation of women in the late nineteenth century.
17 *Bolton Express and Lancashire Advertiser*, 31 February 1824, 7 February 1824, p. 2, 14 February 1824 (Bolton Reference Library).
18 President of the Royal Society in House of Lords 1807 debate on Samuel Whitbread's Educational Bill, quoted in Cipolla, 1969, pp. 65–6.
19 *Bolton Express and Lancashire Advertiser*, 14 February 1824, p. 2.
20 Pole, *op. cit.* pp. 50–7; Currie Martin, 1924, pp. 13, 32–3, 48, 52; Memoir Books of the Stockport Sunday School 1811–80.
21 Barker, 1837, pp. 13–15; Barker, [1846] 1880. There are many examples of the condemnation and the defence of writing from between 1790 and the 1840s within and outside religious organisations, e.g. Mayers, 1798, p. 10.

22 On Whit Monday and other pro-writing demonstrations, see R. Johnson, 1979, p. 84; Lacqueur, *op. cit.*, p. 124; *Northern Star*, 6 January 1838, 9 June 1838. For the flight from Sunday schools which did not teach writing, see Musgrave, 1865, p. 44.
23 Barker, 1837, pp. 3–5.
24 *Northern Star*, 3 November 1838, 18 November 1848; an article on illiteracy and crime statistics appeared in 18 November 1848 showing 'the predisposing influence of ignorance and crime'. Out of 348 convicted persons, 107 could not write and 154 could only write 'indifferently'.
25 E.P. Thompson, [1963] 1968, p. 787.
26 R. Williams, 1965, p. 29; see also Said, 1991, pp. 126–39, where he discusses the classical roots and meanings of originality in writing in Western culture.
27 Richard Church, V.S. Pritchett and Neil Bell, all exemplify the tradition of those writers who were born towards the end of the nineteenth century, started their working lives in office work and discussed its relationship to their writing in autobiographies. Many more unpublished writers shared this experience. See, e.g., P. Evett, 'My Life In and Out of Print', TS, Brunel University; E. Brown, untitled TS, Brunel University Library. See Burnett, Vincent & Mayall, 1984, which has many references to this route to writing.
28 Gissing's *New Grub Street*, 1891, explores the world of professional writers of fiction and journalism. See also Leavis, [1932] 1965; Altick, 1957; James, 1976 and 1974. For an analysis of the growth of the professional writer, see Cross, 1985, esp. chapters 3 and 4.
29 Ackroyd, 1990, p. 301.
30 Ong, [1982] 2002, p. 79.
31 Barthes, 1983, p. 379.
32 To locate these autobiographies, see Burnett, Vincent & Mayall, 1984, pp. 70, 98, 130.
33 Barrow, 1986, esp. chapter 6, 'Presence and Problems of Democratic Epistemology'.
34 Owen, 1989, p. 79; pp. 171–3; p. 81; p. 171; p. 215; p. 213.
35 *Lyceum Banner*, 1890–8, Vol. 4, No 41.
36 *The Crisis*, April 1832, Vol. 1, No 1.
37 *ibid.*
38 E.P. Thompson, 1968, see especially chapter 16, pp. 782–3.
39 See *Northern Star*, 30 June, 1838; see also 20 July, 1839; 12 September, 1840; 24 August, 1838.
40 Besnier, 1995; on 'incipient literacy', see pp. 16–17, 172–6.
41 E.P. Thompson, *op. cit.*, p. 783, quoting from Adams, 1903, Vol. 1, p. 164.
42 Ong, *op. cit.*, pp. 32–3.
43 Mins of Evidence, SC on Education, 1834, p. 67; Annual Report, Stockport Sunday School, 1825, p. 9; *Monthly Record*, February 1878, p. 28.
44 Vincent, 1989, p. 32.
45 Updike, *Self-Consciousness – Memoirs*, 1989, p. 203.
46 Ong, *op. cit.*, p. 33.
47 Chaplin, 1966, p. 28.
48 Arch, 1966, pp. 110, 121, 137, 146.
49 *One and All*, 1891, Vol. 1, No 7, p. 103; 1892, Vol. 2, No 2, p. 24.
50 Ashby, 1961, p. 1.
51 Dickens, *Great Expectations*, [1860–1] 1985a, pp. 35–6, 73, 152, 75–7, 430, 473–4, 441–2, 473–4, 493.
52 E. Brontë, *Wuthering Heights*, [1847] 1965, pp. 46, 253, 281.
53 Hardy, *Jude the Obsure*, [1895] 1966, p. 35; Kingsley, *Alton Locke*, [1862] 1892, pp. 154–5.
54 E. Brontë, *Wuthering Heights*, 1995, p. 301.
55 Dickens's *Our Mutual Friend*, 1985b, p. 94.
56 R. Williams, 1984, pp. 97–9.
57 Hardy, 'On the Western Circuit', [1891] 1979.
58 Gaskell, *Mary Barton*, [1848] 1970, pp. 155–6, 290, 300, 406.
59 Kingsley, *Alton Locke*, [1862] 1892, pp. 219–20.
60 Leno, 1892, p. 49.
61 Hardy, *Tess of the D'Urbervilles*, [1891] 1965, pp. 22, 106–7, 333, 400.

PART TWO

LEARNING AND LETTERS: WRITING PRACTICES IN THE COMMUNITY

CHAPTER 3

Autodidacts or mutual learners?
Writing, association and the self

I

Among the images and discourses in historical, fictional and autobiographical accounts of working-class learning and writing, two stand out. The first is a romantic picture of the solitary learner, usually a young man. Arduous nights of study by candlelight after long working days are seen as the central experience of the 'autodidact'. He receives little help beyond the possibility of support from the family. In this version of history, the 'working man' learns to write by laboriously practising upstrokes and downstrokes and letter-formation in copy-books or scraps of used paper. He immerses himself in a wildly unstructured programme of reading, which might include *Pilgrim's Progress*, Latin grammars or astronomy. V.S. Pritchett's uncle used Burton's *Anatomy of Melancholy* to learn to read.[1] An autodidact might typically feel stimulated and frustrated in turn, but rarely self-critical or inadequate. Success of any kind signalled a triumph of individual persistence over material circumstances. The patterns of learning were much more complex. Historians have recognised that much of the learning of so-called self-educated people happened in association with other people in networks of mutual support and guidance, made up of fellow learners, family, workmates, political allies, teachers and benefactors. Jonathan Rose has pointed out that 'no autodidact is entirely self-educated' and 'must rely on a network of friends and workmates for guidance, discussion and reading material'. He goes further to say that by 1890 working-class culture was 'saturated by the spirit of mutual education'. Yet the view of the solitary learner, heroic but somehow pathetic, has persisted.[2]

A free evening class at Louth, Lincolnshire, England, taught by Mr Colam for working men. Date: 1862
Courtesy of Mary Evans Picture Library

In *The Country and the City* Raymond Williams questions a contemporary critic's assertion that George Eliot, Thomas Hardy and D.H. Lawrence, whose fathers were a bailiff, a builder and a miner, respectively, were 'our three great autodidacts'. Each, in addition to their independent learning, had a higher or professional education and belonged to prominent literary or philosophical circles. Williams assesses the statement as 'one of the sharp, revealing moments of English cultural history' because:

> *The flat patronage of autodidact can be related to only one fact: that none of the three was in the pattern of boarding school and Oxbridge which by the end of the century was being regarded not simply as a kind of education but as education itself: to have missed that circuit was to have missed being 'educated' at all. In other words a 'standard' education was that received by one or two per cent of the population; all the rest were seen as 'uneducated' or as 'autodidacts': seen also, of course, as either comically*

114

ignorant or, when they pretended to be learning, as awkward, overearnest, fanatical. The effects of this on the English imagination have been deep.[3]

The appropriateness of a learner's aspirations is linked to their level of formal education, their choice of occupation and how their work is received and discussed. The social background of autodidacts and working-class writers has often been more interesting for commentators than what they have to say or how they say it. Until recently, critical responses to the poet John Clare, a Northamptonshire agricultural labourer, typically described his poetry as 'refreshing' but that although it 'compares favourably with his better known contemporaries … He remains, however, a minor poet and his case is one of only partial victory over circumstances'.[4] It is hard to imagine where Clare could have been better placed to write pastoral poems than roaming along the Northamptonshire hedgerows he loved; or over which circumstances he might have sensed victory when he wrote his poem of alienation and loneliness, 'I Am', while living in a lunatic asylum. 'Circumstances' refer obliquely to his lack of formal education and social status as an agricultural labourer. That these work against creative expression hardly needs to be said.

The language of autodidacticism often centres on an unproblematised notion of 'self'. This is illustrated by expressions like 'self-education', 'self taught' and 'self-improving'. A number of commonly-used words characterise the condescending imagery: 'solitary', 'aspiring', 'enthusiasm', 'effort', 'scholar(d)', 'striving', 'struggling' and 'sincere'. There are also contradictory terms which are often used interchangeably with the first group: 'unlettered', 'untaught', 'unschooled', 'uneducated', 'peasant' (poet), 'groping', 'simple', 'illiterate', 'ambitious', 'unsophisticated', 'pretensions', 'rudimentary', 'smattering' (of knowledge), and so on. Both sets of terms labour the image of the solitary learner. Their condescension sometimes feels spiked with dislike, as in Virginia Woolf's view of 'a self-taught working-man, and we all know how distressing they are, how egotistic, insistent, raw, striking, and ultimately nauseating'.[5]

A second way of imagining manual workers learning to read and write focuses on their painful clumsiness and awkwardness faced with a desk, chair, pen and ink. This is exemplified by an HMI report to the CCE, which asserted that good writing was beyond 'the fingers of the rural labourer … the boy that can hold a plough cannot grasp the more delicate handle of a pen' and to educate 'a plodding, hardworking peasantry who do their labour much as the animals they tend' would be to create 'an effeminate class of persons'.[6] Such attitudes were common, expressed in George Eliot's village night school in *Adam Bede*:

> *These three big men, with the marks of their hard labour about them, anxiously bending over the worn books, and painfully making out, 'The grass is green'... It was almost as if three rough animals were making humble efforts to learn how they might become human.* [7]

As education spread, the acquisition and practice of literacy became for many commentators a measure of fully human status. Middle-class writers seemed sometimes to act like amateur anthropologists observing an exotic people. Attitudes towards working-class people learning a craft traditionally practised by powerful social groups suggested they should conduct themselves 'humbly' and were unlikely to go far. The gulf in understanding between the meanings which 'educated' and 'uneducated' writers attached to writing ran deep and wide.

Discussions of autodidacticism have seldom focused on women learners ... an 'autodidact' is often synonymous with a self-taught working man. Self-educated women, especially writers, were seen as even more exceptional. The sexual division of labour throughout the nineteenth century in urban and rural communities and the double burden of paid and domestic labour for girls and women undoubtedly made finding time for learning even more difficult for working-class women. Women had less access to the public sphere than men, particularly domestic servants, or to forms of association which enabled mutual learning in communities. So it was rare for women to be spotted by potential 'sponsors' of their learning. Women's work was much more rarely published and far fewer texts have survived, though some women did manage to write for an audience, producing articles for newletters, poems and autobiographies. Despite the stereotype of the male autodidact, the nature of women's lives meant they were the solitary ones, isolated in their learning, particularly in rural life and domestic service. Where women did manage to learn together with others it was most commonly through church organisations, the colleges for 'working men' and, later, the WEA. The Adult School Movement, Sunday schools or institutions like the People's Colleges, Birkbeck College and the Working Men's College, mainly in towns and cities did attract women to reading, writing and more advanced learning in serious numbers.

Many working-class writers used language which has encouraged a view of their learning as simple and straightfoward, as this passage from the autobiography of the Chartist activist and intellectual Thomas Cooper illustrates:

> *My first poem — for it was sure to come, sooner or later — seemed almost to make itself, one evening as I walked in the valley below Pringle Hill. I give it here, be it remembered, as the first literary feat of a self-educated boy of fifteen. I say self-educated, so far as I was educated. Mine has been almost entirely self-education, all the way through life. From that time forth I often struck off little pieces of rhyme, and made attempts at blank verse, but all such doings were really worthless, and I kept no record of them.*

Elsewhere in his autobiography, however, Cooper showed that he was not solely 'self-educated', and described writing as coming to him so naturally it could 'make itself'.[8]

The most commonly-used texts and the emphasis of much historical analysis has fostered generalisations about working-class culture and the balance of personal aspiration and political motives in learning. The idea of an essential creativity and imagination rarely features. Most scholarship on working-class writing has leant towards a generic understanding of working-class writing: sorting, classifying and identifying the shared attributes of a genre. The picture looks different if writers' individual experiences are explored, unearthing the meanings of literacy learning and practices; the nuances of social-class position; why people wrote; writing styles; gender differences and the variety and complexity of the conditions in which writing was produced. Notions of simplicity, humbleness and the unnaturalness of writing and images of ill-directed solitary learning have perpetuated distorted accounts of cultural and educational practices despite the well-documented evidence of association between people as the bedrock of informal learning and cultural expression.[9]

Charles Shaw, a potter from Tunstall in the Black Country, describes his learning in detail and at first appears to support autodidacticism as a solitary, unguided pursuit:

> *We had in our house a small room over 'an entry'. This entry afforded a passage from the street to the backyards of the cottages. This room was about three to four feet wide, the widest part being a recess near the window, the other part of the room being narrowed by the chimney. I got a small iron stove to warm the room on cold nights, and I fixed up a small*

desk against the wall, and two small shelves for my few books. I don't know what a university atmosphere is. I have dreamt of it, but I know when I entered this little room at night I was in another world. I seemed to leave all squalor and toil and distraction behind. I felt as if I entered into converse with presences who were living and breathing in that room. I had not read many authors then, but such as I had seemed to meet me with an unspoken welcome every night. My life there was strangely and sweetly above what it had been during the day. It was often from nine o'clock to half-past before I could enter this room after walking from my work and getting my tea-supper, the only meal since half-past twelve at noon ... As soon as I entered that room, I was as a giant refreshed with new wine. Its silence was as refreshing as dew, and exhausted energies seemed refilled with vigour and pulsed along with eager ardour. Unfortunately, I never acquired much in the way of knowledge. As I have since found out, I was on the wrong track and had no-one to guide me. But what I failed to get in acquisition I got in inspiration and communication with some of those 'sceptered sovrans who still sway our spirits from their urns'. I made the mistake of climbing trees for golden fruit when I should have been digging and delving in the soul ... I look back pensively and gratefully, however, upon what I did in my little room. I might have done much more in much less time if I had had a guiding mind. Sometimes I read and wrote on till two or three in the morning.[10]

Six days out of seven, Shaw got up to go to work two and a half hours later; on Sundays he was active at a Sunday school.

This passage partly corroborates stereotypes of working-class adult learners. The celebration of 'a room of one's own' as the prerequisite for creativity, away from 'distraction'. The expressions of humility contrast with his suggestion that his room was almost equal to the imagined, dreamlike world of university. Shaw invested this experience with fairy-tale romanticism, 'strange and sweet', casting himself a 'giant' grown to superhuman strength, who met with spirits, climbed trees for golden fruit, and made books come literally to life. This passage contains not only the language of earnest, apologetic self-improvement but also the language of fantasy, with learning as romantic and Shaw as hero. His room is filled with imagined others, among the furniture and books. He is conversing with writers, and the space between himself and his ideas is buzzing with life. This is no passive learning: solitude gives way to an imagined society of learners.

118

The vision of a solitude in which ideas and writing magically come to life is part of the experience of informal learning for many writers, which discourses of individualism and plodding social realism miss when autodidacts are plucked out of their connecting social relationships and learning associations. The imaginative inner life of learners and the electric connections with ideas and writing are obscured if only a social or mass phenomenon is recognised, rather than unique human beings connected with their communities and social class. Learners' connectedness is rarely prominent, even for those enrolled in Mechanics' Institutes, mutual improvement societies or literary institutes. It is as if the associations which supported their learning cannot be given legitimate status because they are not capital E Education. Their explanations and apologies are taken at face value. They ultimately 'fail' (or are ignored) in terms of their writings, because their educational and literary achievements are valued more for what they tell us about working-class life. Their creativity and knowledge remain relatively neglected.

Autodidactic learning does not quite fit literary rags-to-riches stories. Autodidacts were unlikely heroes or myth-makers. The drive to self-publish pieces of writing that fell short of brilliance could be subjected to greater condescension than comparable work compiled in total obscurity, then discovered by a philanthropic patron. A complexity and depth of feeling about learning emerges from the recorded experiences and perspectives of new users of literacy, who had no vested interest in a system of 'flat-patronage' and no truck with public narrow-mindedness about how the poor should be educated. Writers sought out and applied themselves questioningly to methods of learning, writing styles and the knowledge that mattered to them. They explored their own creativity and potential. Over the century though, they increasingly carried the knowledge that, however highly they prized their own learning processes, including their time in Sunday schools and the widely-condemned dame schools, others saw their learning as amateur and even pathetic, compared to the emerging elementary school system. In the heyday of informal learning, the inspectors were at work, and the multiple and diverse forms of independent working-class education were being reshaped and channelled into state-run and middle-class directed conformity. Informal learning associations and their autodidacts were not listened to. They expressed a sense of loss as well as gain about the advent of the state education system, and to understand that ambivalence, we need to locate the practice of 'self education' within the social relationships and communities that supported it, and respect the minds and motives of people who were previously without much or any literacy, who were expected to remain silent, their lives and opinions unrecorded and who decided to write about it.

Perhaps the best and most spirited definition of autodidacts is Logie Barrow's 'persons who were making their education their own affair, irrespective of social superiors'.[11] This does not necessarily mean learning alone rather that what people learned was not subject to a higher authority. 'English plebeians', the argument runs, made concerted efforts to create their own, democratic, definitions of knowledge: a 'democratic epistemology'. This notion of autodidactism allows for mutuality and cooperation in learning. It encompasses collective self-education, formal or informal such as the activities in a Northeast England mining community in the 1830s where education was, as in many social movements, an integral part of trade union and community activity, organised by and for working-class families.[12]

Most adult learners began with the knowledge and language held in common by the communities around them. The technical starting points for learning to write described in autobiographies like Adam Rushton's or John Clare's – for example, the strokes which make up the letters of the alphabet – had a set of names that related to everyday life, such as pothooks, ladles, tarbottles and sheephooks.[13] First, strokes would be drawn, then letters, followed by sentences with moral messages, homilies, proverbs, poems or lines from psalms. The Bible, which vast numbers of households owned, was a source of text, together with popular reading primers.[14] Learning to read from the Bible provided an integrated approach, offering both a graded reading scheme – with the tenth chapter of Nehemiah as the summit of achievement – and a 'real book', whose stories and meanings were a central part of life and literature for adults and children.[15] This has a familiar ring in relation to the debates and changing fashions in the twentieth- and twenty-first-century school system about which methods of teaching reading work best. As autobiographers remember, they advanced to books which were read across society: *Pilgrim's Progress*, *Paradise Lost*, *Robinson Crusoe* – as well as sensational literature, flysheets of poetry and ballads and other ephemera, tracts, chapbooks, fairy tales and poetry books. Increasingly, local libraries, established by Sunday schools, cooperative societies, Mechanics' Institutes and other organisations provided materials for education and cultural activity for working people. One in five Sunday schools boasted a library by 1834. Libraries grew steadily in size: one typical library at the Bolton Working Men's Sunday and Evening School wrote to the *Chartist Circular* in the 1840s to celebrate their initial acquisition of '119 volumes'. As they spread after the establishing of the Rochdale Pioneers in 1844, cooperative societies were encouraged to spend up to 2.5 per cent of profits on education, and between 1870–90 there were more cooperative libraries than public ones.[16]

Stories, poems, myths and legends were learned through oral traditions as well as popular literature from neighbours, family, friends, itinerant workers and visitors. Thomas Cooper remembered the tales which pedlars and beggars staying at a nearby lodging house told him. It is not surprising that writing by people who had learned in these ways reflected their range of reading. For many people, reading was the direct inspiration to start writing themselves. This includes celebratory uses of what they had learned. New writers did not see clear traces in their writing of the sources which had inspired them as a problem. Their problem was lack of education, which they were doing something about. Their confidence was not undermined by fears of plagiarism or a lack of originality. There is often a sense of surprise at the fact of its being written at all. However, working-class writers and poets are often criticised for the transparency of the sources from which their writing was derived, or for their overuse of cliché, or for repetition of the same word in a paragraph or poem. John Clare is almost alone in escaping his confines as a peasant poet, perhaps because, rather than in spite of, his use of local language, with its distinctive terminology for nature, and the way in which he blended these with inherited traditions of poetic diction. Comparing Clare's 'The Skylark' with Thomas Cooper's early poem 'A morning in Spring' (see the start of it in n. 8) would be one place to begin. Reading and writing poetry were popular in working-class life. Poetry-writing was prolific and poems were sold on street corners across the country and read aloud in public and private.

One commentator suggests that Clare's poetry was 'helped' by his reading of eighteenth-century verse. At the same time, his wrting is seen to be flawed by repetition. 'Derivative', 'imitative' and 'overambitious' are some of the critical adjectives often attached to working-class cultural production.[17] Such views of writers and autodidacts have constructed writers as people who distanced themselves from their communities and culture and at the same time lumped them together as a phenomenon, as writers who find an individual voice only with great difficulty. The suggestion is that middle-class authors and working-class writers do not feel the same tension between their social, linguistic and literary inheritance and their individuality – in Williams's words 'the specificity of all individuals and the formative relevance of all real relations'. Working-class writing has been overwhelmingly discussed in terms of an autodidact's circumstances at the expense of 'individual autonomy' and generally at the expense of critical analysis of the writing, the text, itself.[18] Perhaps a retrieval exercise such as that done for autobiography could be attempted. Much more work is needed on surviving working-class poetry – for its qualities as poetry and as literature, exploring rather than dismissing difference.[19]

II Learning associations in the community

Association and communal activity were essential to the way learning was anchored and developed as a shared activity which supported members' own purposes. This section discusses Charles Shaw's autobiography at some length and draws on several others, to explore some of the characteristic ways informal learning and literacy practices in communities worked and how it was remembered in autobiography. Shaw is not exceptional among working-class learners. Many autobiographers tell a story which bears out Shaw's approaches to learning.

Charles Shaw, born in 1832, grew up in Tunstall, Staffordshire, a pottery town with a population which he estimates at between 7,000 and 8,000 during his youth. His childhood was marred by a terrible event. In 1842, the family were sent to the workhouse as paupers and ' "The golden gates of childhood" were thus rudely and suddenly closed'.[20] In other ways, his experience is not, on the surface, untypical of working-class life in a small industrial town. His schooling began at the age of three or four at 'Old Betty W's' day school. He left aged seven, when he had 'finished his education'. Children were still often seen as small adults. A Huntingdon man in the 1870s reported that 'Arter I were about nine year old, I got real ashamed o' going to school when other folks went to work … I used to get into the dykes and slink along out o' sight in case nobody should see me and laugh at me'.[21] At Betty's, Shaw learned to read, to spell – which meant sounding out, dividing words orally into syllables – and to

122

knit stockings. Knitting was an important skill often taught to both boys and girls as part of a family economy. Writing, as in many private neighbourhood working-class schools, was not included in the curriculum. In many private schools, writing and arithmetic were taught later if at all. Attendance at such schools was often brief, and many people left school able to read but not write. Betty's school was fairly typical of the private working-class schools of the period, although many autobiographical accounts of similar schools are less glowing, and Shaw may have retrospectively romanticised it. In his estimation, Betty laid the essential foundation for the next possible stages of learning:

> *She and her class did two things – they made night schools possible for those who wanted to go further, say to learn writing and arithmetic; and they made it possible for Sunday School teachers to have less elementary drudgery.*

Like many other 'little workers', Shaw's 'childhood' was soon over. Once working life began, weekday schooling was out of reach. For many children, the next stages of learning were acquired through an increasingly secularised Sunday school curriculum. Before leaving Betty's, Shaw had already progressed, aged six, to an advanced Bible-reading class at Sunday school and he could 'never remember any difficulty in reading or spelling except, of course, very exceptional and long words in the Bible'. The credit for his success is given to Betty's 'method of teaching'. The two institutions, day and Sunday school, are honoured as the source of a flow of possibilities: 'The former soon ceased to flow directly, but never indirectly, while the latter, Nile-like, has spread its fruitful waters over all my life.' Shaw describes a structured and hierarchical learning process which offered a foundation on which to build. Other options followed. In a chapter called 'The Pursuit of Knowledge Under Difficulties' he describes 'the methods of my own educational development'. This meant learning with other providers, sponsors and companions. His first significant helper, William Leigh, was a fellow potter from a more affluent family.

> *He found out, from seeing me reading at nights when he came to our house, that I was fond of reading, and up to the time of going to the workhouse he regularly supplied me with books, and these were as precious as the bread he gave us. It was he who first opened to me the great*

world of literature and from that day I have known 'the world of books is still the world'.

Shaw singles out three people at Sunday school who stretched his education beyond the bare bones of its official curriculum. The school's superintendent Daniel Spilsbury heard him read and 'smiled pleasantly upon me, and stroking my hair … said the Bible I had read from … I could take home as a present'. Ralph Lawton was a teacher whose 'tender interest', as well as his quality of 'unspeakable serenity', is still so vivid to Shaw that 'sixty years after, the vision of his ecstasy would be like a "bright cloud" hanging over an old scholar's life, at once an inspiration and a joy'. Lawton attempted to reintegrate the Shaw brothers into the class after they returned from the workhouse 'branded' because they were wearing a parish 'brat' or apron, and were rejected by their school fellows. Taunted and ostracised, the brothers leave. For several weeks, Shaw hides at home but his 'passion for the Sunday School' leads him to try another school. As the brothers lean against the wall of the chapel outside, a young man with a 'gentle face' invites them to join the school. His name is George Kirkham, and 'in his hands I was a plant carefully tended, nurtured and watered. He lent me books. He gave me counsel. He breathed his prayers for me.' Kirkham's support for the next six years is lovingly remembered. His intervention is a transformative moment, which turns 'shame and fear' to hope, darkness to light. Education was Shaw's religion, and his 'saintly' guide worked the miracle of 'giving him a dawning interest in a larger world … like the blind man in the Gospel, I had begun to "see men as trees walking" '. When Kirkham suddenly dies, 'I felt a loneliness which chilled me.' He is left bewildered by the loss of guidance to deal with the 'many questions whose dimness spurred my interest in them'. Shaw survives this 'perilous interval' during which he fears he will lose everything he has learned. He stays at the Sunday school and develops friendships with young men 'a little older than myself'. Together they form a learning group, the basis of his next phase of learning.[22]

William Leigh, Daniel Spilsbury, Ralph Lawton, and George Kirkham are significant sponsors for Charles Shaw, inspirational and intimate friends. Shaw's narrative fuses good teaching and practical support with sainthood, love and salvation in ways that would be treated with suspicion today. Shaw describes dimensions to growing up and learning in communities, which supplement or supplant family and school, and take on significance in a developing sense of self in the

124

learning process. Alternative or complementary 'parenting' through the intervention of a neighbour or outsider who becomes a sponsor, offers another way of looking at community in this period. Familiar figures from local networks close to home, church or workplace also crop up and offer help; middle-class benefactors as well as fellow workers or neighbours. Total strangers, encountered at moments of crisis or change, who become guiding friends frequently walk into narratives of learning. For people who then go on to publish autobiographies, the repeated naming of such significant figures appears to have a ritual meaning in the development of a self-identity as someone whose learning has been achieved through relationships with others.[23]

In a world where birth parents or older siblings were hard-pressed to provide the essentials of life, and could not offer longed-for emotional or educational support, it was often other adults, met sometimes apparently by chance at moments of crisis, who fulfilled missing elements of parenting. For Catherine Drew, going to school to learn to write at the expense of a gentleman sponsor was far superior to lessons from her father, who took over her learning after her parents' illness forced her to leave school. Strangers or mentors within the community provided less complicated encouragement than parents. They could be – and often were – serially replaced by another sponsor, allowing each individual to retain their romantic aura, unaffected by the compromises of family relationships and daily life. The sponsor as 'parent' figure exists solely in relation to the developing subjectivity of the writer's remembered young self, and there is seldom a wider characterisation. In some accounts, significant figures are constructions of undiluted goodness, intellectual strength, with heroic, almost magical qualities. In other versions, the relationship with them is about human solidarity, often associated with belonging to working-class organisations. And in a few accounts, strangers combine power and influence with menace, to be explored in the final chapters of this book. Most often, the solidarity experienced is akin to affectionate mentorship, and a feeling of mutual support and goodwill between members of small groups who shared scarce resources, and provided safe environments in which to explore knowledge away from the imagined contempt of the well educated.

In his autobiography, John Bedford Leno, the poet and activist born in 1826 in Uxbridge, pays tribute to significant people and events in his 'ambition to become a scholar and master of my trade'. Aged 14, Leno was apprenticed in a printing office where at first his literacy skills were 'miserably deficient for such an occupation and my first proof occasioned roars of laughter'. His loyalty to the early education his mother had provided in the dame school she organised, inhibits and confuses him. Faced with ridicule, he makes little progress. But the impasse is broken when 'the cleverest man in the office' offers to teach him.

> *Mr. Kingsbury 'conceived a great liking for me, and, at his invitation, I stayed at the office beyond the usual hours . My half-hour's schooling over, I used to accompany him to the 'Dolphin' on the Moor where it was his custom to give me one half-pint of ale. If, interested by the conversation, I by chance dawdled over the drinking of the said half-pint I was quietly reminded that my time had expired.*

Like Shaw's Kirkham, Kingsbury's adoption of Leno is mythologised through the presentation of his interventions as an inexplicable 'mystery': 'I know not how it occurred.' Despite Leno's subsequent meetings with prominent figures such as Kingsley or Morris, Kingsbury remains without equal 'for general intelligence and all round ability'.

Leno describes how his education and political activism flourish from this moment onwards. He forms a Chartist branch and a mutual improvement society; he organises song evenings and begins a career writing and publishing songs, poems and pamphlets. He co-edits and co-publishes newspapers such as *Spirit of Freedom* and *Working Man's Vindicator*, contributing to many more, including the *Christian Socialist*. His first publication, an impromptu song, is also mediated by a clearly-recalled helper who 'it so happened' was present to hear his performance at a 'Falcon Harmonic' meeting. The old gentleman (a retired Scottish physician who had 'known Burns personally') invited Leno to write his words down and 'had them printed, and for days afterwards, he might have been seen in the loitering shops of the town ... pointing them out as something truly wonderful'.[24]

The positive mood which suffuses writings about intellectual parents, sponsors or learning associations is sometimes in stark contrast to subdued descriptions of family. The latter are noticeable for their brevity, or phrases of dutiful, bland praise, though in some writing, there is also abiding resentment at family members' outright hostility to learning. Hannah Mitchell and John Clare are among many examples of writers whose families opposed their learning. Clare pretended to his parents that the poems he read to them in the hope of helpful criticism were not his

126

own, but simply texts he used to practise copying skills. This met with approval because copying might well lead to better paid work. As he said of his mother, 'She'd be bound, I should one day be able to reward them with my pen, for the trouble they had taken in giving me schooling.'[25] Hannah Mitchell's mother fiercely resisted her learning. Indeed women's autobiographies more often openly explore family conflicts over education, writing in particular, than men's.

At a practical level, significant figures outside the family are remembered as knowledgeable and inspiring teachers, offering systematic guidance and introducng method to haphazard learning activities. Some offered a prescribed course of reading though with no imposed hierarchy linked to technical difficulty. Discussions of texts and writing exercises feature prominently, as do questioning and conversation about topics, and about knowledge itself. George Kirkham, for example, offered Shaw a course of reading through the shelves of the Sunday school library, starting with *Robinson Crusoe* and *Paradise Lost*, and including now obscure works such as Charles Rollins's *Ancient History*, George Gilfillan's *Bards of the Bible*, Gottlieb Klopstock's *Messiah* and Thomas Dick's *Christian Philosopher*.

> *Scientific matters were put before me with such new vividness and interest. I felt far more interest in this than in Rollin's History. Nature, from sods to stars, became to me a temple. The religious tone of the book entranced, and the sublimities of the heavens which it unfolded awoke in me imaginings which thrilled my soul.*

Looking back, he saw this as a 'strange assortment'. Kirkham had no resources beyond the school library, so 'they just happened to fall into my hands'. Three things suggest this was more than desultory reading. He repeatedly drew comparisons between the relative merits of particular volumes. Secondly, he deliberately chose more difficult texts because the 'more elementary and educative books … could not have moved passion in me which these other books did', and thirdly, his reading led to learning to write:

> *I began to feel a desire to express myself about the things I read, and certain forms of expression lingered in my ear as well as entranced my eye. This I imagine, was the first movement of a literary instinct.*

127

He began to write unaided, using the cheapest materials he could find, starting with the least baffling of his strange new tools.

> *I remember my first efforts at composition were made on a slate. I could better manage a slate pencil than a pen. I tried a pen and copy-book now and then, but the exercise proved a weariness to the hand and an irritation to the mind.*

Frustrated by learning without guidance, Shaw finds 'a well-read man who thought deeply on many subjects'. For two years his teacher was this 'old friend', a boot- and shoe-maker. Officially, the lessons were writing and arithmetic, but as the exercises progressed 'slowly and irksomely', the conversation often became so absorbing that 'both teacher and pupil forgot the more mechanical work on which I should have been engaged'. Shaw stopped his writing lessons able 'only to scrawl a little' and 'inside the range of vulgar fractions', but with the benefit of wide-ranging discussion sessions.[26]

Political activity that he witnessed as a young man also motivated Shaw to learn to write. A chapter of the book is about Joseph Capper of Tunstall, leader of the 1842 riot in the town, with an analysis of the political consciousness of the potters. Seeing the riot motivated him to improve his skills so he could write about it; and the enduring technical shortcomings of his writing did not stop him eventually becoming a journalist and autobiographer. For other writers, motivation to learn came from writing itself. Adam Rushton remembers how ideas would come to him by copying out hymns and poems that 'greatly excited' him and prompted him to read.[27] The pace and sequences of learning were a matter of personal choice.

Shaw and his companions begin a course in 'recitation'. Working together is so enjoyable and provides such 'mental uplift', that they form a Young Men's Mutual Improvement Society. More people join them. The preparation for group meetings is demanding and Shaw settles into his night-time study routine. His nostalgic description of their education programme exposes ambivalent feelings about the gains and losses of universal elementary education: 'these more disciplined days'. 'We never dreamt', he writes, 'of any elementary pursuit of knowledge. We met to discuss and criticize all things in heaven and earth, and sometimes even a far deeper province of the universe'. Meeting on Saturday nights, they listen to one person's essay, discuss it, and decide together on the next subject to ensure variety. They discuss 'as if the fate of a nation depended on that night's debate'.[28] Shaw argues for the relevance and momentum that drove successful learning in groups such as this, and many accounts of mutual improvement societies endorsed his view. Such societies for cooperative learning, from those formally constituted to informal getting together in communities, grew fast in the first half of the century, engaging hundreds of thousands of people – at least. As a guide, 19 per cent of the British population was enrolled in Sunday schools in 1888.[29] Diverse forms of association for learning flourished into the 1850s, waned and grew again in the 1880s. However we view it, societies were countless, numbers were massive and they put today's participation in independent adult learning in the shade. Writing was central to learning in all of them.

For another four years, Shaw also belonged to another society. They shared and commented on each other's writing on the essay/discussion model, later adapted for the WEA's tutorial classes for the 'Higher Education of Working Men' which began in 1907.[30] Thomas Cooper's mutual improvement society set up an Adult School to teach reading and writing 'for the poor and utterly uneducated'. This was typical of the way people who were active in education became involved in other, related initiatives through which 'self-educated' people taught those they saw as less advantaged than themselves. Joseph Lawson describes a group which met in a Yorkshire village at five each morning, making 'great progress' despite lack of books. One member then became a substitute teacher at the Sunday school.[31] Such organisations continued to flourish later in the century too. M.K. Ashby, writing of her parents, tells of how 'the use of the pen came pretty naturally to the children, reporting meetings for the local journals, writing papers on exciting authors for a club of Young Methodists or on the Tysoe church for some magazine'. Their father 'taught them to write, as far as anyone can, laughing at a neat turn, looking dark at a silliness, standing between them and crude criticism. "What peaceful hours reading and writing brought!" ' Even as she celebrated her community's culture, past and present, Ashby was aware with what disdain it could be regarded.[32]

Mutual learning groups also formed in workplaces. The case of a group of young workers in a candle factory in Vauxhall illustrates that some employers could be persuaded of the benefits of literacy, including writing skills:

In the year 1847, some dozen boys set an example by starting a night class on their own initiative, 'hiding ... behind a bench two or three times a week, after they had done their work and had their tea, to practise writing on scraps of paper with worn-out pens begged from the counting house'. Their efforts received judicious encouragement from the managing director, and made the beginnings of a well-planned scheme of social betterment.[33]

J.W. Hudson described the formation of the Leeds Mutual Improvement Society in 1844, which resembles Shaw's description of setting up his group, with 'four young working-men, of very humble circumstances, who resolved to meet regularly'. Then 'other young operatives ... asked leave to join them'. They met in a 'garden house' where 'reading, writing, grammar and arithmetic were taught and learned amidst rakes, and hoes, and broken flower-pots ... Poor young men resorted to the garden-house to learn to read. The Society grew from these beginnings, and within six years had eighty members paying 3d a week, a museum and a library of three hundred titles.'[34] In Pudsey, there was a blacksmith's shop where several met to hear and read the newspaper. Thomas Todd and his friends in Teesdale, without a local night school to go to, persuaded the Duke of Cleveland's agent to let them have a library room for 'long, dark winter-nights' of study. This led to the foundation of the local Mechanics' Institute. Most of the myriad examples of self-directed, community-based mutual learning initiatives are characterised by the belief that learning this way, however briefly, gave people's lives deeper meaning. Todd notices that 'old men' often said that 'lives were changed or moulded after reading one or two books'. He adds that 'the influence of only one book has been tremendous in some men's lives'.[35] The emphasis on 'old men' signals again the sense of what had been lost when such institutions, like Adult Schools, steadily declined after school became universally available.

Mechanics' Institutes, often founded by working-class people, became dominated by their middle-class benefactors and subscribers, who increasingly controlled the curriculum. But they remained locally-managed, generally successful ventures. One grew at Filey in the 1840s when a group of fishermen, some over 60, were helped to learn to write, read handwriting, and read the Bible. Writing for business and essay writing also flourished at some Mechanics' Institutes. Birkbeck and other colleges for working people promoted learning which helped learners to 'satisfy their natural curiosity and … aid their intellectual development', remaining distant from the influence of employers who increasingly shaped a more vocational curriculum and forged the reputation of Mechanics' Institutes as organisations serving the interests of industry and the middle-class.[36]

To return to Charles Shaw, criticism of the negligence of government at national and municipal levels toward working-class education runs through his narrative. He does not consistently romanticise the past, seeing the 1840s and 1850s as primitive times, and he was among those who waved their flags for the Empire. But his view of progress also conveys misgivings and doubts, as he attempts to express his enduring anger that Betty W. was providing school for 'a pittance' when 'our rulers were squandering the resources of the nation in less useful ways'. He rebukes the 'powers' for 'lethargy and paralysis' while he and others in his social position took their own steps to get an education. More than that, he surveys the steps since taken by government to introduce education, and judges it to be inadequate precisely because it is elementary, a lower form of education than his own has been. Yet he is keenly aware that it is his own education which will be found wanting. When he writes of 'these more self-conscious days', when the world would sneer in 'wonder and amusement' at the essays produced in the mutual improvement societies, he is not hailing the new structures unequivocally as progressive. He is struck by losses as much as by gains. His book is in part an evaluation of his own educational experience in a new era that was already dismissive of informal learning, which saw self-education in Logie Barrow's sense as the bad which preceded the good – the great institutional changes from 1870. Shaw's ambivalence is evident as he belittles his own efforts and his 'simplicity and sincerity', but he still remains confident enough to celebrate the 'audacity' of people of his class to attempt to create a knowledge of their own and to defend the levels, methods and rigour of their learning.[37]

Thomas Cooper, whose book is similarly filled with accounts of learning friendships and associations, explores with those around him a wide range of subjects including a serious study of astrology. Benjamin Brierley, a founder-member of a local mutual improvement society, refers to such societies in his autobiography as 'modest' universities, at which 'men who have since made their way in the world "graduated" '.[38] Their spurning of the 'elementary' grows out of an entirely different approach to knowledge, as Shaw describes:

We could expatiate about the universe when an examination in the geography of England would have confounded us. We could discuss astronomy (imaginatively) when a sum in decimals would have us plucked from our soaring heights into an abyss of perplexity. We could discuss the policies of governments and nations, and the creeds and constitutions of churches, while we would have been puzzled to give a bare outline of our country's history.

The Board Schools' curriculum, which replaced this and other 'higher' forms of learning, can, on the other hand, certainly be shown to be 'lower': elementary by design, and with clearly-defined and controlled upper limits. But it is the schooling of Shaw and his contemporaries which is subject to condescension. The mood of Shaw's book is of someone speaking to a modern audience incapable of understanding or valuing the methods of mutual learning. The new system, 'through examinations and even by "cramming", has scared away all such lofty flights', he argues. He knows that the efforts of the mutual improvement society to read, think and write together, working towards an understanding of wide ranging subjects would only be seen as 'bombastic pretence'. He is thankful that the 'essays' were not published, 'saving him and his friends from the humiliation of a great misunderstanding'. Shaw was decidedly against a 'hardening and narrowing respectability', which he saw as one explanation for the defeat of the democratic movements of the 1840s.[39] The new education system as he saw it suffered from some of these defects. It was inadequate reparation for past neglect, and had led to the loss of mutual associations for self-directed learning. It was indeed a real loss, and even today the possible outcomes from education are perceived by many as narrower than those which nineteenth-century independent learners hoped to achieve for themselves. In Logie Barrow's words:

What is lacking is a confidence that knowledge, once gained, may enable you to do, discover or help decide something important. However seldom nineteenth century plebeian autodidacts were potentially in such a position ... we shall hardly find them believing invincibly in their own stupidity, or rather ... in their own pointlessness or lack of qualification. Not them: on this score, they – or at any rate those who fill our sources – were decidedly optimistic.[40]

132

In this spirit, George Bourne (1863–1927) criticised the new education from the perspective of a working-class rural community in Surrey. In *Change in the Village* (1912) he wrote:

> *It was sterile of results. It opened to him no view, no vista; set up in his brain no stir or activity such as could continue after he had left school; and this for the reason that those simple items of knowledge which it conveyed to him were too scrappy and too few to begin running together into any understanding of the larger aspects of life ... no English history, no fairy-tales or romance, no inkling of the infinities of time and space, or of the riches of human thought; but merely a few 'pieces' of poetry, and a few haphazard and detached observations (called 'Nature Study' nowadays) about familiar things – 'the cat', 'the cow', 'the parsnip' ... And what could a child get from it to kindle his enthusiasm for that civilized learning in which, none the less, it all may have its place?*

Bourne has a similarly dismissive view of the technical 'night schools' which were aimed mainly at young adults as unlikely to set up any 'constructive idea-activity'.[41] Looking back, some working-class writers felt that the new system was more of a jumble of bits and pieces than the old. Writing skills, which people had learned in order to compose what they wanted to say, was regimented by late nineteenth-century education into a hierarchy of technical skills, with the carrot of the composition lesson remembered even today by many working-class writers as the only space in elementary state education for creative, imaginative work, held out for years as the eventual reward for years of 'parsnips'. Alfred Williams had similar views. His proposed remedy was 'to cultivate strong feelings, sensibilities, and sympathies, real true, living matter, not skeleton forms of elaborate artificiality'. For him, brains without heart was the course on which the education system was set.[42]

In the eyes of most who learned in local associations, state education was welcome but for some, it was a decidedly mixed blessing. As one wrote, 'the people are educated at great cost – but they are neither better nor wiser than the people who were left to educate themselves'.[43] Joseph Lawson looked back in bewilderment from the 1880s, at the loss of the demand and fierce desire for education which had been the lifeblood of learning associations: 'there is something wrong with education when the years of school education are increased and there is less desire for knowledge'.[44]

III

The stories of a diverse but shared experience in the formation of community-based literacies brush against the grain of generalisations that are often used to categorise and label working-class cultural and educational activities. The split between individual and collective modes of learning has been perpetuated from widely differing perspectives. Analyses on the cultural and political left have promoted the significance of organised collective action for education, tending to privilege writing by men, particularly members of social movements. Those seen more as individual autodidacts than as social actors who wrote have often been situated on the sidelines, even if they were involved in political action at some point in their lives. Some have been seen more as captives of an ideology of laudable self-improvement, in an individualistic interpretation of Samuel Smiles's 'self-help', seeking respectability and upward mobility through education. The early nineteenth-century, mainly Tory, view, which demonised collective activism, was sceptical of the value of educating the lower orders, and scorned 'self-education', softened over time to contribute to a romanticisation of the individual learner-writer as a valiant figure, while patronising and weakening 'him' as one who can never quite belong anywhere. The autodidact is both admired and contained in a comfortable fantasy about working-class life. What left and right versions underplay is the experience and impact of associationism.[45] Even if writing a life story was a rarity, which is doubtful given what we know about the scale of present-day writing practices by 'ordinary people', learner-writers in a broader sense were not. Writing was needed and practised increasingly over the nineteenth century. What the diversity of practices held in common was that they were organic to local communities and affiliatons, such as faith or politics. They involved solidarity and support. They were informal associations and therefore involved relationships in which a range of emotions and attitudes informed activity. Who was curious about the value and workings of such complex forms of social engagement outside the learning communities themselves? Perhaps it is little wonder they are so poorly understood.

Although self-education is a social process, there is a sense in which the individual self is important. The articulation and extension of the idea of oneself were doubtless facilitated by writing. The writers in this chapter knew that the self who had no signature and lived without reading and writing skills was voiceless in a world increasingly organised through the uses of literacy. Selfhood became a different state of being for those who could read, discuss and write about issues which affected their lives. The desire for education was fostered by the inescapable presence and power of the literacies around them and by a consciousness of the consequences of neglecting their own capabilities. Education was compelling enough to activate people to seek allies, find and follow mentors, welcome chance encounters, persuade parents, enlist substitute parents, work hard and use their imagination and all the resources they could find. Learners experienced the difficulty, intensity and empowerment of moving through to a different self-consciousness and a greater consciousness of the world through the demanding social processes of critical reading and writing. They used writing, often much later, to locate their own experience and self identity within it. No surprise that they greeted with ambivalence the advent of a huge machine to educate everyone in exactly the same way to the same standard. Pride in their own achievements mingled grittily with envy at the time and space which was now available for children and young people to learn. These feelings were underpinned by a very clear vision of the quality of what had been lost and the relative intellectual poverty of state schooling.

Notes

1 Pritchett, 1978b, describes Burton thus: 'this rambling and eccentric compendium of the illnesses of the brain and heart was exactly suited to his curious mind. He revelled in it. "Look it up in Burton, lad", he'd say when I was older. "What's old Burton say?" ', p. 47.
2 Rose, 2002, pp. 76–9, 83.
3 R. Williams, 1975, pp. 208–9.
4 Klingopoulos, 1982, p.73.
5 Quoted in Hoggart, 1958, p. 302.
6 Quoted in Horn, 1978, p. 128. Horn, 1980, quotes one inspector in 1845 complaining that he often encountered the belief that education 'unfits for manual labour', pp. 135–6. See also Haggard, 1906, Vol. 2, pp. 207–8.
7 Eliot, *Adam Bede*, [1858] 1960, p. 228. See also pp. 229–30 on the writing lesson at night school.
8 Cooper, [1872] 1971, p. 43. The poem is entitled 'A Morning in Spring' and begins: 'See, with splendour Phoebus rise, / And with beauty tinge the skies. / See, the clouds of darkness fly / Far beyond the western sky; / While the lark on soaring wings / And the air with music rings'.
9 See, e.g., Vincent, 1982, Part 3; Rose, *op. cit.*, chapters 1 and 2. For critiques of 'simplicity', see Steedman, 1984, p. 7; Yeo, 1986; and the 'Local History' chapters of G. White, K. Worpole and S. Yeo in Samuel, 1981, pp. 21–42.
10 Shaw, [1903] 1977, pp. 224–5.
11 Barrow, 1986, p. 151. See chapter 6 for his concept of 'Democratic Epistemology', pp. 151–3.
12 Colls, 1976, pp. 79–85.
13 See, e.g., Rushton, 1909, p. 23; Clare, 1983, p. 4.
14 See, e.g., Altick, 1957; R.K. Webb, 1955; R. Williams, [1961] 1965; James, 1976.
15 See, e.g., Lawson, 1887, p. 45.
16 *Chartist Circular*, 1840–1, Vol. 2, p. 229. One of the early community libraries was the Educational Department of the Rochdale Equitable Pioneers' Society (REPS) founded in 1849.

Members had already been 'assembling themselves together after the day was done ... for the purpose of hearing the news of the week'. Magazines, then books, were donated; in 1856 there were 1,000 'carefully selected books', and by 1870, 9,000. Such libraries had short evening and Saturday opening hours. Classes were in art, science and technical subjects as well as reading, writing and grammar. See *Minute Books of the REPS Educational Department 1866–71*; Greenwood, 1877. The Oldham Lyceum was another organisation typically offering library facilities alongside a large programme of reading, writing and grammar. In 1856, 85 men and 24 women attended separate literacy classes which included examinations in writing from dictation; classes in 'essay and discussion' attracted 16 students (*16th Annual Report of the Oldham Lyceum*, 1856, p. 4). See also Rose, *op. cit.*, pp. 62, 79, on Sunday school libraries, cooperative libraries and education.

17 E. Robinson's introduction, in Clare, 1983, pp. xiii–xiv; Klingopoulos, *op. cit.*, p. 73. See also Storey, 1982; Maidment, 1987, esp. pp. 97–100; for a critique of the language and approaches which Maidment's anthology, for example, uses, see R. & M. Williams, 1986, pp. 4–10.

18 R. Williams, 1977, pp. 194, 198; Swindells 1985, pp. 163–83.

19 See Maidment, 1987, which includes discussion of the eighteenth-century forms which influenced working-class poets. On Clare, see Bate, 2003a, 2003b.

20 Shaw, *op. cit.*, p. 137.

21 Horn, 1981, pp. 528–9.

22 Shaw, *op. cit.*, pp. 9, 93, 136, 140, 17.

23 See Brandt, 2001, pp. 18–19.

24 Leno, 1892, pp. 17, 20. See Pritchett, *op. cit.*, for another striking account of an inspirational figure, in his first office job, pp. 168–70.

25 Clare, *op. cit.*, p. 4.

26 Shaw, *op. cit.*, pp. 219–22.

27 Rushton, *op. cit.*, pp. 24–5.

28 Shaw, *op. cit.*, p. 222.

29 Rose, *op. cit.*, p. 62.

30 Study groups and informal meetings to help with the demands of essay-writing in WEA tutorial classes are well documented in *The Highway*, the WEA journal from 1907. See also Mansbridge, 1913.

31 Cooper, *op. cit.*, p. 46; Lawson, *op. cit.*, p. 45.

32 Ashby, 1961, p. 245. Her grandfather, she writes, learned 'a little grammar' at night school, but learned speeches from Shakespeare from his brother, 'in bed at night', p. 21.

33 From the *Quarterly Review*, December 1852, 183, art. 1, quoted in Dobbs, 1919, p. 156.

34 Hudson, 1851, pp. 94–5. See also Dobbs, *op. cit.*, p. 172.

35 Lawson, *op. cit.*, p. 41; Todd, 1935, pp. 43–4. See Tylecote, 1957, pp. 102–3.

36 Tylecote, *op. cit.*, pp. 5–6.

37 Shaw, *op. cit.*, p. 5.

38 Brierley, 1886, p. 50.

39 Shaw, *op. cit.*, pp. 219, 222–3.

40 Barrow, *op. cit.*, p. 152.

41 Bourne, [1912] 1984, p. 131.

42 A. Williams, 1912, pp. 133–4. On the theme of positive reappraisal of the lost systems of education, see also Grant, 1931, where she reflects on the motivation 'our ancestors possessed', and fondly recalls her aunts' stories of the village dame school.

43 Adams, 1903, Vol. 1, p. 109.

44 Lawson, *op. cit.*, p. 77.

45 Yeo, 1987, pp. 103–11.

CHAPTER 4

Letters and letter-writing: meanings deeper than the mere exchange of information?

I

Separation from family and friends was part of the pattern of life in working-class communities, urban and rural. Writers bear witness to the coming and going of family members, domestic workers, labourers, journeymen, pedlars, domestic workers, soldiers, circus people or itinerant visitors. They write of trudging long distances on foot to find or keep work. They tell stories of migration and emigration to escape poverty and seek fortunes; and stories of incarceration in prisons and workhouses. Travelling to meetings or to disseminate documents was built into the activities of associational life and social movements. Decades of upheaval catalysed by the enclosure of land, agricultural reform and the Industrial Revolution made forced and voluntary migration commonplace. In this situation, people wrote letters for many reasons. Prolonged separation from others was a strong enough motive for many people to learn to write. Between family members, lovers, friends and political allies, letters were the only way of keeping relationships alive. Letters also had a role in finding work, applying for poor relief, dealing with disputes, reconciliation, religious belief and public protest. In 1840, chaotic, corrupt and expensive postal services were reformed, revealing the extent of writing practices and opening up possibilities for far greater access to letter-writing. This chapter looks at practices and meanings of letter-writing in people's lives in their family, social and political contexts.

II Postal reform and working-class letter-writing

The introduction of the Penny Post in 1840 was an historic event in letter-writing practices. It meant that for the first time, postage was paid

The General Post Office – One Minute to Six by George Elgar Hicks
Courtesy of the Museum of London

by the sender, not the receiver. It regularised postal services, charges and post offices. Postal systems had been riddled with fraud, corruption, censorship, espionage and controlling interests in high places, not least peers and MPs who controlled much of the postal service. Rowland Hill, an educational reformer whose father's friends included Thomas Paine and Joseph Priestley, started his campaign for a more equitable and open postal system in 1835, presenting proposals in 1837. In the House of Lords, the Postmaster General was vehemently opposed: 'of all the wild and visionary schemes which he had ever heard of, it was the most extraordinary'. Maberly, Joint-Secretary to the General Post Office, agreed.[1] But industrialists, traders and parliamentarians were among the majority in favour. Old prejudices against working-class writing were weakening. There were fears and hopes about making the post more accessible to working-class people, for many of whom the costs of postage had made letter-writing almost impossible. The Select Committee on

Postage which met in 1837–8 and 1838–9 heard from mainly middle-class witnesses, some welcoming change, others stating that working-class people had little occasion to write; yet others feared the social consequences of encouraging writing practices. But many accepted the growing use of writing. As one witness to the Select Committee typically commented, 'common farmers and humble shopkeepers continually have letters to write'.[2]

For many people, writing letters was often the only form of writing they undertook, so that when they were prevented from writing by the high cost of postage, the possibility of keeping up or developing their literacy skills suffered. The liberal MP Henry Fawcett was quoted as regarding 'high postage as a tax on education, which tax he considered to be the worst of all taxes'.[3] One witness, talking chiefly of servant girls, described 'many persons who, when I first knew them, wrote an excellent hand, [but] on account of their scarcely ever practising, now write very badly' and one acquaintance who 'is so much out of the habit of writing, that he would as soon do a day's work as write a letter'.[4] A Liverpool educationist commented that the ability to write to friends would 'stimulate parents … in sending children to school to acquire a knowledge of writing', but that the cost of sending letters ruled out the likelihood of such an attitude change.[5]

The debates in Parliament and the Select Committee reveal a cluster of economic, social and moral concerns. One of the main aims was to quantify letter-writing practices to help them decide on the economic wisdom of a flat-rate pre-paid charge. The Select Committee members in favour of change hoped the Penny Post would increase the amount of letter-writing across the country sufficiently to make it a sound economic proposition. The questioning of the Select Committee's witnesses about working-class writing practices centred on whether the drastic reduction in postal duties which was proposed would be financially neutralised by an increase in writing, and whether that in itself was morally and politically desirable. One way to achieve their aims was to increase letter-writing among working-class people, because it was the largest untapped market. They were aware that those people with access to cheap postage before the Postal Reform Act, such as soldiers, were reported to have 'an extraordinary desire of letter-writing'. It was reported that they learned literacy 'expressly for this purpose' and wrote letters continually once they had the skills, which they also used to seek promotion. Witnesses estimated that about a quarter wrote their own letters, others using a scribe, but that two-thirds of all soldiers could sign their names. One officer reported that letter-writing was 'continually the subject of my attention'. Soldiers sent seven and a half letters yearly, and he concluded that if the population generally had the privileges of soldiers, the benefits of the revenue would be great.[6] Official statistics indicate a huge growth in Post Office deliveries of mail after 1840. In 1839, 65 million letters were delivered in England and Wales, 8 million in Scotland and 9 million in Ireland. By 1850 the numbers had risen to 276 million (England), 35 million (Scotland) and 35 million (Ireland), and by 1872, to 737 million (England), 82 million (Scotland) and 66 million in Ireland.[7] However, evidence of widespread evasion of postal deliveries before 1840 suggests the rise may not have been as spectacular as the figures suggest. Middle-class letter-writers and business carriers may have gained at least as much as working-class people from the introduction of regulated cheap postage. The rise of bureaucracies in government and business increased dramatically in the middle years of the century, reflected in the technology of communications. The railways made the growth and efficiency in postal services possible, and the advent of the telegraph, also linked to the railway system, changed business and social practices. Between 1857 and 1867 telegraph messages grew from 881,000 to 3.35 million and the cost dropped by 50 per cent. And there was a steep rise in secure places to post letters: from 4,028 collection points in 1840 to 26,753 pillar boxes in the 1880s.[8]

In fact, the true extent of letter-writing before the Penny Post is unclear. It was common to use personal carriers and informal, clandestine delivery routes – sometimes in relay – to avoid charges. But such ways and means were complicated and unreliable. Letters were paid for by the recipient, and writers had cause to worry about whether their letter or package would make it through to its destination. One witness to the Select Committee on Postage remarked that when people began their letters, as they often did, with the phrase 'having obtained an opportunity', they meant that a way of avoiding the cost had been found. But many were excluded, for lack of literacy or access to carriers.[9]

The practices working people used to subvert the old systems were varied and inventive, but speak of a determination to stay in touch despite all obstacles. One cheap way of sending letters was to send a blank piece of paper. Samuel Taylor Coleridge witnessed a postman delivering a letter to a woman at her cottage door in the Lake District, and overheard her refusing to pay the postage, which was one shilling. Coleridge paid (reluctantly), but when the carrier was out of sight, the woman revealed that his money had been wasted. The sheet of paper was empty. She had an agreement with her son, who 'wrote' to let her know he was well.[10] Various kinds of invisible 'sympathetic' ink were also used, witnesses told the Committee; and notes were written on the sides of newspapers and printed material, which were carried more cheaply. Another practice was to prick letters and words onto paper with a pin.

The prohibitive effect of high postal charges on literacy practices was raised in the public debate on postage before 1840. Cost appeared to have been a more significant deterrent than illiteracy. The average cost of a letter was 6d but it could be more or less, according to the distance carried, and the weight. One Select Committee witness, an educational publisher of elementary books, reported:

> *I have in service several people, male and female; I know one who has seven or eight brothers and sisters scattered all over the kingdom; I put the question to him the other day, How many letters do you receive from your relations? Not above one in six months, and hardly that. I said, if the postage were 1d or 2d, how many would you receive then? He said, we should be happy to receive one a week and to send one a week; some of them do not receive a letter in a twelvemonth.*[11]

So it is difficult to estimate the extent of letter-writing before 1840, let alone to estimate accurately what difference the Act made to working–class people. It was certainly intended to enable many more people to engage in an activity which was known to mean a lot to them. As Vincent suggests, for those who could and those who couldn't, the variety and meaning of writing and sending letters was as important as the sheer numbers. The posting and receiving of letters was an event. Many memories of letter-writing in autobiographies, describing times before and after the Penny Post, and reports of debates on postage in working-class newspapers, for example in the *Northern Star* in 1838–40, show clearly how cheap postage was seen as essential to the pursuit of greater social justice.

The Select Committee recognised the demand for affordable letter-writing and the pain caused by separation without the possibility of keeping in touch. Cases of young people leaving home to go into domestic service were often quoted. One witness argued that 'the greatest misery takes place on account of their not writing to their parents' for reasons such as that given by one girl that 'I did not like to saddle them with the postage and, for my part, I had no money to spare'.[12] That people suffered acutely when communication was impossible was not questioned. But testimony may have been driven as much by the moral imperative to develop middle-class family values among the working class as by real understanding of the unhappiness of separated people cut off from news, or expressions of affection, mired in anxiety at not knowing what was happening to people who mattered to them.

Many middle-class commentators often assumed that reasons for writing were simple, and that the literacy levels required were equally simple. But the state made little provision for writing skills as the education system developed. It was not until 1871 'three decades after its introduction (that) the children of the labouring poor were to learn how to make use of the Penny Post'.[13] Composition was only introduced at the final stage of state-supported schools, Standard VI, expressly to facilitate communication by letter. The Newcastle Report of 1861 had recommended that boys should be able to achieve sufficient basic skills so that 'if gone to live at a distance from home, he shall write his mother a letter that shall be both legible and intelligible' and 'he shall be able to spell correctly the words that he will ordinarily have to use'.[14] If people had always found ways and means of writing letters without the sanction of the state, such practices were now officially sanctioned – within strict limits.

III   Public letter-writing: social protest, scenes of crime and conversion

Letters, often anonymous, were part of the culture of political and religious movements. Machine breakers in the 1810s and rick burners in the 1820s–1840s commonly sent letters as threats, pinned letters of protest to trees, left behind letters as marks of their work or 'gazetted' their grievances in local newspapers. One letter sent to a senior civil servant in 1812 tells him 'Every frame Breaking act you Make an amendment to only serves to shorten your Days … It is know [*sic*] your turn to fail. Yr Hbl sert &c.'[15] At issue was the right to earn a livelihood and defend the customs and practices of work against the imperatives of the new factory system. Letters have the feel of talismans, elements of a ritualised form of action that dramatised protest. They were often signed by leaders, mythical or real: 'Ned Lud' or 'Captain Swing'. Letters were the work of individuals in movements rather than collectively planned actions. As such they may be read as relating to individuals' desires to solemnify an act. Writing stamped authority and purpose on even the most desperate action. There were at least two kinds of threatening letters in Luddism: the highly crafted letter, laced with Latin phrases which E.P. Thompson attributes to the informally educated artisan; and the work of colliers or village stockingers, which 'somehow carries a greater conviction'. Thompson argues that their authenticity is clear from the tangible sense of the difficulties which attended such writing, with its wild spelling and erratic punctuation.[16] A reader could sense the formation of the letters on the page and feel the effort involved in its production. Errors provided an insight into the decisions taken at each stroke of the pen and testified to a strength of feeling about writing and sending a message which defied all technical writing difficulties. In this way, the writing process was as much part of the message as its content. That many of these letters were barely achieved as pieces of writing adds to their solemnity, menace and power. The scenes of sabotage were political events in which people left their mark by writing. Increased writing skills in many ways shaped protest in the nineteenth century, enabling more effective organisation, communication and coordinated action.[17] Autobiographers describe letters as pivotal to running organisations. Joseph Arch claimed that in the formation of the Agricultural Labourers' Union in the 1870s 'Letters were now coming in by the gross from all parts of the country asking for help and advice'. Success led to 'further organization' and secretaries were hired to deal with correspondence.[18]

It was also common practice to leave a note at the scene of a crime, almost politicising the act. One letter from a thief to his victim found its way to the Dead Letter Office:

> SIR – Tramping thro' London last nite I whish to tank you for your coat, which will keep me warm on my rode to York, a warm coat is more serviceabel to me, so I enclose your check, as it may be a heavy loss to you – you know times are very hard and overcoats are very scarce, so hopin' the return of the check will cover the loss of your coat,
>
> believe me yours,
>
> A CONSIENTOUS BORROWER
>
> P.S. thanks for my breakfast[19]

Mischievous uses of letters feature in autobiography. David Love, from Edinburgh, who wrote poems and sold 'small books' door to door, described how, when he was in the army, he was victimised by a bullying sergeant. From jail, he wrote long anonymous verse letters as a counter-attack. One targeted the sergeant's wife, resulting in a violent fight. At his court-martial he cleverly used several 'hands' to dupe his interrogators at trial. He got off as no proof was possible that he was the writer.[20] Other tragic, dramatic and sensationalised forms of letter were published in broadsheets, as well as radical newspapers like the *Northern Star*, which printed letters telling the true story or last-minute repentance of condemned criminals. Radical newspapers were also a medium for correspondence between political prisoners, their families and supporters. Through newspapers, views were exchanged on many topics by letter, sometimes for months on end by people who may have had no other access to public debate or discussion.[21] And letters were used as a campaigning tool. W.E. Adams recalled his 'first contribution to the press ... May, 1851. It was an appeal on behalf of the fugitives who had been landed in Liverpool. The printing of that letter produced an exaltation that no similar honour has ever produced since.'[22]

Letters played an important part in narratives of religious conversion, with which literacy, especially letter-writing, is closely linked. The two went hand in hand. In the journals of organisations such as Adult Schools, letters from participants ranked the gaining of literacy skills as almost equal to the experience of conversion to a pious and sober life. Letters to newspapers and journals linked to Adult Schools were widely used in efforts to improve the morals, living conditions and literacy skills of the poor. Sometimes in verse, they pleaded the significance of literacy in religious conversion, but also its worldly benefits. A letter by Charles Poole, a boot-maker of Coventry, who learned to write in an early morning Adult School class, entitled 'A Testimony' to his 'Brother reader[s]' explains how he was reformed through learning to read and write.[23] Richard Weaver's autobiography is the story of his conversion from drinking and brawling to religious faith and sobriety, offering a sermon on the transformative powers of writing in changing the course of a life. His mother's faithful letters to him, read to him by a companion, were the catalyst for change. Her words, 'I will never give thee up', startled his reader, who stopped him burning her letter, and took it away with him. He was 'brought to Christ', learned to write and sent a sequence of letters to his family and the woman he wanted to marry. He writes emotional tales of converting others through letters 'adorned with teardrops as the fields in summer are adorned with daisies'.[24] The chance acquaintance who had read his mother's letter returned it years later, with a message that it had been the turning point in his own conversion. Faith and magic combine with the power of letters in narratives of changing lives.

IV   Letters and work

Much letter-writing was practical. One witness to the Select Committee on Postage emphasised the value that working-class people placed on exchanging information about wages, working conditions or the availability of work in different parts of the country, which was more likely to be trusted in written form.[25] Printed items, which would include information about jobs, were prohibitively expensive to receive, but information could also be transmitted through private letters home from people working away from their communities. Patrick McGill, in *Children of the Dead End*, writes back to Ireland to offer friends work digging potatoes in Scotland: 'If you would care to come I will keep a job open for you ... If you will come with me rite back and say so ... your wages is going to be sixteen shillings a week.'[26] Acting on a letter was a quicker and less haphazard way of finding work than walking miles on the basis of hearsay. The Select Committee's minutes in 1838 record the view that 'this tramping would not take place if the persons could write to other workmen in those places, to inquire if there was a frame to let, or they could get employment'. The plight of the unemployed walking in search of work aroused the sympathy of some witnesses: 'We often see poor men travelling the country for work, and sometimes they come back, and it appears they have been in a wrong direction; if the postage were low, they would write first and know whether they were likely to succeed.' Even more systematic approaches to employment were suggested, such as 'direct communication with one another, in place of sending delegates from town to town' to discover the price of labour.[27] The *Northern Star* and other papers advertised jobs, especially for clerks. The long letter which John Warden, a gardener and leader of the Bolton Chartists, wrote to apply for a clerical job in 1841 indicates a growing formality in job recruitment.[28]

John Castle, born in 1819, of Coggeshall in Essex reported walking miles to find work, then back again to avoid writing a letter to his lover because a letter from London to Coggeshall 'cost tenpence'. Later, when he was unemployed again, his family wrote to say that they had 'engaged a loom's worth of satin for me'. The sense of magic in the fortuitous arrival of this letter is palpable. Castle's family had not known he was out of work, yet they had arranged a loom and hired rooms as if they knew that the letter would bring him home. Much later he recalls the letter's significance: 'This seemed to me strange at the time, but after my eyes became opened I could see a good Providence in it'. Castle's sense of good fortune is linked to the act of writing itself, which makes life events permanent in memory: 'while I am writing it is over 31 years since'.[29]

Writing letters often had deeper meanings beyond the overt purpose of communicating. The self-identity of the developing writer is discernible, the consciousness of him or herself as a person who has become literate, using a skill which was once beyond reach. Letters manifested new capabilities and access to a form of communication which bridged the gap between spoken and formally written language. Alfred Ireson, who left home to find work against his parents' wishes, remembered his first correspondence with home which marked the reality of separation – but made reconciliation possible. Ireson recalls his letter and its impact decades later:

> *I now realised that I had separated myself from kind parents and a good home. I sat down and wept. The thought of the anguish of my dear broken-hearted mother gave me great distress. I sat down and wrote my first letter home, pleased to tell them of my luck in finding work ... A reply came by return. The tools and clothes asked for would be forwarded at once ... I have never forgotten that first letter. It was written by my father. How they regretted my action ... The closing lines of that letter will ever remain with me, and although so many years have passed, and life has had so many changes, I still find tears forcing their way to my eyes. 'God Bless you, my boy. Never forget you have a home to come to.'*[30]

Correspondence in separated families was not always sweetly redemptive. Patrick McGill wrote home to his parents 18 months after leaving home because 'I was longing to hear from somebody who cared for me'. His mother replied in an 'angry letter' asking why he was not sending money home. Their exchange of letters reveals the risks and dangers of situational and emotional misreadings of writing. McGill's guilt and disappointment at his mother's response ('I wished I had never been born') and his desperate attempts to find some money to send home are intensified by his parents' pressure and the myth of emigrants earning fortunes and abandoning those they leave behind in poverty.[31]

V Painstaking postal practices: life, luck and loss

Writing and receiving letters was a social as well as a solitary activity in communities. Unofficial scribes were essential to the flow of letters to and from absent people. In many families, one person was responsible for all correspondence, often the mother. Joseph Arch's mother, who taught her son to write, 'was a splendid hand at writing letters. A great many of the poor people who had children and relatives away from home, but who could not write to them, used to come to my mother and ask her to write their letters for them. She did it with pleasure'. Later, it became common for children with a little more schooling to become the scribes for less literate adults. This pattern became stronger for Board School children at the end of the century. Awkward feelings between generations could make scribing a source of family conflicts. In Margaret Penn's fictionalised autobiography her elementary-school educated heroine Hilda plays the role of family scribe, reading and writing letters and keeping the accounts.[32]

The significance of writing and receiving letters was affected by the conditions under which they were produced. The difficulties of the writing process could contribute to a distressing sense of loss. In the life-story of Will Crooks, the joint letter-writing efforts of his mother and one of his brothers illustrate how an attempt to lessen the loss of one person could enable those left behind to grow closer through the ordeal of producing a piece of writing.

> [They] spent nearly three hours one evening preparing a letter to a far-away sister, the mother painfully composing the sentences, the lad painfully writing them down. The glorious epistle was at last complete, the first great triumph of a combined intellectual effort between mother and son. Proudly they held the letter to the candle-light to dry the ink, when the flame caught it and behold! the work of three laborious hours destroyed in three seconds. It was more than they could bear. Mother and son sat down and cried together.[33]

Letters without full addresses were an everyday occurrence and posed a challenge to the postal service. Enormous numbers of letters failed to arrive and ended up in the Dead Letter Office. In his memoirs, G.R. Smith, an official in the office, recalled stories which provided examples of the quantity of lost mail and illustrated what the arrival and non-arrival of letters meant in a society still learning to practise literacy routinely. Letters were cultural and emotional emblems of a person's ability to take action and connect with others in a world in which literacy was becoming central to communication. Two of Smith's stories stand out. The first describes an elderly widow living in a workhouse. She comes to the Dead Letter Office to seek a letter which had been returned by workhouse overseers because her name was misspelt and they might have spent the 2d charge in vain. After 1834, the Poor Law institutionalised the separation of families and little sentiment would have been wasted on the meaning of letters to workhouse dwellers. The woman tells the official how she has not heard from her son who has been at sea for four years. She has sunk into destitution. She is about to leave when she suddenly asks, 'I suppose you haven't got any letters from over the sea for me … ?' After a search, 'strange to say, I did find one addressed to her name among our Ship Letters, sent to an old address'. The woman is 'overjoyed', but confronted with the postal charge of one shilling, 'all I possess in the world', she persuades the official into a reduction of 6d. He softens and she eventually pays 3d after asking him to read her the letter aloud which runs: 'I am on my voyage home, and when I get to old England again I will find you out and make your old age comfortable'. Whether the woman's enquiry was genuine or a piece of theatre to avoid charges, the story illuminates belief in letters as magical and contingent, but also as solid material objects which will deliver their indelible messages of hope or despair. Like the centrepiece of a popular romance, the mere existence of a lost letter offers suspense and emblemises the role of luck in endings which are unequivocally good or bad: destitution and loneliness or happiness and material prosperity. The letter is a device in a fairy-tale narrative, an enabling myth in itself.

Letters could also be symbols of pathos: grim endings as well as fairy-tale ones. The second story from the Dead Letter Office tells of 'a simple-minded girl' in service in London who had posted a packet bearing this address: 'To my dear father in Yorkshire at the white house with the green palins.' She had enclosed a pair of new steel spectacles and a scrap of paper on which was written: 'to help you see better – with lots of love from your dear girl, Bessie'. She had 'trusted too implicitly' in Yorkshire postmen.[34] The letter could be neither delivered nor returned.

148

The separation of parent and child seems final. It is possible that the girl could have returned to visit her father on foot or begged lifts from carriers, although work, money and lack of time would have made the long journey unlikely. Paradoxically, the new access to cheap postage which helped more separated people to keep in touch made absences more unbridgeable for those who did not understand the rules and could not use writing effectively. The old systems of using personal carriers with verbal instructions, however shaky, did not require the ability to write a precise address. In one sense, this story is about the girl's ignorance of literacy techniques and postal conventions, and the consequences she suffered. A more speculative reading suggests that the power attributed to writing as a magical link between separated people meant that to those just becoming literate, letters seemed to offer a way of transcending the solid facts of absence, loss and bare economic survival. Perhaps the girl's letter can also be read as evidence of the belief in writing as a code, the unknown rules and complexities of which do not need to be fully gripped. If writing seems to offer a set of enchanted 'passwords' which can open doors, then if the words do not work, they become symbols of loss, despair and mortality, just as good news by letter becomes fairy-tale closure.

Trust in the quality of postal services grew. The growth of literacy skills was one factor. The systems grew more familiar and reached into communities in personal ways through the postman and post offices. Increasingly, this form of official literacy was regarded as so reliable that the failure of letters to arrive seemed a shocking event, despite the quantities of lost mail in the Dead Letter Office. People became more accomplished at forms of address, and there is evidence that letters in all manner of guises, some wrongly or scantily addressed, did reach their destinations.

VI Letters to and from communities

In villages and small towns, the post office was sometimes the only social centre and source of advice, oiling the wheels of daily life. Flora Thompson, born in 1876 in a small Oxfordshire village, was fairly typical of post office officials in that she came from a working-class family, the daughter of a stonemason and a nursemaid, and worked her way into administrative work before becoming a writer. Her work as a postmistress included writing letters home for itinerant Irish harvesters who came in to send postal orders to their families. The postmaster, postmistress, or the postman himself, regularly read letters out loud to those who could not read them.

If the receipt of a letter was a memorable event, their non-appearance could be miserable, because the regular visits of carriers had to be endured whether or not they had a letter for someone waiting anxiously for news. The arrival of post was a very public affair, especially if a reader was required.[35] Good news was often happily shared among people in the community but equally letters which brought bad news could be a public ordeal. For people with spouses, lovers, friends or children living away from home, or far from home themselves, receiving a letter or the possibility of writing one back brought hope and pride in the ability to overcome separation or homesickness and at least to know what was happening, for better or worse. Flora Thompson described the daily postal deliveries as a key event in a village community which brought into the open the feelings of people longing for letters:

> *There was one postal delivery a day and towards ten o'clock the heads of the women beating their mats would be turned towards the allotment path to watch for 'Old Postie'. Some days there were two, or even three letters for Lark Rise; quite as often there were none; but there were few women who did not gaze longingly. This longing for letters was called 'yearning' ... 'No, I be-ant expectin' nothing, but I be so "yarnin" ' one woman would say to another.[36]*

Postmen knew what people felt. John Bedford Leno, the Chartist and poet who once worked as a postboy in Uxbridge, recalls that he was welcomed wherever he went: 'It was something to have a letter in those days. It was the talk of the villagers. "Got any there for me, postman?" persons would ask, who never had a letter in their lives and turn away desparingly [*sic*] as I answered, "No".' Leno enjoyed his power over others as he read the contents of letters to recipients. He could 'create smiles and draw forth tears'. He understood the power of the scribe in the community and the satisfaction of the dependence of older people who could not read as well as he, a young man, could. He also relished, 'like a crafty statesman, the possession of secret knowledge' he gained from reading the many letters which were sent without the luxury of sealed envelopes.[37] Before 1840, when a letter arrived safely, it had to be paid for according to its contents and the distance covered.

A postmistress or postmaster was well placed to observe the customs and the changes in writing practices. Not all practices were respectable exercises in family communication. Flora Thompson noticed that the old practice of sending 'lace-bedecked' sentimental Valentines changed in the nineteenth century into an outlet for comic cruelty and obscene abuse,[38] and G.R. Smith reported that 'at least one fourth of our Dead Letter Shoal was coarse and offensive, too much so for description'.[39] Autobiographies record the workings of village postal systems. Flora Thompson's account of the tensions surrounding the postman's arrival is typical of how the post featured as a significant part of daily life. Autobiographers, who had worked for the post office, recalled the variety of roles a postman had. Moses Heap (1824–1913) remembered that there was a letter-box but no post office in Rossendale, so stamps had to be bought from the postman whilst he was delivering letters and collecting outward mail.[40] Thomas Cooper remembered how, during the 1811–14 period of the Napoleonic Wars, 'our little town was kept in perpetual ferment by the news of battles, and the street would be lined with people to see old Matthew Goy, the postman, ride in with his hat covered with ribbons … as he bore the news of some fresh victory'. Cooper's 'illiterate' uncle was also the 'weekly carrier', and as a boy he helped him to decipher the directions on letters and parcels.[41] Clara Grant recalls the postman

bringing letters from Westbury, spending the day at some industry in the village and walking back at night, sounding his horn for us to bring our letters out as he passed. In my mother's day the postman worked at tailoring with her uncle, and had his dinner with my grandmother, who got him to put some writing copies in books for her children … [with] some very good morals in them.[42]

Some autobiographers claim that there was little letter-writing before the reforms of 1840. George Herbert, born in 1814, describes the workings of the postal service in 1830s Banbury. A Miss Norton, who kept the post office and the public house, and the postman, Mr Joseph Barrett, enjoyed 'an easy berth' because few letters were sent due to the cost, a shilling from London to Banbury for a foolscap page. In his view the costs were punitive, even though the rules were flexible: 'If the sheet happened to be a thick one they would charge it as a double letter. But if you took the letter back to show it was a single sheet, they would tear the half sheet off and keep (it) and return the postage.'[43]

According to Herbert, the postal service increased in size and rigour after 1840, with a postmaster who served continuously from 1837–63 with his wife and female assistants. The postmaster still retained another job in the shop which housed the new post office. The Banbury post office boasted all the accoutrements of the modernised service, and was visited by Rowland Hill himself. Marianne Farningham, who was brought up in a Kent village in the 1830s and 1840s helped out her father, who was also a Baptist Sunday school teacher, in his work as village postmaster. Before 1840, letter carriers regularly used 'little girls and old women' to carry out letter collections.[44] In the second half of the century, autobiographers remember taking jobs in the Post Office as one of the increasing opportunities for male and female clerks which were becoming available to school leavers who had achieved all the six Standards. Edward Brown, for example, born in 1880, was apprenticed to a local post office as a 'learner'.[45]

VII   Loss, longing and love

In Joseph Lawson's memories of Yorkshire village life, written as 'Letters', he claimed that no one in Pudsey wrote letters before 1840 owing to high postal charges combined with lack of literacy skills, but that this did not stifle the hopes of receiving one:

> *Many people might be heard wishing for a letter from some absent dear one, while adding that they did not know how they could raise the money to pay for it when it did come. Hence it was common to see the working people going from door to door, trying to borrow the postage on the arrival of a letter. Those who could write a little had often to go about borrowing materials to write a letter with; and one or two in a neighbourhood wrote the letters for the rest.*[46]

Lending and borrowing writing materials seems to have been widespread and suggests a strong desire to write, and some of the 'one or two' who wrote letters for the rest of the community will have charged a small fee or service in kind for their writing, which others were prepared to pay. There are curious contradictions in observations of writing practices. Some of those who commented that little writing happened except through scribes, but noted that more and more letters were received, perhaps reflect the drama of the arrival of letters – which must have been written somewhere, and in all likelihood by people in similar circumstances. Sending letters was a less publicly observable event.

The stories of writing and sending letters mask deeper needs for contact among people who had no choice about leaving home. This was often true of girls and women in domestic service, and of many others living in enforced isolation: prisoners, emigrants, soldiers and sailors. They learned literacy to communicate with those at home, as well as to find self-expression writing prose and verse. Without writing skills, longing for contact with home could reach an impasse, especially if there was no-one to help compose or transcribe thoughts onto paper. For those who could write, letters brought relief from the grind of domestic service in large houses and farms, especially the initial shock of living with little privacy, cheek-by-jowl with unknown people, masters, mistresses, housekeepers, other servants, or with too many solitary hours, especially in outdoor work. Such a life was often in stark contrast to the noise and familiarity of home, family and village life. Mrs Wrigley, a plate-layer's wife born in 1858, writes of how she 'fretted very much for ... home', but 'Not able to read and write, I could not let my parents know, until a kind old lady in the village wrote to my parents to fetch me home from the hardships I endured'.[47] Ruth Barrow's letters to her future husband communicate her pain and depression in dialect spelling: 'I am almost ashamed to say it, that I feel very dull and I cannot away with it all ... It is such a great chaing, a chaing that can only be felt by those who have felt what it is to leave all they hold dear and have sought a home amongst straingers.'[48] Middle-class commentators were alive to the dangers which awaited isolated women in their employers' houses. One warned of the problems when servants' 'affections are obstructed' by not being able to afford postage.[49] By implication, blame for the sexually predatory actions of male employers is placed on the inability of servant girls to write.

The dependence on letters to keep emotional bonds intact was described by the Dundee factory boy (b. 1816) whose father was transported to Australia for 'culpable homicide', leaving his mother destitute. He recalls his parents' emotional closeness. His father's letters home even enhance it. He remembers how his mother had received a letter,

giving a graphic account of the sufferings he had endured as a convict and bewailing, in simple though sincere language, the sad misfortune which had deprived him of the society of his wife and little ones. Its affectionate protestations, harrowing details, and passionate love, stained with the salt

> *tears of a contrite spirit, had plunged my mother into an agony of grief.*

Lack of contact destroyed even the memory of attachment:

> *During all this time I had heard no word from my father. A friend had written to Australia to try and discover if he still lived: and in the same letter the melancholy news of my mother and brother's deaths were detailed; but five years had elapsed since this letter was sent off, and no answer had been received. I had almost forgotten about him, not having seen him since I was seven years of age. I can barely say that I felt the warm glow of affection which lights up the hearts of the young in presence of their parents … when I tried to realize him to my mental eye, he faded from my imagination like a dear friend who has long been dead.[50]*

The radical writer, poet and diarist Samuel Bamford (1788–1872), an avid literary, political and personal correspondent, clipped one letter which was published in a newspaper, and included it in his diary as evidence of a husband's conversion from domestic violence. Bamford plays down the 'writer's' regular beating of his wife when drunk. At such times, the wife went to stay with her Accrington relatives, leaving him to look after the children. This is a very short extract from her husband's long, melodramatic and rather unconvincing exhortation to his wife to return home, with promises of written pledges to reform:

> *Mi Hever Deer Betty. I send you theese fu lines hoppin the wil find yu in good elth has the leve me hat pressent, exceptin won hor too pints of hale whitch I av ad whith Hedmun; an won hor too more this hafternoon, hat Jacks, an Billy Meddocroft has rites this … So prithee deer whife kom whom, an dunno make no moor nonsense abeawt hit; an iv hever I sthrike thee ogen, or have a finger at the, Ile sine a stampt papper at Ile be willen to goo to prissen for hit. Mi deer take theese things into Konsitherashun; and pak hop thi klooas, and lyev yore foke … thi hone affectionhate usband. JOHN[51]*

Whether this letter was originally written by 'Johnny Briggs' (the husband's name), or dictated to Bamford who wrote it in a dialect form, or whether it was composed by Bamford himself or a journalist as a plaintive 'Come Whoam to Thi Childer an' Me' letter, the mixture of Lancashire dialect and wayward spelling seem written for effect. Bamford suggests that such letter-writing was a common event, using scribes if necessary. It is intended to evoke the power of letter-writing and the role of letters in processes of conversion to sobriety, faith and self-improvement, complete with written oath. Bamford noted that the wife did return and the husband still had 'bouts' but that he was a reformed family man whose conversion was to be held to the test of a written, signed, stamped pledge to reform. The wife's point of view is absent from Bamford's commentary.

Letters to and from prison, E.P. Thompson pointed out, 'give us some insight into that great area between the attainments of the skilled artisan and those of the barely literate' – although it is not necessarily the case that all highly skilled artisans were highly literate. And some who were highly literate struggled with the skills of their trade. Prisoners' correspondence is mostly by and to political prisoners. The difficulty of writing letters which would pass the prison governor's scrutiny added to inmates' literacy difficulties. Prisoners did have 'unaccustomed leisure', though this kind of enforced idleness was not always experienced as productive time.[52] The correspondence of Samuel Holberry, who was arrested and unjustly imprisoned in Sheffield in 1838 after disturbances following the Newport uprising, draws out many issues relevant to letter-writing in the first half of the century. The *Chartist Circular* published Holberry's letters to his wife and sympathisers. He wrote to protest his innocence and draw attention to his state of health. Holberry came from a literate family, but like many working-class families who wrote letters, the evidence of their literacy has been lost: 'he unfortunately, on a visit to his parents some years later, burnt the letters he had addressed to them while wearing the red coat'.[53] He had educated himself at night school during his life as a soldier. In 1838 he married a woman 'with defects of education' but, he added, 'a mind of no mean order'. This was a combination of attributes beyond the understanding of most middle-class observers at the time. His first letter to his wife from York Castle gaol shows optimism and he asks her to inform the people he hoped would petition for his release. By 1842 (he had been imprisoned for four years) 'he was scarcely able to hold a pen'. As his health deteriorated his letters home became more desperate.

My dear Mary,

I received your kind letter and Mr. Burley brought me some oranges. I feel rather easier this morning, but you may depend I am a poor object. My dear, you say you should like to come to York to see me; to that I cannot give my consent. In the first place, we should have to look through the odious bars and it would only make you more unhappy, to say nothing of myself; besides I have no complaint on me at present that is likely to terminate my existence; that my illness should bring me into consumption is all I am afraid of, but I believe they will not let me die here ... keep up your spirits.

This was his last letter to his wife. The Home Secretary ordered a release but the magistrates prevaricated and mercy came too late. Newspaper reports estimated his funeral procession at 20,000; the Chartists claimed it was 50,000. Holberry's letter-writing campaign from prison triggered other forms of writing. The series of articles which reprinted and commented on his letters was published as if it were an act of political duty, that people might 'never forget the name and fate of Holberry'.[54] One significant act of literacy generated others, which reflected the culture of working-class radical journals of the time. The letters themselves were published as a serialised 'true' story, political, moral and tragic, depicting as a literary event an all-too-common instance of injustice to the innocent and powerless.

A life crisis such as separation or victimisation, which created the need to write, could also bring about a change in material circumstances or a deepened sense of selfhood. For some people, the act of writing a letter, a social form of literacy and often intended as a dialogue, also created a watershed between two versions of self. Writing a letter could signal the acquisition of literacy and at the same time announce a person's new capabilities and their desire to engage in new forms of communication. Many autobiographers include their first or most significant early letter, placing them prominently within the reconstruction of a life which was often full of bigger drama and incident, seeming to point to the significance they accord to literacy in their developing selfhood, as well as to the belief that letter writing is a practice on which much personal and social change depended.

Mary Barber's life story, *Five Score and Ten*, was dictated to an unknown scribe after her return home to Ireland from London, starting at aged 97. She could not read or write at all. She survived to 111 years old and died in 1837. Her autobiography tells of her long journey back from Ireland to London, so that she can see her children again before she dies. She sets out after a long illness during which she discovers that her daughter, with no letters to inform her otherwise, has assumed her mother to be dead. The story of Mary Barber's journey is propelled by a series of letters, each one essential for her next step. Mary Barber needs help with literacy, so before setting off she visits a 'kind-hearted' scribe to write to her daughter 'for a trifle', in the hope of being met at Liverpool. Without literacy skills, she finds it difficult to produce the proof of identity he asks for, evidence itself of the increasing demands of written forms of identification and information-gathering. Eventually she manages to produce a baptism certificate. She has to accept a lift to Dublin before any answer arrives from her daughter. No-one meets her, so the old woman finds another scribe in Liverpool. She 'inquir[es] for a person to write a letter for me ... for a trifle'. After the letter is written, 'I sealed it and gave it him to put in the post', forgetting to instruct the scribe to give her daughter directions. 'In a sad fright', because she has run out of money, she manages to find him and put things right. Then begins a wait of more than three days for the daughter's reply, and she suffers acute anxiety: 'I laid me down on the bed, and almost wished that I could die and end my troubles then and for ever.' The scribe discovers her daughter's reply has been turned away by Mary's landlord because of a confusion of identity. But he retrieves the letter, which contains money for Mary to come to London alone as the daughter is too ill to travel. She starts walking to London.[55]

Mary Barber's story is revealing about letter-writing as well as other literacy practices. Firstly, finding and using dependable scribes to write and despatch letters was essential. The role of scribe went – and still goes – far beyond simply writing down the words dictated.[56] Secondly, this story and other evidence suggests that even in the late 1820s, written forms of identification were becoming increasingly important. This was a contested development at first. In 1801 Censuses began, and in the same period other official documents requiring proof of identity were introduced.[57] Thirdly, letter-writing, as already emphasised, was the only means of communication there was, if meeting in person, directly or through messengers, was impossible. Whilst it may be true that writing played a small role in communication within a local area where talk still ruled, as soon as someone moved away, literacy became central to the course of relationships. Finally, making the right decisions increasingly depended upon a series of letters and the wait for a response. Letters enable Mary to complete her journey, but the whole process depended on knowing how things work and the rituals to be followed, which Mary did not completely grasp. And letters inherently carry the constant threat of their own unreliability and potential untimeliness. The only second chance if things go wrong is another letter. Writing skills, money and time were essential, all or some of which were likely to be in short supply. Mary Barber's story demonstrates utter reliance on letters and the additional anguish of working in a medium you can't afford. Once she manages to access it, *Five Score and Ten* describes a fast and efficient postal service, with replies expected within three days, the safe arrival of cash with letters, and the re-delivery of refused items. Her story casts light on the complexity of literacy events, particularly before 1840, but it also conveys the mixed feelings of wonder and anxiety attached to literacy by those who needed others to write for them. The significance of writing itself partly eclipses the remarkable story of her 206-mile walk from Liverpool to London, a journey so astonishing for a penniless woman in great old age, that she and her editors felt it necessary to have its truthfulness publicly 'attested' in her book by its aristocratic patrons.

Tiny amounts of private letter-writing have survived. Official sources of evidence of how much people wrote to each other, whether in 'real' writing or through scribes, or in the kinds of codes unearthed by Select Committees, is scanty and often contradictory. Many people persisted in thinking that, despite evidence to the contrary, working-class life was overwhelmingly lived in tight-knit local communities, with little geographical separation between people. In this view, there was little perceived need to write, and therefore little writing happened. What writing there was was widely assumed to be instrumental. As the down-to-earth Joseph Lawson wrote of Pudsey, 'There is no such thing as writing love-letters! It is as well it is so: otherwise courting amongst the common or working people would be impossible, as a letter costs a half day's wage; but there is no need of letter writing in making love, as the parties generally live near each other.'[58] In these circumstances, it was assumed that most information was exchanged in person. Letters which have survived often deal in deeper meanings than the mere exchange of information implies. They mark key moments, convey feelings, qualify information, make demands, threaten, convey ideas and tell stories. People excited by the arrival of the postman and motivated by the hard-won ability to write, both widely witnessed, were likely to want to use their literacy to write notes, however rudimentary, with whatever 'scraps' of materials they could find, and send them if they could afford to. Private processes and products are difficult to monitor and trace. It seems likely, given the large numbers of people affected by separation, the availability of supportive family and community networks and scribes to help write, carry and deliver post, that writing may have been far more widespread than has usually been accepted. The extent of the references to letters in Victorian paintings and fictional writing as well as autobiography and official reports, suggest that letter-writing was a cultural presence, perhaps for the majority of people. Among the letters which have survived, some richly express the experiences, feelings and imagination of writers. They are historical and social accounts of lived experience, but they invite analysis as literature. This love letter, written on 9 September 1868, is drawn from a daily correspondence between David Jones, a grocer's assistant in Rhymney, and his beloved, Mary Ann, who worked as a shaper in the hat trade. The spelling is as reprinted in Thomas Jones's *Rhymney Memories*:

Dr Polly,

… I am happy to inform you that I have received your kind letter this morning and was very glad to here that you were safe and that you are quite happy but I have not the least doupt than you be much happier if I was a long side of you with the arms of love guiding you and a faithful heart to comfort thee.

… I have sent you a short note yesterday. I hope you have received it with the everlasting love to the one that write it as his for ever and ever to you. Last night no place to go put bed to comfort myself and soon as I got to bed my mind was running over the mountains towards the viaduck of Crumlyn and the heart of yours. Somehow it wouldn't sleep put it was telling me that the mind was lonely and no moonlight to accompany us both. Bed by myself but after all my eyes was still with me to I have nothing so do put try and look through the window and there I was listening to hear if I could see something but before long I could see the Bird in all colours come and told me you have a friend and the last word she said tonight after prayers was that she have a friend in Rhymney has a plant of love in his heart for which I wish you to comfort him before dark and tell him the secret that I am his for ever. I cannot tell you how I spept after that. I hope you possess such feelings, my dearest Polly.[59]

As Barthes put it, the spoken and written language of lovers is a hidden and 'forsaken' form, rarely surviving to be read by others. This lover's intimate discourse soon breaks with the conventions of its awkwardly formal start, and from conventional or clichéd patterns of love letters, to engage with the language of the senses in kaleidoscopic images and metaphors of longing. The letter itself, as it conjures its painful sense of the other, explores desire, the pleasure and pain of waiting and resentment at the threatening possibility the other person might be happy without him. The 'Bird' appears as a shared erotic symbol, curiously juxtaposed with 'tonight after prayers', which feels a rather dutiful fixture in this prose-poem of love.[60]

VIII

The tapestry of working-class letter-writing seems to have been richer, more varied and more widespread than evidence from the postal reform process suggests. Like much working-class writing, letters were ephemeral and only a tiny fraction survive as manuscripts or incorporated in publications. The private spheres of daily life and the imagination have left few traces. The examples we do have hint at a lost world of writings, discarded either with indifference, or with a lack of confidence in its value to others, like so much evidence of working-class life, at least until recently. The true extent of writing can never be known for certain, even though unlikely documents from the past have a strange habit of resurfacing. Things turn up. Sometimes against the odds they are kept and may still lie in library boxes. Margaret Llewellyn Davies gave two reasons why so much working-class writing gets lost. She said that only 'sometimes' did she receive letters from Women's Cooperative Guild members which she 'could not bring herself to burn'. But that if she did find them interesting, it was 'as if to expose them to other eyes were a breach of confidence'.[61] The work of retrieving and analysing evidence which sheds more light on the complexity, depth and variety of literacy practices is difficult. Coming to conclusions about the limits to literacy based on the scant material we now have is easy. Research on emigrants' letters has grown since the classic work of Thomas and Znaniecki on *The Polish Peasant in Europe and America*, including recent work on nineteenth-century letters to and from Canada, Wales and Australia. David Barton and Nigel Halls's work on letter-writing as a social practice includes nineteenth-century perspectives. Most recently, Alistair Thomson's *Moving Stories* describes twentieth-century working women's experiences of emigration from the UK to Australia, much of it through letter-writing before phone-calls were an affordable reality. People separated by force of material circumstances created literacy-based cultures and practices through letter-writing, creating 'writing relationships' to intervene in their own and their correspondents' lives in the hope of changing their circumstances, however small those changes might be.[62]

Notes

1   Hill, 1880, p. 279.
2   PP: SC on Postage, 1838, p. 111.
3   Baines, 1895, Vol. 1, p. 105.
4   PP: SC on Postage, 1838, p. 216.
5   PP: SC on Postage, quoted in Vincent, 1989, p. 36.
6   PP: SC on Postage, 1838, pp. 334–9.
7   B.R. Mitchell & P. Deane, 1962.
8   See Vincent, op. cit., p. 39; Weller & Bawden, 2005, pp. 782, 786, 791.
9   PP: SC on Postage, 1839, pp. 261–2.
10   Quoted in Hill, 1880, p. 239.
11   PP: SC on Postage, 1839, p. 278.
12   PP: SC on Postage, 1838, p. 216.
13   Vincent, op. cit., p. 89.
14   Report of the Commissioners appointed to inquire into the State of Popular Education in England (The Newcastle Report), 1861, quoted in MacLure, [1965] 1986, pp. 80, 75.
15   Binfield, 2004, p. 1.
16   See E.P. Thompson, [1963] 1968, pp. 783–7; Hobsbawm & Rude, 1973, chapter 10.
17   Vincent, 2000.
18   Arch, [1898] 1966, p. 58.
19   G.R. Smith, 1908, p. 51 – spelling as reproduced in the book.
20   Love, 1823, pp. 51–7.
21   See, e.g., Northern Star, 20 July 1839, and letters and petitions from prisoners reported in issues 4 July 1840 and 7 September 1840.
22   Adams, 1903, Vol. 1, p. 271.
23   One and All, May 1895, p .118; December 1894, p. 180.
24   Weaver, 1913, p. 29.
25   PP: SC on Postage, 1839, pp. 261–2.
26   McGill, 1914, p. 45.
27   PP: SC on Postage, 1838, pp. 213, 136, 200.
28   Letter of John Warden to D. Urquart, Esq., 1841, Bolton Reference Library.
29   John Castle, 1961, 'The Diary of John Castle', TS, Bishopsgate Institute, London, pp. 14, 10, 14.
30   A. Ireson, 'Reminiscences', TS, Brunel University, p. 47.
31   McGill, op. cit., pp. 116–17.
32   Arch, 1966, p. 22; Penn, 1947 (see chapter 7 for references).
33   Haw, 1907, p. 18.
34   G.R. Smith, op. cit., pp. 7–9, 150.
35   F. Thompson, 1973, pp. 101, 398, 470–1, 514.
36   F. Thompson, op. cit., p.101.
37   Leno, 1892, p. 8; see also G.R. Smith, op. cit., p. 4, where he describes how letters 'were generally written on sheets of paper which doubled, measured about 9 by 6 inches; and … had to be folded to the size of the ordinary Post-letter, the edges being tucked in and fastened with wafers or sealing wax'.
38   See Briggs, 1988, for accounts of the rise of postcards and other personal ephemera connected to literacy; also Vincent, 1989, p. 44 for further evidence of changes in Valentine practices.
39   G. R. Smith, op. cit., p. 46.

40 Heap, 'My Life and Times', MS, Rawtenstall District Central Library, p. 19.

41 Cooper, [1872] 1971, pp 11–18, 20–42.

42 Grant, 1931, p. 2.

43 Herbert, 1948, pp. 82–5.

44 PP: SC on Postage, 1838, p. 162.

45 Brown, Untitled TS, Brunel University Library.

46 Lawson, 1887, pp. 39–44.

47 Quoted in Llewellyn Davies, [1931] 1977, p. 58.

48 Quoted in Horn, 1986, p. 105.

49 PP: SC on Postage, 1839, p. 258.

50 Anon., *Chapters in the Life of a Dundee Factory Boy*, 1850, pp. 39, 69.

51 A clipping in Bamford's unpaginated manuscript 'Diary' shows that this letter appeared in the *Manchester Weekly Times* in October 1858, taken from an original which had been written about 20 years previously.

52 E.P. Thompson, *op. cit.*, p. 786.

53 *Chartist Circular*, 1841–2, Vol. 2, No 117, pp. 261, 266.

54 *Chartist Circular*, , 1841–2, Vol. 2, No 120, pp. 270, 278.

55 Barber, 1840, p. 14.

56 Mace, 2002, and Kalman, 1999, explore some continuities in scribing practices across time and place and the nature of relationships in the writing process.

57 From the early nineteenth century the collecting of information concerning personal identity grew. The ten-yearly census which began in 1801 in Britain exemplifies this growth in controlling forms of state literacy. See Manzoni, *The Betrothed*, [1828] 1972, pp. 271–4, 316–17, 360, for his imaginative representation of the anger with which the intrusion on personal liberty by authorities was received, particularly by those who could not write.

58 Lawson, *op. cit.*, p. 10.

59 Jones, 1938, pp. 36–7.

60 Barthes, [1977] 1990, Preface, writes of the need to bring 'lover's discourse' out of its 'extreme solitude'. It is a language which is 'warranted by no-one', even though it is spoken by 'thousands of subjects (who knows?)', 'disparaged' or 'ignored'. The love letter is central to his 'affirmation'.

61 From Virginia Woolf's introduction to Llewellyn Davies [1931] 1977, p. xxxi.

62 Thomas & Znaniecki, [1918] 1984. See also diaries and letters, such as those recorded in T. Thompson, 1987; Fairman (2000) explores paupers' letters asking for poor relief before the 1834 poor law; and research on letters between emigrants and immigrants and their families and friends at home, including A. Thomson, 2011, pp. 205–13, on how letters were shaped by 'writing relationships'.

PART THREE

WRITING LIVES, DIFFERENT SELVES

CHAPTER 5

Telling the truth: fact, memory and special pleading

Why did the autobiographical form best suit nineteenth-century working-class writers? Raymond Williams saw the roots of autobiography in a complex cultural inheritance:

> Though they had marvellous material that could go into the novel very few of them managed to write good or even any novels. Instead they wrote marvellous autobiographies. Why? Because the form coming down through the religious tradition was of the witness confessing the story of his life, or there was the defence speech at the trial when a man tells the judge who he is and what he has done. These oral forms were more accessible, forms centred on 'I', on the single person. The novel with its quite different narrative forms was virtually impenetrable to working-class writers for three or four generations.[1]

The autobiographical form was also the best means of conveying the life experience of people whose literacy was hard-won. Barthes's exploration of the differences between the meaning of 'authors' and 'writers' suggests the possibility of distinguishing 'authors' who write, intransitively, from 'writers' who have something to say. Williams engaged with the distinction historically, tracing the concept of authorship from one in which 'authority' derived from God informs 'a sense of decisive origination', to that of someone who owns 'literary property'.[2] Authors' status differs from writers' in the uniqueness of the property, and because the term 'writer' can also mean an activity or process. The majority of the autobiographers in this book define themselves as writers. This does not

165

The instruction reads 'Make a fair copy of the following passages in the time, writing distinctly, correctly, neatly and as rapidly as you can & writing out all abbreviations at full length.'

From Keefe's Copying M.S.: extract from the examinations for Boys Clerks, 1891, exercise XVI, about an autobiographical text mean that ownership or uniqueness of style and the literary casting of writing are not part of their purpose. But in their reconstruction of a life, many writers are more urgently concerned with the material to be conveyed than with the mode of conveying it. Their self-consciousness about style is often apparent in apologies for their lack of it, or the expression of a desire for a literary voice. Some writers adopt a set of imagined literary qualities or conventions. But mostly, style and form come second. Writing is first and foremost the ambition to put the record straight, to break the almost total silence about working-class experience as part of a national culture; and to dare to explain, justify and celebrate one's own self. Further, autobiographers want to announce they have become writers and how they made this happen.

For some writers autobiography was the right genre, not only because it best expressed the complexity of their purposes, but because it could include other kinds of writing they had practised. The majority had already written letters, notes, diaries and poems; some had written essays, articles for magazines, lines for epitaphs and hymns. In several autobiographies, early pieces of writing and their first writing tools lay on the writer's table as she/he wrote – aide-mémoires and emblems of a writing journey. This material was often interpreted and used in the construction of a life history. Since the inner and public 'self' to be created is to some extent also an imaginative, fictional 'character', these pieces are not simply factual material or evidence for the story. A writer may have had clearer ideas of how she/he could use them to support the narrative than would be possible in constructing a novel. The pieces of writing themselves are unassailable facts; adding legitimacy to the self or selves being constructed.

The sense of pleasure in writing and astonishment at the writing journey is, as already stressed, particularly inviting to people whose writing skills have been hard to acquire and time has always been in short supply. Some autobiographers were still living out a working life as they wrote. Their dual identity and selfhood as workers and writers is another discernible dimension to autobiographical writing. In the complexity and stress of working-class experience, therefore, autobiography was the mode best suited to situating, constructing and explaining the self in context. In any case, fiction was not available as a cultural resource for working-class writers – reading it, let alone writing it, was widely frowned upon. A better starting point for reading and critiquing autobiography is to take it on its own terms rather than to see it as something it is

167

not: less than fiction, or a substitute for the novels writers would have written if they only had the imagination and literary skill. This approach allows readers to engage with the extent to which writers managed to synthesise the qualities of 'author' and 'writer', to tell stories and convey messages about society to society, about how a sense of self develops over a life, and how writers engaged with the literary world and worked through the pleasure and pain of crafting writing for writing's sake.

Writing a life story makes possible a relatively safe focus on the self. The substance and the authority of an autobiography are difficult to challenge except on the grounds of 'truth or falsehood'. As an adult literacy student expressed it in modern times:

> *It's easier to write about yourself … That's one subject you are an expert on … If you've written about your life somebody can say: 'Well, I'm your brother and you didn't do that.' You can say: 'Well, I did. That's how I felt. It happened.' It's a stronger argument. If you're writing pure fiction somebody can criticise it and say: 'It's boring, it's slow …' They might be right.*[3]

The charge of weak narrative tension in autobiography is to miss the main point for writers, which is to create a truthful account of their lives, exploring and justifying personal change. For them, what is factual will be believed. The view of autobiography as a genre that is based, however selectively, on fact, reality and lived experience provides, paradoxically, the freedom to develop an episodic narrative which will carry all the writer's contradictory and digressive personal and public preoccupations, alongside their characterisations of self and others: 'true' stories enhanced by literary techniques. There is freedom in the form as well as the content: autobiographies contain essays, poems, handed-down stories, official letters, treatises, documents or parts of them, rich variety within the apparently unassailable organising principle of telling the truth.

Another important motive for writers was to ensure a wider understanding of themselves as a people who had been socially, culturally and economically disempowered. While offering a version of self which seeks to be faithful to events and feelings, nineteenth-century autobiographers also sought to pre-empt criticism of the style of writing as well as to challenge attitudes to working-class people. One way of doing this was to adopt language dismissive of themselves. Writers repeatedly describe their own work as 'efforts', as unliterary, matter-of-fact or simple, and urge readers to concentrate on the story. These apologies can also feel like a necessary ritual, which also contains an indirect critique – having a go at elaborate literary or novelistic styles sideways-on, grounded in a belief in the virtues of 'plain' language and pointing out the writer's social circumstances in order to be better understood.

Working-class autobiography is never only about the 'I'. It offers more than the remaking of a personal past, namely a sequence of experiences and events lived through a complex inner emotional life shared closely with others – and presenting them, however oddly assembled, as a single life. The life being constructed in writing is invariably lived in recurrent tension with strong external currents and pressures that criss-cross the personal, cut across motivation and hope and present choices – or more often inevitabilities. Writers lived within – and often against – a family and a community, as well as within a subordinated social group with and against other, dominant, groups. Autobiography urges as a minimum the visibility of 'ordinary' life in addition to an understanding of particular experience. These prefaces of working-class autobiography, like M.A. Ashford's, express the wish to be known and understood through the 'facts' of a life:

> In the month of July 1842, as I was passing the site of the Royal Exchange then in course of re-erection after being burned down, my attention was caught by one of the very numerous bills with which the boards … were covered: it ran thus – 'Susan Hopley, or the Life of a Maid Servant'. This book, I thought to myself, must be a novelty; for although female servants form a large class of Her Majesty's subjects, I have seen but little of them or their affairs in print: sometimes, indeed, a few stray delinquents, from their vast numbers, find their way into the police reports or the newspapers; and in penny tracts, now and then a 'Mary Smith' or 'Susan Jones' is introduced, in the last stage of consumption, or some other lingering disease, of which they die, in a heavenly frame of mind, and are duly interred. In a short time after, I procured the 'Life of Susan Hopley' and felt disappointed at finding it to be a work of fiction. It occurred to me that the various events of my own life – not merely 'founded on facts', as is sometimes expressed, but the real truth – might afford amusement to matter-of-fact persons.[4]

Alfred Williams, a Swindon railwayman who was a prolific writer of prose and poetry, wrote in the preface to *A Wiltshire Village* (1912):

> *I do not fear to confess I am not a novelist. My intention was, before everything else, to be faithful, to write what I have seen, to tell that which I know. Accordingly, the characters that figure in these pages are not imaginary ones, but are, or were, real persons, blunt and plain enough, it may be, and unliterary also.*[5]

Mary Ann Ashford catches the stereotypical image of the working-class woman and derides it as simplistic and sentimental. She defines the audience for her 'real truth': matter-of-fact persons, rather than those looking for novelty or flights of fancy. Alfred Williams, too, refuses to court his readership with any apology that his project or his style are inferior. It seems to him it would be a failure of the reader's imagination and human sympathy if they could not appreciate the stories of 'real persons'.

Confidence in the form and substance of a life story is connected to its purpose: that is, the writer's wish to tell truths which are unknown to the wider world. In this way autobiography permits a kind of 'special pleading', a trust that the reader will understand, or identify with the writer once they have read the truth, sympathised with mistakes and misfortunes. Nineteenth-century novelists were aware of the power of the autobiographical form. Dickens used it for *Great Expectations* and *David Copperfield*; Kingsley used it for *Alton Locke* and Charlotte Brontë used the conventions and cadences of the 'special pleading' of autobiography in *Jane Eyre*, and here in *Villette*:

> *Religious reader, you will preach to me a long sermon about what I have just written, and so will you, moralist; and you, stern sage: you stoic, will frown; you, cynic, sneer; you, epicure, laugh. Well, each and all, take it your own way. I accept the sermon, frown, sneer and laugh; perhaps you are all right: and perhaps, circumstanced like me, you would have been, like me, wrong.*[6]

Brontë's stress on the first person in *Villette*, Williams argued, 'is really: the world will judge me in certain ways if it sees what I do, but if it knew how I felt it would see me quite differently'.[7] Virginia Woolf wrote disdainfully of special pleading as a weakness of women's and working-class writing, because the writer intrudes as 'someone resenting the treatment of her sex and pleading for its rights. This brings into a woman's writing an element which is entirely absent from a man's, unless, indeed, he happens to be a working man (or) a Negro'.[8] She dismisses special pleading as a distortion of perspective, throwing the reader solely into the subjective with no refuge in a more detached register. For Williams, too, special pleading does have a weakness in that 'persons outside this shaping longing have reality only as they contribute to the landscape, the emotional landscape of the ... recommending character'. But another way of seeing it is to focus on its 'power: the immediate personal and creative form: the inclusive sharing of what had been an unspoken voice'.[9] Working-class writing helps to include more voices expressing their truth, with a sense that the 'recommending character' is an individual who also carries a collective, even archetypal set of experiences and feelings, which emerge from, and are shaped by, the conditions of writing. For Carolyn Steedman, in autobiography, the writing process itself can be described as a form of resistance. In this argument, the distortions involved in special pleading might more creatively be seen as part of the difficulty of expressing resentment. Indeed they voice the difficulty of placing the self at centre-stage, as hero or heroine, when the actions and feelings described fall outside 'the proper and fitting set of feelings' for working-class people to own, as well as outside dominant notions of the heroic.[10]

Perhaps the problem for working-class women or black writers, historically and today, lies in the term 'special pleading' itself. The Oxford English Dictionary defines it as 'a specious or unfair argument favouring the speaker's point of view'. Chambers defines it as 'aiming at victory rather than at truth'. But these definitions do not adequately convey what is intended in much working-class writing, which has more stature than a plea, since it aims formally to address the problem of a deeply-felt social and cultural imbalance. This chimes with a legal definition: 'pleading with reference to new facts in a case'. It takes as read that the prosecution has already stated its case, or does not even have to, because all the assumptions and opinions have already been formed in its own dominant language, representing its own interests. Special pleading ignores the existence of a powerfully-articulated 'other side of the argument', or other experience. Writing from disempowered groups assumes an imbalance of volume in favour of those whose articulate voices are already publicly heard and their experience understood. Such writers are well aware of the expectation that only a few voices, or representations of their experience (and these often only in fiction), resonate in a wider cultural context or become central to society's images of itself or its understanding of what constitutes literary expression. As such, much working-class

171

autobiography can be understood as insisting on speaking out loud, as a form of cultural resistance.

Rethinking special pleading raises issues about the preoccupation with telling the truth in working-class life stories. The sense of a real living audience is one compelling reason for a careful concentration on accuracy in autobiographical work: 'Those … who wrote for their local community upon whose subscriptions they were dependent, were likely to have every moment of their autobiographies interrogated by a readership far more informed than any subsequent student can hope to be'.[11] Whether or not family members or the local community were always the intended primary readership (in many cases not), awareness of local scrutiny is still likely to have been present in the author's sense of audience. If a truth goes beyond the self and seeks to represent one's own community or social class to another more powerful social class, the burden of accuracy on the connecting relationships between the narrator to her/his community is heavy. There might be envy, pique, or competing versions of the truth, as well as pride that someone is telling the world how 'we' live. In *The Book of Laughter and Forgetting* Milan Kundera proposes that writing a book is an attempt to universalise experience; that a universe is marked by its uniqueness and is therefore naturally threatened by the existence of another universe: 'Two shoemakers can live together in perfect harmony (provided their shops are not on the same block). But once they start writing books on the lot of the shoemaker, they will begin to get in each other's way; they will start to wonder, is one shoemaker alive when others are alive?'[12] But Dave Douglass's article about the working-class writer Jack Common has a view grounded in social solidarity:

> *When a working man writes about working men he writes for them, on their behalf. He writes to give voice to the dumbness of the silent majority. Every sentence is a struggle rarely satisfied. A struggle to explain, to give some sense to an otherwise seemingly irrational, brutish blind bitterness. Sometimes a writer achieves it, and upon reading the passage all one can do is sit back, put the book down and say 'that's so right'. For this reason working-class writers are never rivals.*

A third view is offered by a member of a present-day working women's writing group who sees the truth as 'powerful':

> *Truth either does a lot of good or a lot of damage. There is no in-between with truth. At first I thought, I can't write this book, because I'm not going*

to be very popular with my family, or it's not going to make me a bright shining woman that I'd like to be deep down. If I'm going to divide it into what people expect, and what I want to write, I'd never write the book. After a lot of soul-searching I thought 'I'd like to write a book in all truthfulness, you can always tell when people are edging over things. Just write it as I see it, as I feel it, and sod 'em.'[13]

Autobiographers presented telling the truth as their literary virtue. Theirs was a realism which differed from a social realist novel, and was even hostile to it. In working-class communities, the novel was known to be a compelling and popular form but it was deeply distrusted, particularly in non-conformist religious circles as immoral, not only for the alleged depravity of characters and plots, but precisely because its narratives were imaginary: not true; fancy not fact. Thomas Jones of Rhymney, born in 1870, described how chapel preachers denounced fiction as 'the disgrace of English literature' and took pride in the fact that 'they did not take' with Welsh readers. Jones writes of his parent's experience of novels; his mother read her first novel aged 50 and never fully grasped the nature of fiction or drama:

My father saw in a shop window a book called 'The History of Tom Jones' by Henry Fielding ... My mother read it. She believed every word of it and could not conceive how a man could sit down and invent the story of Squire Alworthy and Sophie and Tom out of his head. So did Robert Owen ... read Robinson Crusoe and Richardson's novels and believe every word to be true.[14]

Suspicion of novels strengthened the conviction that autobiography was the natural and best medium in which to express the conditions of production of writing, the material to be turned into literature and to satisfy the particular hoped-for audience. As the wheelwright Antony Errington wrote in 1823: 'The reason of my wrighting the particulars of my life and Transactions are to inform my family and the world ... I write this from pure motives of justice and truth, and that whether with or against myself'. Wrighting = writing = righting was the formula which motivated him, and others.[15] To this was added the comforting belief that the writing of factual material was of higher moral worth, avoiding the vanities and profanities of fiction.

Writers often dwell on the external facts of lived experience, for which 'the truth' was a shorthand. Autobiography is a form which strives to be factual, or at least based on fact. It claims the status of a map and a written record of real life, more than it claims to be a literary construction, even if it is absolutely that. Nineteenth-century autobiography could create a unique record because barely any other accounts of working-class life, which were told, or even authenticated, by its historical actors, exist to this day. But difficulties arose for writers because they had to choose between and try to reconcile different personal and social truths. Sometimes they could not know fully what had happened in a particular event, and had to piece the parts together and interpret them. Telling the truth sometimes meant dramatising or playing with the truth. Tension and dissonance arise in much writing as a result of attempts to reconcile loyalties, sensitivities and others' viewpoints.

In autobiographies, by men in particular, the strong emphasis on shared experience, ordinariness and the material conditions of life often feel like efforts to externalise as well as universalise what is being said about the self, and keep emotional experience and the deep inner self in the shadows as material which is too difficult to incorporate into narratives which see the facts as the most important messages to convey. And if the discussion of feelings is not part of the discourse of a family, or friendship and community circles, the language to explore feelings seems difficult to access and use. But the life stories in this book show that emotional life was not dulled by the struggle for survival. For some it was sharpened. The view that loss and grief were not so deeply experienced as they are now, that multiple loss deadened the senses, is emphatically not reflected in autobiographies. However, if the utterance of deep and conflicted feelings and imaginative expression are perceived to some extent to belong to an alien fictionalised culture which expresses middle-class values and anxieties as they are expressed through novels, it is unsurprising that the emotional sphere in autobiography is embattled, forces itself out from between cracks in the tough surface of daily life or that its expression flows faintly and intermittently. Traces of partially successful attempts to squeeze out or bury emotional life are often visible, however, and the last section of this book will explore this through the autobiographies themselves.

Perhaps it is the categorisation of literature itself which forced writers into stating the boundaries of their chosen genre. The problem as Williams saw it arose from 'a falsification – false distancing – of the

174

fictional or the imaginary (and connected with these the subjective) ...
And [from] a related suppression of the fact of writing – active signifying
composition – in what was distinguished as the "practical", the "factual",
or the "discursive" '.

Following this argument, understanding what autobiographers
meant by 'telling the truth' means understanding where they are placed in
relation to a 'complex series' of possible permutations of reality permitted
within a chosen literary form: 'what really happened; what might (could)
have happened; what really happens; what might happen; what essentially
(typically) happened/happens. Similarly, the extreme negative definition
of "imaginary persons" ... "who did not/do not exist". The range of
actual writing makes use, implicitly or explicitly, of all these propositions'.
How aware a writer might be of boundaries imposed on a particular
form, in this case autobiography, or how obedient to such boundaries,
might be added to this 'series'. 'History, memoir and biography use a
significant part of each series, and given the use of real characters and
events in much major epic, romance, drama and narrative, the substantial
overlap – indeed in many areas the substantial community – is undeniable'. Williams goes on to argue that:

> The range of actual writing similarly surpasses any reduction of 'creative
> imagination' to the 'subjective', with its dependent propositions: 'litera-
> ture' and 'internal' or inner 'truth'; other forms of writing as 'external'
> truth ... the range of writing, in most forms, crosses these artificial
> categories again and again ... autobiography ('what I experienced',
> 'what happened to me') is 'subjective' but (ideally) 'factual' writing; realist
> fiction or naturalist drama ('people as they are', 'the world as it is') is
> 'objective' (the narrator or even the fact of narrative occluded in the form)
> but (ideally) 'creative' writing.[16]

Patrick McGill's fictionalised autobiography *Children of the Dead End*
(1914) engages with Williams's 'complex series'. McGill conceals his own
thinking about life-story writing behind a simple association of fiction
with moral untrustworthiness, describing his writing apprenticeship as
'Five truthful and exciting incidents of my navvying life, and I was not
clever enough to tell lies about it'.[17] But elsewhere he analyses the
supposed differences between the novel and autobiography:

> The threads of a made-up story are like the ribs of an open umbrella, far
> apart at one end and joined together at the other. You close the umbrella

and it becomes straight; you draw the threads of the story together at the end and the plot is made clear. Emanating as it does from the mind of a man or a woman, the plot is worked up so that it arouses interest and compels attention. Such an incident is unnecessary; then dispense with it. Such a character is undesirable; then away with him. Such conversation is unfitting; then substitute one more suitable.[18]

So McGill set out why he chose autobiography, while acknowledging he manipulated it by occasionally taking up 'the pen of the novelist'. He rejected the simple idea that the novel was impenetrable to working-class writers. For him, it was a containing structure which provided a neat and orderly framework but allowing much more freedom over content. He saw autobiography by contrast as fragmentary, chaotic, problematic and constrained by the compulsion to be truthful, without conventional closure and therefore also less controllable as story. It is impossible, McGill argued, to write a pure autobiography. The genre of autobiography has to permit the harnessing of factual personal truth to general, typical truths. It is ultimately a necessity for the autobiographer to use the techniques of the novel.

Most of my story is autobiographical. Moleskin Joe and Carroty Dan are true to life; they live now, and for all I know to the contrary may be met with on some precarious job in some evil-smelling model lodging house, or, as suits these gipsies of labour, on the open road. Norah Ryan's painful story shows the dangers to which an innocent girl is exposed through ignorance of the fundamental facts of existence; Gourock Ellen and Annie are types of women whom I have often met. While asking a little allowance for the pen of the novelist it must be said that nearly all the incidents of the book have come under the observation of the writer: that such incidents should take place makes the tragedy of the story.[19]

The driving force behind autobiographical writing for Patrick McGill was to display and convey to others the truth of 'what really happened' – where necessary, although not often conceded as a conscious technique, emboldened by what does or can happen, essential, typical truth. How does this emphasis on the truth tally with the notion of a reconstruction of the self, of selectiveness and choice in narrative? McGill tackled this issue too:

In this true story, as in real life, men and women crop up for a moment, do something or say something, then go away and probably never reappear again. In my story there is no train of events or sequence of incidents leading up to a desired end. When I started writing of my life I knew not how I would end my story; and even yet, seeing that one thing follows another so closely, I hardly know when to lay down my pen and say that the tale is told. Sometimes I say, 'I'll write my life up to this day and no further', but suddenly it comes to me that tomorrow may furnish a more fitting climax, and so on my story runs. In fiction you settle upon the final chapter before you begin the first, and every event is described and placed in the fabric of the story to suit an end already in view. A story of real life, like real life itself, has no beginning, no end. Something happens before and after; the first chapter succeeds another and another and another follows the last.

In his choice of autobiography as his chosen genre, he acknowledged that truth would be a construction, an interpretation or fictionalising of experience in the service of a general truth – at least as much as it would be remembering or reconstruction of historically verifiable facts. It seems he was attracted exactly by the difficulties of the genre as well as the freedoms it offers. Despite contradictions in his argument, McGill also thought autobiography had greater dramatic possibility – offering stories and characters which might be dismissed as implausible in fiction. In autobiography they would be undeniable. Ultimately, he saw a moral purpose to working-class autobiography, which was to address social justice.

I, writing a true story, cannot substitute imaginary talk for real, nor false characters for true, if I am faithful to myself and the talk imposed on me when I took to writing the story of my life. No doubt I shall have some readers weak enough to be shocked by my disclosures; men and women who, like ascetic hermits, fight temptation by running from it and avoid sin by shutting their eyes to it. But I merely tell the truth, speak of things as I have seen them. Truth needs no apologies, frankness does not deserve reproof. I write of ills which society inflicts on individuals like myself, and when possible I lay every wound open to the eyes of the world. I believe that there is an Influence for Good working through the ages, and it is only by laying our wounds open that we can hope to benefit by the Influence. Who doctors the wounds which we hide from everybody's eyes?[20]

As for others, there is an overt political meaning in telling the truth for Patrick McGill. Will Thorne drives this home in his determined appeal to readers that 'You will begin to understand'.[21] Their belief is in the importance of being understood, as essential to the progress of history, from which working-class people will only benefit if they make themselves heard. Writing is a crucial means to emancipation. McGill, like others, urges a working-class readership to take up their pens as tools of change. Indeed the 'truth' that was to be written down was in itself a tool of change. Autobiographers like McGill, in their own way, shared the Victorian insistence on the superiority of fact, epitomised by Dickens's killjoy Mr Gradgrind in *Hard Times*. For the Victorians, as W.E. Houghton commented, 'truth is not only absolute, it is attainable. And once attained, it is of course asserted dogmatically.' 'Inspired insight', Houghton argued, was characteristic of most Victorian writers, and set deep in the nineteenth-century literary tradition.[22] If writers like John Ruskin claimed the status of absolute truth for their opinions, and an authoritative statement of theory was seen as 'inspired and absolute truth', then a writer like Patrick McGill could feel on firm ground expressing lived human experience as unassailable truth. He felt reason to hope that once the truth had been conveyed, action might also be taken to improve matters.

In this sense the motivation and intentions of writers like McGill were very different from the portrayal of twentieth-century working-class culture and consciousness in Hoggart's *The Uses of Literacy*, in which he argued that working-class people make little use of generality, or exhortation to serve the general good, because they do not consider themselves affected by it. They see themselves in a more limited way, as 'the ground base of society, they know; normally they go on living their own kind of life … the local and concrete world is what can be understood, managed, trusted'. The weight of expressive forms is therefore on 'the intimate, the sensory, the detailed, and the personal'.[23] Hoggart described a class-consciousness he saw as changed by the dramas and technological advances of the twentieth century: one where the general is the other, for example the state; not a generality of conditions in which their own cultural activity could make a difference. In McGill's view, the working-class writer can harness attachment to detail, materiality and social connection – and manipulate them comfortably precisely with the idea of great movements for change in mind: educational improvement, recognition of lived experience or the struggle for better living conditions.

McGill's writing lends support to the place of special pleading within the genre of working-class realism or autobiography – or a hybrid of the two – which may be aligned more closely to other literary forms of realism than exclusively, or self-referentially, to other autobiographies. In *My Favourite Books* (1900) Robert Blatchford argued against realism as a reliable portrayal of 'things as they really are'. He proposed instead that a realist writer is 'one who describes things as they actually appear to *him*. Such a "Realist" is a literary witness who tells the truth'. He values the faithfulness to the 'spirit' of a subject rather than 'a slavish and laboured delineation of externals – as if a painter should offer an accurate anatomical study of a corpse as a picture of a living athlete'.[24]

Besides attempts to use autobiography for a new form of working-class realism, the flexibility people saw in it also meant it could carry a plurality of intentions, desires and forms of expression. Hannah Mitchell wished her autobiography to be a social, a personal and a psychological history as well as the means to a measure of fame for herself.

> *An autobiography is perhaps not quite the place for a dissertation on social reform, except in so far as one's own efforts have been devoted to such matters, but it is a glorious opportunity to talk about oneself. I have therefore tried to present a fairly comprehensive picture of my struggle to obtain some measure of personal freedom, and to leave some mark, however faint, on the sands of time.*[25]

The blending of facts and quotes from favourite books or poems with the subjective reconstruction of a life leans strongly towards the pleasures of writing about the self. For Hannah Mitchell the purpose in telling the truth is inseparable from the desire to be remembered and to be famous – and other autobiographers declared this as their first purpose. As Thomas Cooper put it:

> *If there be any gratification to be derived from the reading of my book, I think I ought to share it … if I had thought a share of such gratification would be denied me, I would not have written the book at all. Thus the reader will see that I have let the truth out, at once: I have written the book chiefly to please myself. And that, I suspect, is the chief reason why anybody writes an autobiography.*[26]

Notes

1   R. Williams, 'Commitment and Alignment', in *Marxism Today*, June 1980.
2   Barthes, 1983, pp. 185–93; R. Williams, 1977, chapter 8, 'Authors', pp. 192–4.

3   John Glynn, interview with U. Howard, Gatehouse Books, Manchester, 1985.
4   Ashford, 1844, Preface.
5   A. Williams, 1912, Preface.
6   C. Brontë, *Villette*, [1853] 1979, p. 228.
7   R. Williams, 1984, p. 74.
8   Virginia Woolf, *Women and Fiction*, 1929, quoted in Steedman, 1988, p. 3.
9   R. Williams, *op. cit.*, p. 74.
10 Steedman, *op. cit.*, pp. 2–3.
11 Vincent, 1982, p. 5.
12 Kundera, 1979, p. 105. Kundera makes a distinction between 'human being and writer' in terms of audience: 'Tamina feels that the eyes of a single outsider are enough to destroy the worth of her personal diaries, while Goethe thinks that if a single individual *fails* to set eyes on his lines, that individual calls his – Goethe's – entire existence into question.'
13 Douglass, 1976, p. 207; Margaret Bearfield, Brighton, taped interview with U. Howard, 1993.
14 Jones, 1938, pp. 42–3.
15 A. Errington, 'Coal and Rails, the Autobiography of Anthony Errington', TS, Brunel University Library, p. 1.
16 R. Williams, 1977, pp.147–8.
17 McGill, 1914, p. 229.
18 *ibid.*, p. 112.
19 *ibid.*, Foreword.
20 *ibid.*, pp. 111–12.
21 Thorne, 1925, p. 13.
22 Houghton, 1957, p. 144.
23 Hoggart, 1958, p. 104.
24 Blatchford, 1900, pp. 222–33.
25 H. Mitchell, 1977, p. 239.
26 Cooper, [1872] 1971, p. 2.

CHAPTER 6

Cracked bobbins and showers of frogs: connections in creativity

I

One aspect of his childhood which the Chartist Thomas Cooper describes with passion is his musical education. His longing to understand music seems to stand in for all his regrets, unfulfilled hopes and dreams:

> *How often I have wished that the dulcimer had been a violin, or a pianoforte, and that I had been taught music by the notes … Such wishes are vain; but I have them, and of various forms. 'Oh that I had been trained to music – or painting – or law – or medicine – or any profession in which mind is needed; or that I had been regularly educated, so that I might have reached a University!' – I say, I often catch myself at these wishes still – even at sixty-six.*

Elsewhere Cooper writes of other enthusiasms: how he 'fell upon the project of drawing with slate and pencil; but became still more attached to cutting out shapes in paper. With a pair of scissors, I used often to work for hours, making figures of men, horses, cows, dogs, and birds'.[1]

This chapter explores the creativity of working-class writers, whose work has generally not been associated with creativity or originality. Writing a life story (or a fragment of one), a diary or a poem is a creative process, but to assert the nature of creativity or what counts as literature is not straightforward. As Williams wrote in *The Long Revolution*, 'it would be a brave man who would say … that he is sure … what "creative" quite

181

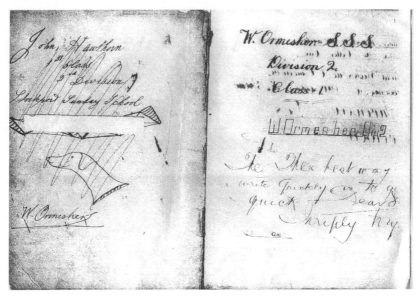

Sunday school learner W. Ormesher's copy book, illustrating his efforts at writing styles and drawing. The book has been passed on from previous users
Courtesy of Stockport Local Heritage Library

means'. To understand what motivated people who were not socially or culturally well-placed to take up drawing or expressive writing to go ahead and do so, we need a definition which assesses their work in terms of creativity, as well as skill, and as art as well as a social phenomenon. The concept of 'culture' may enable the inclusion of a wider range of writing as creative. It becomes 'cultural production', part of a culture or way of life. Seeing working-class writing as cultural production counteracts those condescending commentaries which have simultaneously praised and undermined writings as laudable efforts made in unpromising contexts; which view autobiography as an unreliable historical source in its own right, useful mainly for corroborating or challenging official, documentary sources; or which do not dwell long on the content of writing, beyond its authentic illustration of working-class life. My aim is to explore writings as imaginative literature as well as life stories, focusing on the creative processes, tensions and forces which shaped narratives, both by obscure writers and those who did achieve critical recognition.

182

Working-class autobiography reveals what Williams calls 'a vital imaginative life and the deep effort to describe new experience'. Autobiographies are 'intense forms of general communication' demonstrating that the struggle to 'remake ourselves … is often very painful'. Williams includes communication as an essential element of creativity in contrast with theories of romanticism or modernism, which value only 'special inspiration', the revelation of 'superior reality', and an exceptional 'uniqueness' of vision as the essential qualities of the creative mind. Williams's theory of creativity, taking account of the communication of new experience, is sweepingly inclusive in comparison with the paradigm of art as original, individual work which has generally assumed a middle-class frame of reference: an elite or meritocratic education, time, privacy and space. Working-class writers believed passionately in their writing precisely because they wanted to describe and interpret experience which was new as art, written by people new to art and original in the sense that it had never been voiced before. Their motivation to write is clear from the introductions to hundreds of autobiographies, which explain and justify the search to find a voice, 'the means by which the experience could be shared'. Williams's argument that art and culture are 'ordinary' implies paradoxically that far more people's writing needs to be seen as extraordinary. 'There are no "ordinary" activities if by "ordinary" we mean the absence of creative interpretation and effort'. Communication, 'the process of making unique experience into common experience', is the missing conceptual piece which facilitates a theory of creativity which is inclusive.[2] This creativity is also the making of common group or class experience, through the process of writing, into a unique communication about the nature of social and individual experience from a class, gender, or ethnic position. Nineteenth-century working-class autobiography is a form of social and individual creativity. It is the reconstruction of a life and a selfhood, using memory and imagination as well as such facts as can be garnered. Most writers acknowedge their connections with others in coming to write in positive and negative ways. They are conscious of the ideologies and circumstances within which life has been lived, and the powerful structures which make writing difficult and unexpected. The actual production of writing can therefore become a disconcerting, even subversive event.

I will explore creativity from several overlapping angles: the relationships between writing, drawing, reading and other forms of artistic expression; the relationship of education to creativity; the significance and complexity of memory in writing life stories; the use of imagination, hopes, fantasies and day-dreams in life stories; and the role of others in developing creativity and the impact of becoming a writer on social belonging; and finally creativity and the process of writing itself.

II   Art and writing: sources of inspiration

I told everyone I spoke to that I wanted to be a writer. Or a painter. I had brought a box of water-colours with me.[3]

In working-class autobiography, writers often drew striking connections between the significance of writing and other art forms in the emergence of their view of themselves as possessing creative energies. In the quotation above V.S. Pritchett makes connections between the creative fields he wants to explore. First, writing is not his sole creative interest, which is also true of other writers. Writing sometimes seems to serve as the carry-all for the development of other talents, such as drawing, painting or music, which were even more often denied for lack of time and money. More positively, writing sometimes emerges as an enthusiasm which has been inspired by other art forms. Thomas Cooper plays with different outlets for his creative energies during his childhood, clustering music, art and medicine together as areas in which his hopes for self-expression were dashed. He pays little attention to writing as a preoccupation of his childhood years. But writing is the only element of his longing for creative achievement which could be realised to the point of public recognition and as a means of livelihood. This is true of many writers: a livelihood in music, theatre or a circus life was among the dreams which faded because leaving the neighbourhood was impossible, and such activities were suspected as disreputable compared with writing, which was woven into the fabric of local educational and religious activities.

Even if writing was the only possible creative outlet, art offered at least some training in producing images and developing the imagination. Many working people learned crafts which involved making things from wood, stone, iron, cloth and much besides: buildings, furniture, household objects, clothes, decorative artefacts and many more. A visual sense was needed for many traditional crafts. For Cooper and many other working-class writers, his visual sense was strongest. The drawing of images was essential to pre-literate written communication. For some,

184

intimate knowledge of the nature and the local countryside offered vivid imagery which they later used in writing. For Cooper, the sense of an unknown natural world glimpsed through exotic displays at seasonal travelling shows fed a lifelong pleasure in visual representation, and coloured the imaginative landscapes of his childhood. Cooper describes the early experiments with shape which these inspired:

> *I have many pleasant remembrances of the time that we lived in the house in front of Sailor's Alley. Miller – my close companion – began, like myself, to cut shapes in paper, and to draw and colour. Our greatest incitement to drawing was the exhibition of pictures on the outside of the wild-beast shows at the Mart … To run and look at these pictures, and come home, and imitate the figures of elephants, lions, tigers, leopards, zebras, and gorgeously-coloured tropical birds, formed a busy occupation … and to copy and improve upon our pictures was an enthusiastic employment for many weeks after.*

Cooper also uses descriptions of tropical fruits and birds which he hears about from a neighbour – and his own collections of wild flowers, which he 'could worship for several days', enchanted by their names – as ways of allowing his imagination to roam freely, as well as to develop technical skills and factual knowledge of the natural world. He also remembers the pleasures of writing and painting as connected activities. He wrote about how his uncle, an illiterate letter-carrier whom Cooper helped after school hours, reading the directions on letters and parcels, helped him in return:

> *He made much of me … always gave me a few coppers for my writing papers, lead pencils, and water colours; and indeed showed every disposition to indulge me. I thus became greatly attached to him … plain, unlettered man though he was.* [4]

Imaginary landscapes were also an escape from the limitations of real ones. Fred Kitchen, a farm labourer brought up on a country estate in Yorkshire at the turn of the century, connects roaming the woods, reading and fantasising as central to his memories of childhood:

> *At an early age I learned of a world beyond the boundary-wall of the park, and in fancy I journeyed in Lady Brassey's Sunbeam, or got*

185

*wrecked on The Coral Island ... Being fond of reading and drawing, and
the study of nature, it was the opinion of my elders and betters that I ought
to be put to something ... But circumstances arose that made of me a farm
labourer, and I never regret being one.*[5]

Connections between writing and art, particularly drawing, are often
made in autobiographies. William Wright recollects winning competitions, set up by the eccentric mill-owner, for poetry and 'drawing animals
or anything we liked'. Wright's interest grew into a 'taste for sculpture in a
primitive kind of way'.[6] He developed his art by carving figures from large
stones smuggled into his bedroom, and this eventually led to his apprenticeship to a stone-mason. He later worked in the theatre, developing his
skills as a 'scenic artist', and designing posters and advertisements which
he set to rhyme. Over time he wrote more poetry and was able to sell his
work to the local press.

William Lovett describes how his mother encouraged his writing,
drawing, carving and digging and his creation of a flower garden from an
old ruin next to their home. Despite their poverty, she prefers to find
money for creative pastimes rather than risk his falling in with 'vicious
associates'. He describes drawing sketches of birds and flowers, 'more
showy than natural', and provides a meticulous description of his experiments with art materials:

> *My first colours, however, were only bits of different coloured stones, which
> I found on the beach, or dug out of the rocks when the tide was out, and
> which I rubbed down on another stone. But having copied out some bills
> for a German quack doctor, who ... gave me some information about the
> names, and the mixing of water colours, as well as the place and mode of
> purchasing better drawing materials at the market town ... I went and
> bought a few brilliant sorts, and the very showy productions these enabled
> me to make, soon met with a ready market among the neighbours.*[7]

Lovett carves birds, birdcages and boats, raising money for new items from
the sales of the previous ones. He shows how someone who later became
a writer interpreted and used his environment to follow a child's curiosi-
ties creatively. His rural community becomes a complex of networks in
which one individual could engage in all sorts of ways. Activities overlap
and feed each other, so that there is no rift between creative and
mechanical skills.

Patrick Barclay was the son of an Irish rag-and-bone collector in Leicester. He started work aged eight and stayed in unskilled work all his life, learning at Sunday school, night school and the working men's college. He became a socialist, writing and lecturing on social issues. Barclay links his ability to write with his talent for drawing, believing that his 'propensity to draw and sketch [was] brought over from some previous generation' because 'I never saw father draw nor sketch and mother never could write her own name'. Her first language was Gaelic, and however poor her writing skills were, she taught him to 'read and spell' in English. His first attempts at writing and drawing were scratching marks on bricks with slate splinters. His first remembered creative impulse was a desire to paint: 'I want to be a painter and with the painters stand. I study a book of replicas of engravings by Michelangelo; I paint the Blessed Virgin in water-colours, positive, red, blue and yellow; roses in cheeks, halo, and smile, and perfectly regular young features … idealised out of all semblance to reality.'[8] His long list of enthusiasms includes becoming an actor, a monk, a student of theology and Latin, a musician and an entertainer. He both celebrates and caricatures his ambitious childhood self, but has a sober realism about the limits to ambition for unschooled workers. It is easy to dismiss aspirations like Barclay's as fast-moving fantasies, the 'wanting it all' of childhood. But they express a wider view among those who learned informally of human creativity, which was not about specialist fields of expertise. They saw their own creative learning extending across a rich landscape in which their practices somehow flowed into each other. For them, it was not innate lack of talent or drive which frustrated a flowering of potential: their energies were destroyed by other forces and other people's decisions. Much later, V.S. Pritchett observed the connection between the natural world, painting and writing. Here he describes an episode in Suffolk during his turbulent childhood, where the pictures hanging on his aunt's wall and his walks in Barlow Woods educated him about Gainsborough:

> I liked painting and I wondered, when I walked to the lane where Gainsborough had painted his elms, whether some of that influence would fall upon me. The thought of being a writer had not occurred to me. I did feel that I could choose some studious kind of life but the barriers to knowledge seemed to me far too great. I would not have to read or know, to be a painter. A picture took one instantly through a door into another world, one like our own but silent. There were no raised voices … In

187

*Ipswich, in that peaceful interregnum of my boyhood, the idea of being a
painter began to dawdle in my mind.*

But we left.

Pritchett's attempts to pursue different ambitions faltered because of a
series of setbacks: 'midnight flits to avoid the landlord' or the lack of a
dictionary to decipher the twopenny Latin primer he buys. Then, an
eccentric teacher introduces him to the *English Review* and 'converts' him
to writing. The writers he reads in it are 'as alive as Barlow Woods … In
Ipswich I had been drawn to painting and now in poems and stories, I saw
pictures growing out of the print … the art of writing became a manual
craft as attractive – to a boy – as the making of elderberry pipes or
carpentering. My imagination woke up.'[9]

The links between writing and visual art were reinforced at school.
Pupils were asked to approach handwriting as a graphic form in which a
socially-appropriate aesthetics of handwriting applied. 'Ladies' Hand' was
best for women; elaborate flourishes for those whose signature needed to
be impossible to forge; legal hand for lawyers' clerks; neatness for
commercial copying; rudimentary round-hand for elementary or Adult
School learners. Rapidly-changing fashions were driven by aesthetic,
social, behavioural and educational considerations. School-based writing
exercises emphasised the visual properties of writing, asking pupils to
draw before they wrote, either abstract strokes or stylised drawings of
animals or ships. These were designed for accuracy and conformity more
than individuality, but they entrenched the association between writing
and drawing. The tools for writing and drawing, as writers recall in detail,
were often the same. In *The Trodden Road*, Albert Mansbridge, founder of
the WEA, remembers

*writing with a slate pencil a reproduction of a story about a rat taking
refuge on a swan's back during a flood. The teacher much admired my
effort, and I can still see that swan. If subconsciously I start drawing on an
agenda paper at a committee, it is always a swan.*[10]

There is a long history to the links between writing and drawing in the
emergence of alphabetic scripts from hieroglyphics and other image-
based systems, and in the gradual encoding of pictures or tallying devices
into the abstract symbols of an alphabet. By the nineteenth century,

writing had long become record, transaction, communication between people and the main medium of imaginative expression. Drawing had become technical, mathematical and illustrative (of writing) and above all art. As literacy spread across Europe, the reading public grew. Only the working-class and peasantry were not expected to write. Among these, people who desired writing but found it difficult to access seem to have connected visual imagery and verbal expression as they made their first attempts at writing. The person learning to write may have related to writing and drawing in ways comparable to those experienced by whole societies when the original transformation to alphabetic literacy was taking place. They were comfortable with objects and pictures. While literacy progressively became part of daily life, the images and shapes of representational drawing remained part of their experience and ways of shaping meaning. Perhaps people new to writing were still positioned between pre-literate and literate cultures.

III   Reading and writing

If art was crucial to writing, so was the interaction between reading and writing in the creative process. The connections between reading and writing are visible in many autobiographies. The absorbing of ideas and images from reading and their influence on a person's ambition to write and the processes and craft of learning to write (the literacy and literary aspects) are sometimes explicit in autobiographies, and sometimes unacknowledged but still discernible in the style of writing. The influence on emerging writers of their range of reading deserves a full study of its own. Images, ideas and writing styles they had absorbed clearly made their mark on writers, resources with which they grappled to produce their own literature. This short section and the many places in which a writer's reading history crops up elsewhere in this book, cannot do justice to such a rich area. A few instances serve to illustrate how important and energising reading was for autobiographers and other writers: access to books; time to read; the range of reading; what was valued and what was avoided. These examples provide glimpses into ways in which the power of stories and imagery associated with reading influenced the development of writing.

In Alice Foley's *A Bolton Childhood*, the connecting image between her reading and writing is a cracked bobbin, which rolled about the floor while her father, 'who had managed to scrape the twopence per week

189

required for his basic schooling', read aloud Dickens and Eliot to the family.

> *During these sessions her mother, who could neither read nor write, firmly held an old, cracked bobbin inside the heel of a stocking, zigzagging the needle of coarse black wool across a gaping hole. Now and again … the bobbin slipped from her lap and, with an odd chuckling sound, rolled wickedly away on its one remaining flange. We children … hailed the fugitive bobbin with glee.*

For Foley this emblem holds deep meaning. Her mother's name for it was 'throstle bobbin', which added a romantic association with song birds. It sparks a connection between the rare creative and comforting times in a childhood otherwise portrayed as harsh – and the emergence of Alice Foley's own creative self. The 'little cracked treasure' becomes the emblem of a dual identity. She identifies herself with her stoic mother but also with the creative public self she has forged. The cracked bobbin evokes 'fragmentary, yet imperishable moments, crystallised by the passing years, of a mother's … endurance of the sum of human frailties and fecklessness – a strange blossoming of spirit in an odd corner of strife and poverty'. The 'spirit' and the memory are hers. It is 'a' mother, as well as her mother, she describes.[11]

Jack Lawson claims that reading aloud taught him to write. It was his duty as a child, because he was the most literate family member, to read to his family, 'all the grim tragedies, trials, and accounts of hangings … But I little knew, as I read to my mother hour after hour, week by week, that I was learning to articulate, to emphasise the dramatic, and that I was also learning the ways of mankind'.[12]

These two examples show the enduring power of reading aloud as an inspirational medium, in oral and literate cultures. But the pleasure and struggle involved in reading to oneself, or as part of mutual improvement societies, are also dominant themes in autobiography. Dickens stands out as the author most often acknowledged as inspirational by autobiographers. George Gissing wrote that 'for at least five-and-twenty years of his life there was not one English-speaking household in the world … where his name was not as familier as that of any personal acquaintance, and where an allusion to characters of his creating could fail to be understood'. When Charles Shaw referred to himself as being refreshed 'like a giant' in his solitary space, he used the same phrase Dickens used for places he could 'think and dream'. *Great Expectations* in particular appears as a book whose autobiographical mode and social-class themes of learning and difference were relevant to autobiographers.[13] Despite the well-documented suspicion of fiction in working-class culture, often announced by autobiographers, the full picture of reading practices which emerges is much more complex. Perhaps working people read more fiction than has been thought, but did not want to say so for fear of moral disapproval. Perhaps Dickens, Kingsley and those writers who represented life from a working-class perspective are exceptions. It certainly seems that Dickens was more avidly read among working people than histories have suggested. The serialised form of his novels made them more accessible and affordable than books, so people of every class could get caught up in the public mood of excitement and a sense of belonging to a culture which read and talked about popular fiction. Working-class readership of fiction grew later in the century as attitudes towards it softened over the generations, and this is reflected in autobiography. Since reading slips into writing at unconscious levels as part of the language we hold in common, Dickens seems to have lodged himself in writers' minds, just as their experiences were lodged in his.

IV   Creativity in working-class schooling

From the mid-nineteenth century, the methods of teaching writing and drawing in school were very different from the ways of informal, community-based education. Drawing was valued as an important component of the official school curriculum. It was a preparatory subject for writing, and judged to be useful 'in after life, to the carpenter, the mason and the mechanic in every branch of labour'. To help to prepare for writing lessons, school inspectors encouraged drawing with chalk on blackboards, and one inspector wrote of monitors 'scrawling outlines of objects, on slates' and 'the cheerful application of little hands in chalking, scrawling, writing and sewing'.[14] As learners progressed, the teaching of writing and drawing focused more on their ability to draw straight lines, rectilinear forms and curves. Schools where drawing was not sufficiently technical drew criticism from HMIs. For the first ten years after the introduction of the Revised Code in 1862, the curriculum shrank to those core subjects which attracted government grants. It was only gradually, after 1870, that subjects such as figurative drawing, and the 'object lesson', put back elements of the visual into schooling, though in very controlled forms. The history of education in this respect is again about gains and losses. The growth of state-controlled popular education provided more opportunities for skills acquisition for more people, but at the cost of creativity and self-expression.

Later in the century, childhood experiences of art and writing were less likely to have been related to home and community life or the stimulus offered by the local countryside. There may well be a connection between the decline of interest in art and poetry, as evidenced by the number of references in autobiographies to the poverty of official curricula, and a lack of interest in artistic expression or 'idea-activity' from the 1860s in elementary and continuation schools. After the arrival of state elementary schools, families who knew their children were going to school were under less pressure to give away pennies from a survival budget than when they were the sole supporters of children's learning. They still had to pay towards writing and drawing materials in schools, and most could scarcely have afforded additional materials. Before the era of state schooling some parents may have provided children with better incentives for imagination and curiosity than the curriculum designers and teacher-trainers of state-run schools.

Education in state-supported schools also contrasted with the diverse and sometimes contradictory motives of informal adult learners. Thomas Cooper for one tried to combine his desire for artistic development with his wish to learn the skills of political journalism for his livelihood. The purposes of the state were simpler. The knowledge the state considered necessary and attractive was knowledge which would be useful to society, and it has been argued that 'by the late 1840s the failure of attempts to improve the artistic skill of British workmen by means of evening classes in schools of design had been recognised'. Many Mechanics' Institutes gradually became, like schools of design, the preserve of the middle classes, which could explain why working-class participation did not flourish evenly in them. The last decade of the century saw legislation which enabled local state funding for vocational education and reinvigorated the Mechanics Institutes' role in working-class education.[15]

Artistic talents were not always crushed under the weight of institutional priorities. But in autobiographies, celebration of the creativity of self-education or community education is sometimes muted by ambivalence and a loss of confidence after the advent of universal schooling. What is apparent in some written responses to state education is a gap between the experience and meaning of creativity to those writers who

192

have managed to tell their stories of schooling, and the professional educators for whom writing or drawing was more a mechanistic means to an end. Only a minority of inspectors viewed drawing as valuable in developing an artistic sensibility or a skill in its own right. Drawing was built into the school curriculum overwhelmingly as a technical subject – good preparation for employment. By 1855, 18,988 children were learning drawing under the regulations of the state's Science and Art Department.[16]

Methods of teaching handwriting from the 1850s re-emphasised the links between the learning of writing and drawing as art. Stokes's writing manual reversed the customary order of learning skills, claiming that the art of writing led to a taste for drawing. Stokes illustrates his ideas with pen drawings based on the waning custom of drawing stylised flourishes. By the turn of the century, theorists of handwriting were beginning to espouse methods which used a child's love of free 'scribble', drawing and making shapes. In *A New Method of Teaching Writing to Infants*, Burke emphasised that the teaching of writing should 'follow Nature's plan', bringing scribble 'within bounds'.[17]

New ideas about education emerged towards the end of the century, which aimed to release the imagination, including those of the influential socialist educator Margaret McMillan. She was concerned with physiological functioning, as well as sensory awareness and imagination. The large free movements she advocated aimed to train motor control by first allowing children to write 'almost with the whole body'. Small-hand copy-books were to be replaced with large surfaces for drawing and writing. Subsequently, controls would be gradually introduced and effected through setting smaller and smaller scale exercises, enabling children to shrink and shape their work into conformity. The aim was to correct the errors of earlier times when children were taught to write by first exercising tight control of the fingers and movements. McMillan argued that if taught to draw freely, a child is eventually more likely to write well, because 'he has not learned the things that stop him, or make his hand feeble'. Freedom serves the purpose of eventual discipline, by using children's natural movements and inclinations in order to rear the rational and neat adult worker.[18]

Even the Pestalozzian concept of 'sense-impressionism', which lay at the heart of the object lesson, aimed to offer elementary science and skills in detailed observation rather than imaginative development or knowledge of the natural world. The object – the cow, the squirrel or a piece of calico – was displayed in isolation from any context. The object lesson involved the drawing of images on the blackboard or from copy-books. It was intended to inculcate facts about unfamiliar creatures or objects, although some commentators felt pupils would be 'open-eyed and receptive' to the novelty of teachers drawing rather than lecturing.[19] These strategies were also symptomatic of an increasingly urban education system, introducing 'Nature' to children who lacked any experience of the rural world. Many autobiographers would certainly have agreed that a purely urban childhood left a fundamental gap in human experience. They remember rural childhoods and express a sense of a lost world in romantic reconstructions of the hours they spent wandering in lanes and fields. In political discourses from the sympathetic to the damning, working-class urban life became a site of moral danger and deprivation in contrast to the benign influence of rural ways of life. McMillan's concern to reintroduce imagination into schooling focused on drawing, composition and nature study. She too saw the 'artificial conditions' of an urban working-class education as a serious problem. Children should draw, model, write and build, releasing powers of speech and imagination which in turn would enable an understanding of science. In this approach, drawing was a subject which connected science with humanities.

V   Writing and memory

Writers explore the terms 'memory' and 'memories' as essential components of their creativity. Memory is frequently presented as a consciously and deliberately-used instrument: as recall, as a set of unproblematised recollections. Memory is also cited as an active agent, cajoling a person to write. The act of writing itself generates more memories. Other versions and interpretations of memory are also evident, but less often acknowledged is the idea of memory as theatre, but muted, unconscious and involuntary, urging a person to write, but more elusively. When someone starts writing a life history, different levels of memory are activated, from well-remembered and rehearsed events and feelings to traces from deeper unconscious levels, which may be faint but are still recoverable. Recalling, reconstructing and excavating are all at work. Memory is fertile soil and active agent. Well-remembered, prominent sets of events coexist with half-buried or forgotten events and feelings which writing has unearthed in narratives conveying a version of a life where outlines of a less composed self can be glimpsed. Working-class autobiographers created a

194

self in memory and through memory. Texts are littered with clues: images, lists, and awkward juxtapositions. The past is re-enacted and re-formed through processes which echo Walter Benjamin's description of the workings of memory:

> *Memory is not an instrument for exploring the past but its theatre. It is the medium of past experience as the ground is the medium in which dead cities lie interred. He who seeks to approach his own buried past must conduct himself like a man digging.*

In this way, autobiographies reflect what Benjamin called the 'cautious probing of the spade in the dark loam'. The exposed material might possibly be seen as 'merely the inventory of one's discoveries, and not this dark joy of the place of the finding itself'.[20] But the choice of which events or feelings are mentioned, and which are skirted over or just hinted at, exposes the creative processes of the search. Some writers were clearly conscious of the significance of material which is hidden in memory, pushing against the pressure to conform to a mode of working-class autobiography shaped by conventions about recounting 'memories' rather than exploring the deeper meanings of memory.

In order to write about a life rather than merely to make a record of events, half-remembered dreams, fantasies, hopes, dreads, pleasures, pain and the lyricism present in any life have to be reconstructed. It was a harder task for writers to re-explore the deeper meanings of any of these than simply to dust off memories like objects standing year after year on the mantelpiece. Though autobiographers may have been conceptually unaware of the complexity of memory, they showed its workings in the writing process. Freud's concept of screen memory enriches understandings of the pattern of memory and language in writing life stories. In the soil of memory lie not only whole objects, but, following Benjamin's metaphor, archaeological fragments: traces of earlier, more deeply significant, events, which have been repressed. Apparently insignificant memories are mapped onto some actual memory-trace which acts as a point of contact for the screen memory. Reading autobiography demands alertness to these traces because they enable significant points of creativity to become visible: the forming and crystallising of the meanings of childhood experiences at different points. This theory suggests that a significant, then repressed, memory is not formed at the point of experience at all. It is formed later, either in childhood, when an association with it is made, or as late as old age, when it could surface, mediated through writing. Freud wrote:

> *One is forced ... to suspect that in the so-called earliest childhood*
> *memories we possess not the genuine memory-trace but a later revision of*
> *it, a revision which may have been subject to the influences of a variety of*
> *later psychical forces. Thus the 'childhood memories' of individuals come in*
> *general to acquire the significance of 'screen memories' and in doing so offer*
> *a remarkable analogy with the childhood memories that a nation preserves*
> *in its store of legends and myths.*[21]

It is not only for personal reasons that, as Freud suggests elsewhere, 'distressing memories succumb especially easily to motivated forgetting',[22] but also because they do not conform to national legends or myths. In the case of working-class autobiography, the pressure of social conformity is also attached to the pressure of class loyalties, myths and legends.

On the surface, autobiography appears to have offered an unproblematic form for the chronological unfolding of memories and changing material circumstances. People did not choose autobiography as a way of working through conflict or to 'raise' forgotten memories hibernating in the unconscious. The act of writing, however, can reactivate dormant experiences, feelings and traumas. The writing can then become a struggle to keep feelings in their place, concentrating on material from the memory which is seen as salient to a public narrative.

Hannah Mitchell remembers a sweet-natured, enviably well-educated and submissive blind girl who lived close by and died while Hannah was still a child. Mitchell's idealised portrayal of her neighbour's accomplishments, femininity and frailty contrasts with her still-angry account of her own transgressive self and her punitive, forbidding mother, whom she cannot love or own as a role model although they are both strong-minded, angry female actors. In adulthood, her mother nursed Hannah through a breakdown and their shared emotional brittleness is understood. But Mitchell still cannot fully gain access to or accept the connections between her mother, her own angry childhood self and who she has driven herself to become.[23]

Adam Rushton, presents a different understanding of how memory works in the development of a creative self:

My strongest impulse to write, I think, comes from the great cloud of witnesses which memory presents to view. Under memory's vivid light my life course spreads out before me like a map, with numerous pathways displayed, along which innumerable beings come and go. There, clearly marked, is the road I trod in childhood's days, leading to lonely woodlands where birds built their nests ... There it was I passionately desired to live and learn, and labour all my days. But from that happy pathway I was rudely torn, and thrust on to a rough and dismal road which broke my health and broke my heart.

From a young age, day-labouring on farms, and factory and warehouse 'slavery', consumed his energies until he devised ways of learning to write, starting with Sunday school. His own desires and fantasies lived on but his problem was to find the means to act on them. For Adam Rushton memory is light itself, enabling him to see the past as a map. Writing is the hard-won skill which he sensed early on would matter if he was to use the map to set out his story. Rushton's use of his metaphorical map is close to Benjamin's digging out of a buried past. To write his life story, Rushton dug out his own collection of earlier writings, books and the pictures on his walls – the pieces of archaeological debris underneath the map: 'piles of old letters are beside me, bringing vividly to view the forms and aspects of the writers ... Heaps of diaries crowded with sketches, narratives and experiences are also there' where he has recorded 'facts and fancies, joys and sorrows, successes and failures'.[24] The artefacts here are all writings or drawings which interact with memory to give him the materials for his life story.

Memory is always at play in the decision to write after long periods have elapsed between lived experiences, early hopes and dreams and the time when writing is possible. Memory not only helps to reactivate and reconstruct stories, fantasies and regrets from the past, but is also a motivating force which drives writing. Mary Luty wrote in her autobiographical fragment, 'My Life has Sparkled', that 'memory urged me vigorously to get pen and paper, and record something of the days now long past'.[25] Memory seems to be many things at once for writers: an instrument for exploring the past; the theatre of the past; the director of the script; and the way of realising the meaning of a life by transporting both writer and audience back into the past. For 'Lord' George Sanger, in *Seventy Years a Showman*, it makes the writer the holder of a magic box from which memories which have been stored can be spilled out:

A long, long, day is waning at last. Here in the waning shadows of the Garden of Life I pause awhile. I want to drink in the scene. I want to realise the full meaning of it all. Rest – yes, I can rest now … I shall carry you with me back to the days of my boyhood, when the conditions of life for all classes of workers, and for show-folk in particular, were harsh and hard to a degree unknown to the present generation. You shall be shown how the peep show carried in a box on the back of the showman grew into a wagon, and the wagon into many caravans and a great combination.[26]

VI   Dreams, day-dreams and daily life

Autobiographies express the longing to develop creative possibilities, while making it very clear how unlikely this is in the unrelenting demands of working life which begin to invade the spaces for learning and imagination even in childhood. The worlds of work and play, reality and dreaming, are in constant dialogue in early memories, teasing out how the fantastical is at play with the mundane, until the realisation of the meaning of adulthood and the unremitting struggle for economic survival crowd out playfulness almost completely. Not until the relative leisure of old age is the recapture of some of the essence of childhood creativity possible.

Two passages in Thomas Cooper's book highlight how in nineteenth-century working-class childhoods, nature – fields, hedgerows and wildlife – offered romance, freedom and mysterious happenings, despite being the same places where people laboured for a living. Fantasy and reality merged and fed the imagination. One passage in his book describes waking up at night in the carrier's cart to see hundreds of 'small, dull, strange-looking lights, scattered over the wide field', which his uncle tells him are a curiously large number of glow-worms. For Cooper this moment is an abiding 'vision of wonder'. In another story, Cooper fends off rational explanations of natural phenomena:

I saw a shower of live frogs. I record this, because I have read … in … books affecting great fidelity to facts in science, that such a sight is impossible. I am as sure of what I relate as I am of my own existence. The minute frogs, jumping alive, fell on the pavement at our feet, and came tumbling down the spouts from the tiles of the houses into the water-tubs.[27]

He wants the frogs to be a magical visitation. Vincent observed of little-schooled writers that 'the exercise of the imagination was the greatest and most persistent incentive for gaining a command of the tools of literacy, and their first and most satisfying application'.[28] Writing and drawing were also ways of extending imaginative life in diverse ways. And gaining literacy itself was a powerful element of an imagined world of pleasure and creativity – as much the object of desires and dreams as the means of expressing them.

Freud's 'Creative Writers and Day-Dreaming' explores the meanings of fantasy in creative writing in ways which help to facilitate thought about autobiographical writing in the nineteenth century. Autobiographies may often claim to be concerned wholly with material facts and circumstances, yet they reveal deeper psychological layers of life experience. Imagination, longing and desire exist in autobiography in a different way to fiction. But psychic, linguistic and emotional connections between the adult writer and the young self about whom he or she is writing are expressed directly and indirectly. Freud writes that 'every child at play behaves like a creative writer in that he creates a world of his own, or, rather, rearranges the things of his world in a new way which pleases him'. For the adult, he argues, 'fantasy' replaces play. 'He builds castles in the air and creates what are called "*day-dreams*". I believe that most people construct fantasies at times in their lives.' A writer 'softens the character of his egoistic day-dreams by altering and disguising it, and he bribes us by the purely formal – that is, aesthetic – yield of pleasure which he offers us in the presentation of his fantasies'. However, the material on which any writer works, following Freud's argument, is similar in many respects. It is the 're-fashioning of ready-made and familiar material'. In this material, the hero, male or female, represents the egoistic day-dreamer, or, in the psychological novel, many characters represent parts of an ego, which the writer through self-observation recognises to be split. In this way the conflicting currents of his/her mental life can be better captured. The material and context for the day-dream or for creative writing are derived 'from the popular treasure-house of myths, legends and fairy tales', whether based on individual fantasy or part of a collective fantasy which has become myth. For Freud, the true artist 'understands how to elaborate his day-dreams'. They can become part of stories which are interesting to others.[29]

The influence of psychology at the turn of the century opened up space for ideas about how to nurture the imaginative life of working-class children. Margaret McMillan took up Freud's idea in *Education through the Imagination* (1904), arguing that 'daydreaming, reverie, hallucinations, etc., are abortive forms of imagination'. Imagination was a 'creative power', and regularly active in everyone except 'the lowest type of idiot'. She saw fulfilled creativity as a two-stage process: 'all our vague hopes, our shadowy schemes represent ... the twilight of creative energy'. These 'obscure' activities of mind could be enhanced into clarity by 'the effort and desire' of the conscious mind.[30]

The exacting material circumstances which held up the working-through of ideas and imaginative fantasies into writing until much later in life make Freud's concept of day-dreaming problematic for creative expression. A full-time professional writer has time to allow day-dreams to emerge and crystallise into meaningful ideas. Working-class writers had precious little time for contemplation. But what they reveal is sometimes surprising. Some thought their long hours of working life and poverty as positive rather than negative influences, as we will see in later chapters. Work which is more physically than mentally exacting arguably allows more room for creative thought and fantasy than detailed clerical work. Nevertheless, lack of time and opportunity for developing the creative self pervades much writing. The autobiographer J.D. Fox is typical in the sense that his 'daydreams' and 'strong desires' in childhood are interwoven with a sense of loss about becoming adult, reducing space and time for creativity to 'spare moments', writing that 'I have come far short of those dreams'.[31] The reflective aspects of autobiography which explore the deeper sources of a desire to write and convey more of the inner self are often detached from the main narrative in prefaces, childhood sections and postscripts. The preoccupations of adult life, especially in men's autobiographies, are dominated by work, external events, family matters, social and political engagements, hurdles crossed, achievements and disasters. Interior life or emotional conflicts, when they appear, are often interruptions to another story, or recognisable as abrupt endings, signifi-cant silences or oblique associations with difficult childhood experiences and remembered feelings. Writers often know what is going on. The suffragette, factory worker and Ruskin College correspondence course student Annie Kenney wrote that: 'My life has been varied and restless, and yet underneath all the outward restlessness there is a silence that is deep and real.' The best time of the day for her was the time after her mother had ordered, 'Silence, children!': 'Then I was happy. I began my real life, far more real to me than the life of the day. All through my life, the day's work over, I have lived in dreams.'[32] Florence White, a working cook, traces her love of day-dreaming to the death of her mother and a romantic longing to join her in the afterlife: 'Soon the next world became as real to me as any other place I had never seen … Ever since, I have had two lives; one in my imagination and one in my ordinary everyday life'.[33]

In *Chapters in the Life of a Dundee Factory Boy*, the anonymous writer's childhood was shattered by his father's transportation for murder. At several levels, dreams were important to him, and he was influenced by 'The Dream' in *Pilgrim's Progress*, 'the glorious dream'; and inspired by his own greatest dream – to be famous as a writer: 'To write a book that young and old read and admire, and the character of which becomes familiar as household words, is surely the greatest triumph.'[34] Much of the Dundee factory boy's writing was gleaned from fairy tales, adventures and myths, as well as readings of *Pilgrim's Progress*, *Robinson Crusoe*, *Roderick Random* and other books which inspired him, including autobiographical novels which, like Dickens's *David Copperfield*, tell stories of escape from harsh and unpromising childhoods.

For Annie Kenney or the Dundee factory boy, writing after their public life was over, day-dreams may have drifted in and out of their minds during the years they had no time to act on them, keeping alive unsatisfied wishes, difficult early experiences, traumas and triumphs which they later worked on through writing. In Freud's sense, day-dreams, 'the constructions of folk psychology', myths, legends and fairy tales, are 'vestiges' of wishful fantasies of whole cultures. These 'secular dreams of youthful humanity' could be the creative sources for reimagining lives: from the dreams, playfulness and longing experienced in restless, tough and painful childhoods to the harnessing of past and present realities and fantasies through writing a life story decades later.

Some people managed to write and occasionally publish while they were still relatively young. It was more likely to be poetry than extended prose pieces. Otherwise they practised on pieces related to daily life or social affiliations: letters, minutes, essays or articles.

Outlets for creativity during working life came through participation in religious, political or social organisations; or through informal learning, including mutual improvement societies. Activism helped people to explore life beyond work, responsibility and rest and offered opportunities for writing. But even in supportive contexts, creative momentum easily faded through unemployment or feelings of depression and anxiety, as the diary of John Ward of Clitheroe illustrates. Ward was a liberal activist and a supporter of Mechanics' Institutes. His mental state and economic hardship prevented him from writing, 'It is nearly two years since I wrote anything in the way of a diary. I now take up my pen to resume the task … The principal reason why I did not take any notes these last two years is because I was sad and weary.'[35]

Sustained pieces of writing came with the opportunity to reflect, sift, reconstruct and reshape dreams, experiences and feelings which were available through memory. Their synthesis was constrained by the customs and limitations of autobiography and its readership. Annie Kenney waited for decades after her public life was over before she wrote her life story, which concentrates on her years of militancy as a young suffragette in a movement in which activists took sides with lingering bitterness. The Factory Boy's shaping of dreams has a different purpose. He writes about 'our hours of solitude, when thoughts of bygone days arise in the soul' and recreates a romanticised, dreamlike and innocent state of childhood before his father's trial. 'Special pleading' is part of his desire to be known and the consequences of traumatic change to be understood:

> *Can the reader blame me then, when I affirm that I think the little cottage where I was born was the sweetest spot on earth. The tidy garden, the river, the thick plantations, over which towered the grey turrets of the ancient castle of Glammis [sic], the soothing solace of an affectionate mother's love, and all the innocent amusements and prattling of youth's warm existence, rush in on my memory.*[36]

There are other ways through which writers seem to link memory, imagination and dreams. One is that memory appears to work in tension with other creative dimensions of writing, close to day-dreaming, but located both in historical time and in cultural history. It is a paradox that many texts are plotted in ways that are congruent with the idea of a time 'before the Fall'. Childhood memories in autobiography are often presented as imagined prelapsarian utopias. The Fall, the rude shock of irreversible adulthood, announces a shift in the register of a text. Expressions of loss or anger subside into the recounting of a more socialised, public phase of life. It is a social fall which is being described. The paradox lies in the duality of the text in which the complexities of a historically-located, remembered community – and of oneself in that community – are plotted together with a deeper, seemingly transhistorical, poetic narrative structure, though one which is itself part of the cultural history of redemptive spiritual thought and feeling. So images of an unfallen world and millenial ideas which centred on seeing what salvation might emerge from the present, imperfect social grown-up world, were created by writers by both imagining and remembering. The history of such imagery goes back as far as the seventeenth century, to poems like Thomas Traherne's 'News' and 'Eden'; or, in nineteenth-century utopianisms, there is Wordsworth's *Intimations of Immortality*; and later William Morris's *News from Nowhere*. Autobiography is another expression of the cultural histories of which it is part.

The idyllic possibilities that autobiographies describe are pastoral and retrospective, placing them in an English 'structure of feeling' or sensibility. As Martin Wiener argues, a love of the rural world across social classes intensified from the mid-century. The Great Exhibition was seen as 'the high water-mark of educated opinion's enthusiasm for industrial capitalism'. Dickens, Carlyle, Ruskin and other writers who are associated with the 'liberal march of progress' also expressed a 'powerful ambivalence' and alienation from the values of commmerce, urbanisation and industrialism. They sought and constructed another quintessentially English way of life embedded in the idea of an enduring rural tradition.[37] The nineteenth-century creation of sanctioned ways of teaching people to read and write grew from the 'fallen' worlds of society and state. But in the memory of writers, they had also created their own agency and means of changing their lives – through learning. In this way, learning to write was part of a mythologised selfhood, the fairy tale in which anything could happen, as well as of the social world around which other authorities drew a narrow educational map and from which decades of labour drained and dissipated creative energy almost beyond recovery. Visionary, unfallen states of being are remembered and imagined from the experience of a socialised, material, historically-changing world. It is at least possible to say that working-class autobiographers reveal complex identities which move between personal, individual and mythologised selfhoods.

Another way of linking memory, imagination and dreams is that during the active decades of working life, those who later wrote also acted out their dreams whenever they could. Picaresque tales of adventure are common, from journeyman travels, to joining circuses, to world travel. Mary Luty's autobiography consists almost entirely of an account of her years as 'a penniless globe trotter'.[38] William Wright recollected how the 'romantic and nomadic' style fascinated and infatuated him, and he joined a circus. Accounts of lives in search of adventure or work include chapters which describe restlessness, moving away from home, going to sea or joining a political campaign as impulses or responses to dissatisfaction, poverty, loss or grief – but they are also about hope, desire and hunger for new experience. For some, adventures and life events were momentous by anybody's book. For others, changes might be the smaller dramas and mishaps which disturb daily life in any community.

The desire to write was not always frustrated or abandoned for lack of time or space. For Hannah Mitchell, being both a writer and a suffragette fed her desire for a public voice and audience. Though she could not realise her dreams of writing, her identity as a writer was a constant presence. For most writers a sense of identity as a writer was less clear, as James Burn articulates:

> *Amid the universal transformations of things in the moral and physical world, my own condition has been like a dissolving view, and I have been so tossed in the rough blanket of fate, that my identity, if at any time a reality, must have been one which few could venture to swear to.*[39]

VII   Living on both sides of the frontier: writing, the self and other people

For some writers, an inner sense of self came through the actual process of writing. Their identity as writers is often associated with difference. Some emphasise the awkwardness and ambivalence of belonging to a relatively powerless social group while also adopting the powerful position of speaking for the experience and identity of others as well as oneself. Consciousness of the dual identity of being 'one of the multitude', and feeling the oppressive and homogenising concept of 'the masses', acted as a motivator to live out and demonstrate difference: to hold an audience rather than be only a member of an audience. There is abundant evidence of this feeling in autobiography:

> *I spent Sunday afternoon – along with the other lads – catching sparrows, or rat-hunting … Maybe some lad would have a copy of Police News – a terrible paper it was … So we got sensation, entertainment or jollification; but never a line of good reading, for which I longed. I was too timid to bring my school-prizes out for the other lads to jeer at, for I knew Lady Brassey, Captain Marryat, or my book of poetry, would be considered 'rammie' … So I shut myself out of the world of books and hunted rats.*[40]

or:

I got to read fairly well and write a little and somehow was looked up to as something alien to the common class of young men.[41]

Narratives also reveal the psychic pain of rejection and a sense of invisibility and insignificance, although some writers were spirited in their resistance to a view of themselves as simply part of a 'mass', or as ordinary, and kept on asserting their difference from other people. For some of them, a decent education or the bold step of publishing a book constituted a move away from community, literally or metaphorically. For others, the wish to be 'other' seems to have been more about the wish for a different subjectivity: to be a writer was the key to recognition and a richer selfhood.

In V.S. Pritchett's phrase a writer 'splits off from the people who surround him and he discovers the necessity of talking to himself'.[42] In autobiography, someone else is the self or character the autobiography constructs. Some working-class writers literally moved away, as if the climate was more conducive to writing somewhere else – to Grub Street or a foreign city like V.S. Pritchett's Paris. Yet there is still a strong sense of belonging, held in tension with such self-conscious acts of distancing. Some writers attribute their imaginative life to a working-class experience. For them, the tension between sameness and difference was addressed without the urge for flight. In John Bedford Leno's poems 'Crowded Court' and 'A Modern Inferno' he defended Drury Lane as a place to write in from the 'wonder' of a writer in the Athenaeum. 'Why not? If I am able to write at all? Any artist will tell you that there can be no good picture without a shadow; and that in no few, it forms a chief factor.'[43] Those who stayed home could defend it, as Fred Kitchen does: 'I know that farm lads are not credited with much wisdom but perhaps the general opinion is wrong, for who knows what a farm lad is turning over in his mind as he walks along his furrow?'[44] Kitchen is conscious of those who dwell disdainfully on the extraordinariness of writing a book, so as not to disturb their sense of the ordinariness of everyone else.

As many autobiographies testify, a working-class woman may write, provided work and family are not neglected. She will rarely be seen first and foremost as 'a writer' or seek such a bold new identity as someone with an individual, creative life. This was not always a tension. Many writers, women and men, did not see the many facets of their lives as tugging in opposite directions. Some saw their creativity as part of their 'destiny', rooted in a place, not somewhere else, somewhere better. They wanted to be with, as well as unique among, workmates, family and community. Alice Walker celebrated the association of women's writing with daily life in an essay on Buchi Emecheta, 'A Writer Because of, Not in Spite of, Her Children'. 'She finds time for writing by getting up at four every morning, before the demands of children and job take over' and believes that she would not be a writer 'without [the] sweet background noises' of her five children. Walker argues that 'the notion that this is even remotely possible causes a rethinking of traditional Western ideas about how art is produced ... which separates the duties of raising children from those of creative work'.[45] In a different era, the Blackburn poet and factory worker Ethel Carnie wrote that 'all my poems came into my head at the mill'.[46] As chapter 8 will explore, men also drew inspiration from the noisy machines or blotted inkpads of their places of work.

Autobiographers often acknowledge the people who first proposed they should write. They convey a feeling that without the intervention of sponsors, the desire to write might not have formed itself and, even if it had, the confidence to act on it might have faltered. Daniel Chater describes this situation:

> *It may be that the poor victim had never contemplated ... the suggested action, or if he had been tempted he did not fall, having dismissed from his mind the action suggested as being beyond his powers of performance. With the return of the fermentation comes the realisation ... that ... practical recognition of its existence is the only way in which peace of mind can be obtained. With the desire for the comfort of mental peace, as that desire becomes more insistent, and more imperative, the necessity for surrender becomes more apparent, and leads to the triumphant victory of the idea germ.*[47]

The significant others who influenced a witer's education and creative development included Sunday and day school teachers, older relatives or siblings, neighbours, friends, postmistresses, grandparents, work colleagues, employers and middle-class benefactors. For some writers, the enigmatic appearance of a complete stranger at the door was the most significant moment of change. These could be messengers, itinerants, carriers, passing ramblers or postmen. At a simple level, such people offered encouragement or even skills. Sometimes the intervention of sponsors – friends or strangers – featured as a counterpart to the lack of support provided by immediate family or slights from other people who deliberately or casually undermined their efforts. Parents could often be discouraging or helpless in the face of their children's desire to learn. Despite that, negative interventions experienced in childhood fired some people to write in later life, and the details of earlier conflicts were central to the story of a developing selfhood. Walter Benjamin offered an interpretation of significant figures in writers' creativity and their func-tion in memory. He suggested that through writing, at moments of particularly clear recall, answers to questions about the significance of others could be 'inscribed, as if of their own accord, on a piece of paper'. For him, this act was unique, and could not be repeated, since when he tried, the clarity was lost and the map became a 'labyrinth'. He argued that in trying to navigate the 'enigmatic centre' of memory, patterns of relationship could be discovered which would repeat themselves throughout life, but were sparked off by 'primal acquaintances', who were 'graphic symbols' of people encountered in significant situations and key places. The people met 'through neighbourhood, family relationships, school comradeship, mistaken identity, or companionship on travels' seemed relevant to the ways in which autobiographers placed significant figures. The concept of 'primal acquaintances' is a key to the emergence of a more autonomous, creative self, in that these figures are not met 'through other people', but are 'entrances' which provide a function related not to external, daily life and its constraints, but to recognition and guidance of a person's own potential and the 'hidden laws' which govern individual existence and difference.[48] Writers seemed to understand well that the sponsors who released their imaginative and expressive powers knew how unlikely it was that their creativity would be widely recog-nised. The next fear, especially for women, was that it would be destroyed again by discouragement, punishment or endless external claims on time and energy.

Some of the experiences and feelings of nineteenth-century writers can be captured by the phrase 'if only'. 'If only' is the recurrent lament of writers who believed that their class position had cheated them of creative fulfilment. It was about the persistence of a belief in what might have been. Developing a sense of potential involved the rejection of a sense of inherent inferiority. 'If only' was expressed in emotional registers ranging from anger to determination, wistfulness or resignation. 'If only' was 'special pleading', fuelled by injustice. It was not always retrospective regret; 'if only' also led to action, such as joining learning groups or social movements. Allegiances, oaths and pledges, associations and movements symbolised a sense of possibility and hope: 'If only I/we take hold of our lives, we can change them'. 'The Pledge' was a key instrument of change in working-class life. It was a way of pitting energies against the forces obstructing one's development and confronting human weakness and destructive habits through empowering associations with like-minded others. The most common expression of the Pledge was the temperance movement, but oaths of allegiance containing written promises were part of religious conversion, education, clubs, friendly societies or trade unions. Membership was a serious business. Belonging to organisations was not possible for everyone, or not for long. Some Adult School participants attended for a few months, others for 50 years, but they all made pledges at entry, and the majority of working-class autobiographers took part in associations which brought some recognition of their creative potential and the possibility of being with people who offered mutual support.

VIII   In and for itself: being able to write

As already discussed, most people's early schooling did not include writing, and it hardly featured as a compositional subject, even in the Board Schools. It is not surprising that accounts of learning to write by one ingenious means or another are particularly vivid, and often more prominent in autobiography than descriptions of learning to read, spell, knit or do arithmetic. A longed-for skill which was hard to come by was bound to feel significant. There was another reason for remembering childhood writing well. The majority of working-class writers, well into the twentieth century, experienced difficulty and frustration with spell-ing, shaping sentences and sculpting their thoughts into writing. This is clear from editors' prefaces and the many manuscripts held in archives and reference libraries. The adult writer, still experiencing the multiple challenges of the task, was likely to identify actively with those aspects of early struggles to learn which are nearest to her or his current struggles for self-expression. The basic technical skills which were needed to recreate the complexity and structure of a life story might so easily not have been learned at all. The recurring theme of 'what if' balances 'if only'. It expresses a still-precarious achievement. At the moment of forming words on a page, the remembered facts and artefacts of learning to write are a vivid record, items of proof, like framed photographs of a special event, a rite of passage. Writing and its essential tools emphasise the difference between oppression and empowerment, permanence and oblivion, immortality and transience. Writing an autobiography is a task involving choices, a sensitivity to characters and audiences, dead and alive, the presence of friendly and unfriendly readers, a sense of being exposed. The time spent writing meant living with vanity, keeping up confidence alongside the doubts and dreads of ridicule or condescension. These feelings may have been especially strong for writers who almost universally announced their lack of education, stressed their ordinariness, their lack of spectacular achievement, their 'humbleness' and their debts to others. They were only too aware of the increasing power of writing over the spoken word.

As a writer squeezed out words, rushed at ideas and lost them again, and as uncomfortable or happy past events jostled with each other and converged with the ebb and flow of a writer's confidence, it is not hard to understand why his or her first attempts at writing would have felt powerfully present. Memories of first attempts at writing were among the earliest expressed memories of a family's hopes for or opposition to learning, and sometimes the site of other, displaced emotional and material struggles. The difficulties of writing which workng-class writers experienced, and of which we know so little, should not be underestimated for all the evidence of their self-belief.

The connection between writing – or not being able to write – as a child, and writing as an adult is not always explicitly made. In many autobiographies, the construction of a life through memory, however fashioned, contains only a fragmentary reconstruction of the writing life itself, with gaps and silences and carefully-selected memories. There are single sentences which have the feel of broken lumps of rock jutting out from a stream. But further back or further on, other fragments can be found and pieced together as another layer of the story. These fragments and writing incidents are part of a writer's consciousness that what he or she has achieved has been a difficult process and that some things cannot be held up to the light. They also reflect their knowledge that their work may be misinterpreted, creating a need to justify and hide as well as explain and interpret their experience.

Notes

1   Cooper, [1872] 1971, pp. 16–17, 8.
2   R. Williams, [1961] 1965, pp. 31, 40–4, 51, 54–5.
3   Pritchett, 1978a, p. 226.
4   Cooper, *op. cit.*, pp. 17, 21.
5   Kitchen, [1940] 1983, pp. 11–12.
6   Wright, 1893, chapter 3, 18 June.
7   Lovett, [1876] 1967, p. 23.
8   Barclay, 1934, pp. 23–4.
9   Pritchett, 1978b, pp. 82, 95.
10 Mansbridge, 1940, p. 12.
11 Foley, 1973, pp. 12–13.
12 Lawson, [1932] 1949, p. 12.
13 Quoted in Tomalin, 2011, Preface.
14 Mins CCE, 1842–3, p. 258; *ibid.*, 1845, pp. 234–5.
15 Ball, 1983, p. 76.
16 *ibid.*, p. 76.
17 Burke, 1909, p. 3.
18 McMillan, 1904, pp. 115–16.
19 See, e.g., Bacon, 1895.
20 'A Berlin Chronicle', in Benjamin, 1985, p. 314.
21 Freud, 1975a, p. 88.
22 Freud, 1975b, p. 199.
23 Cora Kaplan's paper on Mitchell's story of the blind girl (Psychoanalysis and History conference, London, June 1985) suggested 'screen memory' as a way of understanding the incident.
24 Rushton, 1909, p. 9.
25 Luty, 'My Life has Sparkled', undated TS, District Central Library, Rawtenstall, chapter 1, p. 1.
26 Sanger, 1910, Author's Preface, p. xxix.
27 Cooper, *op. cit.*, pp. 20–1.
28 Vincent, 1989, p. 226.
29 Freud, [1908] 1985, pp. 131–2, 133, 139–40, 141.
30 McMillan, 1904, p. ix.
31 J.D. Fox, 1914, p. 20.
32 Kenney, 1924, p. 4.
33 F. White, 1938, p. 42.
34 Anon., *Life of a Dundee Factory Boy*, 1850, p. 51.
35 J. Ward, 'The Diary of John Ward', in Burnett, 1974, pp. 84–5.
36 Anon., *Life of a Dundee Factory Boy*, 1850, pp. 3, 33.
37 Wiener, 1980, pp. 33–5.
38 See the published account of Luty's travels: Luty, 1937.
39 Burn, [1855] 1978, p. 2.
40 Kitchen, *op. cit.*, p. 73.
41 Lovekin, 'Some Notes on My Life', MS, Brunel University Library, p. 32.
42 Bowen, 1948, p. 23.
43 Leno, 1892, p. 65.
44 Kitchen, *op. cit.*, p. 11.
45 Walker, 1984, pp. 66–70.
46 Carnie, 1907; also quoted in *The Woman Worker*, 26 June 1908, p. 109, where Carnie writes: 'It might be as Miss Marianne Farningham said to me … that my occupation has something to do with the rhythmic forms into which my thoughts shaped themselves.'
47 Chater, 'The Autobiography of Daniel Chater', TS, Brynmor Jones Library, Hull University, p. 1.
48 Benjamin, *op. cit.*, p. 319.

CHAPTER 7

Being different: women's lives in writing

I

Working-class life writing has been criticised as naïve, lacking individuality or emotional depth. In an autobiographical account of her own mother, Carolyn Steedman argued against the 'psychological simplicity of the lives lived out in Richard Hoggart's endless streets of little houses',[1] where there is a blurred vision of uniformity in working-class experience and consciousness – men's and women's. If notions of sameness do not hold up for men's writing – to be explored further in the last chapter – what does women's writing show us? This chapter explores the patterns of learning, the emotional landscapes and relationships which characterise working-class women writers' lives. Their autobiographies have been relatively neglected. Studies which have stuck mainly to men's writing have made it easier to portray a collective class psyche and oversimplified depictions of women, especially mothers, who are often sentimentalised in men's autobiography, lacking individuality or emotional depth. Portrayals of girls and women tend to focus on the multiple social roles they will occupy as wives, mothers and working women with little challenge to characterisations of single and childless women as the eccentric, wronged or pathetic figures of Dickens among others. The autobiographies in this chapter point to the awkward and multifaceted life histories of women who did not fit notions of a collectively definable, and progressive female working-class selfhood.

The five women autobiographers explored here are: Janet Bathgate and Marianne Farningham, both born early in the century; Hannah Mitchell and Louise Jermy who were born in the 1870s and Margaret

'Girl in a cottage window' by Norman Garstin
Bridgeman Art Library

Penn born in1896. Their lives encompass urban and rural life in different regions of Britain over a century of fundamental social, educational and economic change. Their writing reveals the social, educational and economic circumstances of their lifetimes through their experiences as working-class women. Theirs were also individual projects to develop a selfhood, both public and interior, beyond anyone's expectations of them. Writing was at the heart of their longing and their plans for change. They were driven by determination with little, if any, support. On the way, they exposed emotional and psychological theatres of conflict in which writing itself was the carrier, expression and cause of discord, disagreement and collision – and sometimes aspiration and pride – in families and communities about the possibilities and risks which literacy offered. Writing was an act of defining difference as well as social belonging. Women writers tell of the peculiarities of a particular life among others, including the role of writing itself, as key elements in the nature of their

212

difference from others. What they had to say in writing and the circumstances in which they wrote are clear but complex: historical, literary and
psychological.

II Janet Bathgate

Janet Bathgate (1814–98) was born near Yarrow, Selkirk in the Scottish
Borders. Her father was an agricultural labourer. She initially intended
her autobiography, *Aunt Janet's Legacy to her Nieces – Recollections of Humble
Life in Yarrow in the Beginning of the Century*, to be no more than a
manuscript, read by relatives and friends. But an ambitious book was
published, followed by a book by her publisher about the making of her
life story, and four editions of her autobiography were printed in the
1890s. Religious belief is her declared motivation for writing, and she
emphasises the teachings in her childhood to fear God, and that her book
is guided by his 'beneficent power over all'. Though Bathgate's God did
not protect her from acute unhappiness and difficulty, he does get some
credit for offering comfort. Her purpose in writing is also to proselytise,
helping the younger generations among her friends to deal with 'trials and
difficulties' like hers in the 'battle of life' by looking to the 'Father' for
comfort and strength. She gives her faith rather than personal gain as the
reason for seeking, in the end, a wider audience. Her book was also 'a
record of the common every-day events of a life begun 80 years ago in the
quiet pastoral valley of the Yarrow'.[2]

Bathgate used literary devices to engage her readers. 'Aunt Janet's
Legacy' was written in the third person, as if to fictionalise it and distance
herself from her main character: the child 'Janet' becomes 'Jenny', creating
an intimate emotional register. This has the effect of generalising her
experience for a wider readership than those who knew 'Aunt Janet',
freeing the subject of the narrative from the responsibilities of the 'I' of
autobiography, and the pressure of telling the truth to 'you'. Bathgate used
the present tense, lending dramatic immediacy to her life-story. She also
used direct speech in remembered or imagined dialect conversations, and
cried out to her readership for understanding: 'special pleading' is part of
her repertoire.

Poverty, conflict and unhappiness mingle with high spirits and the
security of a loving family in Janet Bathgate's earliest memories. She
remembers moving house to 'miserable looking quarters', singing songs
and ballads and reciting poems in the cart. Her clearest picture of early

213

reading was the familiar working-class childhood memory of reading a verse inscription on a gravestone when she visited a churchyard near her new home. Tombstone epitaphs, names and dates were her reading materials – essential texts, since costly books and paper were out of reach. Epitaphs were accepted as legitimate sources for children's reading: sacred and morally uplifting. They were also locally accessible and attractive as personal and poignant scripts, hinting at relevant local stories in ways which the Bible and other reading materials could not. Most working-class children had direct experience of death in the family and community, and gravestones were emblems of loss, and of inherited identity in a world otherwise without writing, as for Pip in *Great Expectations*. But visits to graveyards were also associated with play and freedom. Many writers recalled them as short, borrowed moments of intense pleasure away from work and duty. Perhaps the mystery and macabre nature of a graveyard heightened the excitement and provided a fertile site for a child's imagination. Perhaps because writing itself is not alive like speech as a communication which can develop between people, it had an irreversible finality, fixing in time a thing, idea or human being which does not move or change. It is not surprising then that for working-class writers gravestone inscriptions were a metaphoric reference point, a form of writing that offers layers of different meaning, from innocently fluid play to the finality of death.[3]

The early sections of the book demonstrate the dilemmas many nineteenth-century working-class families experienced about their own and especially their children's education. So many had ambitions for their children to become literate, and kept faith with the possibility that reading and writing would bring benefits in the long-term. But they had to put the immediate need to feed the family first. Bread, knowledge, and then freedom, was their realistic order of priority. So it was that the central experience in Janet Bathgate's remembered childhood was being forced to leave home on her own at the age of seven to do farm work near Selkirk and support the family income. She tells the story dramatically, showing the profound effect the upheaval she suffered had on her future life and her feelings for her family and God. She starts with the arrival out of the blue of the mysterious outsider of romantic fiction: 'a tall man; his hat is drawn well over his brow'. Although she explains that the appearance of ironically-named stranger, Rob Shortreed, has been ordained by God, she makes the evil portent of his visit plain. He proposes that Janet goes to work as a domestic servant for his family. Her mother protests, but

214

in a feeble and ritualistic way. Her misgivings are Janet's age and lack of schooling: she has only just begun to give her daughter lessons. The stranger assures her that his brother and their helpmate, 'baith guidish scholars', would teach her to read. Still concerned about her age, Janet's mother is reassured by her father, a vague and distant figure, who convinces his wife that Rob is a 'tool in the hand of Him'[4] and agrees to release her. In her construction of this scene, the 80-year-old writer revisits her bewilderment and terror at leaving home and her fear of an unassailable powerful God. She still cannot allow herself to vent her mortal fury that her father cannot even own his decision. The pious acceptance of a surrogate authority seems to rob Janet of the right to be angry with him. But the way she recalls his words reveals her feelings – as a child and adult – and her awareness of how faith and all-too-human feelings interact in religious families at times of acute stress to explain and soften painful situations they cannot avoid. And her father's shifting of responsibility onto God offers the space for a consoling bond between father and daughter, for a mutual understanding of how to contain emotions which might otherwise threaten the family's economic survival. Janet's emotional generosity does not extend to her mother. Her father's decision carries God's authority, but her mother's weakness is her own, and she is made to bear responsibility for her daughter's misery.

In contrast with the surface blandness of many male autobiographers' representations of their mothers and step-mothers, and their remembered compliance with a harsh decision, emotional struggles and clashes of will are prominent in women's life stories. The unfinished dramas of childhood are not over for the adult writer who searches simultaneously for private and public acceptance of a past through conscious exposure to emotional currents which still feel radioactive. Writing seems to be an attempt at reconciliation, both in the actors' lifetimes and after their death, and also offers a way of calming clamouring emotions, setting them down. Writing offers the possibility of letting go, perhaps even forgetting.[5] But arriving at that detached state of being can mean a tough journey. Though Bathgate presents her childhood self as a powerless victim, she offers some resistance as well as prayer. She tries to make herself too ill to be sent away, running naked in the snow at night, rubbing it on her chest, face and arms. The shock treatment does not work and she describes breakfast with her mother before she leaves, interweaving her mother's imagined feelings with her own:

Her heart is sore; the porridge will not go down, her mother observes; and she easily understands the reason; her heart is sore likewise, but she tries to be cheerful. She speaks of having something fine for dinner when her lassie comes home with her twelve shillings, but Janet cannot smile. She thinks her mother does not love her, or she would not be so cheery, and this adds to her grief … Oh! If her mother would but look sorrowful, Janet could endure the rest; but her mother acts the merciful hypocrite and smiles as she bids her lassie good-bye.

It is not possible for me to describe Jenny's anguish. Oh, let mothers be true to nature; love never hurts anyone; open rebuke is better than secret love.

The grammar of this passage is strikingly complex. Bathgate disposes at first of the more formal Janet, the girl who could 'endure', and she becomes Jenny, the collapsed infant, then finally the writer, 'me', speaking directly to her dead mother – perhaps all mothers – as if in recognition of the helplessness of any child in the face of an implacable, unreadable parent incapable of openly showing affection.

The needling rebukes – she will even have to pay for her homecoming celebration dinner herself – and the melodramatic reproaches seem, through the pronoun 'me', to express an emotional distance between the miserable child and the woman writer who finally has a voice. But they also express the intensity of residual feeling. In the act of writing, memory seems to have collapsed the intervening decades. The pain is still present in the woman, inhabiting the hurt child who is part of her adult selfhood. She can admonish the inadequate mother, but does this as an adult who wields an authority which is derived in part from her skills at writing. Yet a sense of instability about the identity and subjectivity of the writer seems to remain, in her identification with both the child and her young mother back then, and the wise-woman and still-angry daughter here and now. There is also a sense of self-reproach at her lack of ability to 'read' the mother towards whom she nurses such ambivalent feelings. Bathgate's childhood feelings of desperation are matched by a spirited, and intransigent animus she expresses towards a God whom she could not love 'as well as she loves her mother'. Her mother, less powerful, is ultimately more forgivable.

In the twenty-first century, a child's enforced separation from home and family and an instant transition to adult working life at the age of seven are known to be deeply traumatic events, even though still routine in many parts of the world. The lack of attention given to the psychological or emotional lives of working-class people in the nineteenth century seems to reflect common responses to events far away in time and place. Historians have argued about whether loss and grief are less painful because they were more common and accepted as an inevitable part of life. The stories in this book suggest that to think people then were more inured to emotional pain than now is a consoling narrative of class. Janet Bathgate's experience is an argument that the pain of separation and loss is not necessarily milder because they are commonly experienced, even in communities where there may have been support for an individual person's suffering because experiences were better understood. Above all though, this childhood experience illuminates how difficult it is for people from more powerful social groups, when they gather evidence, sum up, unify and collectivise working-class experience and consciousness, to understand meaning and feeling and to grasp the psychic and social experiences of individual people and their different subjectivities.

In Janet's new life as a domestic servant in a farming household, the promised reading and writing lessons do not materialise. Her working day is 5am–10pm except on Sundays, which she spends 'sitting among the hills from 5 o'clock in the morning till eight at night, trying to keep the Sabbath day holy, by reading, or rather trying to read "The Single Question", the only book she possessed'. Although she reports leaving the job without any more teaching, one of the women on the farm, Katie, spends time with her, telling witch stories and 'wonderful tales about ghosts and fairies'.[6] She is taken to a second job by another 'stranger' wrapped in plaid, where a farmer's wife helps her to read, offering her money as an incentive, which is sent back to her family. The terms of the job after that include a daily lesson, which consists of learning sections of the Bible by heart, again with money as the incentive for success. But she makes little progress.

The book's middle chapter, 'A First Attempt at Letter Writing', forms a watershed between childhood and adulthood and shows how essential writing was to Bathgate's developing sense of herself as a subject, her desire to be educated, and her later construction of herself as an agent of change. Janet's desperate efforts to assert her will in childhood are left behind, and now she assembles the pieces of learning she has achieved thus far. She shows how her stubbornness, persistence and refusal to bow to the will of others become useful once she can harness them to new

217

ways of communication. Through writing she tries to overcome her isolation and take charge of her own education.

Janet has had a long separation from her family. She is acutely homesick and longs to tell them about her life.[7] During the long, solitary hours she spends at work sitting on 'a gray stone' beside a 'loch', she is overwhelmed by loneliness and anxiety. The release of emotion sparks a creative idea. She decides to draw a picture of her circumstances. She has been taught sampler stitch by a local woman, 'Peggie Hogg', who has given her 'a piece of thin green cloth and some yellow silk thread' to practise with. She sews a map of the loch and its surroundings, 'beguiling many lonely hours' to send it home as a piece of embroidery. She then realises that the map will not be understood on its own and hatches another plan – to take the map home herself. But she has no money, and no permission to leave work. Janet bitterly regrets that she has never learned the skill which would enable her family to interpret the 'picture' of her life: 'How she wishes she had learned to write.' She decides to overcome the problem by learning to write there and then. In her pocket she 'rediscovers' a letter from her father to her employer asking after her welfare, which she has kept to use for reading practice. After re-reading it 'for the twentieth time or more', she attempts to copy the letters she is sure of, then to shape her own words from these, helped also by her reading book. She learns by searching out familiar letters of the alphabet, from which she forms words. There were several she did not know and she couldn't easily tell 'E' from 'F'. She invents her own writing materials. For paper, she tears a corner off her father's letter; for a pen, she takes a pin and, raiding her book for letters, 'pricks with the point of the pin their form and thus "writes" a letter to her father': 'My dear father and mother I am well thank God Peggie is kind to me I hope you are all well God bless you Your daughter Janet'. Janet's desire to learn to write is not associated with other learning, like the songs, ballads and fairy tales that have always been part of her life, nor with her partly-acquired reading skills. Her writing is self-taught from scratch, to meet a need.

The way in which she organises the despatch and delivery of her letter illustrates the serious obstacles to communication between separated working-class families at that time. Even if her family could afford to pay the postal charges, unless they recognised the origin of the package, they would have no incentive to pay for it. She finds a way round this possible obstacle. She ties up her letter and map in a rag, unaddressed and gives it to a local carrier with verbal instructions to hand it to the baker at

218

Selkirk who is to make sure her family receives it. When her parents get the odd little bundle, they can't decipher the 'two obscure documents' although they realise that they come from their daughter. At first, they interpret the paper as an attempt to draw flowers. But the letter is correctly read by the two Miss Pringles, local middle-class girls who have been making 'friendly visits' to the family. Bathgate credits them, rather than her family, with fully understanding that the encoded message really meant that Janet's desire for education was just as strong as her longing to be in touch with her family. The two sisters urge her parents to bring Janet home and send her to school.

As a seasonal worker, Janet might just have been able to return home at the end of the harvest and she looks forward to the possibility of some time at school in the winter, but her employers want to keep her: she is a good worker with a 'quiet biddable manner'. She also assumes that the drop in her father's wages during the recent hard times will convince her parents that she should stay away and earn money. They had a large and growing family including a new-born baby to keep. The letter itself might not have been enough to hasten her return, but for the intervention of philanthropic neighbours. Her father relents and sends a letter to her employers – Janet is to come home and attend the local school. This is a story of motivation to learn and belief in the possibility of agency through literacy, and also a story common to many people who contrived to get some time in education: rescue by local patrons.[8]

The literal and metaphorical senses in which Janet's letter reaches home had 'a great deal to do with shaping her future history'. Writing is invested with magical properties as an alternative source of authority, but one which only technical skill can activate. Her letter initiates a long chain of changes in her relationships with family and friends. The period that follows her return is remembered as a domestic idyll with her mother and siblings, learning lessons and singing to the baby. In fact the bout of schooling is brief, and of a pattern in working-class childhoods of the time: it is followed by another period of paid work, then another two weeks of schooling. After that, Janet has to rely on local networks and patronage to support her learning. Fortunately, her next employer, a clergyman's widow, lends her books to read.

It is difficult for Janet Bathgate to accept responsibility for changing her life by learning to write and the progress of her life is not straightforward. She suffers a breakdown that she describes in part as a crisis of faith. She recalls a 'giddy dance which passed midnight on a Saturday, and joining others in mocking Jesus'. She describes feeling terror and doubt about her ability to manage her life. The self-belief she has gained undermines cultural expectations of girls and women. The traumas she associates with God's will shake the religious beliefs which give her family their moral framework and justification for hard decisions: 'whatever she has gained in strength and worldly station she has lost in piety'. Janet recovers and receives a letter offering her a post looking after the children of a family returning from India: her first reaction is to express distress at the story of the separation of her new charge from her 'ayah'. In this displaced narrative of abandonment she is confronted again with her feelings about God as authority, about the terror of separation and loss, and she is troubled by anxiety throughout adult life.

The identity Janet achieves is historically and socially located. She discovers the imaginative power to gain the then more masculine and middle-class craft of writing, achieving this through the feminine and domesticating skills of embroidery. She begins a process of externalising her feelings and representing herself. Through her embroidery she depicts herself in a landscape. She encodes, abstracts and 'frames' her meaning. Her map breaks the tension between containing and communicating feelings. She can recognise that, for her, writing is the key to socialising and acting on experience.

Much later, Janet Bathgate opened her own school at the suggestion of a benefactress – reluctantly, because she felt her education was inadequate. She remembers 'her first letter and the green map',[9] still conscious of the distance she has travelled to her present social status. She celebrates breaking out of her subordinated existence and shaping her own life. And she empathises strongly with other people going through comparable conflicts and difficulties. She suggests that there is a high cost to becoming different, through writing, to become a girl who acts on her own behalf. Janet Bathgate still belonged to a specific class, community, place and time, but the nature of her belonging changed.

III   Marianne Farningham

Marianne Farningham – the pseudonym of Marianne Hearn – was born in the village of Farningham in Kent in 1834, a postmaster's daughter, the oldest daughter in a large family. Her life story, *A Working Woman's Life. An Autobiography* (1907) also identifies writing as central to her hard-fought struggle to gain an education. She remembers her first act of writing, signing the 'pledge', a significant writing ritual in many working-class organisations and non-conformist churches. Her father guided her hand as they jointly pledged her name, an act of writing significantly associated with decisiveness and resolve, but also a binding duty to obey.

Both parents taught at the Baptist Sunday School in Eynsford, a larger village a mile away. There was no school in Farningham, and as soon as Marianne could walk to Eynsford she began Sunday school with her four brothers and sisters. The nearest dame school was also at Eynsford, but apart from a brief spell there, her childhood education was entirely informal. With the Bible as lesson book, she was taught to read by her paternal grandmother, 'who thought beautiful thoughts, and expressed them in beautiful language' and who wrote poetry. As many life stories illustrate, there was little perceived need for girls to develop writing skills during the first half of the century. There were few, if any, opportunities to earn a living from writing, and spells of schooling were too short to include writing. Like others, Marianne Farningham refused to give up and resorted to studying in secret. This way of learning avoided disruption to family life or employers. If a girl made progress though, and her achievements offered prospects, learning might be sanctioned, and per-mission given to practise literacy to help other people with writing as a scribe in the family or community, or to develop writing skills for teaching and, later in the century, clerical work. If a family was hostile to learning, support might be forthcoming from local well-wishers. For women, as for young men, church organisations were perhaps the most common source of support, or if a girl were lucky, middle-class benefac-tors.

Writing was not designed to be part of Marianne Farningham's education. She persistently asked to be taught to write, recording this as her first outright demand. She describes herself as an insubordinate girl who disliked the long hours of domestic labour she was burdened with at home from early childhood. But like Janet Bathgate, a childhood memory of literacy is linked to playing among graveyard inscriptions in which writing is the essence of ceremony and rites of passage. The ability to write was longed-for.

My first attempt at rhyming was an epitaph on a dead toad which we found in the garden, and which we put in a match-box and buried with great solemnity. I could not write the epitaph, for in the matter of writing I was quite behind the other children of my age. My ignorance in this respect

221

was a sore burden to them with my continual cry, 'Teach me to write'.[10]

Marianne Farningham writes of herself as a disobedient, angry child and her desire to write is her way of turning tempestuous behaviour into constructive action. She knows that her desire to learn is as challenging to her allotted place in the family as her waywardness, but her parents' initial response is positive. Her family provided nearly all her teaching but stopped short of teaching her to write. It is possible that they felt that their own writing skills were inadequate or that they were unsure that writing was appropriate for a girl – most girls didn't write. However a cousin, Isabella Rogers, hears of her 'childish desire', and offers to teach her. Her father agrees reluctantly, but he also 'took great pains with a little box in the shape of a book, which he made to hold my copy-book, pen ink ruler and pencil and which I proudly carried under my arm when I went to receive my writing lesson'. Again, as other chapters have shown, the tools of writing feel important in writers' memories of childhood.

Farningham closely links her happy memories of learning to write with her love of rhyming. This is echoed in passages which describe an 'awakening' of the spirit immediately following the story of her determination to learn to write. In a magazine which her grandmother gave her to read while minding her baby brother, she finds a poem expressing 'strange, sweet emotions' entitled 'The Better Land' by the popular poet Felicia Hemans. The poem is a fantasy about life after death in a heaven of 'coral strands', 'sands of gold' and 'ripe dates', which fuels Marianne's fantasies of a better life in this world.[11] It encourages hope and reconciliation to a Christian death and doubles as a utopian vision evoking restlessness and longing. She recalls feeling 'overcome with faintness' and rushing to the door for fresh air, but she is soon recalled to her 'duty' by the baby's 'loud cries'. The tension between her wish to indulge playful fantasies and her mother's constant calls to duty causes nagging resentment. After discovering the poem she describes how 'Nature claimed me'. Lyrical descriptions of idyllic hours among the meadows, trees and flowers take on the tone of an ecstatic religious experience: 'I have many a time imagined groups of angels and the "innumerable company" moving about in the masses of white and golden clouds … often I have stood with tears in my eyes and my heart throbbing with love and gladness'.[12]

The hard work of learning writing skills is as laden with romantic longing as the eulogies to nature and day-dreaming. The connections Farningham makes between these different aspects of learning are expressed in juxtaposed paragraphs on learning how to write and the explorations of selfhood that develop her private world of fantasy, nature and poetry. With regard to the latter, she pits the quiet support of her grandmother against the uncomprehending disapproval of her mother:

I was never allowed to stay long enough to satisfy me, for the cheery voice of my mother would call me into the house to amuse my brothers and sisters, or do some work. I am afraid she was grieved at my evident love of standing still and gazing. On one or two occasions, to my utter shame, she broke in upon me when I was talking to myself, and ordered me to sweep the carpet all over again, or showed me some article of furniture which I ought to have dusted. Dear mother! she did not like my always having a book in my hand or pocket, and would have been better pleased if I had been equally fond of the brush or the needle; but she did her best to keep me at work all day, only letting me have books and magazines when my tasks were done.

In contrast with Janet Bathgate's passionate rebuke, Farningham interprets her mother's heavy-handed treatment of her as well-meaning. 'Dear mother!' is remembered as 'grieved', rather than angry. But her 'cheeriness' in this context is not fondly recalled. It is reminiscent of Bathgate's wretchedness at her mother's unwillingness to respond to her distress, and her anger at the repression of feelings which make it easier for her mother to send her away. Janet's mother's powerlessness is not accepted as an excuse. Farningham expresses unresolved ambivalence towards her mother subtly, and perhaps her hesitancy in expressing negative emotions directly is still swayed by her mother's untimely death in 1846. The consequences of this tragedy for the pattern of Marianne's daily life – and her learning – were severe.

Marianne's motivation to learn and the family's response to it are informed by gender as well as social class. Though male working-class 'autodidacts' were often characterised as earnestly naïve, and their learning met by a blend of admiration and condescension, by the 1840s the idea that education was inappropriate for working men was waning. Their learning had recognisable purposes. But a woman's wish to go to school and even to learn to write was not understood in the same terms. Women could not take practical steps towards self-improvement, a better job or acquiring a body of scientific or literary knowledge with others, in the way that members of mutual improvement societies did. Farningham's narrative of her progress in adult life, once she had won acceptance in a social world, might sound similar to such men, but in her childhood such routes were not open to her. Her recreation of growing up in the mid-century is a psychological narrative of longing and day-dreaming which exalts the possibilities of poetry, imagination and the private fantasy world of a solitary child's play, to act as a counterpart to the repression, anger and resentment in her hardworking everyday life. From her mother's perspective, presented as no better or worse than prevailing attitudes to working-class girls' learning, schooling and books were still deeply suspect. While her independent-minded grandmother supported all her aspirations at home, the only places to learn which her parents did accept as reasonable were Sunday school, and the weekday British school – but only when day school did not interfere with domestic duties. Sewing and other feminine skills were learned at home. For some families who aspired to a degree of gentility for their daughters, drawing, music and even writing Ladies' Hand were learned, but Farningham's family did not entertain such ideas.

Farningham's conflict with her mother is about who owns her time. She longs to wander, absorbed in nature, but 'I was never allowed to stay long enough to satisfy me'. Her mother disapproves of 'standing still and gazing', though she remembers her mother also loved to play with her 'pretty and clean' daughters. Her memories of reading are echoed in other autobiographies. Mary Smith wrote: 'I was now a girl of eight years of age, with a great love of books and a very good capacity for reading. My poor mother looked upon reading, even when I was a little child, as a species of idleness; very well for Sunday or evenings when baby was asleep and I was not wanted for anything else.'[13] So for many girls, reading was censored: it was time-consuming, reflected self-centredness and involved spending time alone and, worse, unavailable. In the same period, Florence Nightingale wrote bitterly in 'Cassandra' that middle-class girls and unmarried adult daughters were expected to be occupied in ways which ensured they could respond to the demands of others for practically all their waking hours. Middle-class girls were to be occupied with social or philanthropic activities, accomplishments and conversations; working-class girls were expected to be occupied with domestic duties, childcare or paid employment. For a girl to move against these expectations simply because she wanted a different life for herself was virtually beyond comprehension in the rigidly-gendered socialisation of daily life. If some girls and women in this period did rebel, their actions were the first stirrings of changes which began to evolve. A more public questioning of the narrow confines of middle-class girls' activity began later in the century. Any measure of independence was the hard-won reward of a tiny minority of women and girls, or the unavoidable, economically-determined lot of spinsters or widows.[14] Loneliness was the experience of many; solitude the blissful experience of a few.

As the century progressed school became a legitimate means of release from drudgery at home or in service, and less short-lived. For girls like Marianne Farningham in the 1830s and l840s school was only a brief escape, experienced in constant fear of incurring displeasure. When a new school was built in Eynsford by the British and Foreign School Society in 1843–4, which she describes as a triumph for the nonconformists, she and her siblings were among the first pupils. Her schooling means a brief respite from adult responsibilities, and she also behaves like a child there: her memories of school are dominated by stories of her wilfulness and bad temper.

Aged ten, Marianne's life changes fundamentally when her mother catches measles nursing her sick children – including Marianne. She never recovers and dies two years later. Her death is followed shortly by the death of the aunt who arrives to take her place. The family is poor and her father does not remarry, so Marianne, the eldest daughter, has to care full-time for the younger children and her schooling ends abruptly. The shift from a relatively normal, if unusually spirited, girlhood, to adopting the role of mother is traumatic and burdensome. In the psychic drama of Farningham's narrative, guilt and resentment dominate her feelings. Marianne has begrudged her mother the hard work that followed her illness and death, and longs to abandon her tasks. Her mother leaves her a complicated emotional legacy. She feels guilty of causing her death. But she is also even angrier, feeling that her mother has taken revenge by bequeathing her the life of drudgery that has always threatened to rob her of any freedom. She has 'killed' her mother only to find that her punishment is to be a 'mother' to her siblings, and a substitute 'wife' – helpmeet and housekeeper: 'My father often said that I never had a girlhood, but grew at once from a child into a woman.'[15]

Tension between father and daughter escalates. There is a cool defiance in Farningham's account of the time after her mother's death as she conveys the difficulty of living without the comfort of friends her own age, or women who could provide role models for her longing to escape:

> *I still think it was a bad time for a girl to pass through. Reading was my consolation, and I had not much time for that. My father gave us two monthly magazines … the 'Teacher's Offering' and the 'Child's Companion'. In one of these was a series of descriptive articles on men who had been poor boys, and risen to be rich and great … Every month I hoped to find the story of some poor ignorant girl, [her emphasis] who, beginning life as handicapped as I, had yet been able by her own efforts … to live a life of usefulness if not of greatness. But I believe there was not a woman in the whole series. I was very bitter and naughty at the time. I did not pray, and was not anxious to be good.* [16]

Her fury is a defence against trauma, a survival strategy rather than a positive trait or form of self-identity. Her mother has been cast as adversary rather than model, guilty of stifling her creativity. Memories of her mother's femininity and sweetness, compared with Marianne's own moodiness and hankering after masculine pursuits, complicate her emotional inheritance. In Farningham's later life, she finds a pattern of living which is as far from her mother's life as possible. She does not marry and pursues her professional life whenever possible away from Kent. She never ceases to work at her writing. Anger and bitterness are channelled into determination and agency. Once she is her own authority, she too can be 'cheery' without being hypocritically sweet. In one significant memory, she recalls her mother giving her a piece of writing, a will she has either written herself or has had written for her. She divides up her few possessions and provides a 'legacy', entrusting her children's goodness and well-being to God. In law, her mother would have had no possessions of her own. It was 1882 before the Married Woman's Property Act was passed for England and Wales. This episode hints at the practice of 'will' making as a ritual form of family 'law' which could carry respect in communities regardless of its lack of legal status. Farningham keeps the 'pathetic document' all her life. This recollection serves to emphasise the powerlessness of her mother's generation of women and the pathos of illiteracy in a now increasingly literate world. Harbouring a fragment of significant writing for decades serves as a reminder of the limited literacy Farningham would have achieved had her mother's influence prevailed. She can write the words 'pathetic document' from her position as an author of popular books, the triumphant outcome of insisting on being taught to write.

226

How did Marianne learn to write? Her father was more present in her everyday life after her mother died, but the struggles over her education, creativity and desire for solitude continued. As is often true of working-class autobiography, her father has seemed an absent, undercharacterised figure, limited to his position of authority, which is displayed in occasional acts of discipline or benign attentiveness. Once he is the sole parent, he becomes the parent whose authority Farningham challenges. She turns to her teacher at her Sunday and British schools, Miss Eliza Hearn (not a relative), who becomes her mentor and role model. She resumes – irregular – attendance at school, 'that I might be with her'. Farningham's interest in writing at that time was channelled into helping her father at the post office: 'whenever there was an address in a particularly good handwriting, I copied it and tried to imitate it'. She was later criticised for having no individual style to her handwriting. Individuality and freedom from crushing uniformity are what she achieves through writing, making visible her sense of difference. Stylish handwriting would have been a prominent badge of that difference, but it remains irksomely lacking.

Although her 'ignorance was a constant burden' to her, indifference and hostility compounded by her long working day made it impossible to concentrate on lesson books. One summer she gets up at five o'clock every morning and sits in the woods and meadows, but exhaustion overcomes her, and her father expects her to be at work before seven o'clock. She begins to 'burn the midnight tallow'. She is sent to bed at ten o'clock but keeps herself awake by the 'immoral device' of drinking strong tea kept back from the afternoon's brew. She is overwhelmed by feelings of guilt at her deception and fears that her studies will provoke her father's disapproval and anger. Bit by bit she internalises a sense of shame about learning. She is discovered when a customer in the post office asks about the bedroom light shining after midnight. Her father orders her to produce evidence of what she's been doing, which consists of 'some cheap copy books with badly written pages, full of descriptions of the places that I had dreamed about, and never hoped to see'. Through her secret study of fact-laden geography books, she has continued to explore her private fantasy of heaven on earth, 'A Better Land'.

Her father rebukes her for the dishonourable act of saying goodnight under false pretences and setting a bad example to the other children. In this aspect of the drama of disobedience between parent and child, his

response is absolute. About her learning, he 'did not think such knowledge would ever be of much use' to her. Contemptuous of her hopes and
dreams, he only values education that is useful to their station in life. The
meaning of his daughter's life is expressed in terms of the moral absolutes
of duty, service and care of the family. Marianne's father was not unusually
cruel. It would have been an exceptional working-class parent in the 1840s
or 1850s who valued or sanctioned learning for girls which went beyond
practical skills. Marianne piously agrees that secret studying is sinful. But
she is much too committed to stop for long, and eventually 'yielded to
temptation once more'. She goes on writing and reading at night, often
falling asleep and waking at six in the morning with her clothes on and
the candle burnt out. One night she wakes to find her room on fire and
her father calmly extinguishing the flames. The symbolically elemental
ending to a clash of wills becomes a moment of reconciliation, and it
transforms their relationship. Marianne acquires the status of an adult in
her father's eyes, and a language of reciprocity and support replaces
fighting, subterfuge and inflexible parental authority.

Her father 'began to consult with me' about a return to school. The
compromise they reach is for Marianne to divide her time between
half-time work as a shoe-binder and half-time at school. She is to make
contributions for board and lodging. From this time, her study and
writing activities take precedence. She has a series of teachers, all
connected to the Baptist church and its institutions. She studies religious
and scientific subjects, including astronomy. Her education changes from
a solitary, secret process into an autonomous, social process. And the
subjects studied move closer to those often chosen by male autodidacts.
Marianne participates in social circles of teachers and friends connected
to the Baptists, which provide the setting around which working-class
cultural, educational and social life in the community clustered. She
dwells on names, places, subjects, debates, the attraction of religion and a
growing sense of belonging, as her points of reference move away from
family and into a public world. Her father's acceptance of her activity
challenges views of the uniformity of the rigidly repressive moral values of
Victorian fathers and non-conformist families. Marianne's father was able
to develop respect for his daughter's determination and her difference
from many other girls, and strike a compromise rather than cling to his
given authority. The elasticity in their relationship is essential to Marianne's escape from the domestic sphere towards a public, social sphere in

which she can steer her own education and desire to write as a legitimate part of her developing selfhood.[17]

In small communities like Eynsford, religious organisations – most frequently non-conformist churches and Quaker meetings – fostered networks where a degree of freedom in social and cultural life and learning could be enjoyed. The secular activities they organised sometimes challenged the moral certainties of their own Sunday rituals and prescriptive interpretations of the Bible. Certainly in education for both children and adults, religious and voluntary organisations were often at the forefront of rapid changes taking place in social and cultural life. In her next phase of learning, Marianne's mentor is the Reverend J. Whittemore, Eynsford's Baptist minister. He is a published writer and stimulates her interest in literature. During Marianne's years as mother-sister, she has 'written rhymes for friends' birthdays and other local happenings'. Now she and other young people become influenced by Whittemore: 'His talk about books and newspapers and publishing matters generally quickened in the minds of several young people a latent desire to write.' He introduces her to Shakespeare and gives her a copy of *Jane Eyre*, 'a book, my girl, which is thrilling everybody'. He suggests she reads fiction, which she had been taught to think of as 'wicked'. In encouraging her engagement with literature, he presents a novel written by a woman with a female heroine, suggesting alternative possibilities just at the point when she is poised between living a traditional village woman's life or pursuing her ambition to write: ' "if you can write like this you will do something". Alas! I only wished I could and have been wishing it ever since'.

To her irritation, even Whittemore could not resist condescending and sarcastic responses to her writing. He reads out her poems, pointing out their weaknesses with 'most aggravating scorn in his voice'. She becomes afraid of his opinion and once again retreats into writing in secret to improve her style, addressing his criticisms. Eventually a moment of vindication arrives, which confirms for her his hypocrisy and misuse of power:

> *A little girl, connected with our family, died, and I wrote some verses and sent them to the child's mother, a lady of fine intellectual ability. She wrote a short account of her daughter and put my verses in it. Mr. Whittemore read this account during his funeral sermon. There was no name attached to the verses and he, believing them to have been written by the lady herself, said before reading them, 'I do not know the author of these lines,*

229

but they are very beautiful.' I was quietly sitting in our pew at the back of the chapel, with my father, and I had a moment of keen joy, not unmixed with pride, for I knew that nothing would have induced him to speak thus had he known the words were mine.

She takes pleasure in this tribute to her writing made in the presence of both of the male authority figures who have tried to frustrate her ambition – as well as reaching, if anonymously, her first public audience. In all her phases of learning to write, the experience of humiliation motivates rather than discourages her, and forces a temporary retreat through which she regathers strength and confidence. And not once in the whole book does she express any doubt in her own ability. She is not afraid to be different and never apologetic about doing something others might see as inappropriate. Her concern is getting to know people who can help her and gaining the economic independence needed to realise her ambitions. She is energised by anger that this is harder for girls than it is for boys. She experiences humiliation but is never humbled, and does not respond to praise with gratitude: for Marianne, her writing is worth recognition, she has worked for it, and she takes pleasure in the deception necessary for success.[18]

She continues to write poetry and take lessons. She leaves home to become a teaching assistant in Bristol. Later, when she is forced to come home to look after a sick sister, she resents it as the end to her 'best prospects in life'.[19] Eventually she becomes a teacher and later still a member of the Northampton School Board. She writes continuously, gives lectures and travels the country to participate and perform at public events. She finds her first publisher independently of Whittemore. By the time he asks why she has bypassed the journal he edits, she is ready to confront him with his destructive criticism and establish a collaboration on more equal terms.

Throughout her life, writing is the means by which Marianne Farningham develops a sense of agency and the means to find a private and a public voice. Her writing is the weapon with which she assails powerful authorities and manoeuvres herself into a position of autonomy. When, in 1867, she decided to write for a living, her books included biographies of Grace Darling and Livingstone; and appreciations of Harriet Martineau, Elizabeth Barrett Browning and Charlotte Brontë. She wrote a fictional story arguing for the abolition of capital punishment and finally her autobiography. She wrote regularly for literary magazines and her choice of subjects is telling: legendary women of heroic valour; adventuring pioneers and feminists; rebellious and romantic poets; and a novelist whose work pushed at the boundaries of what was morally acceptable. In her choice of romantic feminine subjects, in her reviews of working-class women poets and in her preoccupation with justice, rights and Christianity, Farningham leaves behind the burdens of domestic duty and grafts her imagined world of exoticised otherness, romance and female heroism onto the morally responsible sensibilities of her public life in educational, religious and voluntary organisations. These allegiances socialised her passions. Through learning to write for a living, Farningham brought together her sense of social responsibility, her creative energy, independent life as a single woman and the hopes, dreams and fantasies of her inner selfhood. Her choice of subjects also reflects the costs and pleasures of creativity experienced by working women. Reading *Jane Eyre* is a milestone in her literary education. Brontë offered legitimacy for a 'subjective, single and immediate' voice for 'lonely unexpressed feeling'. Her form of 'special pleading' in *Jane Eyre* and *Villette* offered a model for working-class women's constructions of their individuality and selfhood. Williams called this the power of 'the immediate personal and creative form: the inclusive sharing of what had been an unspoken voice'.[20] It is a plea and a challenge to the external world to understand a writer's wayward actions and feelings in the context of their class and gender: 'Perhaps, circumstanced like me, you would have been, like me, wrong.'[21]

Writing enabled Marianne Farningham to develop her interior creative self. She used writing to create an authoritative voice as a person who had moved from a put-upon girlhood to a single woman living an unusually independent and socially-engaged life with a respected voice. She weaves the threads of her early steps in learning into a story in which writing practices are always significant – an emphasis in many autobiographies. She writes of acting as scribe for other people; of her delight in new writing materials such as stylographs and pads. She refers to spelling and quotes poems and hymns which were important to her learning. In these ways, her journey as a writer is charted meticulously from beginning to end. In small details and minor events, as well as grand emotional turbulence, the meaning of the scale of changes that literacy could bring about is revealed.

IV   Hannah Mitchell

Hannah Mitchell grew up in rural Derbyshire in the 1870s in a family of tenant farmers, the fourth of six children. She became a public figure in the suffragette movement, active in the Independent Labour Party (ILP), and a Manchester city councillor and magistrate. During her political work as a prominent working-class speaker in the Women's Social Political Union (WSPU) she was also known for her writings. Her autobiography, *The Hard Way Up*, reconstructs the emergence of a formidable creative and public selfhood from a childhood lived in poverty, in which she was equally starved of affection and the education she hungered after.

Hannah Mitchell claims she was persuaded to write her autobiography by a friend, who remains nameless. She acknowledges him at the end of a book which reveals bit by bit the sporadic development of her writing life and creative ambition: ' "You say you wanted to be a writer," he said. "Well, you *are* a writer. Go home and write your autobiography." '[22] Long before this passage, her desire to be recognised as a writer emerges in the spaces between her political life and private life, first as single working woman, then as wife and mother. In the first pages she announces her preoccupation with literacy, with getting an education and with her selfhood as a writer with an interesting story to tell.

Hannah Mitchell's childhood home was 'hidden away in a cleft of the hills in the wildest part of the Derbyshire moorlands'. Her mother, a former maidservant, was pretty, charming, well-dressed and could 'sing like a lark', but had terrifying outbreaks of violent temper which lasted several days, growing worse with the arrival of each child. Mitchell's autobiography is an emotionally-rich narrative which can be read as a psychic as well as social history. Hannah's own enduring anger is a defence against her pathological mother, and hardly a word of understanding, let alone remorse, softens the harsh portrait of her mother as she writes her autobiography decades later. Her memories of her mother are unforgiving, though her adult life as a feminist and socialist points towards her mother as an unacknowledged source of the fighting spirit and energy Hannah needed for political and social action. Her mother has squandered her own gifts and failed to channel her force of character: Hannah has learned the lessons of those failures for her own life. Even so, 'many years had to pass before I found some solution of the riddle in the complexities of my own nature'.[23]

232

The autobiography explores thoroughly the role writing, and her fierce desire for learning and books, played in the emergence of her adult self from her embattled childhood. Early on, Mitchell tells the story of a blind girl who lives on the next-door farm, using the imagery of an idealised, accomplished femininity and physical damage, against which Hannah's powerful and brutal mother is positioned. The blind girl is the object of compassion and envy. The story functions as a 'screen memory' in relation to the images of powerlessness and frailty in Hannah's childhood experience.

> *This blind girl was an object of much sympathy to my young mind. She had been for some years at a school for the blind, where she had been taught, not only to read and write, but many other useful arts as well. She could do the most intricate knitting patterns, and could wash dishes, and clean up the house as neatly as her sighted sister ... she was not the least morbid about her blindness, and used to get my sister and me to shut our eyes and try to follow her, laughing merrily when we stumbled into the furniture indoors.*[24]

The episode also suggests that to be literate and accomplished bring happiness which outweighs frailty and disability. When the blind girl and her mother die – briefly and factually reported – when Hannah is ten, her family take over their house. These events are juxtaposed with Hannah's account of her own mother's merciless 'scoldings and beatings' because her daughter did not have the stamina for a 16-hour day working on the new house. Hannah 'would have collapsed' had her brother not intervened to rescue her, and in this way the blind girl's death is associated with Hannah's recovery of the harshest memories of childhood, but also her own survival, overcoming vulnerability.

The opportunity to learn 'for some years' like the blind girl and the example of how education need not be at odds with domestic skills and duties excite wonder in Hannah and exacerbate her frustration that her mother is denying her aspirations for education. The episode feeds the psychic drama between them. She sees her father and his family history differently, beginning with their 'foreignness'. Her father's parents 'had earned their living in other ways' and given their children a 'fair education': not only could he read and write, he was artistic and interested in birds, flowers and country lore. Although her mother had also learned to read and write in Sunday school, her bad temper, irrationality and hostility to education are contrasted with her father's gentleness, courtesy and attention to education. Hannah identifies with the 'foreign' side of the family, who teach the children literacy:

> *My uncle taught me to write and I taught the two younger ones to read and write by a rough and ready method of my own invention, writing words of one syllable, such as 'cat' and 'dog', on a slate. I showed them how to copy these words until they learned to recognize them as they would a picture. Then by degrees I gave them bigger words until a whole sentence was built up. It was a long and difficult task as neither of them were keen on learning, and only came to their lessons to please me. But it was effective as they learned to read and write at the same time.[25]*

Hannah's story is not unusual in that families formed part of a tapestry of learning episodes and events in most localities; and everywhere, some families helped and others hindered those seeking literacy skills. Hannah's parents decide to send the children to school in turn because the costs are high, involving school fees and lodgings (the nearest school is five miles away) as well as the loss of free labour. Unsurprisingly, the older brothers attend first. Hannah uses her waiting time well, exchanging domestic tasks in return for her brothers' promises to bring books home from school and teach her at weekends. Meanwhile she plunders neighbours' libraries and her reading includes theology, cookery, horror stories (*The Castle of Otranto* 'haunted my dreams for many a night'), Gaskell's *Cranford* and *Adam's First Wife*, which 'raised some doubts in my mind as to Adam's innocence in the pre-apple days' and seems to prefigure her later feminist and secular beliefs. Her grandmother is a powerful figure: a competent, crisply-aproned community midwife who also tells her strange stories of Druidic life, converses with her dead husband and makes herbal remedies from her beautiful garden.

Hannah then describes her distress at not being allowed to join her sister 'for a bit of schoolin' after all. Her family's prosaic term is contrasted with her own enchanted vision of school as 'the magic key which would admit me to the treasure-house of learning'. She wears down her mother until she relents, and records making great progress with her learning, but a harsh winter and no heating in the schoolhouse mean both children soon fall ill and are kept home. In the spring her uncle takes charge of her learning again: 'He bought exercise books and set lines for me to copy – "Procrastination is the thief of time"; "Never put off till tomorrow what

234

you can do today" '. These typical examples of the moral adages used in published copy-books seem well chosen as an ironic commentary on the frustrating delays to her schooling. The significance of recalling them could be that while they are commonly-held maxims, and their status as folklore lends them timeless authority, they are also a call to human agency.

The connections Hannah makes between learning to write and the power of mythic language seem to herald the arrival of a stranger at the farmhouse door, seeking shelter from the rain. As in Janet Bathgate's and other working-class life stories, change – for good and ill – is catalysed by outsiders, mythic strangers, nearly always men, whose essence lies in their unknown provenance and their dislocation from time, place and community:

> *Among other matters he carried several books, and seeing my eager interest in these, asked if we liked reading poetry. We hardly knew what he meant. The only poetry we had read were short poems in the local paper, which my mother called 'verse'. But I knew it meant reading matter, so I said quickly: 'Yes, we like it'. He then took from his knapsack a copy of 'Wordsworth's Poems', saying that he would leave the book with us until he came again. Then whichever of us knew most of the poems by heart should have the book for their own.*

While she is writing her autobiography, Mitchell rediscovers the book, remembers seeing him 'write something on the fly leaf' and finds that the signature of the stranger belongs to a 'model employer' whom she had later known as a magistrate in Manchester. His role in her life has been 'a little act of generosity' in a 'long and useful life'. So the episode becomes a social reality in time and place, coexisting with her intuitive sense of the stranger as a magical harbinger of change. In the creation of a mythic structure in many women's autobiographies, the benign outsider is often a middle-class man. And although class-consciousness, rooted in social, political and economic life, is a strong element in reconstructions of self, the factual and historical are sometimes suspended to allow such mythical agents of change to transcend and make good the limitations of material realities. If the energy to transform circumstances cannot be found from within real-life situations, it may come instead from a dehistoricised 'other', a visitor from outside the mundane world of human struggle, frustration and defeat. The stranger's intervention is a brief appearance or apparition, a magical visitation, which cannot be a continuous relationship. A stranger can represent a subversive form of messenger from God or the Devil – for Hannah Mitchell, bringing good, for Janet Bathgate, misfortune. The stranger's appearance may remain inexplicable in ordinary social historical terms. Its mythological meaning, however, is central to a story in which personal change and attainment can only be explained as fabulous and extraordinary. But this contradiction works both ways. The stranger is also credited with initiating processes of change and attainment in the social, material world, which, although activated by a mysterious visitation, are also associated with ordinary life.

This stranger has walked into the tension between mother and daughter and unknowingly escalated their battle of wills, which is now about time 'wasted' in reading and memorising Wordsworth. Like Marianne Farningham, Hannah associates her discovery of poetry with her desire to learn to write. She is depressed and demoralised by feelings of ugliness, frustrated ambition and the long working day imposed on her by her mother. The blind girl, a possible role model for overcoming handicap, has died. Her brother is the only person who can bring calm between her and her mother and she flees to his house when she runs away from home: 'ill-equipped for the battle of life. Uneducated, untrained'. She feels driven out by her mother whom she 'never quite forgave ... for my lack of education'. Mitchell uses an unattributed quotation from a book on child psychology to accuse her mother: 'Would you hammer back the apple blossom and insist that it became a pear?' Her flight from home feels essential, but also painful and equivocal. It is only her mother she wanted to leave and she records her misery as she 'tramped over the hill, hardly conscious of the distance, blinded by tears and full of grief at leaving my father and uncle, and the two younger children', conscious that she has 'left her childhood behind for ever'.

Hannah's story is more complex than the portrayal of herself as heroine and victim – misunderstood, mercilessly driven out and finally roused to violence by endless provocation. It is also a narrative of self-absorption and self-will, an insistent moving against a mother's opposition while she is fully conscious of her own cussed nature. More than that, she concedes that 'in my desire for education I was determined and ruthless, rating my own intelligence probably much higher than it really was'.[26] These characteristics are precisely those she has inherited from her mother: they colour her imagination, feed her passion and belief in justice, and provide her with the energy she needs for a life of hard work and arduous, enervating campaigning. She never directly acknowledges their temperamental affinity. But she touches on it once, in a bemused tribute to her mother, who comes to live nearby after her father's death. When Hannah later falls ill with a nervous breakdown it is her mother, who she claims has no time for 'ordinary illness', who understands her suffering and helps her through a year of mental illness. Projecting her own feelings, she can see that 'perhaps some latent insight into her own temperament gave her the clue as to mine'.[27]

After leaving home Hannah goes straight into domestic service and earns extra money dressmaking. She borrows books from the local library, and continues to carve out time to read. She uses her free time and money to buy exercise books to improve her handwriting. One episode in this section describes seeing the first ever photograph of herself, in a group, and its meaning to her is as

> *a milestone in my life, showing me to myself, for the first time, as an attractive girl ... I did quite honestly believe myself to be unattractive, and was so painfully conscious and ashamed of my ignorance, that I did not fully appreciate the knowledge I possessed. I could not sing or dance, or even make conversation like my friends.*[28]

Hannah's confidence grows through political work for the ILP and the suffragette movement: reading, learning and public speaking. But during an exhausting schedule of campaigning and public speaking for the WSPU, she collapses during a public meeting at the 1907 Colne Valley bye-election. She has suffered a nervous breakdown, and she contrasts the support of her mother and her working-class women friends and fellow campaigners throughout the year she needed to recover with the middle-class WSPU leadership by whom she felt neglected and abandoned.

Two chapters explore her continued preoccupation with writing and her pursuit of an audience. The chapter which follows 'Breakdown' tells of an incident in which she hears a man say 'with a sneer: "Hannah Mitchell! Oh! she's a sort of Dickens in petticoats" ', which she receives as a great compliment, confidently taking issue with 'sort of'.[29] Although this is a digression from the main narrative of public political work and Mitchell's reflections on WSPU strategy and tactics, and the incident takes up just five lines, she calls the chapter 'Dickens in Petticoats'. The scene exemplifies how divergent strands of activity and preoccupations are not always woven together into linear patterns, but co-exist, scattered through a text in episodic and abrupt transitions. They are not just interesting digressions from a straightforward social history of a working-class WSPU activist, but must be interpreted through another symbolic register to excavate meaning. At the point of the 'Dickens' incident, her writerly self is emerging strongly, associated with growing confidence in her creativity – just at a moment when she is recovering from illness. As Mitchell puts it: 'a nervous breakdown is like breaking a spring which may be mended, but never again has the same resilience'.[30] Writing becomes associated with what is pleasurable, and with the easing of her life after the First World War. Like Marianne Farningham, she became a respected, socially-engaged citizen, serving as a Manchester city councillor and a magistrate. She also became a member of the Lancashire Authors' Association. She wrote dialect sketches, which were published in an ILP paper. She entered literary competitions, and wrote a booklet on local history for a Methodist group. In recalling its publication, she again draws comparisons with Dickens, who she often quotes and whose powerful significance for Mitchell is shared by other working-class writers, for example Margaret Penn.[31] Hannah Mitchell emphasises the differences between herself and Dickens, but confidently asserts the view that there are characteristics all writers share. It is a statement which expresses her feelings about belonging to a new group.

> *I'm sure that Dickens with all his fame never felt so proud as I did viewing that little pile of books, bearing my name, but I think he would have understood my bit of simple vanity. Only the truly great writer can enter into the feelings of the untaught, struggling against great odds to express themselves. The little booklet sold well and I felt that in a very small way I had become a writer.*

In this passage she presents herself as the fraught little girl, but she also has a new identity as a professional writer who can sell her work. In the final chapter of her autobiography, 'The Kitchen Sink', Mitchell examines the tension between the opposites of duty and freedom; untaught child and writer; constraint and adventure; the domestic and public spheres; material reality and 'the early dreams, secret hopes and half-realised ambitions of one very ordinary woman'.[32] Working within opposites, her whole book is an argument for women's empowerment. Walking up a long steep hill against harsh winds means struggle as well as the pleasure of getting at least half-way up. This life story is an exposition of the ways in which writing itself can motivate and give depth of meaning to hard-fought personal change. She says of the conditions of writing *The Hard Way Up* that its production under the threat of Second World War bombing raids focused her mind on the search for the 'brotherhood' which aimed to make war impossible, and on trying to discover through writing how such a project could be reborn.

> *This thought enabled me to keep my courage during those long, dreadful nights when it seemed as if morning would never come. With pencil and paper I set down roughly this story of my life, and asked myself what life had taught me.*[33]

V   Louise Jermy

Louise Jermy was born in 1877 in rural Hampshire, daughter of a stonemason's foreman. Her mother died a year later. After her father remarried, the family moved to Dalston in East London. Her schooling was intermittent. In a childhood marked by unhappiness and psychological distress as a result of bitter conflicts with her step-mother and her obsession with revenge, writing became both the focus of her troubled circumstances and the means of dealing with them. Jermy's presentation of her developing selfhood in a difficult family context is characterised by her strong sense of difference: a desired, embattled and finally celebrated otherness. She presents her ability to write, to say something unique, as positive proof of her difference, confirmed by other people and associated with her possession of irrational powers as well as more ordinarily explicable talents. This brew of characteristics is reflected in the passage below in which Jermy moves between persuasive versions of herself, 'she' and 'I', from the imagined perspectives of others:

> *It has been suggested that I write the story of my life. I am wondering if the one who made the suggestion has said to herself, like many others have done, 'She', meaning myself, 'is not like other people', for I have heard this remark passed so often that I have come to believe it … I have often been told that I possess the gift of second sight, if there is such a thing. I have often been called 'A Witch'.*[34]

The people who suggested she write her life story were women in the respectable world of the Women's Institute. Her autobiography is said to be the first by a W.I. member. And the dutifully type-casting title of her book, *The Memories of a Working Woman*, gives no hint of the emotional storms at the heart of her story, of the demonic reaches of the feminine she embraces in 'She' and 'Witch', or of her insistence on difference. She does not want to be known as just another working woman: any reader's expectation of ordinariness or sameness in working-class experience is soon confounded. Her determined awkwardness is signalled by more nicknames which draw attention to her defiance of traditional class and gender roles: 'The Lady Louisa' at work because of her contemptuous manner; and 'Dynamite' to reflect her wild and transgressive temperament. The book title follows a generically self-denigrating formula: it assumes a cultural predisposition to casting working-class people in the same mould. But this is challenged by her insistence that she is telling the story of a unique and complex life; a working-class person is drawing attention to the existence of 'A Woman', a particular woman, who has a life as a writer as well as a worker. Even the simple title may seek to say something more complex, and Jermy is in good company among autobiographers. One example is George Acorn's *One of the Multitude* (1911), which includes a piece of 'special pleading' for his readers' understanding of the lived contradictions for working-class writers as they deal with their multiple identities which are individual and related to belonging to a social class. On the one hand there is a sense of singularity and of being chosen: the 'One'. On the other hand there is a humbleness, but also a challenge to the language of the multitude or increasingly 'the masses', which emphasises from on high the ordinariness and sameness of working-class life:

> *I have called it ONE OF THE MULTITUDE but it is probably one of many such; – isolated souls struggling in obedience to inner promptings, which are at first a nuisance, and later recognised as some divine mystery or miracle … The book is but an imperfect record, – a poor thing, maybe, but 'One's' own; and perhaps the public will recognise that experiences LIVED, and written down however poorly, are of more real value and interest than imaginary fictions beautifully disguised.*[35]

In Louise Jermy's writing, the play between 'I' and 'She' and others is complex. Her adoption of the position of a legitimising outsider in references to herself as 'She' provides a commentary which somehow substantiates her identity and position in society in relation to the

240

benefactresses and companions in the Women's Institute who encouraged her to write and facilitated the publication of her book. The detached 'She' also hints at 'She-Devil': not just different from but powerfully threatening to the respectable rural social world. Her life story reveals her transgressive ways of being different in the working-class world of her childhood and how she becomes a modern 'New Woman', engaging with the fearful misogynistic world, popularised by Rider Haggard, with a degree of relish and her own twist on women's roles and relationships. The third person also allows Louise to express her ambivalence about owning the self which she professes other people see in her. Yet her book justifies and celebrates the actions in which she throws acceptable feminine behaviour to the winds. Playing with a novelistic convention of 'she' gives her a way, in Barthes's terms, 'of building the world in the way [she] chooses' and cocking a snook at convention.[36] In more conventionally-constructed first-person autobiography it is more difficult for the 'I' to be the sardonic and righteous spectator of her own story.

The writing process itself offers meaning to Louise's 'gift of second sight'. The use of imagination, the crafting of stories and self-discipline are all as important as sorcery and revenge in expressing power. Through writing she can invest her embattled life with meaning and through writing she can unravel the tangled knots of her early life, and deal with uncomfortable relationships and memories of an isolated childhood. Writing is asked to explain a life, but it is also its apprenticeship. It is the skill through which she is able to transform the sour relationships which threaten her emerging subjectivity into relationships through which she can forge, defend and justify a transgressive female self.

Archetypal roles and the rhythmic elements of fairy tales characterise the narrative style. As for Farningham, the key event of Louise's early life is the death of her mother when she was less than two years old. Though she has no conscious memory of her birth mother, she re-enacts her final illness and death as theatre, and after death her mother becomes a magical presence in her life. One day while her mother is ill, their employer, 'her Ladyship', passes her in her cart as she walks along the road and offers her sympathy, which is accepted, melodramatically: 'I am cold, my Lady, you see I walk so slowly'. 'Her Ladyship' wraps her dying mother in her own 'beautiful coat and cloak all in one of white wool and threaded with blue silk'. After her mother's death the coat 'vanished'. But aged 15, Louise rediscovers it, re-dyed and outmoded. She ties black ribbons to it and wears it 'as long as I possibly could' regardless of the mockery she attracts:

'I didn't care, I went my way in silence'. She is never parted from the cloak, and, as she writes her life story, she still possesses fragments of it. The mythical mother, herself once rescued by a fairy Godmother, seems to be present through this emblem to provide a conspiratorial 'warmth' and approval for Louise's version of her embattled girlhood. Despite the 40 years between them, Marianne Farningham and Louise Jermy and her sister Amy experienced a similar pattern of schooling: a mixture of attendance at the British school, home teaching and complete neglect. The unevenness of access to education persisted in urban and rural communities long after 1870. Although Louise describes going to school in happily vivid terms, 'I can see us in fancy now as we would run through the town', family members are remembered as effectively the main teachers of her sister Amy and herself.

> *Mother taught us both to knit and I took my stockings to knit even in the infants' school, and although I could do that, strange to say, I could not learn to read and finding that I could not get on, my father taught me to read himself, as my sister could read even before we ever left Romsey … and he also bought me a Mavors spelling book, and so many words as he marked off I had to learn every day.*

Louise's childhood is dominated by her relationship with her step-mother, although the grandmother who 'taught her verses' and hymns is still significant and positive, associated with aspiration and creativity in ways her parents are not. For some years her step-mother is depicted as warm and protective, a teacher to her, and a human shield from her father's harsh treatment. Moving to Dalston in East London brings her sense of being different to crisis point, marked by the 'strangeness' of her uneven progress in learning, her 'crying fits' when she is scolded, particularly by her beloved grandmother, the fact that her 'mother' is her step-mother and her father's wish that his children should better themselves and not 'mix with so many rough children'. They are sent to a school where Louise remembers the high standards and the 6d per week fees. She lists the tools, materials and books they had to buy themselves: 'slates, copy books, pens, rulers, poetry books, geometry sets'. The remembered list of commonplace but costly tools seems to double as an incantation of the mysterious totems of writing.[37]

Unfortunately for their father, although Louise and Amy flourish academically, they exhibit exactly the rough unfeminine behaviour from which he has been trying to shield them. They fight viciously with each other and disgrace themselves. On one occasion Louise throws a knife at her sister. The fragile family relations, which contextualise Louise's self-characterisation as a bewildered, violent and vulnerable girl in an aspirational working-class family, revolve around a harsh father, a volatile step-mother increasingly sick with a tubercular hip disease and a strong, healthy sister who retaliates against brutality and unkindness – in contrast with Louise's own physical frailty and chronic ill-health. Louise's family relationships are a kaleidoscope of changing alliances: kindness replaces severity in her father, spite replaces protectiveness in her step-mother. A story of losing her memory and her bearings is one signal of her psychological disturbance and dislocation. Louise describes becoming 'lost' while out alone on a simple errand, finding herself again miles away in a street where the family had previously lived. Other writers prided themselves on their tempestuous nature. The suffragette mill-worker Annie Kenney hinted that Emily Brontë's life and work was a legitimising role model for behaviour driven by elemental passions:

> … *storms, surging floods, windswept moors, lightning and terrific thunder, in fact the militancy of nature rouse within me emotions that in themselves are enough to sweep me away in their surging dreams and yet, as though to save me, deep down there is always great stillness. A passionate and big personality alone appealed to me. A militant movement alone could satisfy such a tempestuous nature as mine.*[38]

In some respects, Louise's father is a powerful figure, far from the feeble father of traditional fairy tales. But in family conflicts he conforms to the stereotype: he is weak and faltering and cannot effectively intervene on behalf of Louise. Ultimately he is a minor character in the drama of Louise's childhood. The struggles Louise remembers are exclusively female events involving mother, sister, friends – and in the pivotal events, her step-mother. Though she is ambivalent about her own family, Louise loves her Sunday school teacher and embraces religion. Her step-mother's opposition to Sunday school marks the rapid deterioration of their relationship. This struggle with her is at the heart of the search for a solid emotional space among shifting sands, one in which a developing self-hood can be nurtured without being uprooted by distressing confrontations and the unpredictability and high-handedness of powerful others.

Louise's step-mother denounces her religious fervour as 'crazy' and tries to prevent her from reading Sunday school literature at night as a wasteful use of light. Louise resorts to secrecy. The conflict escalates when her step-mother discovers her reading the Bible, and 'swept all my books – Bible, Prayer Book and hymns and text book – into her dirty apron'. Louise makes her point by way of the classic nineteenth-century association between ignorance and uncleanliness. They quarrel violently and exchange bitter words. Louise refuses to accept her step-mother's apology and any suggestion of reconciliation. Instead she swears revenge, and throughout the book refers to her oath of vengeance, looking to build suspense as in a novel. Eventually, her step-mother returns the books and Louise sees that she is crying. Nothing is said for years: 'then I brought it home to her with such a biting force, that she declared with tears and distress, that what I had said had broken her heart. I said it was a mere nothing, that she had broken mine years before and cursed my life ever since.'

Jermy recalls that a few years later, on her seventeenth birthday, her father gave her a Bible, which she interprets as a curious and magical act of recompense because her father supposedly knew nothing of the earlier incident. Throughout the book Jermy presents herself as a difficult, uncompromising person with mysterious powers, as well as a lost, mistreated child. The contradictions in her combination of cruelty and loyalty to her step-mother reflect attempts to sustain a complex sense of self which enables her to persist in challenging attempts to suppress her spirit, while allowing loving feelings to co-exist or be serially replaced with hostile ones. The pressures on her, and on nineteenth-century working-class girls generally, combine to inhibit any straightforward emergence of a sense of agency, dispersing and displacing the elements of an emergent self into resentment of the overriding demands of others. The selfhood she constructs seems both an acknowledgement of and challenge to these pressures: an inner selfhood which could hold fast in such circumstances was bound to be complex, contradictory and split, forged both with and against significant others.

Despite her father's educational aspirations, Louise's working life starts aged 11, first in domestic service and afterwards as a knitter. At 14, she begins an apprenticeship as a dressmaker. But the hostility between Louise and her step-parent continues, now expressed through money. 'There were very few days in which my stepmother did not tell me that it was three guineas thrown away, and that it was a pity that I had not got to work for my living like other poor devils.'

244

An independent place of work offers Louise the relative privacy she needs to write, which is the way she works through her feelings:

At this time I wrote my first piece, scribbling it down in the workroom while I was waiting for my work to come back from the fitting room. It all came about from a few words said to one of the girls who happened to say to one of the older ones, 'I am sorry, I'll unsay all I said', and the reply, 'You can't, it's not much use to be sorry afterwards'. You understand the title.

BITTER WORDS

Bitter words in anger spoken,
You cannot recall again.
Time is past, the heart once broken
Sighs and tears are all in vain.
Perhaps in time they are forgiven,
But the thought will still remain,
And the words so harshly spoken
Will return to you again.

After a few minutes' thought about it, I added the next lines, which leaves no doubt as to what I wished if only I could have carried it out.

Let us never then in anger,
Pierce a heart with words unkind,
For in after years they may be
Often called again to mind.

Well I thought, I'll copy it out neatly when I get home, and they will help me to remember, which I did, watching my opportunity when I was alone, as I thought. It just shows how closely I was watched; I had written it out and just folded it and slipped it into my pocket, when my stepmother came in, and demanded to see the letter I had been writing. She had been watching me through the half-open door unknown to me. I told her it was not a letter, and nothing much, but that I didn't want her to see it. Said she, 'It's some chap you are writing to, I suppose?' I said, 'No, it's really nothing much, it's just something I didn't want to forget.' Said she, 'It's something you are afraid for me to see, or you are ashamed of, or you

245

would give it to me, but I want to see it, so take it out of your pocket and give it to me.' Well, I was only shy about it, and I didn't want her to have it, but I handed it over to her without a word. She read it and read it again. It was something so different from what she'd expected, so utterly unlooked for from a girl not yet seventeen. It showed how I looked at life and also how bitter had been the experience to me to be able to put it so plainly. The paper was handed back without a word and I never knew what she thought about it. She never mentioned it again, neither did she ever accuse me of writing to chaps on the sly.[39]

This incident takes place not long after the 'rediscovery' of her birth mother's old cloak. As she deals with contradictory feelings towards her step-mother, she is strengthened by her symbolic 'inheritance', a comforting connection with her birth mother. This helps her to distance herself from her step-mother enough to make a considered gesture towards her. The second part of the verse appears to take responsibility for her part in the drama which she already knows has deeply disturbed her step-mother ('I saw that she was crying'), but she is also pointing the finger – yet her step-mother, as reader, could interpret it as regret as much as blame. Louise's actual words in the original row are never disclosed, and the wording of her poem permits her to orchestrate events: to present herself as enigmatically powerful, avoid responsibility for the quarrel and present herself a victim. Louise alludes to the oath as devastating, and her repentance and pious regret, if such they are, are comparable to the sentiments of a Sunday school hymn or copy-book homily. Her writing conveys the pain of her revenge pledge, as well as the paradoxical feelings of freedom and terror at the power she holds in the relationship. Writing is the conduit for changing the terms of her relationship with her step-mother – possibly luring her through the 'half-open' door, but certainly wrong-footing and silencing her. Writing also enables her to make a point about the relative power of writing and speech. Though she sees the verbal utterance of her oath as irreversible and unforgettable, through writing she finds a new voice.[40] She can construct herself as wronged heroine, but also as the actor in charge of the scene.

Louise is not yet finished with her step-mother and she finds her moment to complete the drama.

For the revenge I took after waiting my chance about seven years, I've no excuse save that honour thy father and mother could not mean to me what it once had done, seeing that the Book which taught it, along with "Vengeance is mine", had been condemned by her as damned rubbish.

When Louise eventually goes into domestic service she resumes her education, reading poetry and learning French with her employer. Frail health soon forces her to return home, but in the meantime she has learned important skills and is committed to women's suffrage, influenced by her employer's political ideas. During yet another quarrel with her step-mother, when she advocates the right of women to smoke, she sees her chance to strike:

I saw in a flash the day of reckoning had come. In quite a quiet tone I asked her did she remember the day when she had taken away my Bible, and what I had said ... She visibly shuddered as she realised at last, how near to utter disaster she had brought us both ... she said I had broken her heart and with biting mockery I laughed and told her it was nothing.

Shortly after taking her revenge, Louise writes an ambiguously-entitled story, 'The Answered Prayer', in which she protests her belief in God, despite the failure of her prayers that her books would not be taken from her. She re-emphasises the existence of another 'self', split off from the socially-adept, vulnerable and physically frail person: a tough intransigent self whom others must eventually meet if they test their will against hers. Her personal power is sustained by secrecy, will-power and duplicity: 'my step-mother and myself went everywhere together and in general we were very good friends and I am sure no-one would ever have suspected that there had been such bitter trouble between us in the past'. Louise constructs herself as the lurking evil-doer in her drama, plotting the moment of attack, half-revealed to a wondering audience but cloaked in an innocence that dupes the victims she appears to befriend. She is also the cruelly-treated heroine, unhappily deserted by her lover and exqui-sitely delicate in health. When her troubled courtship ends disastrously, Louise suffers a breakdown, feeling 'the most extraordinary fear of the future and dread of change', and has a 'premonition' of the course events would take. Her step-mother is the only person able to care for her 'because she saw what no-one else did, that I was slowly losing a grip of myself and that I was not fit to go about alone'.[41]

Louise believes in her own feelings of empathy with her step-mother as a fellow human in pain, and she believes that her step-mother understands her own will to self-destruction. Just as Hannah Mitchell was briefly reconciled with her mother during her mental breakdown, she acknowledges that her step-mother is the one who nurses her to recovery. Their shared physical frailty becomes not only an additional source of mutual suspicion, but an unwelcome mirror on her own life. Her step-mother's illness with cancer opens their locked relationship and becomes the catalyst of reconciliation, but first creates another twist in their operatic family relations. When Louise marries John Jermy, a gardener, she writes letters to her step-mother. Her father withholds them, for undisclosed reasons, while her step-mother 'grieved at her negligence'. She dies five months after her step-daughter's marriage and Louise is then reconciled with her father. She can only accept, or is only allowed, one loving parent at a time. All the actors in the narrative, as the hidden letters suggest, are complicit in sustaining this unhappy pattern.[42] Each blocks and prevents the possibility of an accord, which might have enabled Louise to come to terms with feelings of early loss and abandonment and their consequences.

The deep structure of Louise Jermy's narrative is formed by writing itself. Writing permits a degree of self-revelation, distinct from the telling incidents themselves. Writing offers Jermy the means to create the self-justifying story of her life. Writing facilitates her attempt at synthesising multiple, conflicted selves – the witch, the heroine, the villain and the victim – and allows her to develop into the awkwardly-placed, but creative, active, socially-responsible woman and mother. Writing empowers her to discover her voice and publishing adds another dimension of legitimacy for her story. Writing is significant throughout Louise Jermy's life because it marks critical moments in the development of a selfhood which developed through difficult relationships with others, whether hated, loved, despised or respected. Above all, writing justifies and gives voice to Louise Jermy's sense of otherness. The series of incidents is rooted in undercurrents of unhappiness, discord and emotional volatility. Writing empowers Jermy to use the material of emotional discord to develop a powerful, complex and uncomfortable subjectivity, and the tools with which she can explore and justify it.

VI Margaret Penn

Margaret Penn's *Manchester XIV Miles* is the first of an autobiographical trilogy, which tells the story of Hilda Winstanley. In a third-person narrative, Penn moves between the social historical facts of working-class life in a Lancashire village and the construction of a semi-fictionalised heroine, in ways which stretch and cut to her own pattern the genre of autobiography. Hilda is born in 1896, the illegitimate child of 'a gentleman' and his servant. She is adopted by a farm labourer's family, Joe and Lizzie and their two sons, who live in 'Moss Ferry', near the Mersey estuary. The title implies the desire to move away: Manchester may be close geographically but it is a sophisticated, faraway place. The facts of her birth are unknown to Hilda, and Penn creates a drama in which she is set apart from her community. It is a version of the classic story of an orphan discovering noble parentage, eventually restored to her rightful *niveau social*. Hilda pushes herself up the social ladder, excelling at Board School and gaining a dressmaking apprenticeship at a fashionable Manchester department store, acquiring the trappings of glamour. She tries to address the growing differences between the language and culture of her family and her self-promotion into 'the ranks of the professional workers'.[43] At the point where her training reaches a higher level and family relationships move towards irrevocable discord, the 'proper relations in London' are introduced, and her journey to the literary world of her father's family, who are London booksellers, provides closure. The romantic heart of the story is not marriage to a prince but the realisation of Hilda's desire to be educated, to write, and to belong to the middle-class. Her fantasy is complicated by her absent father's identity as her mother's rich seducer. For girls like Hilda, with access through local libraries to romantic fiction, reading a different, vivid narrative of self.

Hilda's development as a character and her problematic relationships in the Moss Ferry family can also be read as an exploration of the meaning of literacy in class relations in the age of Board School education. The book explores the intergenerational and gender-related tensions resulting from children becoming more literate than their parents, dealing with increasingly indispensable literacies and wielding greater authority over the demands of written communication as they invaded everyday life.[44] Hilda's belief that she is different from her family is unshakeable. For one, in her adoptive mother's words, she had 'allus been that self-willed'. Before her opportunity to leave home finally materialises, she has created such tensions within the family that the closure is an escape from escalating conflict caused by Hilda's desire for a skilled job, a city life. Hilda's first inkling of her different status comes when she discovers the names of all the Winstanley family members inscribed in their Bible, drawn up in her eldest brother John's handwriting, in order of age. Although she is not the youngest, Hilda's name has been entered last, 'as an afterthought'. Peeved at the slight but intrigued, she soon afterwards picks up village gossip which deepens her sense of some 'mystery concerning herself'. She confronts her mother with 'this exciting news'. In the exchange that follows Penn accentuates Hilda's difference through their language. Hilda's mother speaks in an exaggerated regional dialect, in contrast to Hilda's standard English. The working-class family becomes patronised and exoticised. Hilda's language is the norm, justifying her rejection of them. Penn uses Lancashire dialect in family dialogues as a tool of social positioning and to display Hilda's grasp of two cultures. Her speech, in agreement with the grammar of the narrative, places her as 'normal' (standard), and also as the writer (objective), explaining working-class life to an imagined middle-class readership. Her 'special pleading' tries to justify her rejection of working-class life and the fantasy of belonging to the imagined refinement of middle-class life.

In the course of telling Hilda about her parentage, her mother boxes her ears and makes dismissive pronouncements which Penn simply declares 'irrelevant'. Hilda's sharpest invective is reserved for illiteracy, stupidity, uncouthness and the links between them. Hilda praises her father and her eldest brother John, respected as good-tempered and intelligent and who 'read a Sunday newspaper and could talk quite knowledgeably about politics'. By contrast, the younger brother Jim:

> *was tall and big-boned like his father, but in looks took after his mother, and he had her quick, easily roused temper. He was able to read and write, but, as his health had kept him away from school for long periods, he could only do these things slowly. He used to spend whole evenings reading* The Family Herald, *following the lines closely with his finger.* The Family Herald *was taken by John and was the only paper that came into the house ... Between Jim and Hilda there was continual strife. With her book-learning she could always get the better of him in arguments, and many and bitter were the fights they had. Sometimes as she watched him reading painfully through* The Family Herald *she would jeer at him unmercifully, provoking him to such a towering, lunatic and bestial rage that he would jump from his chair and pursue her with murder in his eyes. Only then, when she sensed the awful physical danger she was in, would she run to her mother for protection. Once, when in rage he roughly pushed his mother aside in his desire to choke the life out of his sister, she*

had barely time to bound up the stairs to the little room which she shared with Lily. She managed to shoot the rickety bolt, and stood braced against the door, at which he was shaking and pounding. She could hear him slobbering, and quaked with terror lest the gimcrack fastening gave way.

Penn's characterisation echoes fictional depictions of literacy already discussed in which the physique and ways of life of working men are seen as incompatible with the delicacy of touch required for writing. From this, other characteristics are extrapolated. Here, Jim's illiteracy is also associated with instinctual irrational behaviour. His efforts at reading mean nothing. Jim's primitive nature and slowness are like a slumbering beast, capable of murderous aggression when aroused. Hilda is the damsel in distress, fearing that 'she would, if he ever got his hands on her … be crushed like a blown eggshell'. In contrast to Jim, Hilda is allowed the subtlety of a moral conscience and a capacity for remorse, if not compassion, expressed from behind the safe borders of her subsequent good fortune. Hilda's demonisation of illiterate people extends to representing a good working-class home as an unsafe environment, separated only by a flimsy curtain from the jungle beyond. Stronger still is her confident sense of the higher state of being conferred on her by elementary schooling, relegating those who have no literacy to a status less than fully human:

With his laborious pothook-writing, his slow reading and his dirty physical habits, he disgusted her. For though he washed himself just as thoroughly every night as John and her father, his clomping farm boots brought a strong smell of manure into the kitchen, and his corduroy trousers, which he tied just under the knees with a thick rope of straw, smelt of sour milk and other farm peculiarities. She could not understand why Jim should smell so horrible when … Joe always smelt natural – of bracken and hay and clean straw, and he always rubbed his boots well in the long grass by the roadside.

Apart from clean straw, the rural world is represented as an offensive working environment. For Penn, nature is not the romanticised childhood pastures of Farningham or Bathgate or Clare. Jim's presence confronts Hilda with the sweat and smell of human work and bodily functions; and by association with the sensual circumstances of her own origin. Jim is an affront to her attempts to adopt middle-class social mores, but also offers her the opportunity for a display of genteel squeamishness.

The problem for Hilda is that Jim belongs, in writing, as a socially-documented fact on the Bible's flysheet, whereas she is a scribbled 'afterthought', and this situation provides the impetus she needs to realise her dream of professional and social success.

Jim also epitomises the embarrassing gulf between home and school life. Hilda shines at school, but home increasingly becomes a place of ambivalent feelings:

> *Hilda was excited at having a friend home and everything was going well till Jim clumped in with his smelly boots. She saw Cissie's face wrinkle at the offensive odour, and when she put away her unfinished sandwiches in her little basket Hilda could have died from shame. Cissie never came again, preferring to eat in the warm clean classroom.* [45]

Hilda's childhood highlights the increasing stigma attached to illiteracy brought about by the establishment of Board Schools in the 1890s. Autobiographies rarely suggest that illiteracy was experienced as a serious stigma before this time, though middle-class commentators frequently projected shame onto illiterate people. Some embarrassment seems to have accompanied brides and grooms not being able to sign the marriage register, and some – especially women – are likely to have signed with an 'x' so as not to show up their illiterate spouse.[46] But Hilda's parents, who never had the opportunity to learn and could neither read nor write, are treated as objects for her charitable help. Her own success is measured by the failure of others in a new educational environment which has become more systematically competitive than the community-based schooling so common for much of the century.

Hilda's pride in her educational progress is focused on writing. In minute detail she tells the story of her first public performance, a paper on 'Spiders' presented to the newly-established 'Moss Ferry and Kilnbrook Mutual Improvement Society'. She gathers information from *Chatterbox*, her regular annual and, until the opening of a local cooperative library, her main reading matter apart from the Bible and *From Log Cabin to White House*. She describes working

> *unceasingly, pruning it and polishing it until she had got it to her liking, quite certain that not a single question could be asked to which she had not memorised the answer. Finally she copied out the paper neatly in a*

penny exercise book with ruled lines, and waited as patiently as she could till her turn arrived.

She relishes the public performance and applause without a trace of coyness, satisfied with her calm handling of critical reactions which she dismisses as malicious envy.

Like many Board School children of illiterate parents, Hilda becomes the scribe and mediator of family literacy practices, managing personal and business correspondence. In many families, keeping accounts and running the family's transactional and social communication was women's — by now often girls' — work. John could have performed the role, but instead he read any letters to himself, then left Hilda to read them and she 'eagerly assented' to writing the few letters the family needed to send. The rare arrival of a letter involved a ritual: it waited, propped against the tea-caddy until tea-time when Hilda was asked to read and re-read it until her mother, then her father, had learnt it by heart. Jim could not read the letters and Hilda enjoyed 'impressing her loutish brother with her cleverness'.[47] Hilda's open delight in her skills and the reversal of parent–child responsibilities for literacy practices are met in the family with a mix of pride and fear that she is 'getting above herself'. Hilda is 'top in spelling' and her essays are read out to the class. Her mother, 'who had no idea what an English composition was, showed that she was pleased but nevertheless warned Hilda not to go getting above herself'. Her father celebrated her individuality and achievement: 'Aye. Reckon she's got it in her. There's nowt like being a good scholard when all's said and done'.[48] Each response voices classic phrases of working-class homage to education. Her mother fears the moral consequences of inappropriate ambitions in a girl and her ambivalent response is both more damned and more respected. For Penn, literacy is a divisive cultural process between working-class siblings. As Hilda becomes more educated and begins her dressmaking apprenticeship, the consequences of literacy are re-emphasised in conflicts between parents and child. A mix of shame and unease about her attitudes to her parents surfaces in outbreaks of remorse and an urge to make reparation. She decides to improve her parents' education: 'Although she loved her mother and father, their illiterate ways made her feel ashamed'.

Literacy carries the burden of improving the way of life that her parents feel Hilda has rejected. They associate literacy with ambitions and vanities which are incomprehensible. This informs the intensity of their 'startled and embarrassed' response to Hilda's proposal to teach them to read and write when she gets home from Manchester each evening. She assures them they are capable and they reluctantly agree. Hilda plans her lessons carefully, providing spelling manuals and reading materials. Some progress is achieved, with Hilda teaching 'very slowly and patiently', but the project founders:

> *Trouble swelled up, and the climax came when she purchased a penny copybook for them to write in. Her father was the first to backslide. He had tried hard to master the fearful business of forming words egged on by the reward which Hilda assured him would be his when he could write, easily and confidently, his own name – Joseph Winstanley … but when he saw the neat ruled lines of the copybook he took fright. His kind red face hardened stubbornly, and with a hopeless gesture he pushed the copybook away from him.*

The focus on names in their attempts to learn literacy are powerfully reminiscent of Joe, Mrs Joe and Pip in *Great Expectations*, a book whose 'magic' has captured Hilda's imagination.

Like Joe Gargery, her father regrets his lack of schooling and gives up. Her mother accepts the pressure to become literate but understands the psychological, class-related complexities of their learning situation and angrily defends her husband. The exchanges between mother and daughter confirm Hilda's socially-aspirational femininity, defined as personal cleanliness, groomed elegance and individual freedom. Hilda's wish to own her own comb is as baffling to her mother as her insistence on buying pink scented soap. Her mother attacks the elementary schools which she is intelligent enough to know are permanent institutions, because they challenge family and community relationships: 'Nobbut a waste of time. And it's not for *you* 'Ilda Winstanley, to go setting yourself up above us.' Like millions of others, both parents know that if they do nothing about their literacy, something which has been a relatively unproblematic reality of life would now become a stigma and drag them down socially. It is ironic that it was often children coming home from school to read family letters who shattered adults' innocence about what skills people were increasingly expected to have. And in this narrative, Hilda's different social status, as the daughter of a middle-class father with the stigma of illegitimacy, complicates the class-related discourse of literacy.

The literacy lessons take place during Hilda's three years of apprenticeship, for which all the costs of promoting her into a different class are borne by parents who fear that the 'lady-like' ways she is learning in Manchester will bring her to a 'bad end'. Hilda's sporadic, but growing, self-criticism of her acquired selfhood, 'spiteful', 'shameful' and 'uneasy', contrasts with her depiction of her parents' honesty, generosity and loyalty, however harshly expressed.[49] Penn explores her own projected feelings about the 'good' and 'bad' parent(s), and Hilda's gradual consciousness of what her adoptive family has meant to her. Hilda is not Pip, but there are many echoes of Pip's material and psychological journey in *Manchester XIV Miles*.

At a different level, this is a book about modernity and changing possibilities for women. Separation from family and social mobility through work (and, in Hilda's case, a fairy-tale middle-class family as well) was a newly possible step towards independence for women. Gissing's 'odd women' – trained teachers, shopworkers or office girls – might earn their own income and live separately from their parents without being married.[50] Hilda's dream is just feasible and finally becomes a calculated plan. She decides to leave home after the end of her apprenticeship, when she can earn enough to support a life in 'lodgings'. In the end, the planned reward for three years of hardship are overtaken by the book's romantic closure. Hilda is magically whisked away to a metropolitan life in London with the politically progressive, literary middle-class relatives who arrive out of the blue to claim her, though her troubles are far from over. A central irony of *The Foolish Virgin*, the sequel to *Manchester XIV Miles*, is that Hilda's relationship with her Lancashire family becomes dependent on literacy, but she is forbidden by her London relatives to write to them.[51]

VII

Despite their differences, shared issues emerge in the construction of each of these five narratives. The writers are women who wish to be 'read' as eccentric and whose agency, won through their persistence in learning and practising literacy, has made them different: admired and respected, but also awkward, menacing, strident or subversive for the families and communities around them. In their writing, literacy itself becomes at times a more important authority than mother or father. Parental opposition was there to be flouted or overcome. They persisted in pursuing secular forms of reading and writing despite its association with moral danger, betrayal or worse. They associated literacy with faith and crises of faith as well as the chance to determine the direction of their lives. Attending school, especially Sunday school, was one way of trying to reconcile two competing forces: the desire for material progress and the pleasure of learning, creating and communicating on the one hand; and pressure to submit to parental authority on the other. These life stories share a subversive quality, challenging and undermining oppressive authorities through learning and practising literacy and pursuing knowledge.

All five women confronted difficult choices and conflicts in order to realise their ambitions for literacy itself and for the making of the self which they believed literacy had facilitated. The experiences of Janet Bathgate and Margaret Penn are nearly a century apart. The social and emotional meaning for each of them of a life without literacy would therefore have been very different. For Bathgate, illiteracy would have meant a life much like other girls of her class, as a servant or in manual work. Margaret Penn grew up in an age when illiteracy already carried a stigma and meant living a more restricted life than her generation of working-class girls. But throughout their overlapping lifespans, ways of achieving a degree of agency were found through their ability to manipulate existing education systems and available tools for writing. By acknowledging and recognising their own potential and by their determination to act on this self-knowledge, they externalised and socialised their longing for change and achieved for themselves an authoritative selfhood of their own.

Longing for a different, self-determined life can be seen in all these life-stories as a crucial reason for remembering the events of the past. The skills of writing were at the centre of that longing, offering possibilities for self-expression as well as communication. Although the way learning happened changed over the century as schooling lasted longer, there are common patterns of remembering learning to write which were woven into these accounts. Significant objects and tools related to writing and agency are kept and sit on the writer's desk decades later as she writes her life story, long after they have stopped being useful. Favourite books and their characters stalk the pages. They escape memory and context to become tool, weapon, aide-mémoire and talisman in the development of self. Books and other objects emblemise the deeper meanings of literacy and other life events, giving metaphoric energy to set pieces of experience, conflict and growth.

Feelings of loss and abandonment are common to these narratives. For working-class women who managed to learn literacy, writing offered a way of moving on from the self who had been abandoned by separation or death or who experienced emotional and educational neglect, a self who might have lived out a passively subordinated life of material hardship and underachievement. The self who was recognised to have emerged through the process of writing retained a residual anger towards powerful others or structures but moved beyond this to celebrate the self whose more powerful existence was proven and celebrated by the writing of the book itself and reaching an audience. As Elizabeth Ham (1783–1852) wrote, 'I shall now endeavour, at sixty-six, to recall the history of my past life, in order to try if I can to trace out the influences that were most active in forming the present individual *Me* [*sic*] out of the little neglected girl of my earliest remembrance.' A short version of her book, starting with her Dorset childhood, was first published nearly 100 years after her death.[52]

Women writers explored the psychic dimensions of parent–child relationships through literacy, which often became the theatre of contests about authority and the place of girls and women in society. The notion of surrogacy also seems central to these narratives. Writing is posited as a significant cause of conflict, working on layers of emotion which cannot be exposed to light except through the controlled interpretations which writing offers. Writing plays a multiple role in this respect. It is the site of emotional displacement. It points towards personal conflict and ambivalent feelings as well as the contextual constraints of social class and gender. At the same time autobiographical writing focuses self-referentially on itself as a hard-won, skilled and powerful practice which can equally reveal and hide. It makes possible play between the unconscious and conscious arenas of a life. These narratives include the expression of meanings beyond those which are consciously known or fully understood. Meanings which have been hidden from a writer can surface through the act of writing. Writing a life is a set of processes and events in the making of a self. These produce alternative versions of selfhood for interpretation, rather than determining and controlling a particular reading, and give voice to the transformative possibilities of a life event and, more ambitiously, to the transformation of the self which writing has made possible.

These women writers seem aware of the risks of expressing ambivalence about their community and gender as people rooted in working-class life, but sharing it with people whose horizons they think are more limited than theirs. They have staked their future on literacy and learning, and seem not to recognise fully the complex humanity in those they have overtaken. Autobiography demands a self-centred exploration, which can eclipse the complexity of other reconstructed characters, especially those who have opposed their progress. These narratives are partly protests against a female socialisation which glorifies selflessness and subordination. Their task is the creation of a self who was not supposed to flower educationally within the class-bound, gendered framework of their time. Their difference remains extraordinary to them and defines them, whether their different lives are lived out on familiar streets or not. Perhaps the continuing realities of hard work, responsibility and disappointments are paradoxically why writers often displace their story-telling into the mythic timeless structure of a fairy tale, the quest for a life which is transformed from poverty into wealth – wealth of education and meaning as much as money. These are narratives of 'Once upon a time there was a woman who', which are self-justifying, not only because the writer has become a school-teacher, political agitator, magistrate or stalwart of the Women's Institute. Their self-justification is more about becoming literate, the rare achievement of becoming a writer and the triumph with which their writing selves look back to view the distance they have travelled.

Notes

1 Steedman, 1984, p. 7.
2 Bathgate, 1894, Preface, p. 1.
3 See, e.g., Ong, [1982] 2002, pp. 80–1, where Ong interprets Plato's view of writing as inhuman, 'things-like' and destructive of memory, and points to many related influences on this view, including the Bible: 'the letter killeth but the Spirit gives life'.
4 Bathgate, *op. cit.*, pp. 51–3.
5 See, e.g., Rousseau, [1781] 1985, p. 328. John Mortimer's autobiography has an interesting account of the process of letting go and forgetting: 'I had collected memories of my father, and written lines for him, so that a man who had filled so much of my life seemed to have left me and became someone for other people to read about' (Mortimer, 1982, p. 13).
6 Bathgate, *op. cit.*, pp. 58, 50, 71.
7 *ibid.*, p. 104. See also Horn, 1986, chapter 6.
8 Bathgate, *op. cit.*, pp. 104–6, 108, 126–7, 132.
9 *ibid.*, pp. 126–7, 132.
10 Farningham, 1907, pp. 13, 20.
11 *ibid.*, p. 20. The poetry of Felicia (Mrs) Hemans is mentioned in a number of autobiographies. Wright, 1893, 18 June, chapter 3, thinks of Hemans's 'There is no place like home' when a homesick sailor. See also F. White, 1938, p. 42. Mrs Hemans was a popular poet whose works

were reprinted in many editions. 'The Better Land' seems derived from Goethe's 'Mignon' ('Kennst Du das Land wo die Zitronen blühen') and 'Erlkönig'. It is a poem depicting heaven, but was also read as a vision of utopia whose natural and material riches appealed to the fantasy worlds of working-class children:

THE BETTER LAND

"I hear thee speak of the better land,
Thou call'st its children a happy band;
Mother! oh, where is that radiant shore?
Shall we not seek it, and weep no more?
Is it where the flower of the orange blows,
And the fire-flies glance through the myrtle boughs?"
– "Not there, not there, my child!"

"Is it where the feathery palm-trees rise,
And the date grows ripe under sunny skies?
Or 'midst the green islands of glittering seas,
Where fragrant forests perfume the breeze,
And strange bright birds on their starry wings,
Bear the rich hues of all glorious things?"
– "Not there, not there, my child!"

She is a poet associated with working-class culture, and is mentioned for example in Gaskell's *Mary Barton*, [1848] 1970, p. 259.

12 Farningham, *op. cit.*, pp. 21–2.
13 *ibid.*, pp. 22–3; M. Smith, 1892, p. 26.
14 F. Nightingale, 'Cassandra', a fragment from the second volume of her *Suggestions for Thought to Searchers after Religious Truth*, written in 1852, in Strachey, [1928] 1977, pp. 395–418. It was a social rule that it was not for women to express an individuality. Kingsley, *Alton Locke* [1862] 1892, p. 224, for example, expresses the view that 'It was woman's nature – duty, to conceal her feelings'.
15 Farningham, *op. cit.*, p. 43.
16 *ibid.*, p. 44.
17 *ibid.*, pp. 39, 45–50.
18 *ibid.*, pp. 71, 61.
19 *ibid.*, p. 67.
20 R. Williams, 1984, pp. 71–4.
21 C. Brontë, *Villette*, [1853] 1979, p. 228.
22 Mitchell, 1977, p. 241.
23 *ibid.*, pp. 37, 40.
24 *ibid.*, p. 38; Cora Kaplan, 'Autobiography', unpublished paper to Psychoanalysis and History Conference, History Workshop, London, June 1985.
25 Mitchell, 1977, pp. 38–9.
26 *ibid.*, pp. 43–4, 49–51, 57, 63–4.
27 *ibid.*, p. 170.
28 *ibid.*, p. 72.
29 *ibid.*, p. 177.
30 *ibid.*, p. 175.
31 Penn, *Manchester XIV Miles*, 1947.
32 Mitchell, 1977, p. 193.
33 *ibid.*, pp. 239, 241.
34 Jermy, 1934, p. 1.
35 Acorn, 1911, Preface.
36 Barthes, 1983, pp. 48–9.
37 Jermy, *op. cit.*, pp. 3, 10, 18–19.
38 Kenney, 1924, pp. vi–vii.

39 Jermy, *op. cit.*, pp. 58–9, 62.

40 See Barthes, 1983, pp. 378–404, on the irretrievability of the spoken word.

41 Jermy, *op. cit.*, pp. 97, 106.

42 Portraying one good and one bad parent is common in autobiography. It is less common to find them alternating in these roles. Foakes, 1972, and Johnston,1867, both describe their hatred of a despised father or step-father.

43 Penn, 1947, p. 176.

44 See, e.g., T. Thompson, 1981, pp. 69–70, where Annie Wilson of Nottingham recalls helping her grandfather to write a letter and 'guid[ing] his hand to sign his name at the bottom'. She also remembers hiding books 'because you see reading was a vice. You've got something better to do than put your nose in a book. That was the expression you see. But I did love it' (p. 94). She and her sister taught their mother and father to read and sign their names. Foley, 1973, pp. 25–6, describes her role as 'mother's official reader'.

45 Penn, *op. cit.*, pp. 10–12, 16–18, 177.

46 Vincent, 1989, pp. 29–32, argues that little stigma attached to illiteracy before the establishment of state education, although a degree of self-stigmatisation motivated people to learn. The assumption of universal literacy by 1914 changed and broadened the nature of the meaning of illiteracy in a world of fast-developing communication systems. See also pp. 270–80.

47 Penn, *op. cit.*, pp. 63, 76.

48 *ibid.*, p. 95. Although 'composition' had been an element of schooling under inspection since the 1830s, it only became officially part of the curriculum in 1871. Pupils were taught to write a 'short theme or letter or an easy paraphrase'. See Vincent, 1989, pp. 224–5. 'English' was an even later official subject, appearing as part of the vocabulary of elementary schooling in, e.g., the Revised Instructions of 1892. Hilda is thus expressing her command of standard English, the only sanctioned form as schools attempted to teach children a uniform language separating them from regional and class varieties of the English language.

49 Penn, *op. cit.*, p. 175.

50 See, e.g., Gissing, *The Odd Women* [1895] 1980, which describes both the hardships and challenges of life for single women in late nineteenth-century and early twentieth-century England, when an expansion of urban job opportunities provided work for the surplus of unmarried women, as teachers in small private schools, clerks and typists, or low-level retail workers. These were often wretchedly paid. For patterns of women's work in nineteenth-century England, see John, 1986.

51 Penn, [1951] 1982, pp. 39–40.

52 Ham, 1945, Preface.

CHAPTER 8

Moving through material worlds: men's lives in writing

I

This chapter explores the relationship between the public and private worlds of a number of writers, mostly men, and the significance of literacy to both. Work, politics and public life take priority in working men's reflections on learning and using literacy. The deeper meanings of writing sometimes disturb more surface stories: psychological and emotional realities emerge within classic tales of progress from poverty and obscurity to public prominence. Fragments of interiority are revealed among portrayals of material hardship and obstacles overcome against the odds. Childhood experiences are still alive in stories dedicated to the public side of life, some of them happy, some uncomfortable and painful. Writers choose which 'truths' will be told in their autobiographies and often declare that they tell nothing but the truth. Their consciousness of the part writing has played in their public lives and wider social being is evident, but so also is a sense of the power of writing to bring back forgotten memories, good, bad and ambivalent. As part of the process, memories of learning to write find their way into the story. Writers convey their sense of the precarious nature of literacy for people in their circumstances and the impact which becoming literate has made on their sense of self.

II   Writing and working life

The poet John Clare, born in 1793 in Helpston, Northamptonshire, recalls how a childhood lived in unforgiving rural poverty is injected with

261

Work-related writing exercise from the Stockport Sunday School.
Courtesy of Stockport Local Heritage Library

hope and enjoyment when his parents start to help him learn writing and arithmetic:

> *every winter night our once unlettered hut was wonderfully changed in its appearance to a school room the old table, which old as it was doubtless never was honoured with higher employment all its days then the convenience of bearing at meal times the luxury of a barley loaf or dish of potatoes, was now coverd with the rude begg[in]ings of scientifical requ[i]sitions, pens, ink, and paper one hour, jobbling the pen at sheep hooks and tarbottles, and another trying on a slate a knotty question in Numeration, or Pounds, Shillings and Pence, at which times my parents triumphant anxiety was pleasingly experiencd, for my mother would often stop her wheel or look off from her work to urge with a smile of the warmest rapture in my father's face her prophesy of my success, saying 'shed be bound, I should one day be able to reward them with my pen, for the trouble they had taken in giveing me schooling'.*[1]

262

Family pride, the enjoyment of writing and hope for the earning potential of literacy are all present. Clare's parents wanted material rewards for their investment in his schooling, hoping that their son might become scholar enough to be a clerk if not a schoolteacher. This was a tall order. Schooling at that time was rarely seen as relevant to the skills and trades of rural life, although the possibility of better work already influenced literacy learning. Clare's family could not afford an apprenticeship or his leaving home to work. In any case, Clare's one brush with clerical work in a nearby town convinced him he never wanted to work indoors.

Clare's habit of wandering off by himself was seen as an early sign of deviation from appropriate childhood pastimes, and led to early speculation about his mental stability:

> [when I used to] wean off from my companions and stroll about the woods and fields on Sundays alone conjectures filld the village about my future destinations on the stage of life, some fanc[y]ing it symptoms of lunacy and that my mothers prophecys would be verified to her sorrow and that my reading of books … was for no other improvement then quallyfiing an idiot for a workhouse.[2]

Although at the highest point of his public success, John Clare's parents were proud of his writing, in his childhood the family fretted over which kinds of writing were legitimate for him to learn to the point of outright conflict. His parents wanted him to concentrate on practical forms of literacy. But Clare was beginning to read avidly and to write poetry. During his first job driving a plough, he writes that he finds inspiration from his friend John Turnill, who 'dabble[d] in poetry', and, like other newly-literate people, wrote gravestone epitaphs.

> Here I got into a habit of musing and muttering to ones self as pastime to divert melancholly, singing over things which I calld songs and attempting to describe scenes that struck me tis irksome to a boy to be along and he is ready in such situations to snatch hold of any trifle to divert his loss of company.[3]

Clare hides his poems, but his mother finds them and reuses the paper, thinking it to be discarded handwriting copies. Eventually his desire for an audience makes him bolder, confident that his work surpasses the 'wretched composition of those halfpenny ballads' which his father sings at home. But his parents meet his compositions with scorn and alarm and he stops writing – soon taking it up again secretly and finding cunning ways to seek his parents' views, without revealing his authorship:

> *I had written it out of a borrowd book and that it was not my own the love of rhyming which I was loath to quit, growing fonder of it every day, drove me to the nessesity of a lie to try the value of their critisisms and by this way I got their remarks unadulterated with prejudice – in this case their expressions woud be, 'Aye, boy if you coud write so, you woud do.'This got me into the secret at once and without divulging mine I scribbld on unceasing for 2 or 3 years, reciting them every night as I wrote them when my father returnd home from labour and we was all seated by the fire side.*

For a poor family, the fear of learning the wrong kind of writing was about wasting precious money. Their sacrifices could make the difference between survival and ruin. Learning to write was a risky venture as well as a luxury. It singled out the Clare family in their village. They could not imagine one of their family writing poetry, let alone see it making any money. Clare's biographers have pointed to his family's qualified support for his education – which was common in working-class families. Writing was valued as a set of skills for work which was both respectable and promised upward mobility. Opportunities for this kind of employment were gradually increasing. The writing skills clerks needed were good handwriting, accurate, neat copying and note-taking, but Clare's gifts lay in using his own words, rather than copying out other people's. Neither did he ever want to flee rural life: he wanted to give expression to it. Village life and the natural world of animals, plants and birds formed the inspirational sources of his writing – although later, his disturbed inner life and imaginings become his (darker) material.

Many working men and women recalled similar troubles at home about which literacies were appropriate. The journal of Ellen Weeton (1776–1849), a governess, echoes John Clare's experience:

> *I shared so strong a predilection for reading and scribbling rhymes that my mother, who had for some time been much delighted with what she considered my striking talents and encouraged me with unbounded praises, began to think that I should be entirely ruined for any useful*

purpose in life … and treated all my efforts … with a decided discourage-ment; so much so as to dampen my spirits for ever.[4]

Clare and those few other working-class poets whose writing has achieved recognition as literature only emphasise by their exceptional status the social division of mental and manual labour in cultural produc-tion. Imaginative and discursive writing were for the educated and cultured; technical and mechanical writing were for the uneducated. There were good economic reasons why so many working-class people accepted this split. For Clare, to have joined the ranks of lawyers' clerks would have made him a good 'hand', and earned him a better wage. Remaining in low-paid manual labour permitted him to live freely in his head and produce poetry of interest in literary circles, but poverty would always be with him.

The everyday practical aspects of writing absorbed Clare as they did many others. In his later memories of writing poems in his autobio-graphical sketches, Clare lingers over the writing materials he managed to assemble: 'shop paper of all colors', the spaces 'between the lines of old copy books', 'any paper I coud get at'.[5] He spent money intended for sweets and fruit on his secret creative activity. His detailed memories of these objects – what they cost, the trouble they brought him – and how he learned the skills and craft of writing often feature in autobiography and suggest that the material conditions of production are linked with deeper subjective meanings. The craftsperson's respect for the tools of his/.her livelihood is present, but there is also a suggestion that the tools of writing have a symbolic status and cultural power, part of a consciousness that writing is an extraordinary activity beyond the reach of nearly everyone like them. Barthes explored the meaning of this reverence for objects in a way that helps understand layers of meaning in autobiographies.

Why do some people, including myself, enjoy in certain novels, biographies and historical works the representation of the 'daily life' of an epoch, of a character? Why this curiosity about petty details: schedules, habits, meals, lodging, clothing, etc? Is it the hallucinatory relish of 'reality' (the very materiality of "that once existed")? And is it not the fantasy itself which invokes the 'detail', the private scene, in which I can easily take my place?

This was not, for him, a 'theatre of mediocrity' but rather of 'grandeur'. He suggested that to omit 'insignificant notations', such as the weather, is to foreclose pleasure: without such details grand narratives are limited.[6] The materials, the details of daily life, the lists, the repetitiousness, the 'clichés', for which working-class autobiography has often been criticised are seen instead to be essential, as they are in naturalist fiction. Writing materials and alphabetic and language skills are the same, whether they are used for manual copying or cerebrally creative aspects of writing. What separates them are social and cultural definitions of the value of each. For the writers discussed here, the factor which invests the memory of 'insignificant' or mundane writing tools with powerful meaning is the presence of the writer reflecting with 'relish', as the imagined reader as well as the re-creator of an earlier self, on the moment when those tools were part of realising the desire to be actively literate. Many years later, those functional objects still represent desire, determination and luck. Without them, writing would have remained out of reach. They are ordinary but also fantastic, because they also carry the writer's sense of wonder at developing an imaginative life: not just learning basic literacy, but producing literature.

At the end of the century, Patrick McGill wrote bitterly in his fictionalised autobiography about the conditions of writing for people who do heavy manual work, and explored the complex self-identity of such writers:

> *I hope you will have more pleasure in reading these verses than I have had in writing some of them. Imagine a navvies hut, fill it with men shaggy as bears, dressed in moleskin and leather, reeking of beer and tobacco. In a dark corner of the hut aforesaid place your humble servant scribbling for dear life on a notebook as black as his Satanic Majesty, while on one side a trio of experts in fisticuffs discuss the Johnson–Jeffries match and on the other side a dozen gamblers argue and curse over a game of banker, and you have a faint idea of the trials of a versifier.*[7]

McGill is the solitary outsider, observing others. At the same time he is inside his own picture: his writing is just one of the activities happening in the room. His writing materials are dirty and he refers to his work in the diminishing terms often used to describe working-class writing: he is a 'versifier' rather than a poet. He associates writing with the illicit: dark corners and devilishness characterise the setting. By emphasising both belonging and difference he shows how complex the social conditions of production are, suggesting that the person who emerges as any kind of writer from these conditions is an extraordinary human being.

A common portrait of a working-class writer is that of the talented individual who transcends the circumstances which stifle creativity. The Chartist poet Gerald Massey commented that 'poverty is a poor place to write poetry in', and many have since agreed that cultural production is inevitably hampered by the 'difficulties of overwork, a lack of privacy or leisure, inadequate education and a lack of intellectual encouragement'.[8] Those who wrote of the countryside at least chose themes that were in tune with prevailing ideas about appropriate subjects for literature. A rural working environment was comprehensible as an inspiration for poetry. By contrast, the routines of factories and mills have rarely been subjects of poetry. Blake's 'dark Satanic mills' were a bewildering new phenomenon in early nineteenth-century life, not yet the focus of literature or painting. Yet working in factories and mills could inspire people to write. Nearly a century later, when Marianne Farningham reviewed the work of Ethel Carnie, the Blackburn mill-worker and poet who composed some of her work in the factory, she argued that Carnie's 'occupation had something to do with the rhythmic forms into which [her] thoughts shaped them-selves'. Most reviewers of working-class writing found this connection startling, including Robert Blatchford. Not so the writers themselves. The factory worker and poet Ellen Johnston 'was a weeping willow' at her step-father's home, but in the factory she was 'pensive and thoughtful, dreaming of the far-off time when I would be hailed as a "great star" '.[9]

In his vision of socialism, the factory worker R.M. Fox, born in Northampton *c.* 1894, developed the idea that working with heavy machinery was itself a creative force for emancipation. In *Smoky Crusade*, he writes that for him factory work and poetry dovetailed: the 'rude rhythms of the workshop – the regular beat of the engine, the syncopated clatter of the machines – made me write verse'. He wrote while he worked: 'alongside the number of minutes allowed on each drilling job, I jotted down scraps of verse with a stump of pencil'. The rhythms of a poem could be precisely calibrated with a manoeuvre in the factory. The redrafting and editing of his poems is fitted into the dinner break. Poems and drilling notes are set out just as they appeared in his workshop notebook representing free time and expropriated factory time. The connected layout suggests that the flat and precise technical facts and the verse interrelate: they are awkward together, but they do not jar. They form a creative contradiction: an alienated working life and the hope and creativity it both cramps and inspires, out of which the longing for a socialist utopia is born.

Handwheel Bkts
Time allowed 9 mins

   I sing of men who gather
     In factory, forge and mill
   Warming their hands by the fire
     In the morning, grey and chill.

Wormwheel Bkts
Time allowed 35 mins   *Warming their hands for a little*
(1) 1/8 oil hole 15 mins   *while*
(1) .1 hole 71/2 mins   *Strong hands at the Fire of*
(2) 7/8 holes 121/2 mins   *Life:*
Jig No T13289   *Serving, hoping and working*
                       Mid the din, the stress and
                       strife.

   I sing of the cold and the dark
     Of fog and damp and gloom,
   Of roads that the workers journey on
     Which end for them in doom.

   Whatever the roads they travel
     In search of life and bread,
   They see the sun in the evening
     Dyeing the sky blood-red.

Over the hills in the morning
Rises the golden glow,   *Nut Clamp Bolt*
   Bringing them hope and courage   *Time allowed*
   To strive for the things they   *7.5 min*
know.

Flange for Trunnion
Operation (1) 3/8 hole 1/4 Recess (1.5)
Time allowed 10 min 3/8 " (1.5)

> *Out of the dark to the sunlight*
> *Forth from the slum to the glen,*
> *We are the sons of the future*
> *Men and the children of men.*

The shape of the 'stanzas' on the page creates spaces amidst the grind of everyday working life for the co-existence of harshness and hope that both factory life and nature embody. There is self-respect for the skills and craft of factory work and the warmth of its fires; nature is gloomy and 'blood-red' but also offers a refuge from toil in its sunlit valleys. Hope for the 'sons of the future' lies in the sweetness and light of the imagined unspoilt countryside, the utopia that will be socialism.[10] The intrusion of modern motor manufacture, with its flanges, trunnions and rigid time constraints, into lines that observe poetic conventions also sharpens the meanings of the lyrical lines. The fantasy becomes knowing, and the sense of a shared 'journey' away from the drudgery and oppression of expropriated time and relentless factory rhythms becomes less sentimental. Hopes, beliefs and imagination can originate in the alienated workplace and are sustained because 'the workers' are 'we'. Shared oppression fuels creativity. Idyllic places where time and nature belong to you are part of a utopian vision, as well as the search for pleasure and redemption.

For Fox, the workplace also determined the process of writing. He belittles his way of composing writing in the factory in language more often used by educated people to depict working-class writing: 'clumsily and painfully'. And yet: 'sometimes I would be pulling at my machine handle, with the sweat pouring down my face, when words would form themselves to the medley of sounds'. He recalls memorising key words that will trigger the remainder of a line when he has time to write in breaks from work. He likens the shaping of language to the welding process, 'bending the hard material of words to something like the shape I wanted', cutting across the division of mental and manual labour as he likens processing words to processing hot metal. He refers to the 'technicalities of poetry', of which he claims to know nothing. Yet he also makes poetry out of the technical:

269

> *The Roar began with the refrain 'This is the Machine Age, We are the Machines.' All through it the machines triumph over humanity, which serves them and is crushed by their weight. Fragments of this chant came to me as I stood by my machine, listening to the shrieks and wails of metal as the machine teeth bit into it, the high crescendo chatter of the milling machines, the steady pound of the engine … The factory obsessed me with its power. It had the fascination of a giant octopus and I was fast in its clutches.* [11]

Fox loathes the factory but pays homage to it as the source of his inspiration, expressing the ambivalence of a committed socialist writer. He longs to leave work and studies persistently, overcoming several setbacks to win a scholarship to Ruskin College, Oxford. For Fox the factory is the site of and metaphor for capitalist oppression, but also creates the conditions for political and cultural struggle against it. He for one could leave it for a better life.

Writers explored the relationship of writing to their progress in working life. Fox's motives for writing and for leaving manual work were to change the world for manual workers. Others grasped at writing as a way to escape manual labour, and for some it was also a means to serve social organisations in practical ways. J.D. Fox (no relation to R.M.) describes how he became a mill-worker in the weaving trade and a telegraph messenger in his spare time. Fox was born in 1849 in Bingley, Yorkshire, and had virtually no schooling. He gained some education in Primitive Methodist classes and the Band of Hope, a temperence organisation for children. He was 'anxious to get out and on' and 'used to have day dreams as to what I would like to be and do'. After working in the weaving trade, he applied for a job as 'Curator, Secretary and Librarian' at the Mechanics' Institute. He persuaded his mother and other family members to take care of the cleaning side of the post, and applied himself to the writing side as secretary and librarian. [12]

As Fox shows, working life changed substantially as the need for literacy grew. Literacy practices in the workplace became more complex as increasingly high levels of writing skills were required. [13] The voluntary organisations, in which people who had little or no formal education engaged, needed increasingly high levels of literacy to cope with the quantities of written communication they produced and consumed. The notes from one lobbying committee of working men in 1862 state that 'one thousand six hundred postal communications, including letters, petitions forms, circulars, acknowledgements & etc., have been sent during the two years' effort'.[14] That this information was recorded points to literacy's power to lend weight to the organisations and associations of working people. The significance of such acts of writing is emphasised by iconic references to documents. People represented by such organisations appropriated the totems of cultural power in their struggle for empowerment. Written constitutions, agendas and minute books were part of doing business properly and also a defence against possible attack in ways which were closely related to the fetishisation of procedures, oaths and ceremonies. These had been common to radical organisations and early nineteenth-century forms of trade unions, particularly those banned organisations which had worked in secrecy.

J.D. Fox saw his job as a form of 'compulsory education, perhaps the best I could have had', reminding readers of his limited education and abiding astonishment at finding himself, through writing, in direct communication with those he saw as superior, even illustrious: 'Now imagine if you are a young man under such circumstances having to write to Lecturers, Members of Parliament, and others, asking them for dates, terms, etc. for lectures and to attend the Annual Soiree.' He also had to give lectures ('more difficult for me still – no-one will ever know except myself – was the work of teaching at the Evening Classes'). He did not see these roles as detracting from his development as a writer. He celebrated the interconnectedness of his writing, his need for money and his family responsibilities with pride in the operational planning which enabled him to manage his work and learn at the same time:

> It was during the thirteen years at the Institute that I wrote many of my poems. The salary given for the work of secretary and librarian, coupled with that of curator, having to be divided between my parents and myself, left me about eighteen shillings per week, hence the committee allowed me to undertake a morning delivery of letters. This delivery took me as far as Eldwick every morning, and three times a week as far as 'Dick Hudson's'. My pay for this work was eight shillings per week. Many of my best thoughts for my poems came to me as I walked through the Park to Eldwick, and through the fields beyond, listening to the singing of the birds, and drinking in the fragrance of the flowers, both wild and cultivated.
>
> I have been asked – 'Are poets made or born?' I reply that many thoughts expressed in my poems are certainly far beyond my education. I have often

271

*pleasant memories of conversations held with gentlemen (nature's gentle-
men) who resided within my delivery.*[15]

As well as those who wrote for a living as clerks, scribes or secretaries,
there were manual workers who made money from writing. William
Wright, born in 1836 in Keighley, began writing poems when he was first
sent away from home as a farm-hand. He attended night school and
entered poetry competitions at the mill where he later worked. The night
school teacher whose enthusiasm for Burns inspired him provided his
only memorable learning experience. Wright was an entrepreneurial
jobbing writer who wrote for local radical and satirical papers and a comic
annual. He wrote and performed in plays. He claimed that one of his
pamphlets, *T'History o'th' Hawarth Railway*, sold 100,000 copies. Several
papers he worked for were closed down, one because of libel action and
another because of editorial disputes, and he was brought before magistrates for verse that 'threatened with revenge acts'. On one occasion,
following a magistrate's judgement for misdemeanour and motivated by
their pronouncement that he was an 'impudent scoundrel', he used
writing to reverse his fortunes.

> *The same afternoon, still smarting under a sense of having been unfairly
> dealt with, I set to work with my pen, and wrote a satire on the magistrate
> who took the most prominent part in dealing with my case. By the dinner
> hour on the following day, (Saturday), I was in the market place selling
> copies of the satire. People bought with avidity and before Saturday went
> out I had disposed of a thousand copies at a penny each; which returns
> enabled me to pay the fine and then make a profit out of my prosecu-
> tion.*[16]

The status and uses of literacy were in a constant state of change. This
created a persistent tension between the spread of a range of literacies
which were sanctioned and promoted by the state, and the increasing
practice of other, independent literacies, which could serve practical,
poetic, social or subversive purposes. William Wright's spirited use of
writing for survival and resistance may be unusual, but the proliferation of
local papers, magazines, annuals, pamphlets and broadsheets created and
reflected a market which was open to local writers. Wright's writing
apprenticeship included entering prize competitions, a regular feature of
the journals and papers of working-class organisations. The publications

of the Chartists and Owenites, and later cooperative societies, Adult Schools, churches, the spiritualist movement and many others, provided space for readers' letters, poems, articles and essays and nurtured the ambition to write for money.[17]

III Public prominence, private life

The practice of writing about oneself in the nineteenth century complicated people's lives materially and psychologically. To write about one's circumstances abstracted and distanced the writer from the relations and conditions of daily life. Autobiographers sought to become an authority on their own lives. When the writer also represented working-class people more generically, there was an implicit claim to a wider authority to write on behalf of others. There is a tension between the writer's identification of him/herself with others and the appropriation of others' experience. Autobiography also merges the diversity of voices and characters into a more generalised selfhood. Writing about the self opened up the range of situations and movement between situations in a subordinated class or gender, but also made the limits to change more starkly apparent. It is not surprising that working-class writers sought to place their literacy in relation to the situated culture from which it emerged. Their family, community or social group made their development as writers possible and at the same time their class position threatened to contain or thwart their aims. Simply by writing, working-class writers questioned their ordained place within a world dominated by manual work or servanthood and lack of independence. Writers who asserted an authoritative voice about their own experience contested their specific place in the cultural and social order and took a public stance about the nature of social class.

Some writers expressed their distance from 'the common working man'. Emotionally and psychologically, they became outsiders even though their economic and social position remained working-class, and their cultural position displaced. Those who strongly aligned themselves with their class could not escape distancing themselves to a degree. To be a writer on behalf of others creates cultural power in relation to them. That can be uncomfortable. As Patrick McGill wrote: 'My success as a writer discomfited me a little even. I at first felt that I was committing some sin against my mates. I was working on a shift they did not understand.'[18] In a sense this is the role of scribe, but of collective rather than individual

273

messages. This kind of scribe is also a commentator, and objectifies shared experience rather than solely recreating a self who simply belongs to a social group. The parameters of her/his belonging may change, and the writer therefore has to shift ground. Yet, as McGill put it, a writer also lived with the possibility of being recognised, a triumph to offset any loss of identity:

> *Some day – when I become famous – I will take immense pleasure in reminding the world, like Mr. Carnegie, that I started on the lowest rung of the ladder, or, as is more correct, in looking for the spot where the ladder was placed; … A labourer has one consolation no other mortal has, though he has remote (very remote) possibilities of rising, he can never sink to a lower level in society than the one he occupies.*[19]

As the century progressed, the possibility of social mobility increased, despite the barriers of class and culture remaining firmly in place. Social mobility through self-improvement captured middle-class literary and artistic imagination, and it was of great significance to people learning to write, regardless of the extent to which real mobility or economic security could ever be realised. The reading of Samuel Smiles, which saw his self-help as the creed of individualism, made it an icon of individual self-improvement. The cultural practices of writers suggest they were closer to G.J. Holyoake's notion of self-help through association. Success depended on the patronage of a well-placed 'sponsor', sympathetic family members, a publisher or the support of a voluntary organisation. It was often through associations and networks that working-class writers found a publisher. Writing for a living could change social status. Publishing an autobiography brought recognition, perhaps short-lived, but rarely brought more hard benefits than might be won through more mundane forms of practising writing.

IV   The life stories of three working-class activists

Autobiographies by men can seem to offer less psychological depth than women's. Men who rose to some prominence in the labour movement tell compelling rags to riches stories and describe humble beginnings, work, religious and public life. They explore their class situation more explicitly and seek to represent more than their own lives. But as Vincent commented, although (male) 'autobiographers avoided any discussion of

274

some aspects of their private lives, and wrote with difficulty about many others, their attempts to connect the public side of their personalities with their private emotional experiences are of great value'.[20] While many narratives show how important economic and social circumstances are to their writing, they also reveal, if hesitantly, how closely the external world is connected to private, half-hidden interior experience.

The remainder of this chapter will explore three autobiographies to see how complex psychological narratives can co-exist with simpler, realist ones: John Castle's 'The Diary of John Castle', George Edwards's *From Crow-Scaring to Westminster. An Autobiography*, and Will Thorne's *My Life's Battles*.[21] All three texts disturb the view that nineteenth-century working-class men tended to avoid or tightly contain affective registers in favour of the flatter, solid narratives of progress.[22] Fragments of emotional histories co-exist with the overt purposes of these texts, the chronicling of life in the material worlds of poverty, labour, public and political work. Private histories appear erratically as part of the narrative, as a broken stream which sometimes runs above ground and sometimes disappears down swallow-holes, surfacing in the form of word associations, hints, silences or the juxtaposition of brief disconnected episodes. Buried layers of meaning are exposed through fragile fragments of experience. Memory and writing appear to be the main tools in their excavation. The self-referential narratives of the making of the writer within whole life stories demonstrate how closely interrelated the external world is with the psychological. They show how significant each is to the development of the desire to write and the role of writing in enabling a person to manage different levels of emotion, thought and action in the experience of a life.

John Castle

John Castle was born in 1819 in Great Coggeshall and lived in Essex all his life apart from one episode working in London. His life began in poverty, but he eventually became a respected cooperator in his village. Castle's manuscript life story, his 'Diary', is an explicit argument about writing, and makes clear the significance of literacy to what he made of his life. The unconventional spelling, grammar and unruly punctuation in the manuscript 'Diary' have been retained in the typescript (which I use in quotes). It evokes spoken language, although the ingenuous style and apparently spontaneous narrative structure also function as devices to achieve the social purposes of his writing. Castle writes as candidly about private relationships as he does about his struggles to earn money or win justice for a cause. The 'Diary' is unsentimental, spirited and seems free from the constraints and conventions of morality and values that sometimes infuse the writing of later, more firmly Victorian, autobiographers. The characters of Castle's wives and lovers are presented with sometimes unflattering honesty. There are unsparing accounts of illness, death and the workings of the extended family and local community. A seemingly simple linear structure is broken several times by digressions into disconnected incidents and episodes. By the end of the 'Diary', it is clear that fragments and digressions are part of a pattern which reflects the complexity and fragility of living at the edge of poverty and powerlessness, and also explains how a combination of agency and luck can combine to enable survival and progress.

The details of John Castle's childhood reflect the loss and grief likely to be experienced by working-class people in this period: family tragedy and trauma went hand in hand with economic hardship. Castle recalls moving away from Coggeshall to live in a different village, where, within just over two years, his two sisters and his father die, leaving his family destitute. His mother, who gives birth to a child shortly after these events, feeds the family by wet-nursing, her wage supplemented by the Parish. She manages to send John to Sunday school and a day school. Castle also briefly attends a writing school, but 'filled only two copy books'.[23] At nine years of age he starts his first job in a local silk factory. The first half of his autobiography deals with the continual, exhausting difficulties of finding and keeping work; a period in the workhouse; his first marriage and bereavement. All of this happens within a long period of economic depression, nationally and locally, during which the introduction of machinery into the silk industry cost many people their jobs.

As a young man, John Castle's response to grief or difficulty has been flight or passive acceptance, with occasional outbreaks of resistance or petty sub-criminal 'larking'. His wife's serious illness precipitates his conversion to religion, but is characterised in his account by caustic scepticism about sectarianism. He is unemployed and cares for his wife until her death. At this time he also discovers education, constructing a new identity as a sober and self-improving working man. His new life is exemplified by the way he sets about teaching his wife's young brother to read, spell and write. After his wife dies he proceeds methodically to rebuild his life. He writes to an unknown woman he has glimpsed in a local churchyard, and he marries her after a short courtship. He then departs from his own story to recall a significant episode from this period in his life. This is the story of a friend who was paralysed in an earlier 'rooking' incident with Castle but has now become a successful artist and earns a living painting, drawing and writing with his mouth. This story and other anecdotes, projections perhaps, are presented as inspirational in the restructuring of his life. They offer clues about his motivation and ambition, as well as supplying role models for overcoming obstacles to progress. After ten years, during which he records only his remarriage, the arrival of two children and steady work with one employer, he begins a crucial narrative in the remaking of his sense of self, to which writing is pivotal.

Castle and his fellow silk weavers are threatened by unemployment and the workhouse. The employers propose to rationalise their business due to bad trade. The Colchester workshop is to be sacrificed, and work concentrated 16 miles away at Braintree. The workers resist and their proposed response centres on a piece of writing. Unlike Castle's previous pattern of reaction to setbacks, his retaliation as leader of this dispute is carefully planned and executed. The 40 families affected by the closure are not in a position to move to another town, which has been offered to them, for reasons of money and time. 'We met together and decided not to leave Colchester without a struggle.' Their plan is to send a deputation to London and ask another firm of silk manufacturers to place work with them in Colchester. Castle is appointed with two others to gather local support for their case among 'the gentry and tradespeople' and to raise funds. At this point they decide that a written argument is an essential element of their strategy:

We thought it best to get some competent person to write us a petition explaining our case, a lawyers clerk was thought of, but he was not at home. I asked the question why we wanted such a person seeing we only wanted to write the plain truth? one remarked 'We cannot do it grammatically enough.' 'Hang the grammar', I said, 'Give me a sheet of paper.' I wrote a plain statement of facts, such as would bear scrutinizing. He first took it to the Mayor of Colchester, which was Dr. Williams. This was in 1850. He read it carefully and asked who wrote it? I told him I did. He said it wanted a little polishing. The contents of it he considered it his duty to attend to, as it involved the loss of a trade to the Borough which if once gone could not easily replaced. He promised if we left it for him for

277

one day he would copy it for us. I told him I thought an unpolished document would do best, as there were to many well-polished begging petitions got up. However, we left it. Next day we called for it: the Doctor had become quite converted to my opinion – he simply wrote a note at the bottom to give us a good start.

Castle emphasises the importance of writing to his campaign in several different ways. First, he recognises that a written document in support of the case is essential to any prospect of success. Secondly, he disputes the form of language appropriate to a formal document. His initial reaction to the professionalisation of the petition is defensive, a declaration that independence of words and actions is more important than a correct grammatical text which would involve outside assistance and loss of control over process and product. Castle proposes that their own, ungrammatical, language is more likely to be effective than standard English. Castle goes on to argue that only those directly affected are ever in a position to tell 'the plain truth' and suggests that working-class forms of written language, rather than 'well-polished' language, are the most truthful as well as the most effective medium of communication. Thirdly, the passage stamps the group's authority on the situation, breaking from their initial impulse to seek professional advice and celebrating collective self-help as the way to succeed. Because his chosen way of writing prevails, Castle establishes his leadership of the weavers' struggle.

Literacy 'events' continue to dictate the terms of the dispute. The petition leads to further notes, requests for written verification, signatures, seals, certifying notes, certificates and magistrates' licences to raise funds. All the necessary information is thus gathered in writing, without any direct confrontation with the employers, 'as we knew our movement was not liked by them'. A deputation is sent to London once the money has been raised. Again Castle shows the way in which written language can change the nature of human relations. The deputation does not feel competent to see their action through alone, and writes for help from Castle. Money is sent for the second delegation via post office orders; and circulars are dispatched to various manufacturers setting out the group's proposal. When one offer is made, which the delegation is concerned might not be acceptable to the weavers, they write home to present it and get their reply in writing. Eventually, negotiations prove successful: the delegation writes home to announce they are on their way home, carefully omitting the name of the new manufacturer who is to supply work, 'fearing that something might be done to spoil our success'. Castle is well aware of both the power and the vulnerability of writing, and his fear of committing volatile information to paper shows both realism and superstition at work. He keeps the petition, the notes and the seals which certificated the success in the campaign. 'It remains in my possession till this day, which is over 21 years.'

This action brings about more change. 'This was a link in the chain of Providence to bring about other events in the life of one who felt unworthy of so many merits.' In his recollections of the negotiations that salvaged the local weaving industry, the issue of the post of foreman of the weavers surfaces. At first John Castle denies any ambitions: 'I could see at once that they were discussing the question of a foreman; up to this moment it had never entered my thoughts'. It becomes clear that his desire for promotion is strong, but he has been told by the Mayor that his education is inadequate.

> *'Don't be disappointed, Castle, it will not be you – those gentlemen would have chosen you in preference to any one had you been a better scholar.' Here I felt the importance of education – a chance of rising in circumstances but apparently lost from want of education. Who could I blame? My father? No. He died before I went to school. Could I blame a good mother who suffered hunger to give me as much education as cost her twenty-six shillings – or sixpence per week for twelve months? No; I dare not blame her … I am forced to be a strong advocate for Compulsory Education.*

John Castle's opportunity 'of rising in the social scale' has been achieved through writing, and he uses writing again, this time to contact the employers. Well aware of the difference between the manual and the mental aspects of writing, he tells his intermediary, Dr Williams the Mayor, that 'I considered it not right to judge from the hand-writing a person's competence to keep books, as I considered book keeping laid in the head more than hand'. Eventually he is given the job over a rival whose handwriting skills are superior. This marks another stage of his journey from 'poor tramp' in search of work to foreman, with the power to give work to others. His promotion to a 'new life of bookkeeping and a variety of things quite fresh to me' inspires him to write lines of encouragement to others:

Ahead, then, keep pushing, and elbow your way,
Unheeding the envious who wish you to stray;
All obstacles vanish, all enemies quail
In the path of their progress who nev'r say fail.

This poem celebrates what he has achieved solely through his own agency, despite his lack of schooling. It seems that his ability and determination to communicate his thoughts in well-judged written language showed the people with power that a lack of technical skill does not always correlate with lack of intellectual ability. Castle piles on his own sense of wonder at his achievement with another recollection – of writing a long letter as soon as he was in post to 'Wroth', Chairman of the Workhouse Guardians (punning on his name to match his nature). Wroth had evicted him as a youth and Castle writes now 'to remind him of God's goodness to me, in contrast to his hardness of heart in sending a poor faithless lad into the world with 4/-'. In fact he does not send his cathartic letter, but by now he is experimenting with literacy for all sorts of purposes.

From this point Castle expresses a self-righteous distrust of 'politics or anything else among the working people'. He is annoyed at the ingratitude and envy of people he acts and speaks for, but compelled to be politically active in working-class causes.

> *But why record these things? Does it not generally fall to the lot of those who endeavour to raise their fellow men in the social scale to be slandered and misrepresented such is the selfishness of man, especially those men who have failed after many years in this life to accomplish anything creditable to themselves or beneficial to their fellow men; those men envy another who makes headway in spite of a scanty education.*

Castle organises a weavers' club, and becomes a founder member, trustee and treasurer of Colchester Cooperative Society, which was formed to challenge the perceived dishonesty of independent bakers and other food producers. Written documents propel the action in this conflict, too. Anonymous letters and 'Postal cards of the most foul and libellous nature' are followed by long-distance chases to track down the writers: documents, writs, summonses fly about; and written apologies, 'the most humiliating possible', are printed in the local press and the Society's paper, *The Cooperator*.[24]

The power of writing is central to Castle's uninhibited celebration of his achievements, especially his ability to choose the right form of literacy for the particular requirements of a sensitive situation and set change in motion. However, he recognises the ironies in his new situation, in the self he has become, expressing disdain towards people who were once his equals, and for whom he has become a powerful figure with the capability to represent their interests. His discomfort about these feelings reflects the ambivalence he feels towards his own pre-literate identity, as someone who relied on others to represent him.

Castle draws attention to his 'plain' style of writing, exhibiting the faults and idiosyncrasies which nearly cost him social advancement and political influence. He does not attempt polished Standard English. He remains confident in his own mixture of spoken English written down, together with literary devices that show the painstaking planning he undertook to overcome the challenges of manipulating chronology, topics, changing perspectives and the sporadic appearances of significant characters within both the main spine of the narrative and his many anecdotal digressions. His writing makes evident the struggle to form thought and action into the right wording, and the difficult dialogue which joins his past and present selves.[25]

George Edwards

From Crow-Scaring to Westminster (1922) is the story of George Edwards's rise from a mid-century East Anglian childhood lived in rural poverty to public respect as the Labour Member of Parliament for South Norfolk. The title announces a classic narrative of progress. One clear purpose of Edwards's book is to map the astonishing distance travelled from extreme poverty to a life of comfort; from obscurity to public recognition; from total illiteracy to authorship; and to put on record a succession of struggles on behalf of the labour movement, culminating in his election to Parliament. Edwards's message to others is that personal progress is possible without abandoning beliefs or principles. His success could not have been bought at the price of compromise. It is the reward for 'the strong character I have been able to build up by embracing Christian principles' and 'my one impelling motive … to be true to my conscience'.[26] Beneath the public narrative of heroic integrity, however, there is a private story about experiences that are almost invisible in the public story which has made his autobiography a classic text for social historians.

281

The book opens with a fairy-tale formula: 'In the middle of the nineteenth century there lived in the parish of Marsham, Norfolk … a couple of poor people by the name of Thomas and Mary Edwards.' They are both 'saintly' people whose desperate poverty is the result of injustice. The use of mythic structures can be associated with the continuing vitality of oral traditions in working-class culture. The fairy-tale opening also predicts a ritual closure. Suffering, villainy, loss and death will occur but finally the individual heroes or heroines will achieve justice and lasting contentment. It could be said that this is an appropriate narrative structure for an autobiographical account in which happiness is the reward for a journey to high public status, comparable to Dick Whittington's fabulous achievement. But the structure of Edwards's narrative can equally be read as an ironic commentary on a story which, although it celebrates human agency and achievement, also counts their cost, and acknowledges the persistence of the painful regrets and dissatisfactions of old age. Autobiography as a genre is episodic: a journey of consecutive, sometimes disjointed stories, events, digressions and provisional closures. The unending need for more struggle on different fronts after each episode, whether it has been happy, tragic or unexceptional, mocks the mythic structure, and allows a form of closure, a qualified reconciliation, only when life is almost over. In a sense, closure in much working-class autobiography is the writing of the life story itself, which is an enduring achievement without a troubled future, equivalent to the static and everlasting happiness, often frozen at the point of marriage, which fairy-tale closures present. Closure also provides the means by which some reconciliation of the past with the present is possible in the reappraisal and contextualising of a life – which the writing permits and even demands.

Edwards's father, an agricultural labourer, was enlisted in the army and fought in Spain. He suffered prejudice and discrimination on his return. As Edwards reports, soldiers were popularly seen as inefficient workmen and undesirable characters. His father is forced into a series of precarious labouring jobs and the family falls into poverty and insecurity. The early chapters describe extreme hardship and injustice. This is also a story of maternal abandonment and the trauma he suffered as a baby. Edwards's birth in 1850 comes at a time of near-starvation for his large family. His mother exists on a diet made up solely of onion gruel during her lying-in period, which lasts only a week, after which she abandons breast feeding. As soon as she can get up, she has to start work at the loom and the child is left in the care of a sister 'who was nearly five years his senior', and shakes him when he cries. He records his father as being present for only 'a little while on Sunday'.

It is unclear from whom the story of his earliest days has been passed down. In this episode, Edwards initially uses the third person to describe himself: 'the infant', 'the child George'. By adopting an objective position, he avoids fully owning the infant's experience. Another way of seeing this device is that it relates to the power attached to names and signatures, which recurs in autobiography and is explored in chapter 2. In this story of the first week of his life, Edwards is conscious of the precariousness of infant survival in poor families. Even as an adult, he cannot quite believe his survival until it has been named in writing, through the act of christening, publicly confirmed by formal ritual, 'a record of which can be found in the register of the Parish Church'. His whole life seems suspended between the official proof of his existence and his own account of it, written in old age.

Edwards shifts to the first person singular after the story of his christening. He goes on to emphasise his difference from the rest of the family. His mother, according to family legend, had foretold that his life would succeed in ways unheard of for a 'child of such humble parentage'. Her presentiment comes back to him as he writes: he revisits the village and hears confirmation of his mother's 'gift of vision' from 'an old man who declares that my mother often said that one day her son George would be a Member of Parliament!'[27]

The second chapter, 'A Wage Earner', centres on George's 'first experience of real distress', at the age of six, when he begins to develop a sense of social class identity and a passion for justice. His father has been caught stealing turnips to feed his semi-starved family. Their only other food is blackberries, and George is driven off a farmer's land for picking them. His father is sentenced to 14 days' imprisonment, and George acutely feels the injustice of punishment for trying to secure the family's bare survival. 'The experience of that night I shall never forget'.[28] The family is immediately sent to the workhouse and kept there all winter because the father, 'branded' a thief, again cannot find work. After their release, George starts his first job as a crow-scarer. He works long hours in the fields, getting into trouble for sleeping on the job. He assumes his responsibility as provider for the family, handing over his wage to his mother: 'Now we shall not want bread any more, and you will not have to cry again … I will always look after you.' The facts of that time, scarcely elaborated, expose an unhappiness which stops short of explicit anger or resentment, yet seems connected to the acknowledgement of periods of depression at the end of the book.

As a young adult George Edwards take his first steps towards a better life. He meets his wife who becomes the most significant agent of his social and educational transformation. Through her, he acquires literacy skills, not just for education's sake. Literacy has already become instrumental to his public life as an active local Primitive Methodist. He describes the significant event which is to launch him into a public role and highlights his need for literacy: 'The September Quarterly Meeting of 1872 of the Aylsham Primitive Methodist Circuit decided that my name should appear on the preacher's plan as an "Exhorter" and I was planned to take my first service on the 3rd Sunday in October of that year.' He can neither read nor write at this time and turns to his wife for help. Her teaching concentrates on hymns and sections of the Gospels to be learned by heart for his first public performance, together with rehearsals for the sermon: 'We had spent nights thinking it out'. Once he has learned his lines, he is less concerned about whether or not he 'held the book the right way up'. From then on he celebrates the rapid progress he makes with his wife's teaching: 'She would sit on one side of the fireplace and I on the other. I would spell out the words and she would tell me their pronunciation.' After much practice, he is able to read the lesson and hymns in time to take the Service.

Now motivated to learn more, George Edwards spells out both the value and the cost of education:

> *I was then smoking 2oz of tobacco a week which in those days cost 6d. This did not seem much but it was £1.6s a year. It was a great sacrifice to me to give up smoking, for I did enjoy my pipe. I had, however, a thirst for knowledge, and no sacrifice was too great to satisfy my longing.*

He lists the books which replaced his tobacco: '*Johnson's Dictionary*, two volumes of *The Lay Preacher*, which contained outlines of sermons, *Harvey's Meditations among the Tombs* and *Contemplation of the Starry Heavens*, a Bible, dictionary and a history of Rome.'[29]

For Edwards, literacy was not only about gaining access to existing knowledge and ideas. He was among the many newly literate people with little time to spend on writing but anxious to develop literacy skills. They created a growing market for ready-made texts: dictionaries, grammars, manuals offering advice on writing and anthologies providing model letters for personal or business use.[30] Reading was vitally important. Edwards credits the shaping of his social thought and action to his 'study of theology', through which the 'gross injustices meted out to my parents and the terrible sufferings I had undergone in my boyhood burnt themselves into my soul like a hot iron'. Reading enables him to reconnect his own sense of values with the cauterised scars of childhood traumas. Through literacy and the study of theology he can create a coherent whole from his early experiences, religious beliefs and labour activism.

George Edwards works at several building trades, including brick burning and thatching, as well as seasonal farm-labouring. He becomes an active member of the newly-formed Agricultural Labourers' Union in 1872 – the year of his marriage and the start of a series of agricultural labourers' strikes. For him, union activism goes hand in hand with learning. He had already spoken at his first meeting, 'although I could not read. Still I related my experience of how I was obliged to go to work at the age of six'. Until he can read well, his wife reads the weekly papers aloud. His reading programme continues, because his theological studies have already provided a depth to his political beliefs and passion for justice. After two years, with his new-found ability to read newspapers and growing confidence as a preacher, he is addressing labour meetings: 'preach[ing] my first Labour sermons' during a Suffolk lock-out. Trade union activism is his fight back against injustice and the realisation of his early 'vow' to alter labourers' conditions supported by his interpretation of the scriptures: 'To me the Labour movement was a most sacred thing and, try how one may, one cannot divorce Labour from religion.'

Edwards's study and activism remain closely linked, seen as 'laying up in store for myself some serious trouble, for my employer was a bigoted Tory'. George is given notice to quit his job and house for his activism and he argues he has been victimised. He wins his case, which he sees as a victory not only for his rights as a worker but also as vindication of his struggle for literacy and subsequent education. During the period of his notice, he is offered a lecturing and organising job with the Liberals, which he refuses, partly because of lack of confidence and partly because of a commitment to manual work. Nevertheless, 'At the same time I attended as many political meetings in the evenings as I could and I also read every bit of literature I could get hold of'. His successful case is also marked by the first recorded correspondence of his life. Two letters are reproduced verbatim. One is a letter expressing sympathy and relief from the leader of the Liberal Party in North Norfolk, cited as 'evidence' that his employer had indeed withdrawn his notice; the other is Edwards's carefully composed and uncompromising reply. The correspondence takes on the power of solemnly sealed and signed documents which fasten the truth as irrefutable, but also provides Edwards with the means to occupy the high moral ground above a weighty political figure. Literacy is represented as bestowing equality of status: 'I do not derive the same satisfaction from the withdrawal of the notice as you appear to do ... I will stand by my principles, come what may. Yours sincerely ...'. Writing provides a way of communication which through its crafted formality can offer differences of opinion without rudeness and appreciation without deference.

Edwards's studies, skills and uses of writing continued to develop throughout his life. His book is scattered with texts that were significant to him, quoted verbatim: Labour hymns, poems, his own speeches and reports, and an epitaph for the Tories, delivered during a Liberal election speech: 'Here lay the Party that never did any good / And, If they had lived, they never would.'

George Edwards becomes a paid official of the agricultural labourers' union, the Federal Union, and in 1889 he is elected as District Secretary, writing articles in the weekly papers each week. In this period he works for a Liberal employer who lends him books and supports his education. When the Federal Union collapses in 1897, returning to work as a brick-burner and farm labourer he still writes articles and 'Open Letters'. After the General Election in 1906, Edwards begins to receive letters from workers reporting widespread victimisation by Tories: 'letters kept coming to me containing most pathetic appeals to form another Union. Why I was the one to be written to I attribute to the fact that I was the only one of the former leaders of the men taking any part in public life'. The continued pressure of letters persuades him to restart a union. One stream of memory flowing through the book is his correspondence to and from union members to Labour representatives, MPs and activists. He increasingly feels different from ordinary letter-writing union members. Like John Castle, Edwards is no longer only 'of them'; he has the power to act, or not act, on their behalf. He has himself been a 'letter writer', and now perceives his ability to wield power in ways only afforded by progressive stages of literacy. The emphasis on letters addressed to him, urging action, is thus a significant sign of progress towards an identity as a literate self which marks him out as different from the class on whose behalf he acts.

Between 1920–22 and 1923–24, Edwards was Labour MP for South Norfolk. The last pages of *Crow-Scaring*, first published in 1922, reflect on 'the touch of sadness running through it all', the background 'depression' that accompanied his success. The branding of early poverty on his 'soul', his disappointment at the ingratitude of 'the class' for 'so much sacrifice' and his repeated return to the organisation and representation of labour as 'some overpowering force [which] compelled me to re-enter the field' are all explored. He makes clear the costs of learning literacy and lifelong study. Addressing his readers insistently, he asks them to notice

> *the many bitter struggles I have had coming along this somewhat rugged road of life; how I have battled to lift myself above my environment; how I have laboured to educate myself and to inform myself on all public questions, and I hope they will also detect a burning desire from the first to use the knowledge I had obtained for the benefit of my own class, as I hope, with some amount of success.*

Here is his plea for a better understanding of his journey to a place he has struggled hard to arrive at; his resentment at insufficient affirmation; and the lack of adequate recognition from his own class for the sacrifices made by the public man – the avenger of injustice.

His words conjure up the sad, aggrieved six-year-old boy scouring the hedgerows for blackberries and bringing meagre wages home to his starving family. To these feelings he adds his uncertainty and distress about the beliefs which have driven his actions: 'I am mystified. I cannot understand what has been the overruling power in my life.' At this point he abruptly retreats from the seesaw of self-justification and celebration, doubt and distress, and reveals the 'secret' and real 'reason for the success that has crowned my labours although late in life': the devotion of his wife. He discloses the extent to which he has suffered from depression, recognising how that had meant the suppression of her own feelings to support his 'hours of depression'. Oddly, his writing about her death is perfunctory, hastily moving on, in the same paragraph, to remark that her place has been taken 'at the opportune moment', in public affairs at least, by her niece, 'so much like her in character' and 'even more sympathetic'.[31] There is an unmistakable sense of resentment, hinting at limits to his wife's patient selflessness. The writer invokes the half-starved boy whose fighting spirit is attributed to his mother's example, and whose education is owed to his wife. He exposes the lost, dependent child in the adult, querulously demanding a mother/wife as of right to smooth 'the rugged road of life'. In this narrative, the private sphere intrudes as a semi-conscious melancholy, dissatisfaction is expressed as 'sadness', and both are displaced and channelled, through the support of women, into a doggedly pursued public mission. The death of his father, whose pathetic attempts to feed his family had brought disgrace, trauma and a chain of events that ignited his reforming compulsion, is mentioned as a bald fact. Though in these last pages he acknowledges loss, he cannot find a shift of register to deal with it. His literacy and his politics were learned in a private world but they serviced a public one. Perhaps he had no stomach for writing about grief, or thought it unfitting to broadcast his feelings. He takes account of the sensitivities of what family he still has and retreats quickly into the safer public arena with the readier, more formulaic language of class struggle and Christian belief.

Will Thorne

Will Thorne's autobiography, *My Life's Battles*, places literacy at the centre of working-class activism. Thorne was born in Birmingham in 1857 into a large family and his childhood was lived in extreme poverty. His father, a bricklayer, died when he was seven. His life story has some clear but curious conjunctures and parallels with George Edwards and John Castle. The disgrace suffered by George Edwards's family following his father's imprisonment is echoed in Will Thorne's memory of the trauma of his father's violent death. His father was regularly involved in fights, and his killer was sentenced only to a few months' imprisonment for manslaughter. Thorne associates his death with injustice and oppression, pointing to the coincidence of his father's death with a night of local riots. This account is followed by a detailed memory of his working life as a young child, working 'from six in the morning until six at night' turning the wheel for a rope and twine spinner. Castle and Thorne were each brought up in poverty by a widowed mother. None of the three received schooling, although Will Thorne seems to have picked up a little reading in his youth. Each discovered a motivation to become literate and to use literacy in the labour movement; each was involved as an important figure in the founding and building up of a new union for unskilled workers. Like George Edwards, Will Thorne was a successful trade union leader who became an MP, representing West Ham from 1906–45. And like Edwards, Thorne started his first job when he was six years old. Their narratives share idealised, but contrasting, images of mother as heroine. Thorne's mother rebelled against the inhuman life of young children who combined school and work. She was a role model for endurance and active resistance to injustice. George Edwards's mother is remembered for her accepting perseverance and saintliness. Will Thorne celebrates his mother's show of spirit in defending his interests: 'My mother's rebellion against the way I was being worked is the rebellion of many mothers. It is the rebellion that I feel and still continue to carry on.' Thorne draws his readers into direct dialogue to gain their sympathy:

> *Just think for a moment. There was I, a boy of nine years of age, that should have been in school, getting up in the cold of early morning, leaving home at about 4.30, walking four miles to work and then, after a long 12 hour day, walking back again, a 15 hour day by the time I got home, dead tired, barely able to eat my scanty tea and crawl into bed.*

Without skills or education 'there are few rosy patches, if any, in the fight for bread in the lives of the manual labourer'. The means to education are also seen as dangerous and painful. Education, he argues, in a passage reminiscent of R.M. Fox's factory poem, is pursued by those working-class people who 'dream and hope' and to whom 'God gives … imagination'. This minority of working people, amongst whom Thorne counts himself, experience their gifts as 'more of a curse than a blessing' since 'much wisdom, it is said, brings much suffering'. But he also attributes his promotion to 'semi-skilled engineer' to his membership of this select group.

There is nothing self-abasing in Thorne's version of 'special pleading', which conveys his confident expectation of well-earned attention. The onus is on the reader to relate to his motives and desires:

> *I have often been asked why I am a socialist, and why I persist in carrying on the fight … Perhaps as I tell you my story, which, with variations, is the story of hundreds of thousands of my East End neighbours and of millions of my brothers all over the country, you will begin to understand.*

The reader needs only to 'think for a moment'. Thorne's first mention of literacy is his description of marriage at 22. He uses the written evidence

289

of the ceremony as a device to collapse the time between his later writing and the remembered event: 'I have the marriage lines in front of me as I write. I see that neither of us could write, for both of us made our "mark" on the marriage certificate. It was a Monday morning when we got married. I had been working all night.'[33] In ways resonant of George Edwards's references to his christening documents, Thorne uses his store of writing tools and significant documents to dramatise the key experiences of his life, past memories as well as later facts, and his interpretations of them. They have talismanic significance as objects that have been kept as evidence for his later account of himself. They bear witness to different subjectivities to be traced and constructed in the remaking of a life.

Will Thorne could read at least a little by the time he reached adulthood, despite a meagre education. He works in several trades before becoming a gas worker, including rope-making and building. He claims that ambition, drive and the ability to pick up skills quickly are the reason he gained early promotion at the Saltley Gas Works in Birmingham: 'always striving for something better'. He begins a reading programme which reflects his political commitment, and includes Marx, Engels, Hyndman, Blatchford and Owen. His purpose in reading is to understand 'the economic and industrial system'. His interest in education is harnessed to the concept of class: 'we', the 'workmen' to whom the methods of production are 'a mystery of which we knew nothing. There were few books accessible to the workers'. His reading is structured by meeting and hearing a range of socialists such as Bebel, Jaures and Adler, leading figures in the international socialist movement. His learning is helped most by the 'personal contact I had with great thinkers and working-class leaders'. Specifically, 'Dr Aveling gave me much help and Eleanor Marx-Aveling, Karl Marx's third daughter, used to assist me to improve my reading and handwriting, which was very bad at the time'.

Like J.D. Fox, Thorne's acquisition of writing skills is connected to the workplace. The workplace was his creative motivating force, especially as General Secretary of the National Union of Gas Workers and General Labourers of Great Britain and Ireland from 1889. His politics had earlier been challenged by a foreman at the gas works, who asked him where he had 'learned all this foolish rubbish', and his response underlines the interaction that existed for him between learning and his grounded class experience:

290

I told him that I had learned from books and pamphlets that I had bought with the few shillings I had to spare; that I had learned it in the works where I had been employed; that I had learnt it from bitter experience.[33]

Will Thorne, again like Edwards and J.D. Fox, learns to read and write as part of working life and his political commitment to working-class organisations. All three discuss the centrality of literacy to social movements. Thorne details the daily difficulties he encounters with writing tasks in his union job, especially the 'considerable anxiety' caused by paper work and book-keeping. Exactitude in written records was characteristic of nineteenth-century working-class organisations. He remembers in vivid detail his chaotic office, with no filing system and bills strewn on untidy surfaces. The impenetrability of the complex literacy tasks which challenge him is brought to life through his descriptions of the bewildering array of pieces of paper he faced. Later in life he still feels astonished he was competent enough to keep on top of essential bureaucracy:

The job had to be accomplished somehow. I began by gathering up all papers I could find in the office and sorting them out into a semblance of order. An income of over £3,000 had to be accounted for. There were bills of every imaginable shape and size, written on all kinds of paper, in pencil and ink, a large proportion of them almost undecipherable. Our office then was just one small room, with meagre and primitive furniture, where the whole of our work had to be done, including the holding of committee meetings.

I shall never forget the sight of this room, simply covered as it was in all directions with those papers. It is inexplicable to me how I ever managed to get things together, but I did.

It is almost as if he has spun gold out of straw. He has no training or experience in accounts or report writing. He describes the satisfaction of completing a difficult piece of writing, his first half-yearly statement and report. There is no account of the process of assembling his ideas or the actual process of writing but he recalls 'that was my first report, of which I was justly proud. Since that report I have made many more'.[34]

His workplace is characterised by the sharing of experiences and ideas with others, and by personal experience of learning despite poverty. His class consciousness finds expression as he emphasises the collective nature of his working life and aspirations. He is an individual who wants, like Edwards and Castle, to represent and fight for his class. But Will Thorne is much more confident about his own education and ability to influence. George Edwards's pain and ambivalence about his life circumstances, as well as the fissures in his narrative, make any simple equation of achievement with pleasure impossible. Thorne's more cheerfully self-confident tone only suggests ambivalence when he writes of his own pleasure in learning and knowledge, although he knows it excludes other people in his social group. His comment on a lecture in Canning Town by Bernard Shaw to the Social Democratic Federation – which he belonged to – reveals his awareness of becoming distanced from the East Enders he identifies with and whose interests he represents:

> *His lecture, while very interesting, was couched in such language as to make it difficult for his meaning to be grasped by most of the audience. He spoke to us just as if he was talking to an audience of thousands of people in the Albert Hall. I remember his sharp caustic criticism, and the keen flashes of wit, which, however were mostly lost on his hearers.*

> *The East End of London has never taken kindly to the 'highbrows' although the method of education is gradually permitting the submerged workers of this crowded, over-worked and over-populated district to appreciate the finer things of life.[35]*

He rebukes Shaw for elitism but prides himself on a higher cultural understanding than others of his class. It is Shaw who stands for the finer things of life. Thorne is caught up in the ideology of educational reform and attitudes to working-class culture, whereby the purpose and value of education are to lift working-class people out of their moral and material squalor. Knowledge and culture are to be provided for not by the working class. Middle-class reformers were blind to ideas which might come from working-class people shaping their own meanings, which is how Thorne himself had learnt. Elsewhere he does acknowledge this as a problem, writing that 'all my knowledge, both general and of the great Trade Union and Labour Movement, has been gained by practice, bitter experience', not just by contact with socialist intellectuals.[36]

Will Thorne's sense of the romance as well as the awkwardness of belonging to a more exclusive club is revisited at the end of the book, when he positions himself more subtly. He locates himself as a working-class socialist, at the interface between the condescension of middle-class, Fabian attitudes and the poorly-educated working class. This position is clearly uncomfortable, yet the mixture of class anger, loyalty, energy – and pleasure – in his new life is what he has made of his circumstances, education, self-empowerment and political commitment. Thorne's views of prominent middle-class socialists and liberals with whom he interacts veer between eulogy and gratitude for their patronage and despair at their condescension. His most positive teacher and mentor was Eleanor Marx-Aveling. She taught him to write, supported his reading and provided help with writing and speaking tasks at key moments when his use of English might otherwise have exposed him to criticism. Two events mark her support with the writing tasks needed to run the organisational machinery of the labour movement. During the great Dock Strike of 1889, she and the wife of a socialist agitator 'acted as correspondents for the Committee; they worked long hours and walked bravely late at night, or in the early morning to and from their distant homes'. Then, at the first Annual Conference of his union, 'that very brave and intelligent woman, Mrs. Aveling, was the Secretary to the Conference … and made the work smoother for all concerned'. The significance of Eleanor Marx in Thorne's life, as an admired public figure, intellectual ally and teacher, is brought home in the long and indignant account, which restates his discomfort about the relationship between working-class activists and their powerful intellectual allies, particularly Eleanor Marx's husband Edward Aveling.

An article in a Labour journal by the MP Philip Snowden appears after a speech by Thorne in the House of Commons, which greatly exercises him. Snowden refers to his 'unlettered ignorance and unfitness for Parliament'. Thorne is angry and shocked that Snowden has misused an accepted code of privilege, describing it as 'sad and strange' that he 'saw fit to sneer', given that he 'was born and has always been in favourable circumstances'. Interestingly, Thorne is affected far more deeply by Snowden's inference of his illiteracy than by what he sees as his abuse of class position. He recalls the delayed impact of this 'episode' in terms of a near breakdown:

> *the only one in my career which really threatened to affect my spirit. It was in 1916, and the biennial conference of my union was being held in London at the time. A function had been arranged at a large restaurant,*

and I was called upon to propose the toast of 'Success of the union'. The room was packed with hundreds of people all anxious to hear me, but when I got up I was so depressed that I found myself absolutely unable to commence; tears came to my eyes, and all that I could say was that if I was thought to be too ignorant for the Labour movement I would not continue to be associated with it.

Thorne's satisfaction at having repeatedly crossed social thresholds, starting from his tough childhood and arriving at a position of public influence, results in part from knowing that he has always grasped the complex literacies required in new situations. His confidence is shattered by Snowden's slight. He is bewildered by his confrontation with a rigid hierarchy of literacies and the unseen codes of cultural adequacy. He has come face to face with the fact that the literacy he has attained is not enough. Despite his prominence in the labour movement, and political standing as an MP, he is the butt of a social-class prejudice, which he instantly recognises as powerful but cannot entirely grasp. He knows he is and always will be an outsider, culturally excluded even by, or especially by, middle-class people on the same side of politics. Remembering these events, the response from his own class is crucial. And they offer comfort and affirmation for the achievements in which his self-belief has been so badly shaken: 'The whole audience rose *en masse* and cheered and sang until I recovered myself.'

Thorne rebuilds his belief in his own way of learning: 'while [Snowden's] book learning might count in its proper perspective ... an education such as I have had can only be shaped in the school that really matters. This, at least, is right among the hard facts of life.' He confines Snowden to his 'proper perspective' rather than concede his cultural superiority, hammering the point home with an encomium to the 'kindness of ... two humble souls in Swansea in their poor cottage' contrasted with 'the glittering and luxurious hospitality I have received'. Thorne succeeds in staking out his allegiance, without denying the awkwardness of his position, poised between the 'humble' and the 'luxurious'. His discomfort about his position may be one cause of his 'depression'. His preoccupation with 'proving' his literacy and belonging to the literate world continues. And like so many other working-class writers, he kept all the evidence of his literacy practices. His correspondence is beside him as he writes and several items are published in full: his pledge to the Social Democratic Federation and a personal letter of thanks from Nancy Astor.

Snowden's attack blows open a complex cultural issue. There is widespread working-class acceptance of the importance of activists grasping the 'King's English' in written language, a position Thorne supports. Thorne is not necessarily defending working-class language usages. He is defending the right not to be sneered at while he is learning the 'correct' forms of English to which he aspires. It is the fact that Snowden has inferred that Thorne is illiterate ('unlettered') that is so personally humiliating. Leaving aside the snobbery and disdain with which middle-class socialists treated the working-class people in whose interests they worked, it is the contempt for Thorne's use of English that provides the main theatre of conflict. Thorne points out himself his 'ignorance of grammar' and 'mispronunciation of the English language', and the 'toleration and even humour' of his use of English among his friends. At issue for him is the difference between what is permissible in spoken and in written English: the equation of illiteracy, or the inability to write 'correctly', with non-standard, spoken uses of language, and of the equation of both with ignorance.

The policing of written English in the politics of class action was not confined to middle-class intellectuals and politicians. Thorne's worries about his writing skills mount when he is appointed General Secretary of his union from 1889, defeating Ben Tillett heavily despite Tillett's greater accomplishments (as Thorne saw it). Writing was central to the job. Thorne has an encounter with 'the great John Burns', trade unionist, engineer, socialist (and later Liberal MP for Battersea), who visits him after his appointment to see how he is 'getting along'. Thorne had been in court to listen to Burns's trial for his part in the banned 1887 'Bloody Sunday' demonstration against the Tory government. Burns was revered in the labour movement as courageous, well-read and a thinker. Now Burns is 'down and out' and looking for help. But his visit is interpreted by a touchy Thorne as a check-up on his administrative, clerical and writing skills:

> *Burns … asked me if I could manage the work. I told him that I would work day and night, if it was necessary, to give satisfaction to the members … [I] showed him some of the many letters that I had received during the week, asking for an organiser to come to different places to give information about the union … Burns remarked 'You have a tough job*

on hand'. He saw the bad handwriting of most of the letters, and said 'Some of the writing is worse than yours, and that is bad enough.' This was quite true, because I have never been a good writer, even to the present day.

Thorne reminds him that he has five children to feed on a small wage, but invites him to dine with them and pays his fare home. Thorne recalls Burns's critical comments on the grammar and composition of these letters, and his defensive reply: 'What can you expect?' he tells Burns. 'The writers of these letters are only rough and ready men ... Most of them gas workers that have had to start work from early in life, like their fathers before them. The sons of the craftsmen had a better chance, because their parents were much better off than the parents of these poor labourers.' Thorne interprets Burns's comments as questioning the way the new general unions are run and feels he is being looked down on. Even though Thorne writes as a successful union leader, recognised as the leader who negotiated the working day down from twelve to eight hours, his sense of inferiority about education cannot quite be shaken off, especially when it is echoed by revered fellow activists.

The effect of Burns's visit on Thorne highlights the extent to which written English and grammar were central to power relations, not only in cultural and political conflicts between social classes, but within working-class politics and action. The need to use Standard English to reach wider audiences was accepted. The pressure for conformity of English language use became stronger and attacks on the language and the assumed state of ignorance of the working class more systematic as education became state-controlled. Thorne was well aware of these pressures:

I have seen many ... people who, immediately they receive the confidence of the workers, try to talk differently from their natural and usual method; who try to ape the snobs of the possessing class. I am satisfied to be natural, even though I be rough and blunt and sometimes brutally frank. I have always called 'a spade a spade' and have always found that a few plain, homely words are just as effective and eloquent as flowery, long phrased speech.

Thorne believes, like John Castle, that his 'ill-treating the King's English' and his lack of formal grammar can add to his force as an 'advocate' for his class in negotiations with 'employers' associations'. For him, using working-class language, even as he begins to master other more powerful languages, is part of a conscious alignment of the self, his class and the labour movement. That this has to be repeatedly spelled out points to a deeper, unarticulated discomfort at the tension in his relationship to those he speaks and writes for. Thorne shows how far social divisions within the labour movement were marked by uses of literacy and language; and how the power of literacy could shift feelings and perceptions about belonging.

Will Thorne's autobiography is determinedly, robustly, public, even though he had an unusually eventful personal life, and suffered terrible loss. Despite being widowed, left alone more than once with a total of 13 children to bring up, remarried three times and losing two children, one as a baby and one in the First World War, he describes only that one episode in his career 'which really threatened to affect my spirit': the 1916 toast to the 'success of the Union', described above.[37]

V

If there were inhibitions about expressing feelings and exploring private histories in working-class men's autobiography, there were good reasons for it. Loss, separation, humiliation and other sources of pain were bound up with poverty and social injustice. It cannot have been easy to describe one without revealing fragments of the other. But expressing anger and resentment was complicated for those who knew that their experiences of abandonment, neglect or loss resulted from the odds stacked against their families, who had tried to provide their children with some protection and at least a chance of improving their circumstances. Pride and the fear of betraying the family and working-class experience to an unknown, critical readership must have helped stem the flow of feeling into life stories.

Personal pain is more often projected by autobiographers onto the public sphere. They freely express anger about oppression, class subordination and poverty, which also contributes to their political conviction, sense of injustice, fighting spirit and belief in associating for social change. Some transposing of feelings from one key to another was facilitated by writing. Autobiographical writing was an attempt to understand and present the outer self, while intermittently revealing a deeper, interior self, in Thorne's words a 'projecting of a pencil of light into the darkness of … unspoken memories'.[38] Some memories were too difficult to expose to light for long, and private experience flashes onto public narratives in fleeting and fragmented ways.

Criticism of the simple realism of working-class writing includes the notion that the language used a limited range of registers, stunting subtle articulation of feeling. That is said of working-class men's writing which stayed on the safer territory of work and public life. Reticence about feelings is therefore interpreted in terms of class, of what language was available to writers, rather than their choice of what they felt able to say, what they felt under pressure to conceal, or which literary conventions in autobiography and religious testimony they had inherited and could confidently use. If, too, a writer was speaking for others as well as himself, explanations of what went wrong in a person's life could not plausibly be explained to a working-class readership mainly in terms of personal, emotional experiences. Blame could not be placed largely at the feet of individuals or families in a world where a child had to work from the age of six and teach themselves to write as an adult for lack of schooling. Despite such pressure to be cautious, writers managed to make conscious connections between their external, family and inner lives. They grappled with how to explain the pain of loss, trauma and separation and the humiliations brought about by economic, social and legal forces, such as the Poor Law. They were wary of shouting their triumphs to a less successful, or lucky, readership. But deep personal feelings do appear in these narratives more than has often been noticed. They offer psychological as well as social stories.

Notes

1   Clare, 1983, p. 4. The spelling in this and other quotations from Clare's writing are taken from this edition.

2   John Clare's preoccupation with his physical frailty in early life is an interesting pointer to one possible factor contributing to his later mental suffering. He compares his 'waukley constitution' with that of his twin sister, who died in infancy though 'a lively bonny wench'. His confusions of expression on identity and duality, and his belief that, e.g., his wife is another, earlier lover, Mary Joyce, can arguably be linked to this early splitting and loss. See Clare, *op. cit.*, p. 4, and Storey, 1982, pp. 41–3.

3   Clare, *op. cit.*, p. 7.

4   *ibid.*, p. 10; Weeton, 1969, pp. 13–14. Pritchett, 1978b, p. 185, wrote of how he would pretend to be reading instead of writing.

5   Clare, *op cit.*, p. 10.

6   'The Pleasure of the Text', in Barthes, 1983, p. 408.

7   McGill, 1910, Introduction.

8   Vicinus, 1974, p. 3.

9   Carnie, 1907, Preface; Johnston, 1867, pp. 7–8.

10   R.M. Fox, 1937, p. 78–9; See R. Williams, 1975, e.g. p. 18, where he attacks the view that there had been a centuries old, static country way of life, but that 'a whole culture that had preserved its continuity from earliest times had now received its quietus'. The polarity of country and city has

depended on a romantic notion of the countryside as idyllic landscape, rather than worked environment, constantly changing. Houghton, 1957, p. 79, writes: 'In this environment the romantic love of nature passed into a new phase. It became the nostalgia for a lost world of peace and companionship, of healthy bodies and quiet minds.'

11 R.M. Fox, *op. cit.*, pp. 79–80; Fox reports that *The Roar* was published in the British and American Anthologies of Labour, and that he later found publishers for much of his writing (*ibid.*, p. 294).

12 J.D. Fox, 1914, pp. 20–1. Many autobiographers record working at some point in their lives in the postal and telegraph services, e.g. M. Farningham and J.B. Leno. For them, the association with letters was a key factor in the desire to become a writer; the reader or carrier of post or indeed the postmistress/master occupied a powerful place in the family and community, comparable to a scribe.

13 Writing occupations grew steadily during the nineteenth century, escalating towards the end, but Raymond Williams cites Defoe's note of 1724 that 'Writing … is become a very considerable Branch of The English Commerce. The Booksellers are the Master Manufacturers or Employers. The several Writers, Authors, Copyers, Sub-Writers and all other operators with Pen and Ink are the Workmen employed by the said Master-Manufacturers.' Oliver Goldsmith, a writer who penned poems to pay for his next novel (like William Wright in this chapter), 'converted' Defoe's observations into the line 'that fatal resolution whereby writing is converted to a mechanic trade' (R. Williams, 1965, p. 183).

14 Redfern, 1913, p. 27. See also Vincent, 1989, pp. 276–7, and Steedman, 1988, chapter 5, p. 62.

15 J.D. Fox, *op. cit.*, pp. 22–23.

16 Wright, 1893, 15 September, chapter 15.

17 See, e.g., James, 1976, especially the section 'History and Perspectives', chapters 2 and 3.

18 McGill, 1914, pp. 227–8.

19 McGill, 1910, Preface.

20 Vincent, 1982, p. 39.

21 Castle, 'The Diary of John Castle', TS, 1961 (MS undated); Edwards, [1922] 1957; Thorne, 1925

22 See, e.g., Burn, [1855] 1978. The anonymity of the author is perhaps significant in releasing inhibitions in writing about the private. Another anonymous text, *Chapters in the Life of a Dundee Factory Boy. An Autobiography*, 1850, also unfolds the emotional traumas of early life graphically.

23 Castle, *op. cit.*, p. 1. See Gardner, 1984, for a comprehensive picture of all the different forms of private working-class schools.

24 Castle, *op. cit.*, pp. 21, 22, 24–5, 27–8, 36. The punctuation and spelling are as in the typescript version.

25 Steedman, 1988, analyses the diary of John Pearman, soldier and policeman. Drawing on Vygotsky's argument that written language differs from oral speech in structure and functionality, she suggests that all writers have to negotiate the territory between them. The construction of Castle's narrative demonstrates his awareness of their distinctive structure and usage. As a new writer, his success in manipulating written modes of expression is uneven as the text jerks in non-linear fashion between narrative composition and the transcription of spontaneous speech or thoughts spoken out loud.

26 Edwards, *op. cit.*, p. 235.

27 *ibid.*, p. 15.

28 *ibid.*, p. 22. Edwards's account echoes Dickens's *Great Expectations*, where he traces the roots of Magwitch's life of crime to the archetypal transgression of an unjust society, the stealing of turnips to survive. The subsequent criminalisation of the destitute orphan is inevitable, like the mudlarks of Mayhew's reports. For Magwitch, Pip's 'second father', it was a moment of revelation of identity and his first memory: 'I first became aware of myself, down in Essex, a-thieving turnips for my living … I know'd my name to be Magwitch, christen'd Abel. How did I know it? Much as I know'd the birds' names in the hedges to be chaffinch, sparrer, thrush.' Later Magwitch is taught writing by 'a travelling Giant, what signed his name a penny a time' and begins to use writing for forgery. Writing is responsible for his move into serious crime and for the transportation which then brings good fortune. See Dickens, *Great Expectations*, [1860–1] 1985a, pp. 363–5.

29 Edwards, *op. cit.*, pp. 23, 32.

30 *ibid.*, p. 34. Lists of significant books appear in large numbers of working-class autobiographies of the period. Vincent, 1982, analyses the meaning and scale of the possession of books to working-class people in pursuit of literacy. Edwards's list also contains material helpful to writing: dictionaries and model sermons.

31 Edwards, *op. cit.*, pp. 36–8, 42–50, 98–9, 234–5.

32 Thorne, *op. cit.*, pp. 15, 19, 24.

33 *ibid.*, pp. 62–3.

34 *ibid.*, pp. 99, 103.

35 *ibid.*, p. 55. G.S. Jones, 1983, p. 183, argues that the idea of the working class in London having any 'culture' only began to emerge in middle-class comment in the early twentieth century, for example in 'Charles Booth's observation that the London working class was governed by "strict rules of propriety", but that these rules did not necessarily coincide with "the ordinary lines of legal or religious morality" '.

36 Thorne, *op. cit.*, p. 217.

37 *ibid.*, pp. 85, 125, 219, 78, 7.

Reflections

I   Writing in a divided society

Not being able to write, Frank Smith argued, 'is regarded as an affront to literate society'.[1] Expressed even more starkly, in some societies, in some periods of history, only those who write can be perceived as fully human. This is not to say that those who cannot write, or cannot write correctly, are not human beings who possess complex and valued cultures of their own, but that their social practices and cultures are not valued by dominant cultural groups or the guardians of official literacies. When those in positions of power recognise the power of the literate over people who are illiterate or in the process of becoming literate, writing becomes more central to the social division of labour, defining the terms of exclusion, stratification and the classification of knowledge. Contests of authority take place over the written word and about whose 'conception of the world', in Gramsci's phrase, will be dominant. Language, as he argued, remains at the centre of the 'cultural battle to transform the popular "mentality"'.[2] Writing is at the heart of a divided society because written language carries such a large part of human communication and culture.

In the nineteenth century, writing – the active side of literacy – grew in significance as never before. But as a form of public expression, as voice, it remained available only to a minority. It became essential to be able to write, to the extent that to be without literacy gradually came to be the object of pathos: millions marked the marriage register with an 'x' at the beginning of the century; to do so by the end of the century was humiliating. Working-class 'cultural production' sometimes flourished

A typical page from the Diary of John Ward of Clitheroe, *which was recued from a rubbish heap by a labourer feeding a furnace* independently, but even when it was published remained at the margins of the cultural mainstream. Writing meant many things and only some could make their voices heard in any public sense. These are the paradoxes: only a few can be recognised as writers when literacy is nearly universal; in the case of those who haven't the literacy to write because of institutional failure, it is surely they who are 'affronted' as literate society goes its own way. To be ambitious as a writer beyond the bounds of an expected level and usage of literacy was – and still is – to risk being patronised and seen as exceptional. The fundamental division remains because definitions of what it means to be educated have been continuously readjusted to exclude those with an education which is less acceptable than that of powerful social groups.

By the end of the nineteenth century, although more working people practised literacy at work, more people wrote and sent letters and belonged to trade unions and other organisations than ever before, millions learned independently and wrote privately, a sliding scale of cultural exclusion seemed to operate. The cultural drawbridge was lowered to include writing more fully in education, then drawn up again to preserve the cultural reign of the guardians of national culture. The scale of marginalisation and exclusion is evident in attacks on working-class usage of language and culture, independent working-class education and in the assumption that forms of writing beyond immediate, practical or imitative communication in private or work settings were the province of middle-class culture. The decades just before and after the turn of the century saw a new and vibrant radical politics emerge in which cultural, artistic, social and trade union movements were linked. There was a renewal of social and religious concern and practical action about poverty and the beginning of parliamentary representation of working-class interests. The creative force of William Morris and many others on making things, and realising ambitious social projects for a better world, further affected literacy practices. Literacy was essential to the new general trade unions with mass membership, to the huge and growing cooperative movement, to initiatives for better health, pensions and housing, and self-evidently to the communications revolution as mass-circulation newspapers arrived.

In any account of nineteenth-century literacy practices there is a tension between the narrative of policy-makers and the narratives of other stakeholders. In literacy, commercial interests in particular intensified their hold on popular culture. The slow but powerful evolution of the projects of the state, industry and commerce and established society on the one hand contended with the projects of people, their leaders and their affiliated organisations that learned and practised for their own purposes on the other. The main movement was towards centralism and control of what and how people learned. Once the structures of official literacies were firmly in place, requirements and opportunites to practise literacy increased, but resistance, the exercise of independent literacy and autonomous cultural practices and cultural production became more difficult.

The orthodox historiography of institutional forces and pressures screens other forms of narrative. These are discernible in the experience of learners, and they are different. They speak about conversion, conflict, pain, progress and a journey to a different selfhood, as well as educational and economic self-improvement. By self-help they often mean collective, socialised self-help, rather than the individual self-help of nineteenth-century (and present day) ideology. There are also contradictions in the formal and informal subjective narratives of literacy. Learners' accounts of literacy are political and personal and seek change, while also being internalised aspects of the ideology of hegemonic social groups.

What happens when historical events, discourses and ideologies meet actual practices of reading and writing? The meaning of reading and writing in a particular society at a particular time is recoverable from theory and historical research, but it is also recoverable from the practices of the people who learned. People who wrote autobiographies, as a mode of utterance, declared their identity and their cultural existence.[3] The writings in this book proclaim significant experiences, viewpoints, autonomous practices and myths of their own. Any story or fragment of one may contain multiple elements in the recollection and construction of meanings. My approach to their writing has been hermeneutic. I have tried to interpret the kaleidoscopic, tumbling and colourful elements and meanings in a text and relate them to the structures of power and authority which sought to limit or ignore creative public communication of experiences and knowledge outside dominant forms of cultural pro-duction. The conditions of producing such narratives as these are charac-terised by the always-volatile relations between writers and those who opposed or sponsored their writing. Writers engage in a search for discourses to express their own meanings adequately. They express myths and create new myths as well as memories, of self and others. They convey value and a sense of identity, an inner as well as a public selfhood. The relationship of ideology to all of these conditions of production is volatile for any of these writers. There is no immutable, immanent ideological value to any practice which is not subvertible by someone, through what Jeffrey Weeks, writing of Foucault's theory of knowledge and power, called 'the refractory and resisting consciousness of individuals … deploying one system of meaning against another'.[4] In this book, I have explored the meaning of a self who, through his or her writing, manages to blur the edges of 'cultural division'.

II   Literacy, autobiography and historical evidence

The insights and experiences of the writers discussed in this book work at different levels of meaning, offering a range of 'evidences'. First of all, reconstructions in autobiographical writing are acts of witness, providing reports about and recoverable insights into the meaning of writing practices, and so they serve as authenticating sources for a history of different forms of literacy practice. Autobiography is often questioned as an independently trustworthy historical source: it should be used only to corroborate firmer 'evidences', such as social statistics, official documents, and other published and unpublished materials of historical enquiry. It is much more than that. Autobiography offers its own meanings as a written product, its own interpretation of what learning to write meant to working-class people at different periods of the nineteenth century. My use of autobiography as an historical source has involved trying to dig deeper into one aspect of the worlds that historians have uncovered, asking what is happening in the text itself, how did that text come to appear, and what is the meaning of writing it. The experiences the text narrates are contextualised by the more formal and public history of the teaching and learning of writing. Secondly, autobiographical writing reveals a range of complex meanings about the self in relation to personal writing histories. It serves as a kind of forensic and psychic evidence of changing selfhoods in which writing itself is interpreted as a key agent of change. Finally, autobiography has status as a literary text, evidencing creativities and expressive, imaginative powers. It is open to readings and interpretations of its narrative and its deeper structures as well as the stories it tells.

The ways in which writers communicate reveal how closely all three of these aspects of autobiography are bound together; how each is expressed through the meanings of literacy; and how registers shift within narratives to offer different facets of the possibilities of autobiography. And memory is a critical element. As historical evidence, pure and simple, there are issues of accuracy informed by selectivity and the focus on the self. These can be critically explored. In autobiography, the nature of memory as a problematic player in creating texts of identity becomes part of the psychological drama of what is and is not significant, what is available in the text and what is, or must be, hidden. Memory is at work, too, in the creation of the literary text, one of the strands and motivators to creativity. In working-class autobiography memory is both individual and social; active agent and passive terrain.

III   Writing and the self

The learning and practice of writing changes the meaning of self in a society that is rapidly becoming literate. Where there is a proliferation of the institutions and functions of literacy, it is not neutral either to remain without literacy or to learn to use it independently. To remain illiterate in nineteenth-century England was to court a changing identity in relation to a state, society and culture in which public and private literacies were themselves rapidly changing. The list of changes is long, starting with the growth of a large reading public and a mushrooming popular press as well as books, journals and magazines. Then there were parliamentary and other public information-gathering exercises through censuses and surveys, and an enormous growth in writing in the workplace, at school and in political and social organisations. In everyday life, letter-writing and bureaucratic needs demanded the spread of literacy in families and communities. In this environment, to stay illiterate was to be moved faster and faster backwards, to be written about rather than to write. Conversely, for individuals or social groups to use literacy in ways that state or society would regard as precocious was not a neutral exercise. There was no escaping change. It was not surprising that for individuals and groups, literacy inevitably led to conflict.

Movement from illiteracy into literacy, grounded in the consciousness of cultural change, involved changes of identity in social, material and psychological terms. This accounts for how people who became self-acknowledged writers explain their path into literacy as an essential element of the discovery of the particular kind of self the writer has become, and the precursors of that self as the child or a young adult who acquired literacy. So at one level, this book is a speculative piece of history

306

about the sociology of being. Writing by people from subordinated social groups has been subject to much generalisation, interpreting the meaning of being a working-class man or woman in generic terms. Yet feelings and experiences of class differ to such an extent as to justify more attention to individual, subjective meanings within class structures. This is necessary in order to understand the complexity of individual experiences of class and of the degrees of and limits to social belonging. Further, if literacy facilitates change or entry into another order of social being, what are the framings within which such movements and transitions can happen? And what is the nature of these movements and transitions? I have argued for a movement away from a simple collective identity, a movement which problematises the position of the writer in relation to his or her social group and makes a sense of belonging more elastic.

In autobiographies there is movement from one language into another. This is expressed by writers in different ways. Firstly they communicate the consciousness of their movement from spoken to written language. Then they communicate their confidence about gradually learning more sophisticated usages of written language. They also communicate a consciousness of language and class, and of the attempts from outside to reify the splits between spoken and written languages and to denigrate working-class language as incapable of bridging the two. Pride at having arrived at the other side is tempered for some writers by unease, nostalgia and a reclamation of the value of spoken language and 'plain statements'. There is a consciousness, too, that there is not one written language, but that literacies are redefined as they are acquired and further languages need to be grasped; and that having arrived does not mean being accepted. The apologetic tone in the majority of prefaces to autobiographies seems to bear the weight of the oppressiveness of 'cultural division'. Then there is movement back into a personal past which is selectively remembered and highly conscious of the existence of a differently interpreted and represented present self. Such narratives exhibit traces of uncertainty, in a selective reclamation of lost beginnings and ambivalent declarations of achieved selfhood.

For the majority of the writers whose work appears in this book, the desire for and learning of literacy was a formidable presence in the reconstruction of their early consciousness. This is at one level a reasonable reflection of experience throughout the century. It is born out by the emphasis given to literacy and education by state, church, society and in working-class communities themselves. The genesis of their motivation to learn is complex. Within the community, literacy – and particularly the skills and means of writing – became a strong focus of desire for a number of reasons. First, it was difficult to achieve. Second, there was a growing awareness that literacy could provide the way to a better life as opportunities for jobs for those with writing skills began to grow, particularly in towns and cities. Clamour for writing at Sunday schools and the huge popularity of Adult School writing classes are indicators of the hopes invested in writing. Third, the written word was becoming more and more obviously a means of power and influence in political and everyday life. Fourth, autobiographers celebrated the sheer pleasure they gained from learning and using writing as young people and adults, and the conflicts and difficulties they were prepared to face to practise it. Finally, writing was a more common focus of memories of learning literacy than reading. It was the more controversial element, more difficult to achieve, more costly and more susceptible to longing for the unattainable. Writing was the subject of day-dreams and the expression of a remembered transgressive creative self: the self who wandered in nature, avoided the call of duty, became aware of music, words and pictures, and dreamt of growing powerful enough to change his/her own life and the lives of others, of becoming rich and famous, of reconciliation and redemption. The longed-for imagined self was the self who wrote.

Writing an autobiography, a diary or a fragment of one was a significant act of creativity, however fragmentary, however strongly the writer claimed it was purely factual, and however much it appeared to skate over or hint at deeper meanings. Writers had to work and rework their hard-won skills of writing, to reshape their experience and communicate it. For many, it was the first sustained piece of writing after a long working life. Writing a life story meant that writing skills became craft and art, digging up and reworking memories; revisiting the documents and treasured artefacts of a life; re-imagining lost scenes and people; trying and testing nearly-forgotten sequences of events. Then they had to choose the words to bring everything together in a narrative which expressed a life and communicated it to unknown others. Such complex creative processes are disturbing and often agonising, even if they are also deeply satisfying.

IV Literacy, history and personal myth

Despite the historical specificities of learning to write as a working-class woman or man in a particular period, the possibilities which writing offers are also timeless human possibilities. The creativity of these texts lies partly in the structures and imagery which writers use to convey the depth and strength of the meaning of literacy. The structures are layered. There is a narrative which is historically and socially retrievable and there is also a mythic structure. The mythic nature of literacy lies in the magic of the text itself and the magic of discovery of the possibility of subjectivity and agency through technical competence and the movement from spoken to written language.

The meanings of these autobiographies are also layered, because they are the inheritors of several traditions of expression. First, and most obviously, they are influenced by the oral traditions of story-telling that writers have grown up with. Second, they are produced in an era in which social and critical realism, moralism, positivist thinking and a firm belief in progress infused art and literature. Engaging in the Zeitgeist, working-class writers brought their own culture and their urgent desire to communicate their own truths and knowledge because they sensed how little they were known or understood. At the point of writing, people unavoidably became conscious of the relationships between knowledge, language and power. The language to describe their own experience is, unavoidably, the language also used by others to describe that experience and place it within the framework of the hegemonic culture and its discourses. Working-class people's writing must always be the attempt to marry their own experience and organic knowledge with the language which is used to contain and control them. Discomfort and awkwardness can reflect the difficulty of finding a register in writing that will allow such a synthesis. Third, working-class writers are inheritors of a confessional mode of autobiography in which the conversion experience, religious and secular, which is arguably one of the most powerful themes of nineteenth-century fiction as well as autobiography, is the paradigmatic form. Finally, they are the inheritors of two different traditions of autobiography: the self-representational mode, which may be seen to descend from Rousseau's *Confessions*, and the hermeneutic, or interpretative, mode exemplified in Bunyan's *Grace Abounding to the Chief of Sinners*.[5] In Roy Pascal's classic model of autobiography, the genre is seen as 'a shaping of the past' which 'imposes a pattern on a life', and 'constructs out of it a coherent story, through which the writer takes a particular standpoint at which he reviews his life and interprets his life from it'.[6] Heather Henderson draws these two trajectories together to create another model which may better serve the complex projects of the working-class writers in this book:

> The writing of any autobiography necessarily involves a process of selection: the autobiographer chooses those events from his past which will form a story, a 'personal myth'. For autobiographers since Augustine, that personal myth has frequently been founded on the biblical narratives of conversion and salvation.[7]

The concept of 'personal myth', developed in Jung's *Memories, Dreams, Reflections*, also allows for a synthesis, rather than one or other model, such as the 'French' or 'English' models. He incorporates into the idea of an autobiography elements associated with oral traditions. 'What we are to our inward vision', Jung writes, 'can only be expressed by way of myth … I can only make direct statements, only "tell stories". Whether or not the stories are "true" is not the problem. The only question is whether what I tell is *my* fable, *my* truth.'[8]

Many of the autobiographers in this book write explicit and detailed descriptions of their first and subsequent attempts to learn writing and how they then refine their skills. Their accounts of learning to write, as well as some of their stories of life before conscious memory was possible, reveal typologies which are invested with power and meaning beyond the social, historical interpretations they offer. The meaning of these representations or memories and their interpretation cluster around two phenomena in the texts which I will call 'the mythic meaning of things' and 'the typology of strangers'.

Ceremony and the mythic meaning of treasured things

Freud wrote that:

> a strong experience in the present awakens in the creative writer a memory of an earlier experience (usually belonging to his childhood) from which there now proceeds a wish which finds its fulfilment in the creative work. The work itself exhibits elements of the recent provoking occasion as well as of the old memory.[9]

The power and pleasure attributed to writing manifests itself in many autobiographies in the reverence for inventories of the objects necessary to learning to write and in stories of searching for them, finding them, using and reusing them, receiving them as gifts, being without them and above all keeping them – often to the point where the accoutrements of learning to write decades previously lie on the desk of the elderly autobiographer. Things, the materials of writing, acquire mythic status in autobiography. In one way this is not unusual. Thousands of successful writers testify to the difficulty of writing. They suffer from writer's block, write essays on 'Why I write' and the peculiar position of the writer, in society, but also outside, observing it. The difficulty of writing is always hovering because there is always a fear of exposure of the self into the permanent indelible structures of writing and, in published writing, the visibility of the self to unchosen and untrusted audiences. This is in tension with the pleasure in seeking and finding an audience. For writers from hegemonic cultural groups, the difficulty is more alienated, intangible and fixed in the unconscious although they may learn conscious techniques for releasing creativity. For writers from culturally underrepresented and misrepresented groups, writing – and learning to write – carries different meanings.

Learning to write, as we have seen, seems to have been a more intense experience than learning to read. Reading was less often recalled in such detail in autobiography perhaps because its legitimacy as an appropriate literacy was less controversial. Writing carried significance in other ways. It was a powerfully desired activity. It was more ceremonial than reading. The tools and artefacts of desired crafts, knowledge or rites of passage and their identifying documents, such as membership badges and papers, certificates and pledges, keepsakes, love letters and last letters, carried deep, lasting meanings. Writing involved the ceremony of owning, caring for and using special, wanted things. These objects show that the active making of a life, and learning to write, involved making demands for oneself, in ways which reading the family Bible, for example, did not. Thus in autobiography the artefacts of writing take on the status of emblems, totems and eventually revered relics of a life interpreted as a pilgrimage to a different self. These artefacts are prefigurative emblems of the moment when the acquisition of literacy became possible as a form of conversion, with a remembered and recounted experience of before and after, when choices were made between consenting to what others expected or moving mountains through one's own agency.

Literacy objects also took on the status of iconic symbols about working-class life, from different perspectives. Hareton Earnshaw's inscription over the door of Wuthering Heights exemplifies the way in which the significance of writing was exhibited in graphic representations of uneducated people. In *Our Mutual Friend*, Dickens reproduces a 'facsimile' of Silas Wegg's placard advertising himself as 'a literary man'.[10] In popular Victorian painting, the theme of receiving, writing and posting letters was common, as were explicit representations of literacy such as Richard Dadd's *The Ballad Monger*, or George Elgar Hicks's *The General Post Office* or *Orphan Election*.

Inscriptions and symbolic artefacts also appear frequently in working-class writing. The factory worker, poet and popuar novelist Ethel Carnie describes in her novel *Miss Nobody* (1913) how in her heroine's home 'over the settle, with its Paisley print cover and curtains, was a motto in wool and silk warning the beholder to take count of the golden march of the hours'. A picture of John Bunyan engaged in writing *Pilgrim's Progress* was matched on the other side of the dresser by Milton dictating *Paradise Lost*.[11] Mottoes above the mantelpiece, letters and notes propped against a vase or on the kitchen table appear as iconic symbols of literacy's place at the centre of working-class domestic life. At the same time, whether in letters or paintings, such symbols speak to a viewer, looking through the eyes of an established literate culture, who will see irony or pathos in the importance placed on literacy by working-class people, interpreting writing practices as rudimentary, half-schooled or naively sentimental.

The typology of strangers

Another phenomenon in nineteenth-century autobiographies is 'the typology of strangers', which is a key to understanding the meaning of acquiring literacy. What are the main elements of this theme? It is close to Deborah Brandt's notion of 'sponsors', which offers a social understanding of the range of actors involved in becoming literate in the early twentieth century. The life-stories in this book are complex narratives by people who describe as social practices their own encounters with and their eventual grasp of literacy. In addition, the texts can be read as a sequence of historical evidences and experiences which we can fit into the patterns of other evidences about the growth of literacy and the phenomenon of working-class autobiography and its traditions. Yet we repeatedly find elements of dramatised mystery that are shared, and which are difficult to explain solely in social historical terms. The most common of these is the appearance of a stranger, who intervenes sometimes for better and sometimes for worse in the desired process of learning to write. Not all such 'sponsors' are strangers, but the nature of the representation of their intervention suggests this is an apposite term. They may be local people, for example in Sunday schools, but they are unknown until a turning point in life or learning. They are rarely family, except on occasion a romanticised story-telling grandmother or benign uncle. And they are rarely simply friends from the same social group.

At one level the inventory of such agents acts as a kind of historical demography, a map of the social actors in communities and the wider society. They are the human, social, reality behind the quantitative statistics giving numbers of Sunday school or Adult School teachers. They may be the leaders of social movements, middle-class patrons of working-class communities, quack doctors, itinerants, letter carriers, literate artisans and masters, male and female scribes and many others who helped someone to learn literacy or change their circumstances. Autobiographers illuminate the complex patterns of learning in nineteenth-century communities, showing their significant contribution to an individual's life.

Yet there is another way of reading the role of 'stranger' in a writer's process of coming to terms with literacy. The typology of the stranger transcends and incorporates individual historical identities. The stranger is a mythologised 'Other' with transformative powers, whose fortuitous or portentous appearance places the meaning of acquiring literacy beyond historical contingency. He or she is necessary to the interpretation of self because the significance of the achievement of literacy is discontinuous with the writer's perception of what is historically, socially, ordinarily possible. The typology of the stranger permits the construction of a 'personal myth'.

A dual reading, both historical and mythic, lays open to view the complex ways in which a writer recalls, represents and explicates the material conditions of writing – the social and historical realities. It also allows a hermeneutic approach to the meanings attached to their sense of being. The reader of these texts has historical, interrogative ways of reading, but can also be alive to deeper elements of the narrative structure, which is embryonically and at some points for some writers wholly mythic. This does not mean that these narratives are therefore less trustworthy, rather that they are more multi-dimensional and layered than they are in historically-located texts.

These writings disclose the meanings of structures which are reiterated as a communality of material circumstances. They express shared, situated experiences and events. They reveal the relationship between writing, imagination, conscious and forgotten experience and evidence. So on the one hand there exists a narrative, read to us by historians, in which the writer places himself or herself in family, class and community in relation to oppression and empowerment, poverty and success, illiteracy and literacy, and where all elements are ideologically and materially referable. Autobiography at this level witnesses life in the world of public or social identity. On the other hand there is an intervention. The stranger is recuperable into the public narrative, but nevertheless leaves a mythic narrative intact. The typology of strangers exists across other levels of the narrative and moves all significant other strangers (including more local figures who become known socially) into different roles in relation to the writer and her or his literacy, in ways which go beyond historical ways of seeing. Because the achievement of literacy is the transforming achievement for the self, and the stranger is pivotal to this achievement, the mythic narrative is as powerful as the historicised, social, 'truth-telling' narrative.

In this reading, writing becomes an essential 'personal myth', intensified because for the writer it is an act of self-production. Because writing is perceived as a powerful and alien language which is itself a form of magic, its acquisition is experienced at least in part as mythic. It is represented within the mythic forms available in the culture: fairy tales, legends, magical happenings and magical others – of whom the transformed, writing self is one. There is a consciousness that this acquisition of the language of others is explosive. Its representation can only take shape in unconscious, projected, mythical ways.

I insist that there must be multiple meanings and a plurality of interpretations. As Sue Gardener suggested, to write is to register 'invisible, neglected and unimaginably rich consciousness' in language. To find a language and use it for this exploration is to 'resituate' the self 'socially as well as psychologically'.[12]

V Lost and found

There are many stories, excluded by history and literature, which have not survived. One crucial fact about writing by people without cultural power is that their writing disappears. A substantial body of work has been retrieved by public appeal, resulting in the nineteenth- and twentieth-century 'Bibliography of Working-Class Autobiography', much used for this book. Some is still hidden, and still retrievable. Much more is destroyed. A related issue is how little is known about how writing is produced, from conception to publication. Another problem is that when a piece of writing is found or rights acquired, it is often considered the property of the finder or 'owner' who is deemed at liberty to enclose, dissect, prune and reshape it to fit their own purposes and values. This was long the case for John Clare's legacy, but work on Clare is no longer restricted by the claims of private ownership. In *Essex People, 1750–1900*, A.F.J. Brown uses John Castle's diary. Under pressure to provide evidence about great public themes, he omits from Castle's writing a case study of the conditions for the survival of working-class writing: 'I have omitted the parts not connected with Essex', he writes, and 'some moralising passages and anecdotes, which, though set in Essex, throw little light on Castle or on local society'.[13] Two other works point towards further investigation into the writing and creativity of culturally marginalised people. The first is the story of John Ward of Clitheroe whose diary is discussed in chapter 6. This has survived by the purest chance. His editor writes that 'only by the greatest of good fortune has this fascinating diary been preserved. In 1947 it was picked off a heap of rubbish by a labourer who was feeding the furnace at the Clitheroe destructor.'[14] Even his name was eventually found to be uncertain. An entry in ink on the title page reports that the writer is 'now known as John O'Neal'. The second is the work of Janet Bathgate, whose book achieved such popular success in the 1890s that her publisher, George Lewis, set out to investigate how it was written. The result is a detailed account of how the book came into being, written into six copy-books, two of which were lost, then refound.[15] Such an account is apparently rare, but it points to the possible existence of others. Working-class cultural inheritance is precarious.

Notes

1 F. Smith, 1982, p. 7.
2 Gramsci, 1971, pp. 323–4, 348.
3 Swindells, 1985, p. 122, writes that working-class autobiography produces class consciousness, as well as being produced by it: individual writers are the producers, but the 'conception of reality' is also that of a social group.
4 Weeks, 1982, p. 113.
5 See Peterson, 1986, chapter 1, 'The Hermeneutic Imperative', pp. 7–12.
6 Peterson, *op. cit.*, p. 9.
7 Henderson, 1989, p. 3.

8   Jung, [1963] l983, p. 17.
9   Freud, [1908] l985, p. 139.
10 Dickens, *Our Mutual Friend*, [1864–5] 1985b, p. 88.
11 Carnie, 1913, p. 87. Carnie first wrote poetry, becoming a popular novelist. Under Robert Blatchford's patronage, she wrote articles for *The Woman Worker* and became editor in 1909.
12 Gardener, 1991, pp. 189–91.
13 Brown, 1972, p. 116.
14 France, 1953, p. 137.
15 Lewis, 1894.

Bibliography

Official sources

Nineteenth century

Parliamentary Papers (PP) and government documents:

Digest of returns to Circular Letter from the Select Committee (SC) on Education of the Poor (1818)

London School Board Inspectors' (LSB) Reports (1876)

Minutes of the Committee of Council on Education (Mins CCE), 1839–50, including school inspectors' (HMI) reports

Minutes (Mins) of Evidence to the SC on the Education of the Lower Orders (1834)

Mins of Evidence, SC on Education (1834–5)

Mins of Evidence, SC on Education of the Poorer classes (1838)

Mins of Evidence, SC on Education of Destitute Children (1861)

SC on Postage 1837

SC on Postage 1838–9

Contemporary

Department for Business Innovation and Skills (BIS) (2011) BIS Research Paper 57: 2011 Skills for Life Survey

Department for Education and Employment (DfEE) (1999) 'A Fresh Start: The Report of a Working Group chaired by Sir Claus Moser'

DfEE (2001) 'Skills for Life: the National Strategy for Improving Adult Literacy and Numeracy Skills'. Nottingham: DfEE publications

Department for Education and Skills (DfES) (2003) 'The Skills for Life Survey: a national needs and impact survey of literacy, numeracy and ICT skills'. London: DfES Research Brief RB490

OECD (1997) 'Literacy, economy and society: Results of the International Adult Literacy Survey (IALS)'. Paris: OECD

Unpublished and locally-held sources

(All Brunel University Library MS/TS listed below are cited in Burnett, Vincent & Mayall, 1984–7; page references are to this collection)

Annual Report of the Oldham Lyceum (1856), Manchester Reference Library

Bamford, S. (1858–1861) 'Diary', unpaginated MS, Manchester Central Library

Belcher, W. Untitled MS, Brunel University Library

Bolton History Project, 'From a woman textile worker (b. 1893)', Tape 155a 2(f), Bolton Central Library

Brown, E. Untitled TS, Brunel University Library

Castle, J. (1961) 'The Diary of John Castle', TS, Bishopsgate Institute, London; duplicated from the undated MS, Colchester Cooperative Society, held at Essex Record Office, Chelmsford, donated by the Society for their centenary in 1961

Chase, A.M. 'The Memoirs of Alice Maud Chase', TS, Brunel University Library

Chater, D. 'The Autobiography of Daniel Chater', TS, Hull University Library

Cutts, M. Untitled MS, Brunel University Library

Dark, M.M. Untitled Autobiographical Writing, MS, Bristol Central Library

Ellisdon, L.W. 'Starting from Victoria', TS, Brunel University Library

Errington, A. (1776–1825) 'Coals and Rails: the Autobiography of Anthony Errington', Tyneside Colliery Waggonway-Wright, TS, Brunel University Library

Evett, P. 'My Life In and Out of Print', TS, Brunel University

Frisby, M. 'Memories', TS, Brunel University Library

Gill, E. 'Ellen Gill's Diary', TS, Brunel University Library

Goodwin, A. Untitled MS, Brunel University Library

Heap, M. (1824–1913) 'My Life and Times, or an Old Man's Memories, Illustrated with Numerous Anecdotes and Quaint Sayings', MS, Central Library, Rawtenstall

Howard, U. (1994) 'Writing and literacy in 19th Century England: some uses and meanings', D.Phil. thesis, University of Sussex

Ireson, A. 'Reminiscences', TS, Brunel University Library

Kaplan, C. (1985) 'Autobiography', paper given to the History Workshop Conference, Psychoanalysis and History, London, June

Lovekin, E. 'Some Notes on My Life', MS, Brunel University Library

Luty, M. 'My Life has Sparkled', TS, Central Library, Rawtenstall

Minute Books of the Equitable Pioneers' Society (REPS) Education Department, 1866–71, Rochdale Reference Library

Randall Place School, Logbooks, Greater London Record Office

Stockport Sunday School (1811–80) Memoir Books of the Stockport Sunday School

Newspapers and Periodicals

Bolton Express and Lancashire Advertiser, 1824–6, Bolton Reference Library

The Chartist Circular, Vols 1–3, 1839–43

The Crisis, 1832–4 (Owenite Journal which was retitled New Moral World)

The Highway, 1907–14

Lyceum Banner, 1890–8

Marxism Today

Millgate Monthly (Cooperative movement magazine)

The Monthly Record, 1869–78, Society of Friends

New Moral World, 1834–45

The Northern Star, 1837–52

One and All, 1891–1908, Journal of the Adult School Movement

The Poor Man's Guardian, 1831–5

The Wheatsheaf (Cooperative movement magazine)

The Woman Worker, 1908–9

Womenfolk, 1910

Write First Time, 1974–85, magazine of adult literacy students' writing: archive held at Ruskin College Library, Oxford

Selected publications and further reading for those interested in literacy practices, writing and related areas of adult learning and cultural history

(Published in London unless otherwise stated.)

Ackroyd, P. (1990) *Dickens*. Sinclair Stevenson

Acorn, G. (1911) *One of the Multitude.* Heinemann

Adams, W.E. (1903) *Memoirs of a Social Atom*, 2 Vols. Hutchinson & Co.

Altick, R.D. (1957) *The English Common Reader. A Social History of the Mass Reading Public 1800–1900.* Chicago, IL: University of Chicago Press

Anon (undated) *A Grammatical Game, in Rhyme by a Lady.*

Anon (undated) *Progressive Exercises; or Easy Steps to the Knowledge of Grammar, by the Author of Flora's Offering to the Young.*

Anon (1850) *Chapters in the Life of a Dundee Factory Boy. An Autobiography.* Dundee: J. Scott

Anon (1858) *Writing Without a Master by a Teacher of the New Systems of Writing.*

Arch, J. (1966) *The Autobiography of Joseph Arch.* MacGibbon & Kee Ltd; first pub. 1898

Arnold, M. (1910) *Reports on Elementary Education 1852–1882.* Board of Education, HMSO

Ashby, M.K. (1961) *Joseph Ashby of Tysoe 1859–1919: A Study of English Village Life.* Cambridge: CUP

Ashford, M.A. (1844) *Life of a Licensed Victualler's Daughter Written by Herself.* Saunders & Otley

Ashton, O. & Roberts, S. (1999) *The Victorian Working-Class Writer.* Mansell Publishing/Cassell

Bacon, G.W. (1895) *Bacon's Reform in Handwriting with Hints and Suggestions to Teachers.* G.W. Bacon & Co.

Baines, F. (1895) *Forty Years at the Post Office: A Personal Narrative*, 2 Vols. R. Bentley & Son

Baldry, G. (1939) *The Rabbit Skin Cap. A Tale of a Norfolk Countryman's Youth. Written In His Old Age by George Baldry*, ed. Lilias Rider Haggard. Collins

Ball, N. (1983) *Educating the People: A Documentary History of Elementary Schooling in England, 1840–1870.* Marice Temple Smith Ltd.

Bamford, S. (1859) *Early Days.* Simpkin, Marshall & Co

Bamford, S. (1869) *Passages in the Life of a Radical.* Simpkin, Marshall & Co

Barber, M. (1840) *Five Score and Ten. A True Narrative of the Long Life and Many Hardships of M. Barber, Taken Down from Her Own Dictation, A Short Time Before Her Death, and Who Died at the Advanced Age of Nearly One Hundred and Eleven Years.* Crewkerne: Penny & Makeig

Barclay, P. (1934) *Memoirs and Medleys. The Autobiography of a Bottle Washer.* Leicester: Edgar Backus

Barker, J. (1837) *Teaching the Children of the Poor to Write on the Sabbath Day.* Manchester: W. Shuttleworth

Barker, J. (1880) *The Life of Joseph Barker, Written by Himself.* Hodder & Stoughton; first pub. 1846

Barrow, L. (1986) *Independent Spirits: Spiritualism and English Plebeians 1850–1910.* Routledge

Barthes, R. (1973) *Mythologies.* Paladin

Barthes, R. (1983) *Barthes: Selected Writings,* ed. Susan Sontag. Fontana

Barthes, R. (1990) *A Lover's Discourse.* Harmondsworth: Penguin; first pub. 1977

Barton, D. & Hall, N. (eds) (2000) *Letter-Writing as a Social Practice.* Philadelphia: John Benjamins Publishing

Barton, D. & Hamilton, M. (1998) *Local Literacies: Reading and Writing in One Community.* Routledge

Barton, D., Hamilton, M. & Ivanic, R. (eds) (2000) *Situated Literacies: Reading and Writing in Context.* Routledge

Bate, J. (2003a) *John Clare: A Biography.* Picador

Bate, J. (2003b) (ed.) *John Clare: Selected Poems.* Faber

Bathgate, J. (1894) *Aunt Janet's Legacy to her Nieces – Recollections of Humble Life in Yarrow in the Beginning of the Century.* Selkirk: G. Lewis

Baynham, M. (2008) 'Elite or Powerful Literacies? Constructions of Literacy in the Novels of Charles Dickens and Mrs Gaskell', in M. Prinsloo & M. Baynham (eds) *Literacies Global and Local.* Philadelphia: John Benjamins Publishing, pp. 173–92

Benjamin, W. (1977) 'The Storyteller', in Hannah Arendt (ed.) *Illuminations.* Fontana; first pub. 1968

Benjamin, W. (1985) *One Way Street and Other Writings.* Verso Classics

Besnier, N. (1995) *Literacy, Emotion and Authority: Reading and Writing on a Polynesian Atoll.* Cambridge: CUP

Binfield, K. (ed.) (2004) *Writings of the Luddites.* Baltimore, MD: John Hopkins University Press

Blackburn, F. (1954) *George Tomlinson. A Biography.* Heinemann

Blatchford, R. (1900) *My Favourite Books.* Walter Scott Ltd

Blatchford, R. (1925) *English Prose and How to Write it.* Methuen

Boardman, J. (1810) *An Analysis of Penmanship.* Printed for the author

Bonwick, J. (1902) *An Octogenarian's Reminiscences.* J. Nichols

Boos, F.S. (ed.) (2008) *Working Class Women Poets in Victorian Britain: An Anthology.* Toronto: Broadview Press

Bourdieu, P. (1993) *The Field of Cultural Production.* Policy Press

Bourne, G. (1984) *Change in the Village.* Allen Lane; first pub. 1912

Bowen, E. (1948) *Why Do I Write? An Exchange of Views Between Elizabeth Bowen, Graham Greene & V.S. Pritchett.* Percival Marshall

Brandt, D. (2001) *Literacy in American Lives.* Cambridge: CUP

Brandt, D. (2009) *Literacy and Learning: Reflections on Writing, Reading and Society.* San Francisco: Jossey-Bass

Brandt, D. (2011) *Literacy as Involvement: The Acts of Writers, Readers and Texts.* Carbondale, IL: Southern Illinois University Press

Brierley, B. (1886) *Home Memories and Recollections of a Life.* Manchester: Abel Heywood & Son

Briggs, A. (1988) *Victorian Things.* Batsford

British and Foreign School Society (1854) *The Handbook to the Borough Road Schools, explanatory of the Methods of Instruction adopted by the British and Foreign School Society.*

Brontë, C. (1979) *Villette.* Harmondsworth: Penguin; first pub. 1853

Brontë, E. (1965) *Wuthering Heights.* Harmondsworth: Penguin; first pub. 1847

Brontë, E. (1995) *Wuthering Heights.* Harmondsworth: Penguin

Brown, A.F.J. (1972) *Essex People, 1750–1900: From their Diaries, Memoirs and Letters.* Chelmsford, Essex: Essex Record Office Publications, No 59

Burke, M. (1909) *A New Method of Teaching Writing to Infants.* G. Philip & Son

Burn, J. (1978) *The Autobiography of a Beggar Boy*, ed. D. Vincent. Europa; first pub. 1855

Burnett, J. (ed.) (1974) *Useful Toil: Autobiographies of Working People from the 1820s to the 1920s.* Penguin

Burnett, J. (1982) *Destiny Obscure: Autobiographies of Childhood, Education and Family from the 1820s to the 1920s.* Allen Lane (Penguin)

Burnett, J., Vincent, D. & Mayall, D. (eds) (1984–7) *The Autobiography of the Working Class*, 2 Vols: Vol. 1, 1790–1900 (1984); Vol. 2, 1900–45 (1987). Brighton: Harvester Press

Bynner, J. & Parsons, S. (2006) *New Light on Literacy and Numeracy.* National Research and Development Centre (NRDC)

322

Bynner, J. & Parsons, S. (2007) *Illuminating Disadvantage: Profiling the Experience of Adults with Entry Level Literacy or Numeracy Over the Lifecourse*. NRDC

Carnie, E. (1907) *Rhymes from the Factory*. Blackburn: Denham & Co

Carnie, E. (1913) *Miss Nobody*. Methuen

Chaplin C.S. (1966) *My Autobiography*. Harmondsworth: Penguin

Cipolla, C.M. (1969) *Literacy and Development in the West*. Harmondsworth: Penguin

Clanchy, M.T. (1979) *From Memory to Written Record: England 1066–1307*. Arnold

Clare, J. (1983) *John Clare's Autobiographical Writings*, ed. E. Robinson. Oxford: OUP

Cobbett, W. (1856) *Advice to Young Men and (Incidentally) to Young Women in the Middle and Higher Ranks of Life: in a Series of Letters Addressed to a Youth, a Batchelor, a Lover, a Husband, a Father, a Citizen, or a Subject*. Simpkin; first pub. 1830

Cobbett, W. (1984) *A Grammar of the English Language in a Series of Letters Intended for the use of Schools and of Young Persons in General; but More Especially for the Use of Soldiers, Sailors, Apprentices and Ploughboys*. Oxford: OUP; first pub. 1819

Cole, G.D.H. (1936) 'Life of Cobbett', *International Review of Social History*, Vol. 1

Cole, G.D.H. & Mansbridge, A. (1910) 'Higher Education of Working Men', *The Highway* (WEA Journal)

Colls, R. (1976) ' "Oh Happy English Children!": Coal, Class and Education in the North East', *Past and Present*, Vol. 73, pp. 75–99

Cooper, T. (1851) *The Purgatory of Suicides, A Prison Rhyme in Ten Books by Thomas Cooper the Chartist*. J. Watson

Cooper, T. (1971) *The Life of Thomas Cooper, Written by Himself*. Leicester: Leicester University Press; first pub. 1872

Cowham, J.H. (1888) *Cowham's Mulhauser Manual of Writing*. J.H. Cowham

Cross, N. (1985) *The Common Writer: Life in 19th Century Grub Street*. Cambridge: CUP

Currie Martin, G. (1924) *The Adult School Movement. Its Origins and Development*. National Adult School Union

Cushman, E., Kintgen, E.R., Kroll, B.M. & Rose, M. (eds) (2001) *Literacy: A Critical Sourcebook*. Boston, MA: Bedford/St Martins

De Coulon, A., Meschi, E. & Vignoles, A. (2008) *Parents' Basic Skills and their Children's Test Scores*. Institute of Education, National Research and Development Centre (NRDC)

Dickens, C. (1985a) *Great Expectations*. Harmondsworth: Penguin; first pub. 1860–1

Dickens, C. (1985b) *Our Mutual Friend*. Harmondsworth: Penguin; first pub. 1864–5

Dickens, C. (1986) *The Pickwick Papers*. Oxford: OUP; first pub. 1836–7

Dobbs, A.E. (1919) *Education and Social Movements*. Longmans

Douglass, D. (1976) 'Jack Common, *Kiddar's Luck* and *The Ampersand*', *History Workshop Journal*, Vol. 2, Autumn, pp. 206–10

Edmondson, J. (2003) *Prairie Town: Redefining Rural Life in the Age of Globalisation*. Lanham, MD: Rowman & Littlefield

Edwards, G. (1957) *From Crow-Scaring to Westminster: An Autobiography*. The National Union of Agricultural Workers; first pub. 1922

Eldred, J.C. & Mortensen, P. (2002) *Imagining Rhetoric: Composing Women of the Early United States*. Pittsburgh, PA: University of Pittsburgh Press

Eliot, G. (1960) *Adam Bede*. J.M. Dent & Sons Ltd; first pub. 1858

Fairman, T. (2000) 'English Pauper Letters 1800–1834 and the English Language', in D. Barton and N. Hall (eds) *Letter-Writing as a Social Practice*. Philadelphia: John Benjamins Publishing

Farningham, M. (1907) *A Working Woman's Life. An Autobiography*. James Clarke & Co

Ferreira-Buckley, L. & Horner, W.B. (2001) 'Writing Instruction in Great Britain: The 18th–19th Century', in J.J. Murphy (ed.), *A Short History of Writing Instruction*. Mahwah, NJ: Erlbaum Associates, pp. 173–212

Foakes, G. (1972) *Between High Walls*. Shepheard-Walwyn

Foley, A. (1973) *A Bolton Childhood*. Manchester: MUP and North West WEA

Fox, J.D. (1914) 'My Life', in *Life and Poems of John D. Fox, 'Throstle Nest'*. Bingley, Yorks: Thomas Harrison & Sons

Fox, R.M. (1937) *Smoky Crusade*. Hogarth Press

France, R. S. (ed.) (1953) 'The Diary of John Ward of Clitheroe, Weaver, 1860–64', *Transactions of the Historical Society of Lancashire and Cheshire*, Vol. 105, Lancashire Record Office, Preston

Freeman, M. (2010) 'The Decline of the Adult School Movement between the wars', *History of Education*, Vol. 39, No 4, pp. 481–506

Freire, P. (1972) *Cultural Action for Freedom*. Harmondsworth: Penguin

Freud, S. (1975a) 'Childhood Memories and Screen Memories', in *The Psychopathology of Everyday Life*, Penguin Freud Library, Vol. 5. Harmondsworth: Penguin; first pub. 1899–1901

Freud, S. (1975b) 'The Forgetting of Impressions and Intentions', in *The Psychopathology of Everyday Life*, Penguin Freud Library, Vol. 5. Harmondsworth: Penguin; first pub. 1899–1901

Freud, S. (1985) 'Creative Writers and Day-Dreaming', in *Art and Literature*, Penguin Freud Library, Vol. 14. Harmondsworth: Penguin; first pub. 1908

Furet F. & Ozouf, J. (1982) *Reading and Writing; Literacy in France from Calvin to Jules Ferry*. Cambridge: CUP

Gardener, S. (1991) 'Learning to Write as an Adult', in D. Barton & R. Ivanic (eds), *Writing in the Community*. NY: Sage, pp.167–92

Gardner, P.W. (1984) *The Lost Elementary Schools of Victorian England*. Croom Helm

Gaskell, E. (1890) *My Lady Ludlow and other Tales*. Smith Elder & Co.; first pub. 1858

Gaskell, E. (1970) *Mary Barton*. Harmondsworth: Penguin; first pub. 1848

Gere, A.R. (1997) *Intimate Practices: Literacy and Cultural Work in US Women's Clubs 1880–1920*. Illinois, IL: University of Illinois Press, pp. 59–65, 82–87

Gere, R.A. (2001) 'Kitchen Tables and Rented Rooms: The Extracurriculum of Composition', in Cushman *et al.*, *op. cit.*, pp. 275–89

Gillespie, M. (2001) 'Research in Writing: Implications for Adult Literacy Education', in J. Comings, B. Garner & C. Smith (eds), *Annual Review of Adult Learning and Literacy*, NCSALL, Vol. 2. NY: Erlbaum Associates, pp. 63–110

Gissing, G. (1980) *The Odd Women*. Virago; first pub. 1895

Goody, J. (ed.) (1968) *Literacy in Traditional Societies*. Cambridge: CUP

Goody, J. (1977) *The Domestication of the Savage Mind*. Cambridge: CUP

Graff, H.J. (1979) *The Literacy Myth: Literacy and Social Structure in the Nineteenth Century City*. NY: Academic Press

Graham, B. (1983) *Nineteenth Century Self-Help in Education – Manual Improvement Societies. Case Study: The Carlisle Working Men's Reading Rooms*, Vol. 2. Nottingham: Department of Adult Education, University of Nottingham

Gramsci, A. (1971) *Selections from the Prison Notebooks*, ed. and trans. Q. Hoare & G. Nowell Smith. Lawrence & Wishart

Grant, C. E. (1931) *Farthing Bundles, Fern Street Settlement, E3, Bromley-by-Bow*.

Greenwood, A. (1877) *The Educational Department of the Rochdale Equitable Pioneers Society Ltd., Its Origin and Development*. Manchester Central Cooperative Board

Gregory, G. (1991) 'Community Publishing as Self-Education', in D. Barton & R. Ivanic (eds), *Writing in the Community*. NY: Sage, pp. 109–42

Grief, S., Meyer, B. & Burgess, A. (2007) *Effective Teaching and Learning: Writing*. National Research and Development Centre for Adult Literacy and Numeracy

Haggard, H. R. (1906) *Rural England*, Vol. 2. Longmans, Green & Co

Halloran, M. & Wright, E. (2001) 'From rhetoric to composition: the teaching of writing in America to 1900', in J.J. Murphy (ed.), *A Short History of Writing Instruction*. Mahwah, NJ: Hermagoras Press, Erlbaum Associates

Ham, E. (1945) *Elizabeth Ham, 1783–1820, By Herself*, ed. Eric Gillett. Faber & Faber

Hamilton, M. (1996) 'Literacy and Adult Basic Education', in R. Fieldhouse & associates (eds), *A History of Modern British Adult Education*. Leicester: NIACE, pp. 142–65

Hamilton, M. & Hillier, Y. (2006) *The Changing Faces of Adult Literacy: A Critical History*. Trentham

Hardy, T. (1965) *Tess of the D'Urbervilles*. Macmillan; first pub. 1891

Hardy, T. (1966) *Jude the Obsure*. Macmillan; first pub. 1895

Hardy, T. (1979) 'On the Western Circuit', in *The Distracted Preacher and Other Tales*. Harmondsworth: Penguin; first pub. 1891

Harrison, J.F.C. (1960) *Learning & Living (1790–1960)*. Routledge & Kegan Paul

Hay, D., Linebough, P., Rule, J. G., Thompson, E. P. & Winslow, C. (1988) *Albion's Fatal Tree*. Harmondsworth: Penguin

Haw, G. (1907) *From Workhouse to Westminster: The Life Story of Will Crooks, MP*. Cassell & Co.

Henderson, H. (1989) *The Victorian Self. Autobiography and Biblical Narrative*. Ithaca, NY: Cornell University Press

Herbert, George (1948) *Shoemaker's Window. Reflections of a Midland Town Before the Railway Age*, ed. Christiana S. Cheney. Oxford: B.H. Blackwell & Son

Hill, R. & Hill, G.B. (1880) *The Life of Sir Rowland Hill and the History of the Penny Post*. De La Rue

Hobsbawm, E. & Rude, G. (1973) *Captain Swing*. Harmondsworth: Penguin

Hoggart, R. (1958) *The Uses of Literacy*. Harmondsworth: Penguin

Holyoake, G.J. (1847) *Practical Grammar with Graduated Exercises*. J. Watson, first pub. 1842

Horn, P. (1978) *Education in Rural England 1800–1914*. Dublin: Gille Macmillan

Horn, P. (1980) *The Rural World*. Hutchinson

Horn, P. (1981) 'Country Children', in G.E. Mingay (ed.), *The Victorian Countryside*. Routledge, pp. 522–31

Horn, P. (1986) *The Rise and Fall of the Victorian Servant*. Gloucester: Alan Sutton

Houghton, W.E. (1957) *The Victorian Frame of Mind*. New Haven, CT: Yale University Press

Howard, U. (1991) 'Self, Education and Writing in 19th Century English Communities', in D. Barton & R. Ivanic (eds), *Writing in the Community*. NY: Sage, pp. 78–108

Howard, U. (2008) 'A History of Writing in the Community', in C. Bazerman (ed.), *A Handbook of Research on Writing: History, Society, School, Individual, Text*. NY: Erlbaum Associates, pp. 237–54

Hudson, D. (1974) *Munby, Man of Two Worlds: The Life and Diaries of Arthur J. Munby 1829–1910*. Sphere; first pub. 1972

Hudson, J.W. (1851) *The History of Adult Education*. Longmans

Jackson, J. (1890) *Jackson's New Style Vertical Writing Copy-Books*. S. Low, Marston & Co

Jackson, J. (1893) *The Theory and Practice of Handwriting*. S. Low, Marston & Co

Jackson, J. (1894) *Upright versus Sloping Writing*. S. Low, Marston & Co

Jackson, J. (1895) *Jackson's System of Upright Penmanship and Hygienic Writing: Manual of Handwriting*. S. Low, Marston & Co.

Jackson, J. (1905) *Ambidextral Culture and Two-handed Writing*. Simpkin, Marshall, Hamilton

James, L. (1974) *Fiction and the Working Man*. Harmondsworth: Penguin

James, L. (1976) *Print and the People 1819–1851*. Harmondsworth: Penguin

Jarvis, G.C. (1897) *Semi-Upright Writing. The Golden Mean in Penmanship*. C. Phillips

Jarvis, G. C. (1916) *Handwriting in the Light of Present Day Requirements.* G. Philip & Son

Jermy, L. (1934) *The Memories of a Working Woman.* Norwich: Goose & Sons

John, A. (ed.) (1986) *Unequal Opportunities: Women's Employment in England 1800–1918.* Oxford: Basil Blackwell

Johnson, M. (1970) *Derbyshire Village Schools in the Nineteenth Century.* Newton Abbot: David & Charles

Johnson, R. (1970) 'Educational Policy and Social Control', *Past and Present,* Vol. 49, pp. 96–110

Johnson, R. (1979) 'Really Useful Knowledge', in J. Clarke, C. Critcher & R. Johnson (eds), *Working Class Culture: Studies in History & Theory.* Hutchinson, pp. 75–102

Johnston E. (1867) *Autobiography, Poems and Songs of Ellen Johnston, the 'Factory Girl'.* Glasgow: William Love

Jones, G.S. (1983) *Languages of Class, Studies in English Working Class History 1832–1982.* Cambridge: CUP

Jones, T. (1938) *Rhymney Memories.* Newton: Welsh Outlook

Jung, C.G. (1983) *Memories, Dreams and Reflections,* ed. A. Jaffe. Fontana; first pub. 1963

Kalman, J. (1999) *Writing on the Plaza: Mediated Scribes and Clients in Mexico City.* Hampton press Inc

Keefe, J. (1888) *Civil Service Spelling and Dictation Book.* London

Keefe, J. (1893) *Keefe's Copy Manuscripts.* London

Kelly, S., Soundranayagam, L. & Grief, S. (2004) *Teaching and Learning Writing: A Review of Research and Practice.* National Research and Development Centre for Adult Literacy and Numeracy (NRDC), Institute of Education

Kenney, A. (1924) *Memoirs of a Militant.* Butler & Tanter

Kettle, D.W. (1885) *Pens, Ink and Paper.* Privately published

Kingsley, C. (1892) *Alton Locke: Tailor and Poet, An Autobiography.* Macmillan & Co; first pub. 1862

Kitchen, F. (1983) *Brother to the Ox.* Harmondsworth: Penguin; first pub. 1940

Klingopoulos, G.D. (1982) 'The Literary Scene', in Boris Ford (ed.), *New Pelican Guide to English Literature: From Dickens to Hardy,* Vol. 6. Harmondsworth: Pelican

Kundera, M. (1979) *The Book of Laughter and Forgetting.* Harmondsworth: Penguin

Lacqueur, T.W. (1976) *Religion and Respectability: Sunday Schools and Working Class Culture 1780–1850*. New Haven, CT: Yale University Press

Lansbury, G. (1935) *Looking Backwards and Forwards*. Glasgow: Blackie

Lawson, J. (1887) *Letters to the Young on Progress in Pudsey During the Last Sixty Years*. Stanningley

Lawson, J. (1949) *A Man's Life*. Bath: Hodder & Stoughton; first pub. 1932

Lawson, J. & Silver, H. (1973) *A Social History of Education in England*. Methuen

Leavis, Q.D. (1965) *Fiction and the Reading Public*. Chatto & Windus; first pub. 1932

Leno, J.B. (1892) *The Aftermath: with Autobiography of the Author*. Reeves & Turner

Lewis, G. (1894) *Aunt Janet's Legacy*. Selkirk: George Lewis & Son

Llewellyn Davies, M. (1977) (ed.) *Life as We Have Known It*, introd. Virginia Woolf. Virago; first pub. 1931

Love, D. (1823) *The Life and Adventures of David Love. Written by Himself*. Nottingham: Sutton & Son

Lovett, W.M. (1967) *The Life and Struggles of William Lovett in his pursuit of Bread, Knowledge and Freedom with Some Account of the Different Associations he Belonged to and the Opinions He Entertained*. MacGibbon & Gee; first pub. 1876

Lovett, W.M. & Collins, J. (1841) *Chartism, a New Organisation of the People: Embracing a Plan for the Education and Improvement of the People, Politically and Socially, Addressed to the Working Classes*. J. Watson, H. Hetherington, W. Lovett

Luty, M. (1937) *A Penniless Globe Trotter*. Accrington: Wardleworth

Mace, J. (2002) *The Give and Take of Writing: Scribes, Literacy and Every Day Life*. Leicester: NIACE

MacLure, J.S. (1986) *Educational Documents, England and Wales 1816 to the Present Day*. Methuen; first pub. 1965

Maidment, B. (1987) *The Poorhouse Fugitives: Self-taught Poets and Poetry in Victorian Britain*. Manchester: Carcanet

Mansbridge, A. (1913) *University Tutorial Classes: A Study in the Development of Higher Education Among Working Men and Women*. Longmans

Mansbridge, A. (1940) *The Trodden Road, Experience, Inspiration and Belief*. J.M. Dent

Manzoni, A. (1972) *The Betrothed*. Harmondsworth: Penguin; first pub. in English 1828

Mayers, J.J. (1798) *A Defence of the Sunday Schools: Attempted in a Series of Letters addressed to the Rev. M. Olerenshaw in answer to his 'Sermon on the Sanctification of the Sabbath and on the Right Use and Abuse of Sunday Schools'*. Stockport Sunday School

Mayhew, H. (1985) *London Labour and the London Poor*, ed. V. Neuburg. Harmondsworth: Penguin

McGill, P. (1910) *Gleanings from a Navvy's Scrapbook*. Derry: Derry Journal

McGill, P. (1914) *Children of the Dead End. The Autobiography of a Navvy*. Herbert Jenkins

McMillan, M. (1904) *Education through the Imagination*. Swan Sonnen-schein

Mitch, D.F. (1992) *The Rise of Popular Literacy in Victorian England: The Influence of Private Choice and Public Policy*. Philadelphia, PA: University of Pennsylvania Press

Mitchell, B.R. & Deane, P. (eds) (1962) *Abstract of British Historical Studies*. Cambridge: CUP

Mitchell, H. (1977) *The Hard Way Up, the Autobiography of Hannah Mitchell, Suffragette and Rebel*. Virago

Morley, D. & Worpole, K. (1982) (eds) *The Republic of Letters, Working Class Writing and Local Publishing*. Comedia.

Mortimer, J. (1982) *Clinging to the Wreckage*. Harmondsworth: Penguin

Mulhauser, M. (1842) *Manual of Handwriting*.

Musgrave, J. (1865) *Origin of Methodism in Bolton*. Bolton

National Research Development Centre for Adult Literacy and Numeracy (NRDC) (2007) *Voices on the Page: Stories and Poems by Adults in Skills for Life Learning*. Warrington: New Leaf Books

Olsen, T. (1980) *Silences*. Virago

Ong, W.J. (2002) *Orality and Literacy – the Technologizing of the Word*. Routledge; first pub. 1982

Owen, A. (1989) *The Darkened Room, Women, Power and Spiritualism in Late Victorian England*. Virago

Oxford University Extension Delegacy Tutorial Classes Committee Report (1910)

Partington, S. (1917) *The Future of Old English Words*. Middleton: J. Bagot

Partington, S. (1920) *Romance of the Dialect*. Middleton: J. Bagot

Penn, M. (1947) *Manchester XIV Miles*. Guild Books

Penn, M. (1982) *The Foolish Virgin*. Futura; first pub. 1951

Peterson, L.H. (1986) *Victorian Autobiography. The Tradition of Self-Interpretation*. New Haven, CT: Yale University Press

Pitman (1879) *Domestic Copy Book for Girls*. Pitman & Son

Pole, T. (1816) *A History of the Origin and Progress of Adult Schools with an Account of Some of the Beneficial Effects Already Produced on the Moral Character of the Labouring Poor*. Bristol

Pritchett, V.S. (1978a) *Midnight Oil*. Harmondsworth: Penguin; first pub. 1971

Pritchett, V.S. (1978b) *A Cab at the Door*. Harmondsworth: Penguin; first pub. 1968

Purvis, J. (1989) *Hard Lessons – The Lives and Education of Working Class Women in Nineteenth Century England*. Cambridge: Polity Press

Redfern, P. (1913) *The Story of the CWS, The Jubilee History of the Cooperative Wholesale Society, 1863–1919*. Manchester: CWS

Richardson, M. (1935) *Writing and Writing Patterns: a Teacher's Handbook*. London University Press

Rogers, F. (1913) *Labour, Life and Literature. Some Memories of Sixty Years*. Smith Elder & Co.

Rose, J. (2002) *The Intellectual Life of the British Working Classes*. New Haven, CT: Yale University Press

Rosenberg, S.K. (2008) *A Critical History of ESOL in the UK 1870–2006*. Leicester: NIACE

Rousseau, J-J. (1985) *Confessions*. Harmondsworth: Penguin; first pub. 1781

Rowbotham, S. (1981) 'Travellers in a Strange Country', *History Workshop Journal*, Vol. 12, pp. 62–95

Rowntree, J.W. & Binns, H.B. (1903) *A History of the Adult School Movement*. Headley Brothers

Royster, J.J. (2000) *Traces of a Stream: Literacy and Social Change Among African American Women*. Pittsburgh, PA: University of Pittsburgh Press

Rushton, A. (1909) *My Life as a Farmer's Boy, Factory Lad, Teacher and Preacher*. Manchester: S. Clarke

Said, E.W. (1991) 'On Originality', in *The World, The Text and the Critic*. Vintage, pp. 126–39; first pub. in 1983

Samuel, R. (ed.) (1981) *People's History and Socialist Theory*. Routledge

Sanderson, M. (1991) *Education, Economic Change and Society in England 1780–1870*. Macmillan

Sanger, 'Lord' G. (1910) *Seventy Years a Showman*. C.A. Pearson

Schofield, R. (1973) 'Dimensions of Illiteracy 1750–1859', *Explorations in Economic History*, Vol. 10, No 4, pp. 437–54

Sharp, J.C. (1888) *Writing and How to Teach it, A Manual of Lessons for the Guidance of Teachers*. Allman & Son

Shaw, C. (1977) *When I was a Child, by an Old Potter*. Firle, Sussex: Caliban Books; first pub. 1903

Sheridan, D. (1993) 'Writing for ... questions of representation, representativeness, authorship and audience', in D. Barton, D. Bloome, D. Sheridan & B. Street (eds), *Ordinary People Writing: the Lancaster and Sussex Writing Research Projects*, Paper 51. Lancaster: Lancaster University, pp. 17–23

Smith, F. (1982) *Writing and the Writer*. Heinemann Educational

Smith, F. (1983) *Essays into Literacy*. Portsmouth: Heinemann Educational

Smith, G.R. (1908) *Half a Century in the Dead Letter Offfice*. Bristol: W.C. Hemmons

Smith, M. (1892) *The Autobiography of Mary Smith, Schoolmistress and Non-conformist. A Fragment of a Life*, Vol. 1. Carlisle: The Wordsworth Press

Smith, O. (1984) *The Politics of Language 1791–1819*. Oxford: Clarendon Press

Soloman, J. (ed.) (2003) *The Passion to Learn: an Inquiry into autodidactism*. Routledge

Souch, W.J. (1954) *A History of the Reading Branch of the Workers' Educational Association, 1904–1954*. Reading: Charles Elsbury & Sons Ltd

Springhall, J. (1986) *Coming of Age: Adolescence in Britain 1860–1960*. Dublin: Gill & MacMillan

Steedman, C. (1984) *Landscape for a Good Woman*. Virago

Steedman, C. (1988) *The Radical Soldier's Tale*. Routledge

Steedman, C. (1990) *Childhood, Culture and Class in Britain: Margaret MacMillan, 1860–1931*. Virago

Steedman, C. (1995) *Strange Dislocations: Childhood and the Idea of Human Interiority 1780–1930*. Virago

Steedman, C. (2007) *Master and Servant: Love and Labour in the English Industrial Age*. Cambridge: CUP

Stephens, M.D. & Roderick, G.W. (eds) (1983) *Samuel Smiles and Nineteenth Century Self-Help in Education*. Nottingham: University of Nottingham

Stephens, W.B. (1987) *Education, Literacy and Society, 1830–1970: The Geography of Diversity in Provincial England*. Manchester University Press

Stock, M. (1953) *The WEA, The First 50 Years*. G. Allen & Unwin Ltd.

Stokes, W. (1873) *The Art of Rapidly Teaching Writing*. Roulston & Son

Stone, L. (1969) 'Literacy and Education in England 1640–1900', *Past and Present*, Vol. 42, pp. 69–139

Storey, E. (1982) *A Right to Song: The Life of John Clare*. Methuen

Strachey, R. (1977) *The Cause*. Virago; first pub. 1928

Street, B.V. (1984) *Literacy in Theory and Practice*. Cambridge: CUP

Strickland, I. (1970) *The Voices of Children*. Oxford: Basil Blackwell

Sturt, M. (1967) *The Education of the People. A History of Primary Education in England and Wales in the Nineteenth century*. Routledge & Kegan Paul

Swindells, J. (1985) *Victorian Writing and Working Women*. Oxford: Polity Press/Blackwells

Tawney, R.H. (1914) 'An Experiment in Democratic Education', *The Political Quarterly*, July

Thomas, W.I. & Znaniecki, F. (1984) *The Polish Peasant in Europe and America*. Urbana, IL: University of Chicago Press; first pub. 1918

Thompson, E.P. (1968) *The Making of the English Working Class*. Harmondsworth: Penguin; first pub. 1963

Thompson, E.P. (1971) 'The Moral Economy of the English Crowd in the 18th century', *Past and Present*, Vol. 50, pp. 76–136

Thompson, E.P. (1991) 'The Moral Economy Reviewed', in *Customs in Common*. Merlin, pp. 259–351

Thompson, F. (1973) *Larkrise to Candleford*. Harmondsworth: Penguin; first pub. 1939

Thompson, T. (1981) *Edwardian Childhoods*. Routledge

Thompson, T. (ed.) (1987) *Dear Girl – The Diaries and Letters of Two Working Women 1897–1917*. The Women's Press

Thomson, A. (2011) *Moving Stories: An Intimate History of Four Women Across Two Countries*. Manchester University Press

Thorne, W. (1925) *My Life's Battles*. George Newnes & Co

Tilleard, J. (1855) *Lecture on the Method of Teaching Grammar*.

Todd, T. (1935) *My Life as I Have Lived It. Autobiography of Thomas Todd of Middleton-in-Teesdale, Leeds*. Privately printed

Tomalin, C. (2011) *Dickens: A Life*. Viking (Penguin)

Tylecote, M. (1957) *The Mechanics' Institutes of Lancashire and Yorkshire Before 1851.* Manchester University Press

Updike, J. (1989) *Self-Consciousness – Memoirs.* André Deutsch

Vicinus, M. (1974) *The Industrial Muse.* Croom Helm

Vincent, D. (1982) *Bread, Knowledge and Freedom: A Study of Nineteenth Century Working Class Autobiography.* Methuen & Co.

Vincent, D. (1989) *Literacy and Popular Culture. England 1750–1914.* Cambridge: CUP

Vincent, D. (2000) *The Rise of Mass Literacy: Reading and Writing in Modern Europe.* Cambridge: Polity Press

Vincent, D. (2003) 'The Progress of Literacy', *Victorian Studies*, Vol. 45, Spring, pp. 405–31

Walker, A. (1984) *In Search of Our Mothers' Gardens, Womanist Prose.* The Women's Press

Weaver, R. (1913) *Richard Weaver's Life Story*, ed. J. Paterson. Morgan & Scott

Webb, F. (undated) *Dissected Writing Copies.*

Webb, R. K. (1955) *The British Working Class Reader.* Allen & Unwin

Weeks, J. (1982) 'Foucault for Historians', *History Workshop Journal*, Vol. 14, pp. 106–19

Weeton, E. (1969) *Miss Weeton. Journal of a Governess*, Vol. 1, 1807–11. David & Charles; first pub. 1936

Weller, T. & Bawden, D. (2005) 'The Social and Technological Origins of the Information Society: an analysis of the crisis of control in England: 1830–1900', *Journal of Documentation*, Vol. 61, No 2, pp. 777–812

White, F. (1938) *A Fire in the Kitchen: The Autobiography of a Cook.* J.M. Dent & Sons

White, H.V. (1973) *Metahistory: the Historical Imagination in Nineteenth Century Europe.* Baltimore, MD: John Hopkins Press

Wiener, M.J. (1980) *English Culture and the Decline of the Industrial Spirit 1850–1980.* Cambridge: CUP

Williams, A. (1912) *Life in a Wiltshire Village.* Duckworth & Co Ltd

Williams, R. (1965) *The Long Revolution.* Harmondsworth: Penguin; first pub. 1961

Williams, R. (1975) *The Country and the City.* St Albans: Paladin

Williams, R. (1977) *Marxism and Literature.* Oxford: OUP

Williams, R. (1981) *Culture.* Glasgow: Fontana

Williams, R. (1983) *Writing in Society.* Verso

Williams, R. (1984) *The English Novel*. Hogarth Press

Williams, R. & Williams, M. (eds) (1986) *John Clare. Selected Poetry and Prose*. Methuen

Woodin, T. (2005a) 'Building Culture from the bottom up: the educational origins of the Federation of Worker Writers and Community Publishers', *History of Education*, Vol. 39, No 4, pp. 345–63

Woodin, T. (2005b) ' "More writing than welding": learning in worker writer groups', *History of Education*, Vol. 39, No 5, pp. 551–67

Woodin, T. (2008) ' "A beginner reader is not a beginner thinker": student publishing since the 1970s', *Paedagogica Historica*, Vol. 44, No 1/2, pp. 219–32

Wright, W. (1893) *The Adventures and Recollections of Bill O'th Hoylus End: Told by Himself*, serialised in *Keighley Herald* 2 June–8 December

Yeo, S. (1986) 'Whose Story? An Argument from Within Current Historical Practice in Britain', *Journal of Contemporary History*, Vol. 21, No 2, pp. 295–320

Yeo, S. (1987) 'Three Socialisms: Statism, Collectivism, Associationism', in W. Outhwaite & M. Mulkay (eds), *Social Theory and Social Criticism*. Oxford: Basil Blackwell, pp. 83–113

Yeo, S. (1988) 'Difference, Autobiography and History', *Literature and History*, Vol. 14, No 1, pp. 37–47

Zimmek, M. (1986) 'Jobs for the Girls: The Expansion of Clerical Work for Women, 1850–1914', in A. John (ed.) *Unequal Opportunities – Women's Employment in England, 1800–1918*. Oxford: Blackwell

Index

Note: Page references in **bold** type refer to plates; page references followed by 'n' refer to notes.

mechanics: processes 43; teaching
55
Mechanics' Institutes 25, 130–1,
192
meetings 4
memory 6, 202–4; screen 195–6,
233; and writing 194–8
Methodism 75, 81, 82–4
middle class 4, 116, 153; fervour
48; grammar school boys 40
mills 267, 270–2
minute books 7
Mitchell, H. 126–7, 179, 196,
204, 211; *The Hard Way Up*
232–9
mobility: social 274
monitorial system 33–6, 41
moral education 34, 38, 45
moral judgement 105
Morris, W. 303; *News from
Nowhere* 203
Mortimer, J. 258n
Moseley, H. 39, 41, 42, 46–7, 66
mother 13; ambivalence to 223–4;
leaving 236; memories 232–4
motivation to learn 128
Mulhauser, M. 50–2
Mulhauser method 44, 45, 50–2,
63
Munby, A. 80
Murray, L. 63
mutual education 114
mutual improvement societies 65,
128–30, 132
myth: personal 308–14
mythic structure 235, 282

names: meaning 91; writing 92–4
Napoleonic Wars 3

National Curriculum 17
National Research and
Development Centre for Adult
Literacy and Numeracy 18
National Society 91
New Literacy Studies 9–10
New Moral World 24
Newcastle Report (1861) 142
newspapers: radical 24–5, 144
night school 116; technical 133
Nightingale, F.: *Cassandra* 224–5,
259n
noise: in schools 36, 60
Northern Star 85, 90, 102, 109n,
141, 144, 145
Norton, C. 58
novelists 73; and social injustice 87
novels 7, 172; and autobiography
difference 175–6

observational skills 49
OECD (Organisation for
Economic Co-operation and
Development) survey (1997) 16
office workers 86
Oldham Lyceum 136n
One and All journal 94
O'Neal, J. 315
Ong, W.J. 87–8, 91, 93, 258n
oral cultures/traditions 91, 121
other people: and self 204–8
Overs, J. 87
Owen, A. 88
Owenism 24, 65, 83, 89–90, 91

Paine, T.: *Rights of Man* 4, 38, 77
Palmerston, Viscount H.J.T.(Lord)
53